WOMEN AND THE COUNTRY HOUSE IN IRELAND AND BRITAIN

Women and the country house in Ireland and Britain

Terence Dooley, Maeve O'Riordan &
Christopher Ridgway

EDITORS

FOUR COURTS PRESS

Typeset in 10.5 pt on 12.5 pt Ehrhardt by
Carrigboy Typesetting Services for
FOUR COURTS PRESS LTD
7 Malpas Street, Dublin 8, Ireland
www.fourcourtspress.ie
and in North America for
FOUR COURTS PRESS
c/o ISBS, 920 NE 58th Avenue, Suite 300, Portland, OR 97213.

A catalogue record for this title is available
from the British Library.

ISBN 978–1–84682–647–4

SPECIAL ACKNOWLEDGMENT

The publication of this volume was generously supported by the Ireland Funds.

Printed in England
by TJ International, Padstow, Cornwall.

Contents

Contents

Introduction

This volume of essays brings together new research on the lives and roles of women who lived in country houses in Ireland and Britain from the seventeenth to the twentieth centuries. Drawing from a range of archival sources, the authors present a spectrum of house owners, residents and caretakers who were mothers, wives, widows, sisters and daughters and who were far more than bit players in the history of families and big houses. In addition to their obvious role as matriarchs their lives encompassed the private and the public sphere, and moved seamlessly between the indoors and the outdoors on estates, where men (as fathers, husbands or sons) might be supportive, or in many cases preoccupied with interests of their own away from family and home.

The women presented in these essays were all agents in their own destiny, taking charge of their lives (as much as was possible within a repressive society) as well as influencing the lives of others. They were committed to organizing households, supervising architects and builders, raising families, mobilizing political support, acquiring culinary expertise, assisting husbands or sons, writing fiction, travelling overseas, and, in one instance, undoing a late husband's work. This collection goes some way towards answering the question: 'what did they do?' It faces the reality that some women of the upper classes did live invalid lives; however, debilitating diseases did not necessarily mean that they could not fulfil some, or all, of their roles as the wives of estate owners or peers. What this collection particularly demonstrates is the part women played in the appearance and running of family estates. It has long been assumed that women merely managed female servants, and fulfilled the role of hostess (albeit without always understanding the significance of these resposnsibilities), but this collection unveils a long tradition of female builders and curators of taste.

Amy Boyington reveals how Jemima Yorke, a woman who unusually inherited the title of Marchioness Grey in her own right in 1740, pursued a vigorous programme of house refurbishment in London and at her country seat, Wrest Park in Bedfordshire, in her later years. Earlier in the century she and her husband, Philip Yorke, had jointly commissioned work on the house and gardens at Wrest but as a widow she exhibited a determined, if not restless spirit, to remodel, improve and enlarge her homes during the 1790s, this time without having to defer to her husband.

Catherine Maria Dawson is another example of a woman influencing and directly shaping architectural projects. Judith Hill details her involvement in the building of Charleville Castle, King's County, in the early years of the nineteenth century. Widowed from her first marriage, she was worldly, prudent, educated and free-thinking and in 1798 she married Charles Bury, earl of Charleville. She was steeped in the Gothic, the Picturesque and the Romantic and was an accomplished artist in pencil and watercolour and so able to realize her wishes for Charleville on paper, thereby earning the respect of both her husband and the architect Francis Johnston.

Caroline Dakers chronicles the parallel lives of neighbouring Wiltshire residents Madeline Wyndham and Mabel Morrison. The former married into the aristocracy while the latter married a self-made millionaire haberdasher. Madeline's social and artistic milieu revolved around Clouds, the home built for the couple by architect Philip Webb. Not only had she been instrumental in its design and decoration, she was a practising artist herself. Mabel Morrison's life was very different. Residing at Fonthill, and twenty-seven years younger than her husband, she gave birth to five children but suffered from ill health and, Dakers argues, acquired something of the status of an object in her husband's large collection of art. Widowhood released her from this passive existence and she emerged as a healthy, wealthy, independent figure who set about dismembering Morrison's collections of pictures, books and manuscripts.

Ruth Larsen discusses how sisters formed perhaps the closest of female bonds as they shared concerns over marriage, childbirth and bereavement, and offered one another guidance and support. Her examination of the letters between Georgiana and Harriet Cavendish, daughters of the famous duchess of Devonshire of Chatsworth, reveal a lifelong sibling affection that was not displaced by marriage after they had become 6th countess of Carlisle and Countess Granville respectively. These women also acted as chatelaines, exercising domestic power within the household, and dispensing advice and emotional support at critical moments – marriage, childbirth, bereavement. As sisters, then mothers, and eventually as aunts, they presided over an extended family, and helped knit together a dynastic network that prompted Tory prime minister Sir Robert Peel famously to complain, 'Damn the Whigs they're all cousins'.[1]

The harmonious universe of these Whig households is in sharp contrast to the discordant relations found in the extended Winn family of Nostell Priory, Yorkshire, as chronicled by Kerry Bristol. Here sisters, brothers, husbands, wives, aunts and uncles all seemed bent on family rupture over money, the custody of children and litigation, a tension that stemmed largely from the marriage of Sir Rowland Winn to his Swiss wife, Sabine, in 1761. Her alienation from the family was only partly on account of her resistance to learning English; following the death of her husband, not long after the collapse of his bank, she was accused of mismanaging not only his estates but also the family and its reputation after her daughter eloped with a local baker. The geographical

1 Robert Peel cited in Hugh Cunningham, *The challenge of democracy: Britain, 1832–1918* (London, 2001), p. 40.

separation of the family members led one sister to concede that these fractious relationships were best conducted at a distance, and it is a rich irony that this very emotional and physical distance spawned an epistolary network from which this sorry narrative can be reconstructed.

Philip Bull's discussion of Monksgrange, Co. Wexford, revolves round five women who managed and nurtured the property over the course of 150 years, and he shows how knowledge, experience and commitment to a family could be passed down the generations. In 1868, Dorothea Richards prevailed upon her son Edward to return from the United States and assume responsibility for Monksgrange; in time he transferred ownership to his daughter Adela who gave up her career as a writer in order to manage the estate. During the Irish Civil War she managed to talk anti-treatyites out of burning the house on three occasions, but found her relationship with her daughter-in-law Margaret Richards-Orpen more difficult to manage, especially as the latter did not share her views on the union. With each generation of the family it is apparent that Monksgrange owed its survival to the resilience of its women as opposed to its men who followed legal, military or political paths.

Building on the work of Diane Urquhart, Olwen Purdue and others, Jonathan Cherry and Arlene Crampsie have investigated the role of women in the wave of unionist activism at the time of the third home rule bill. While it is well known that women from the landed classes played a role in shaping opinion and organizing resistance to home rule, their statistical analysis has revealed cadres of women from the middle classes and urban districts who were every bit as committed as their elite counterparts.

Another example of a resolute woman is Lady Harriet Le Poer Trench who married Thomas Kavanagh of Borris House, Co. Carlow, in 1825. After refurbishing the marital home she gave birth to four children but her family also included eight step-children from her husband's first marriage. Widowed at the age of thirty-seven, she raised this large family single-handedly, and managed the estate. But she was a restless spirit and for the next twenty years she travelled frequently to the Mediterranean and the Middle East where she pursued her passion for ancient Egypt, amassing a collection of antiquities. By the time of her death in 1885 she had outlived her eight step-children and three of her own children: her surviving heir was her youngest son Arthur who had been born without any limbs.

Anna Pilz's focus on the arboricultural activities of Lady Gregory at Coole Park, Co. Galway, presents a little-known dimension to this famous literary figure and patroness of the arts. Her interest in, and knowledge of, silviculture was uncommon and was not simply gleaned from relevant volumes in the extensive library at Coole but also from first-hand experience of planting and managing woodlands. For Gregory inscribing names on trees also became a way of creating a literary landscape that was imbued with Celtic and Greek mythologies handed down by oral and written tradition, but her arboreal husbandry recognized the value of woods in the political economy, and the fate of the woodlands following the sale of Coole offers a different perspective on the narrative of the decline of the big house.

The important position of the landed wife can be seen throughout this collection. Unmarried women are a rarer sight among these essays, reflecting their greater invisibility among the family papers of the wealthy elite. Unmarried women often had more unstable living arrangements, making their stories more difficult to discover. It is all the more valuable then, to have the contribution of Lowri Ann Rees, who presents an intriguing microhistory of Jane Walters, an embattled landowner in mid-Wales during the Rebecca Riots. Living in a comfortable house with her sister, these two unmarried women were targeted in the wave of rural unrest that swept the region in the early 1840s. The chapter demonstrates that unmarried women could, and did, take on 'masculine' roles on the estate. Although tollgates were one of the principal causes of anger, rioters also demanded lower rents in a medley of grievances directed at the propertied classes. Jane's family home was besieged but she refused to pay over any money, and the crowd was dissuaded from setting fire to the house. In the ensuing months she wrote repeatedly to the authorities, including prime minister Robert Peel, in her efforts to bring the rioters to justice, but she was also aware that the local magistracy was far from blameless.

Mildrid Darby, the subject of Ciarán Reilly's essay, was a writer, under the nom de plume Andrew Merry. Married to a King's County (later Co. Offaly) landowner she scandalized her husband and his family with her Famine novel *The hunger*, first published in 1910. Reilly contends that her research for the book was extensive, enabling her to represent different levels of society from landlord to middleman, priest and peasant, as well as highlighting the role of women during the Famine. But the novel was a thinly disguised *roman-à-clef* and provoked her husband's ire in its negative portrayal of the landed class especially as his own family had assisted the poor and destitute during the 1840s. However, her desire to 'tell both sides and all versions of the same tale' did not prevent her home, Leap Castle, from being burned in 1922.

Rosalind Howard, 9th countess of Carlisle, was a figure who knowingly courted controversy in her lifetime, acquiring a reputation as 'the radical countess'. Christopher Ridgway charts her commitment to women's suffrage, temperance, the Liberal party, and home rule, and argues that her own upbringing shaped her desire to be politically engaged. Articulate, combative, and renowned for making her own decisions, she is another example of a woman who left a bigger mark on life than her husband.

Regina Sexton pays close attention to a unique manuscript recipe book belonging to the Parsons family of Birr Castle. This compilation, dating from the seventeenth and eighteenth centuries, was the work of several women across the extended Parsons family. It illustrates not just the transmission of culinary knowledge, but the central role women played in the domestic household, in an era when cooks in grand and royal residences were usually men. The manuscript also reflects the influence of English and continental culinary practices on Irish households at a moment when cooking styles and ingredients were beginning to change.

Brendan Twomey discusses another valuable epistolary network, this time between Louisa Conolly and her sister Sarah Bunbury. The collection of letters documents lives at the apex of Irish society, at what is commonly regarded as the greatest of Ireland's country houses. Twomey has space here to discuss just some of the themes covered in these letters, but it is evident that the conversations between Louisa and her sister are a mine of information on social mores, relationships and even the ageing process among the elite.

Fiona White's discussion of Louisa Browne presents another example of a nineteenth-century matriarch married to a husband largely absent from the family narrative, in this case George Moore 'The Historian', of Moorehall, Co. Mayo, who had handed over the running of family and estate affairs to his wife. In her search for advice on raising her sons Louisa Browne turned to Maria Edgworth, and the two women exchanged letters for nearly two decades, with the novelist offering counsel on a range of subjects from education, servants and how to deal with a dissolute son and heir. When George Moore the younger did inherit Moorehall his passion for horse racing remained undimmed but in 1846 his winnings in the Chester Cup enabled him to settle his debts, and finance a relief programme across the estate under the supervision of his mother.

Today scholars, and indeed the majority of the visiting public to country houses, demonstrate an increasing interest in understanding and interrogating the lives of the female occupants independently of, and in relation to, their male counterparts. Providing they were visible figures, recorded in their own words or in the writings of others, then their histories can be excavated; indeed a common thread throughout the volume is the substantial bodies of papers these figures left behind relating to their lives and activities – testimony to the fact that they, or others close to them, deemed these written records worthy of preservation. There is great scope for historians, curators and others to continued to mine these records, in both Britain and Ireland, to further expand our knowledge of such women. Further, exciting work is being carried out by Felicity Maxwell and others to uncover the lives of servants in these houses.

The chronological sweep of this collection is long, and allows a number of themes to emerge, and an understanding as to how women navigated restrictive social codes throughout the centuries. Women throughout this period were tasked with enhancing the prestige and cultural capital of their familics; whether it was through the newest fashions in food or through careful references to Greek mythology when acting as architectural patronnesses in the design of their family mansion, or indeed in attempting to secure deference from an unruly Welsh tenantry. Elite women were conscious of the latest political developments and could contribute to (or attempt to halt) the most important social movements of their day.

At the same time it is not possible to ignore historical circumstance in these centuries. Patriarchy impacted on women's experiences in all social classes, even those who benefitted from a privileged birth or marriage. All of the women discussed here were faced with gender inequality within their society. They were disadvantaged especially in terms of their legal status, educational and professional opportunities, and the sexual double standard which demanded higher levels of morality from women than from men. These restrictions limited their opportunities for social, intellectual and political autonomy. It would be a mistake to endow them retrospectively with modern equivalents of equality, authority and liberty. Still, such a broad collection of essays suggests that women who managed to carve out a sphere of influence for themselves within such a restrictive society were not altogether a rarity. These essays and the many, and growing number of, biographical and collective works on women and the country house across Britain and Ireland that have emerged since the groundbreaking analysis of Amanda Vickery in 1998 demand that the female members of these families be investigated in their own right as important actors in the world of the country house. This work has reaped especially profitable rewards for Britain,[2] where country-house studies have matured as a discipline, but recent work in Ireland has also begun to reveal the female residents of these houses in all their complexity.[3] Before now, however, there has been no collection of essays that reveals the diverse activities and interests of women of the country house across Britain and Ireland from the seventeenth to the twentieth century.

In presenting essays on Irish and British women together, it is possible to decipher similarities and differences in their experiences, and to see how much of a community existed at the pinnacle of society. For the most elite titled members of the landed class, there was no perceptible border along the Irish Sea.

---

2 J. Gerard, *Country house life: family and servants, 1815–1914* (Oxford, 1994); A. Foreman, *The duchess: Georgiana duchess of Devonshire* ([1998] London, 2008); A. Vickery, *The gentleman's daughter: women's lives in Georgian England* (New Haven, 1998); J. Schneid Lewis, *In the family way: childbearing in the British aristocracy, 1760–1860* (New Jersey, 1986); M.J. Peterson, *Family, love and work in the lives of Victorian gentlewomen* (Bloomington, 1989); K.D. Reynolds, *Aristocratic women and political society in Victorian Britain* (Oxford, 1998); P. Jalland, *Women, marriage and politics: 1860–1914* (Oxford, 1988).   **3** A.P.W. Malcomson, *The pursuit of the heiress: aristocratic marriage in Ireland, 1740–1840* (Belfast, 1982); D. Wilson, *Women, marriage and property in wealthy landed families in Ireland, 1750–1850* (Manchester, 2009); D. Urquhart, *The ladies of Londonderry: women and political patronage* (London, 2007); S. Tiernan, *Eva Gore-Booth: an image of such politics* (Manchester, 2012); A. Prendergast, *Literary salons across Britain and Ireland in the long eighteenth century* (London, 2015); R. Wilson, *Elite women in ascendancy Ireland, 1690–1745: imitation and innovation* (Woodbridge, 2015); T. Dooley, *The decline and fall of the dukes of Leinster, 1872–1948: love, war, debt and madness* (Dublin, 2014).

They were almost as likely to marry men on either side of it, and their social calendar could demand frequent crossings between London and the family estate in Ireland. Many Irish peers married women who were born in England and these might view Ireland and the Irish tenantry with a colonialist's eyes. Further down the social scale, social circles were more circumscribed. The north of England families discussed here appear to have had little interaction with Ireland or the Irish, and likewise smaller Irish and Welsh landowning families might have spent most of the year at home, with little interaction with the cultural centre of the empire. For those women with adequate resources and wider interests, their world was not limited to the north-western corner of Europe. Harriet, Lady Kavanagh (1800–85), made extensive journeys to southern Europe, north Africa and the Middle East, the owner of Monksgrange in Co. Wexford (and his daughter) lived part of their lives in the US, and at least one family in West Yorkshire married into the Swiss aristocracy.

The editors are grateful to the authors for their contributions to this volume, which began life as a series of presentations at the Fourteenth Annual Historic Houses of Ireland Conference entitled 'Indoors and Outdoors, Public and Private: Women and the Country House', organized by the Centre for the Study of Historic Irish Houses and Estates (CSHIHE) in 2016. The accompanying exhibition on Airfield House was curated by Dr Maeve O'Riordan, and generously supported by and hosted in the Library at Maynooth University. Special thanks go to Cathal McCauley and his staff, especially Nicola Kelly, archivist in the Office of Public Works–Maynooth University Research Centre.

The editors would also like to record their deep gratitude to Fred and Kay Krehbiel whose generous sponsorship made that conference possible; and also for their wider support of the work of the CSHIHE. We would also like to thank the Ireland Funds for their support for the event and their generous grant towards this publication. As ever, without the support of the Office of Public Works, research, annual conferences and publications such as this would not be possible.

Without the indefatigable efforts of Catherine Murphy, Fidelma Byrne, Jacqueline Crowley and Máire Ní Chearbhaill the administration for the conference, and the numerous tasks related to this publication, would not have been accomplished – all of which were carried out with their customary professionalism and good humour. We are grateful too to Den Stubbs for his design work, and to Four Courts Press.

The stories in this volume are aimed at the general reader, but will also appeal to the specialist, drawn as they are from a rich archival vein, which includes a number of largely unknown images. These narratives serve to confirm, once more, how the vast array of personal papers in country houses, in this instance relating to women, whether professionally indexed and stored in specialist repositories, or cherished by descendants in the family home today, provide an extraordinary testimony that still has much to reveal for present and future scholars. This publication follows on from previous volumes that have grown out of the annual Maynooth conferences, which have focussed on the past, present and future of the country house, and the impact of the First World War. It continues to build on the Centre's core mission to provide a forum for, and a means of disseminating, new research on previously under-explored aspects of country houses and the lives of those who inhabited them.

The architectural endeavours of the widowed Jemima Yorke, Marchioness Grey

AMY BOYINGTON

INTRODUCTION

This chapter will demonstrate that elite widows were as equally capable of pursuing their architectural ambitions as their male peers. This will be illustrated through an exploration of the remarkable architectural endeavours of the widowed Jemima Yorke, Marchioness Grey (1722–97), about whom exists an abundance of previously overlooked primary evidence (fig. 1.1).[1]

Grey was the daughter of John Campbell, Lord Glenorchy, later 3rd earl of Breadalbane and Holland (1696–1782), and his wife, Amabel (1698–1727), daughter of Henry Grey, 1st duke of Kent (1671–1740), and his first wife, Jemima, *née* Crew (d.1728).[2] When the duke of Kent's last surviving son George Grey, earl of Harold (*c.*1732–3), died in his infancy, Grey became the heir to the barony of Lucas of Crudwell, a title that could be inherited by women. At this point the duke decided that Grey should become the sole heir to his vast estates. In May 1740, therefore, the title of Marquess Grey was created for the duke with remainder to the 'heirs male of his body; and in default of such issue, the dignity of Marchioness Grey to Jemima Campbell'.[3] Consequently, when the duke later died on 5 June 1740, not only did Grey succeed to the marquessate, she also inherited the Grey estates which included manors in Burbage (Leicestershire), Colchester (Essex), Crudwell (Wiltshire) as well as the ancestral country seat at Wrest Park (Bedfordshire) and the London house in St James's Square.

On 22 May 1740, Grey married Philip Yorke (1720–90), the eldest son of Philip Yorke, baron and later earl of Hardwicke (1690–1764), lord chancellor and owner of the Wimpole Hall estate in Cambridgeshire. The marriage was a dynastic affair with the aim of uniting the long-established Greys to the socially-ambitious Yorkes. It was a very successful marriage, which produced two daughters, the Ladies Amabel (1751–1833) and Mary (1757–1830). From 1743,

1 This primary evidence is part of the Wrest Park [Lucas] Archive located at the Bedfordshire Archives and Record Service (hereafter BLARS). I would like to thank the National Trust and the Bedford Archives for allowing me to reproduce the images in this chapter, and the Society of Architectural Historians of Great Britain (SAHGB) for kindly providing me with the publication grant which made this possible.   2 James Collett-White, 'Yorke, Jemima, *suo jure* Marchioness Grey (1722–1797)', *Oxford dictionary of national biography* (Oxford, 2004), http://www.oxforddnb.com/view/article/68351 [accessed 4 May 2017].   3 *London Gazette*,

Jemima Marchioness Grey Daughter of John Lord Glenorchy married An.º 1740 to the Hon.ble Philip Yorke Eldest Son of the Right Hon.ble Philip Lord Hardwicke Lord High Chancellor of Great Britain.

1.1 Jemima, Marchioness Grey, by Allan Ramsay, 1741 © National Trust.

the Yorkes lived primarily at Wrest Park, where they commissioned a succession of additions and modifications to the house and gardens during the 1740s, 1750s and 1760s. Throughout her married life Grey was passionate about her ancestral seat (since demolished), determined to make it convenient, tasteful and fashionable. In 1749, for example, the Yorkes commissioned Henry Flitcroft (1697–1769), the architect responsible for remodelling Wimpole Hall (1742–7), to build for them a grand new dining room on the south front, overlooking the gardens.[4] Equally passionate about the gardens, later in 1758 they commissioned the most fashionable landscape gardener of the age, Lancelot 'Capability' Brown (1717–83), to re-landscape swathes of the out-modish formal gardens with his refreshing naturalistic style.[5]

WIDOWHOOD

Following Philip Yorke's inheritance of the Wimpole estate and succession to the earldom of Hardwicke in 1764, the Yorkes split their time between Wrest Park and Wimpole Hall. This naturally meant that less attention and money was spent on Wrest during the 1770s and 1780s. When Grey was widowed on 16 May 1790, she clearly had ambitions to rectify this, as will be demonstrated in this discussion.[6] She immediately commissioned George Byfield (c.1756–1813), architect and surveyor of the estates of the Dean and Chapter of Westminster (from 1803 onwards), to make additions to her London house at 4 St James's Square. Once completed in 1791, Grey then commissioned John Woolfe (d.1793), an Irish-born architect and joint author of the fourth (1767) and fifth (1771) volumes of *Vitruvius Britannicus*, to undertake major alterations at Wrest Park.[7]

Poignantly, Grey decided to embark upon her most costly and ambitious architectural projects as a widow. At the age of 68 she cannot have expected to have enjoyed the finished building schemes for long, which makes her architectural works all the more significant. Her widowhood enabled her to reclaim complete control over her ancestral estate, which in turn provided her with the social and financial emancipation to commission improvements as she saw fit. As her eldest daughter, Lady Amabel Polwarth, was the heir to the Wrest estates it is probable that Grey saw it as her duty to create a befitting architectural legacy.[8] Just as the widowed Henrietta Cavendish Holles Harley, countess of Oxford and Mortimer (1694–1755), had endeavoured to repair

27–31 May 1740. **4** Marchioness Grey to Lady Mary Gregory, 14 May 1749 (BLARS, L30/9a/2/32). **5** Marchioness Grey to Lady Mary Gregory, 3 Oct. 1758 (BLARS, L30/9a/3/20). **6** For a short biography of Grey, see Joyce Godber, 'Grey of Wrest Park', *Bedfordshire Historical Record Society*, 47 (1968). **7** For further information on both architects see: Howard Colvin, *A biographical dictionary of British architects, 1600–1840*, 3rd ed. (New Haven & London, 1995), pp 202–3, 1081–2. **8** Lady Amabel married Alexander Hume-Campbell, Lord Polwarth (1750–81), in 1772.

Welbeck Abbey 'to incline my family to reside at ye only Habitable Seat of my Ancestors', so too did Grey at Wrest Park.[9]

This architectural freedom was also embraced by many of Grey's widowed contemporaries, such as the dowager Lady Leicester (1700–75) with the completion of Holkham Hall, Norfolk (1759–65), the dowager Lady Spencer (1737–1814) with the remodelling of Holywell House, St Albans (1783–4) and Elizabeth Montagu's (1718–1800) house in Portman Square (1771–81).[10] These elite widows counter the traditional perception that women could not and did not involve themselves in architectural patronage. Grey's commissions both at St James's Square and Wrest provide a further fascinating, and hitherto overlooked, example of female architectural agency in the eighteenth century.

ALTERATIONS AT 4 JAMES'S SQUARE

As with most elite families of the eighteenth century, a grand London house was essential for the Greys to maintain their place within society. Number 4 St James's Square had been in Grey's family since 1677–8 when Anthony Grey, 11th earl of Kent (1645–1702), bought the property from Nicholas Barbon (*c.*1640–98), a financial speculator.[11] This house burnt down in 1725 and was rebuilt by Grey's grandfather, the 1st duke of Kent, with the aid of Edward Shepherd (d.1747), a prominent London-based architect.[12] Upon the duke's death on 5 June 1740, according to his will, the house was given to his widow, Sophia, duchess of Kent (d.1748), for sixty years provided she did not remarry.[13] On 21 June 1743, however, she leased the property to the Yorkes for fifty-six years at £300 per annum, and thus it became the Yorkes' principal London house.[14]

There is little evidence to suggest that major alterations to the fabric of the building took place during the Yorkes' marriage. Nonetheless, as was befitting for such a property, the Yorkes adorned the walls with some of the greatest pictures in their collection. Many of these came with the house, but they also commissioned new ones, such as the double portrait of their daughters, 'The Ladies Amabel and Mary', by Joshua Reynolds (1723–92), an influential

9 Draft letter from Lady Oxford to Lady Mary Wortley Montagu, Dover Street, 7 June 1740, as quoted in Lucy Worsley, 'Female architectural patronage in the eighteenth century and the case of Henrietta Cavendish Holles Harley', *Architectural History*, 48 (2005), 158.   10 Amy Boyington, 'The countess of Leicester and her contribution to Holkham Hall', *The Georgian Group Journal*, 22 (2014), 53–66; Frances Harris, 'Holywell House: a gothic villa at St Albans', *British Library Journal* (1986), 176–83; Kerry Bristol, '22 Portman Square: Mrs Montagu and her "palais de la Vieillesse"', *British Art Journal*, 2:3 (2001), 72–85.   11 Conveyance (lease & release), 31 Jan.–1 Feb. 1677[78] (BLARS, L21/94–5).   12 For a discussion on its overall history see, 'St James's Square: No. 4' in F.H.W. Sheppard (ed.), *Survey of London: volumes 29 and 30, St James Westminster, part 1* (London, 1960), pp 88–99.   13 Will of Henry Grey, duke of Kent (3 official copies), 29 May 1740 (BLARS, L32/11–13).   14 Lease, 21 June 1743 (BLARS, L21/124).

1.2 (*opposite*) 'Plan of the Principal Story', 1834, with the additions made by Marchioness Grey in 1790 © Bedfordshire Archives Service.

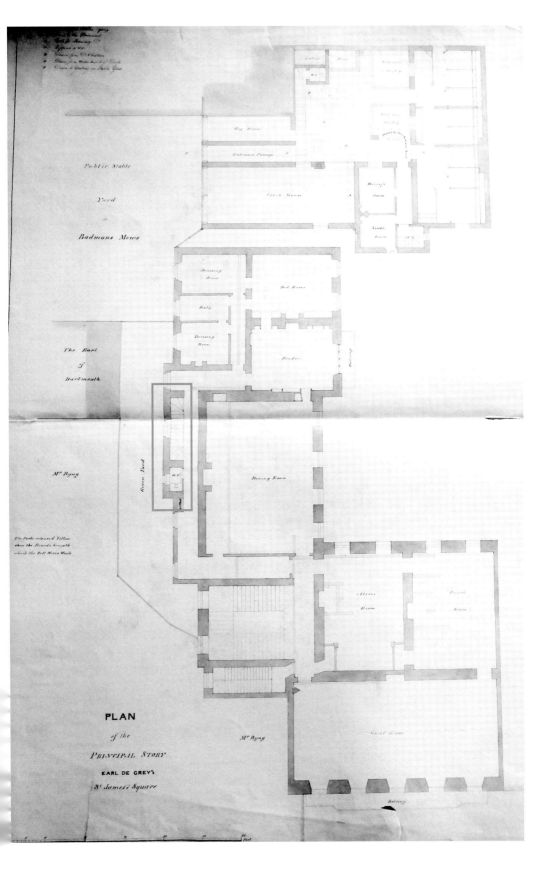

Public Stable

Yard

or

Badmans Mews

The Earl
of
Dartmouth

Mr Byng

The Parts coloured Yellow
shew the Bounds beneath
which the Bell Wires Work

Coy House

Entrance Passage

Coach House

Houses's
Room

Sendt
Room

Dressing
Room

Bath

Dressing
Room

Bed Room

Boudoir

Green Yard

W C

Drawing Room

Above
Room

French
Room

Mr Byng

Great Room

Balcony

PLAN

of the

PRINCIPAL STORY

EARL DE GREY's

St James's Square

portraitist, in 1761, which hung on the principal floor.[15] 'The Great Room' featured famous masters, including nine Van Dycks and one Claude Lorrain, according to Horace Walpole when he visited in 1761.[16]

Following her husband's death in 1790, Grey immediately selected George Byfield as her architect. The immediacy of Grey's commission suggests that she had long wanted to improve her London residence, which might indicate that female architectural agency was perhaps curtailed even within happy marriages. Byfield, in his early country house designs, had advocated a simple neoclassical style, including Bassingbourn Hall, for admiral of the Fleet, Sir Peter Parker (1721–1811), 1st Baronet, in 1784 and Perdiswell Park for Sir Henry Wakeman (1753–1831), 1st Baronet, in 1787–8.[17] His talents for design were not required for Grey's commission, however, as the principal feature of the project was to add a back stairs to the north front. This staircase was to serve all six floors, from basement to attic, and was to be used primarily by the serving staff (fig. 1.2). In addition, a new water closet for Grey's family and guests was inserted near to the new staircase, demonstrating Grey's desire for modernization and convenience.

An undated list of estimates for the building works intended by Grey survives, entitled: 'Particulars and description of the manner of performing and completing the several works to be done for the most noble the Marchioness De Grey at her house in St James's Square'.[18] The estimate is divided into seven sections, detailing the work to be carried out by each trade: the mason, bricklayer, 'plaisterer', smith, plumber, painter and carpenter. The total estimate for this work was £432 3s. 9d. This estimate provides a useful insight into the nature of the alterations and enables one to examine the works that were to be carried out.

Although these alterations were principally functional, care was still taken in ensuring that the end result was sophisticated. For example, the mason was to 'fix in new Portland window sills to [the] window of the new staircase and cope the top of walls with Portland stone similar to the coping over [the] water closet'.[19] This extra expense in using Portland stone suggests that Grey was mindful of ensuring that even the most mundane of architectural alterations were of an acceptably high standard.

Simultaneously, Grey commissioned a series of decorative modifications for the interiors, signifying her desire to keep up with the latest aesthetic fashions. These included the simplification of the colour schemes, as indicated by the details of the painter's estimate:

---

15 Paget Toynbee (ed.), 'Horace Walpole's journals of visits to country seats, & c', *Walpole Society*, 16 (1928), 40.   16 Ibid.   17 Colvin, *A biographical dictionary*, pp 202–3.   18 Estimate for the alterations at no. 4 St James's Square, *c*.1790 (BLARS, L31/276).   19 Ibid.

> To paint all the wood work in dressing closet, bed room, dressing room, dining room and little drawing room five times best dead white. Doors and skirtings to these rooms once extra on account of their being chocolate colour. Gilding over chimney in dressing room, to be cleaned, and chimney piece in the little drawing room, parlour floor, to be cleaned and picked in white. Likewise to paint hall and stair case a fancy colour, the ornament & mouldings dead white. Baluster dead white and new gild them as before; handrail to be grained mahogany.[20]

Except for the main staircase, which was to be painted 'a fancy colour', the improvements involved simplifying the existing decorative scheme to a pure white. This simplification was echoed throughout the project, as demonstrated by the proposed work for the plasterer: 'The ceilings and cornices of dressing room, bedroom and dressing closet to be washed, stopped, and whited, also the ceilings and cornices of dining room, little drawing room, hall and staircase'.[21] This desire for a plainer decorative scheme was perhaps encouraged by Byfield, but it seems more likely that it was Grey's aesthetic preference. This is evidenced by the fact that Grey also decided against re-gilding and painting the balusters on the main staircase, despite Byfield's insistence.[22] Grey's determination for plainness suggests that she was an advocate of the fresh neoclassical aesthetic prevalent at the time, and indicates that she sought to replace the out-modish, heavily ornamented interiors that had been in place since her grandfather's tenure.[23]

Expenditure may also have been a persuasive factor for the simple decorative scheme as demonstrated by Byfield's suggestion for replacing an unfashionable marble side table in the 'eating room' with 'a new mahogany side board', because 'new gilding and painting those heavy frames will be expensive'.[24] While Grey was intent on improving her ancestral London house, she remained conscious of costs and was perhaps deliberately curtailing expenses as she was already planning a far greater scheme at Wrest Park. Grey's ambition at St James's Square can therefore be seen as a conflation of her desire to economically modernize the old house in terms of functionality and ornamentation, while also conforming to the latest aesthetic penchant for the neoclassical taste.

THE REMODELLING OF WREST PARK

The following year, 1791, once the work at St James's Square was complete, Grey turned her full attention to Wrest Park, her ancestral home in Bedfordshire.

---

20 Ibid.   **21** Ibid.   **22** George Byfield to Marchioness Grey, 14 Aug. 1790 (BLARS, L30/9/1/1).   **23** For photographs of the interiors of 4 St James's as it was in 1960, see plates 137–9 in Sheppard (ed.), 'No. 4 St James's Square'.   **24** Ibid.

Wrest Park was a grand, old, rambling house that had been built in a piecemeal fashion since the sixteenth century.[25] Although it had been described by John Macky (d.1726), a Scottish writer and spy, as 'a very magnificent, noble seat, with large parks, avenues and fine gardens' in 1724, by the time the Yorkes occupied the property in 1743, it was very much out-dated.[26] In fact, the house itself had been little altered since its seventeenth-century remodelling, which included the construction of the grand, classical north front between 1672 and 1676.[27] Consequently, in a bid to modernize Wrest Park, the Yorkes commissioned a constant succession of alterations throughout their marriage, which succeeded in making Wrest a much more fashionable residence.

Nonetheless, by the time of her widowhood, Grey clearly thought that there was still a vast amount of work to be done before she died. And thus, as an experienced architectural patroness, she dedicated her remaining years to the improvement and beautification of her ancestral home. Aged sixty-nine, Grey embarked upon her most expensive architectural project, with the estimate for the work totalling a significant sum of £4,888 – eleven times more than her project at St James's Square.[28] This substantial sum illustrates the scale of the project and suggests that Grey was determined to make Wrest convenient and fashionable for her daughter and heir, Lady Polwarth. Further, as the *ipso facto* head of the Grey family the responsibility of re-establishing her ancient family's status and authority fell to Grey; this she chose to do through the medium of architecture. The estimate for Grey's grand remodelling scheme survives, entitled: 'Estimate of the repairs alterations and additions to be done at Wrest House Bedfordshire, the seat of the Marchioness De Grey March 22 1791'.[29] This document provides a detailed insight into exactly how Grey planned to improve Wrest and demonstrates that she had a clear architectural agenda that she wanted to achieve before her death.

GREY COMMISSIONS A NEW WING TO CONNECT THE NORTH AND SOUTH FRONTS

The greatest expense was laid out for 'Building the new room from the vestibule of entrance to the present hall and rooms over it and passage', which was estimated to cost £1,560.[30] This 'new room' was intended to provide a respectable and attractive high-status room, linking the entrance hall or vestibule

---

25 The primary discussion on the architectural history of Wrest Park from 1700 is to be found in James Collett-White, 'The old house at Wrest – part II', *The Bedfordshire Magazine*, 23 (Summer 1991), 4–12. This only briefly touches upon Grey's involvement and is repeated in idem, 'Inventories of Bedfordshire country houses, 1714–1830', *Bedfordshire Historical Record Society*, 74 (1995), 243–51.   26 John Macky, *A journey through England*, vol. 1 (London, 1724), p. 304.   27 Building accounts for Wrest Park, c.1676 (BLARS, L31/230–41); briefly discussed in Collett-White (ed.), *Inventories*, pp 244–5.   28 Estimate for the alterations at Wrest Park, 1791 (BLARS, L31/277).   29 Ibid.   30 Ibid.

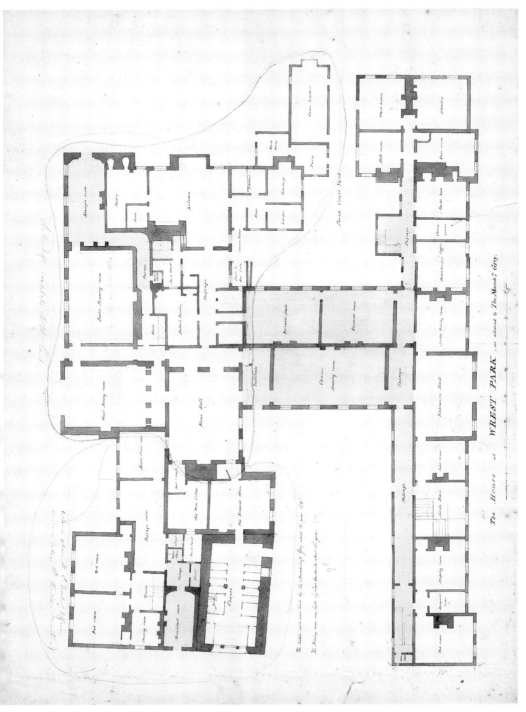

1.3 Plan of Wrest Park, 1824, illustrating Marchioness Grey's additions. The north front is at the bottom of the plan. © Bedfordshire Archives Service.

of the north front to the great hall or 'stone hall' located in the south part of the house (fig. 1.3). Originally, all that had been there was a series of service rooms, and an open wooden colonnade that provided a covered link between the north and south fronts. In a letter from Lady Polwarth to her cousin, Jemima Gregory,[31] a valuable description of this part of the project is provided:

> Lady Grey had it seems always intended to take down the open wooden colonnade in the court and build a room in its stead with a passage (or rooms) over it that should serve as a communication between the two sides of the house. When it was tried to join on this room to the old steward's room, it was discovered that old and new walls would never agree together, the whole west side of the court was therefore laid smack-smooth and a new brick building is raising in its stead, large enough for many a villa near London, with one large room to the court that may serve for a dining room or drawing room in hot weather (as it looks east), a servants' hall and steward's room behind it, with windows to the kitchen court, and two sets of rooms over-head looking to the two different courts, with a passage of communication between them.[32]

The fact that Lady Polwarth states that her mother had 'always intended' to commission this room is significant because it further demonstrates that as a widow Grey experienced an emancipated status that allowed her to pursue her architectural goals. As Amanda Vickery states, widows were the women most likely to 'leave an architectural mark and shape an interior to their personal taste'.[33] Grey was no exception, the new room in question was referred to as the 'Chinese drawing room' according to an early nineteenth-century (*c.*1824) plan of the ground floor, which indicates that Grey decorated this room with fashionable Chinese wallpaper (fig. 1.3).[34] She had long had a passion for *chinoiserie*, as evidenced by the Chinese bridge that she built over the Serpentine canal in 1748, and the Chinese summerhouse she commissioned in 1760. Furthermore, an earlier undated bill for the hanging of 'Indian wallpaper', in Grey's hand, proves that she had followed a similar decorative scheme at Wrest before.[35] Thus, in opposition to Worsley's statement that widows did not commission 'current styles that demonstrate[d] classical knowledge or foreign travel', Grey's advocacy of both *chinoiserie* and neo-classicism demonstrates otherwise.[36]

31 Jemima Gregory was the only daughter of Lady Mary Gregory (*née* Grey) (1719–62), an aunt of Grey, but due to the three-year age difference the two had been brought up together. On the death of Lady Mary Gregory her daughter was adopted by Grey and was brought up with her daughters, the Ladies Amabel and Mary.   32 Lady Polwarth to Miss Gregory, 25 Aug. 1791 (BLARS, L30/23/99).   33 Amanda Vickery, *Behind closed doors: at home in Georgian England* (New Haven, 2009), p. 220.   34 'The House at Wrest Park, as altered by the Marchioness Grey', paper watermarked 1824 (BLARS, L33/149).   35 Bill for hanging Indian wallpaper, undated (but predates 1790) (BLARS, L31/273).   36 Worsley, 'Female architectural patronage', p. 143.

ALTERATIONS TO THE NORTH FRONT

Another aspect of the project included 'building the passage of communication and altering the chimneys in [the] library and rooms adjoining, lowering the floors in housekeeper's room, store room and closet, making good the roof where the chimneys are to be taken away', costing £738.[37] This work was located in the north front and was purely functional, providing a passage for the servants. The early nineteenth-century plan (fig. 1.3) illustrates the scale of this passage, demonstrating that it ran from the north-east corner containing a bedroom and dressing room, passing the north staircase, linen room, entrance hall, south dining room, housekeeper's room, china closet, maids' hall, store room and ending at the laundry at the far north-west corner.[38] In addition, a new staircase was inserted opposite the existing housekeeper's room, to allow servants to access the new rooms above the Chinese drawing room.

By May 1792, enough progress had been made on the north front for Joseph Pawsey, Grey's steward at Wrest, to state that 'some of the rooms in the north front are fit for hanging with paper; and it will be necessary to have a bell-hanger from London; for country bell-hangers never do them to ring well …'.[39] Other rooms were painted, but due to John Woolfe's poor attendance at Wrest, delays occurred as reported by Pawsey: 'I am very sorry Mr Woolfe does not come down with the master of the painters as they [the painters] begin now to be at a loss how to go on, for want of knowing the colours they are to do'.[40]

The estimate also included alterations to the chimneypieces in the library and adjoining rooms, located on the first floor of the north front. The library dated from the 1670s and, except for directing its repainting in 1775, Grey had left it largely untouched.[41] A pencil sketch of the library dated 1831 by John Chessell Buckler (1793–1894), a nineteenth-century architect, allows one to observe its final form.[42] It appears that rather than directing any aesthetic alterations, Grey simply chose to preserve its late seventeenth-century features, perhaps out of respect for her ancestors. Lucy Worsley similarly argues that although Lady Oxford commissioned a succession of alterations and additions to her ancestral home, 'her work at Welbeck certainly did make strong reference to her own seventeenth-century ancestors'.[43] The preservation and celebration of Grey's illustrious lineage can therefore be interpreted as an important aspect of her remodelling scheme. However, far from being beholden to her ancestors' architectural legacy, as Judith Lewis advocates Lady Oxford was at Welbeck, Grey freely pursued her own aesthetic choices and created a house to suit her taste.[44]

37 Estimate for the alterations at Wrest Park, 1791 (BLARS, L31/277).   38 'The house at Wrest Park, as altered by the Marchioness Grey' [paper watermarked 1824] (BLARS, L33/149).   39 Joseph Pawsey to Marchioness Grey, 26 May 1792 (BLARS, L30/9/73/5) 40 Joseph Pawsey to Marchioness Grey, 10 Mar. 1793 (BLARS, L30/9/73/11).   41 Lady Polwarth to Marchioness Grey, 5 Apr. 1775 (BLARS, L30/9/60/50).   42 Pencil sketch of the library interior by John Chessell Buckler, 1821 (BLARS, L33/213).   43 Worsley, 'Female architectural patronage', p. 143.   44 Judith Lewis, 'When a house is not a home: elite English

1.4 South front of Wrest illustrating the extension added by Marchioness Grey on the far left, 1831 © Bedfordshire Archives Service.

IMPROVEMENTS TO THE SOUTH FRONT

On the south front Grey was more ambitious in her directions; there she ordered a new room to be joined to the existing drawing room, which cost an estimated £435 (fig. 1.4). The main reason for this, according to Lady Polwarth, was 'to make the front more uniform' from the gardens.[45] Of the interior décor little is known except that there was a decorative cornice and the windows had ornamental mouldings, as evidenced by a set of dimensions taken of the windows on 5 May 1793:

3 windows in the new room adjoining the drawing room, from the floor to
the top of window moulding: 10 feet 2 inches
and in width are: 5 feet 1 inch
from top of window to cornice: 2 feet 6 inches[46]

women and the eighteenth-century country house', *Journal of British Studies*, 48:2 (2009), 341. **45** Lady Polwarth to Miss Gregory, 25 Aug. 1791 (BLARS, L30/23/99). **46** Joseph Pawsey to Marchioness Grey, 5 May 1793 (BLARS, L30/9/73/14).

Grey also ordered the large bow window of the 1749 dining room to be altered, as evidenced by a letter from Pawsey:

> According to the directions I have had from your Ladyship, the stone masons are at work in cutting down the bow windows of the dining room, which will (with the adding [of] one pane to the length of the lower sashes) be within 16 inches of the floor, they are now 34 inches from the floor.[47]

This work upon the south front demonstrates that Grey was conscious of the classical principles of proportion and uniformity, and with the space that was available she endeavoured to create a uniform façade. To further this principle, Grey directed that all the sashes and frames were to be replaced on both the south and north fronts.[48] A sketch (fig. 1.4), dated 1831, of the south front suggests that Grey did succeed in achieving her ambition, as the front, as far as was possible, appears fairly consistent in its appearance.

DEMOLISHING THE OLD 'QUEEN ANN'S APARTMENT'

Just as the widowed Frances Ingram, Viscountess Irwin's (*c.*1734–1807) architectural changes at Temple Newsam were 'neither timid nor minor', nor were Grey's.[49] Part of her alterations to the east front involved the demolition of a significant portion of the wing (fig. 1.5), as recorded by Lady Polwarth: 'I must add that Queen Ann's Apartment (as vulgarly called) is pulled down and that side of the court will be laid open to the garden, in what manner cannot be determined till we are got a little clear of brick and mortar'.[50] This was the only section of the house that Grey decided to demolish, probably because the wing was now obsolete as modern apartments were being created elsewhere. This again demonstrates that Grey was unafraid of placing her own stamp on the ancestral home, even if it was at the expense of her predecessor's architectural legacy.

GREY'S RELATIONSHIP WITH HER STEWARD AND ARCHITECT

From the surviving twenty-seven letters sent by Joseph Pawsey to Grey, between 1790 and 1796, it is apparent that she maintained a very close watch on the running of her estate, and an even closer watch on her building project.[51] Pawsey consistently wrote to update Grey and ask for further instructions, and it is clear from his deferential manner that he respected her as his mistress. Phrases

---

47 Joseph Pawsey to Marchioness Grey, 10 Mar. 1793 (BLARS, L30/9/73/11). 48 Estimate for the alterations at Wrest Park, 1791 (BLARS, L31/277). 49 Lewis, 'When a house is not a home', p. 353. 50 Lady Polwarth to Miss Gregory, 25 Aug. 1791 (BLARS, L30/23/99). 51 See letters from Joseph Pawsey [steward at Wrest Park] to Marchioness Grey, 1790–6

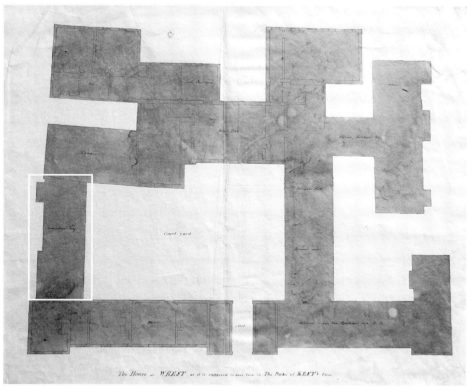

1.5 The 'Queen Anne's Apartment' is indicated by the box © Bedfordshire Archives Service.

including 'it shall be put in a way to your Ladyship's mind and approbation' and 'if your Ladyship approves' demonstrate the clear dynamic between employee and mistress.[52]

In contrast, however, it appears as though Grey's chosen architect, John Woolfe, was not quite so concerned with pleasing his patroness. As the Wrest project dragged on into its third year, the previously patient Pawsey finally vented his frustration to Grey with regards to Woolfe's inefficiency:

> Mr Crease, the master of the painters, came here Thursday evening, and went away on Saturday, but Mr Woolfe (according to custom) disappointed him and did not come to Wrest … this behaviour in him I think very extraordinary, and very rude to Mr Crease, and a total neglect of Wrest House and the works there. He ought to have come and see how the painters go on and seen the plasterer who is now doing the plinth.[53]

(BLARS, L30/9/73/1–27). **52** Joseph Pawsey to Marchioness Grey, 26 May 1792 (BLARS, L30/9/73/5). **53** Joseph Pawsey to Marchioness Grey, 5 May 1793 (BLARS, L30/9/73/14).

Grey's daughters were regular visitors to Wrest and in their mother's absence assisted in directing the workmen, as well as informing her of the progress made. They shared Pawsey's frustration with Woolfe, with Lady Grantham (Grey's younger daughter) remarking in 1792 that 'every room is full of workmen, and none finished'.[54] Organization did not improve, causing Lady Grantham angrily to write to her sister that she was 'much provoked she [Grey] did not rave her stupid surveyor into a better plan, for I am sure with any method the rooms in the north front might have been finished sooner …'.[55]

Lady Polwarth fully agreed that Woolfe had performed poorly, but considered that the immense scale of the project might be the cause of delay:

> I found there were many more additions and alterations in hand than I had imagined, and though I still think Mr Woolfe might have managed better than he has done, yet I less wonder now at the tediousness with which the work has proceeded now I know that it is really on an extensive scale.[56]

Lady Polwarth proceeded to describe the building works as 'very much an image of the Tower of Babel', continuing on to state that her 'sister says the Confusion of Babel has attended all architects and workmen ever since'.[57]

Such comments suggest that Woolfe was not as committed to the Wrest project as he should have been. Although it could be argued that he felt less pressure to please his patroness simply because she was a woman, this seems unlikely because Grey held the power and could easily have replaced him or refused to pay. Moreover, Woolfe was simultaneously engaged with the alterations of 67 (formerly 36) Brook Street for another patroness, Miss Anne White, so his lack of enthusiasm can hardly be blamed on misogynist tendencies.[58] In addition, he was appointed examining clerk of the Works at Whitehall, Westminster and St James's (1790–3), so it would seem that Woolfe had simply overstretched himself by embarking on so many significant roles at once, thus rendering him inefficient in the eyes of his aristocratic employers at Wrest. Furthermore, the fact that he died on 13 November 1793, before Wrest was fully complete, suggests that his poor attendance at Wrest may have been caused either by illness or old age.

IMPROVEMENTS TO THE GARDENS

Despite Woolfe's death, work continued under the dedicated management of Pawsey. As the main projects within the house finally reached their conclusions,

54 Lady Grantham to Lady Polwarth, 28 June 1792 (BLARS, L30/11/240/51).   **55** Lady Grantham to Lady Polwarth, 10 July 1792 (BLARS, L30/11/240/42).   **56** Lady Polwarth to Miss Gregory, 25 Aug. 1791 (BLARS, L30/23/99).   **57** Lady Polwarth to Miss Gregory, 25 Aug. 1791 (BLARS, L30/23/99).   **58** F.H.W. Sheppard (ed.), 'Brook Street: South Side' in

Grey's attention turned to the extensive gardens at Wrest. There she ordered some of the garden buildings to be redecorated, as evidenced by Pawsey's report that the workmen 'shall afterwards paint the Bath House and the inscription over the door, according to your Ladyship's directions; also the Colonnade Seat by Cainhill'.[59]

However, the main impetus of the garden improvements seems to have involved the construction of a sunken wall, presumably a 'ha-ha':

> I expect all the earth will be thrown out of the sunk fence by next Saturday night so that the bricklayers may begin the wall on Monday and on that day, I hope to set on all the labourers we can get to level the Earth ... I will do all in my power to forward that work but am yet afraid it will be too late for planting.[60]

This wall was painted a 'dark Olive' in accordance with Grey's directions. The exact colour chosen by the painters, according to Pawsey, was 'exceeding proper for the purpose of hiding fences'. He was conscientious enough to send Grey the address of the paint company, in case she wished to visit herself: 'the Olive Invisible Green is had at the British Colour Company No. 32 Walbrook London'.[61] Such dedication to detail highlights the extent to which Grey wished to remain informed and in control of her commissions, and further illustrates Pawsey's dedication to his mistress.

GREY COMMISSIONS A 'NEW DAIRY'

Once Grey had completed her extensive alterations at Wrest one might have expected her to take the time to relax and enjoy them. This was not in Grey's character and three years later, a year before her death, she again commissioned a further addition to Wrest Park. A surviving plan (fig. 1.6) of the dairy exists dated 22 May 1796 and states that 'the dairy is 22ft Long and 16ft Wide and 9ft 9i from the floor to the cornice'.[62]

According to an 1818 plan of Wrest, the dairy was located near the old kitchen on the west front, and acted as a screen to hide the service buildings from the gardens.[63] There were two doorways, one facing the service area for the servants to easily access and one located in the south front, allowing convenient access

Survey of London, volume 40: the Grosvenor estate in Mayfair, part 2: The buildings (London, 1980), pp 21–32. British History Online http://www.british-history.ac.uk/survey-london/vol40/pt2/pp21–32 [accessed 4 May 2017]. **59** Joseph Pawsey to Marchioness Grey, 5 May 1793 (BLARS, L30/9/73/14). **60** Joseph Pawsey to Marchioness Grey, 31 Mar. 1793 (BLARS, L30/9/73/13). **61** Joseph Pawsey to Marchioness Grey, 5 May 1793 (BLARS, L30/9/73/14). **62** Plan of the 'New Dairy at Wrest', 22 May 1796 (BLARS, L31/278). **63** Design for a new house at Wrest, superimposed over the plan of the old house, 1818 (BLARS, L33/146).

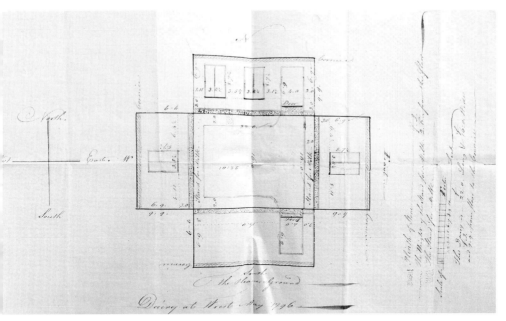

1.6 Plan of the dairy, 1796 © Bedfordshire Archives Service.

from the gardens. It is likely, therefore, that this was included for Grey, so that she could inspect or partake in the dairy-related activities.

Ornamental dairies became increasingly popular in the late eighteenth century, and it is probable that Grey wished to remain at the forefront of fashion. These functional spaces were used by elite women to engage in the traditional, and increasingly genteel, tasks of skimming milk, churning butter and creating crèmes.[64] As a result of the elevated status of the dairy, new, polite and decorative spaces were constructed that advocated clean functionality while also championing the very latest architectural fashions. Contemporary dairies of Grey's include George Sauder's (1762–1839) classical dairy at Kenwood House (1794–6) for Louisa, countess of Mansfield (1758–1843), and John Nash's (1752–1835) gothic dairy (1800) at Corsham Court, built for Mathilda Methuen (1754–1826). Grey was therefore particularly *en vogue* with her final commission which highlights the fact that she evidently took pleasure in architecture.

The architectural style for Grey's dairy is unknown, although from the plan it could tentatively be labelled as classical (fig. 1.6). The positioning of the large sash windows on both the east and west front advocated symmetry, while the positioning of the two sash windows and doorway in the north front maintained a well-proportioned façade. The large windows provided ample light, while the

64 For further discussion, see Meredith Martin, *Dairy queens: the politics of pastoral architecture from Catherine de' Medici to Marie-Antoinette* (Cambridge, MA, 2011).

stone plinth and stand for the milk enabled the dairy to work practically. In comparison to Grey's contemporaries her dairy was certainly not as elaborate or as decorative. That there is no known architect suggests that it was designed and constructed by a local surveyor or master builder, perhaps to Grey's architectural directions.

Less than a year after her 'new dairy' had been completed and only four years since the improvements to her beloved ancestral home had been concluded, Grey died on 10 January 1797. Conceivably out of respect for her mother's architectural endeavours at Wrest Park, Lady Polwarth, created 1st countess de Grey in 1816, did little to alter the house during her thirty-six-year tenure. It is probable that Grey, despite her advanced years, had succeeded in making the old mansion as comfortable as it could be without demolishing it and starting again. That challenge fell to her grandson, Thomas Philip de Grey, 2nd Earl De Grey, 3rd Baron Grantham (1781–1859), who decided to build a grand new house in the French Style (1834–8).

CONCLUSION

The financial independence experienced by Grey during her widowhood provided her with the necessary agency and enthusiasm to finally pursue her architectural ambitions. The wealth of primary evidence illustrates that she had a clear architectural agenda, through which she succeeded in her principal aims of improving the functionality and decorative schemes of both her London and country houses. Grey was evidently conscious of the future and wished to create an architectural legacy that would not only place her on a par with her ambitious ancestors, but would benefit her successors, namely her daughter and grandson.

Families are 'sometimes … the best at a distance': sisters and sisters-in-law at Nostell Priory, West Yorkshire

KERRY BRISTOL

INTRODUCTION

The subject of women and the country house has been a rich field of enquiry in Britain in recent decades. Scholars have investigated the relationships elite women had with their homes, the impact of marriage settlements and female inheritance on the rise of great estates, the hierarchies of life 'above' and 'below' stairs, and women as consumers of exotic goods originating from throughout the British empire.[1] Significant research has also been undertaken on the meaning and membership of the family, particularly the dynamics between husbands and wives, and parents and children.[2] Women operated in many contexts, although perhaps the most difficult for historians to recover is that of the sister who no longer lived at the ancestral seat.[3] Sisters, especially spinsters, are often omitted from the genealogies published in country house guidebooks yet they were never

I would like to thank the staff at West Yorkshire Archive Service (Wakefield) for facilitating my research over many years; Julie Day for alerting me to important documents in The National Archives; Sarah Ledjmi for translating Rowland and Sabine's correspondence from French; and my fellow Nostell enthusiast, George Chambers, for generously sharing his discoveries on the Winn family.
1 See, for example, Christopher Clay, 'Marriage, inheritance and the rise of large estates in England, 1660–1815', *Economic History Review*, 21 (1968), 503–18; Lloyd Bonfield, 'Marriage settlements and the "rise of great estates": the demographic aspect', *Economic History Review*, 22 (1979), 483–93; Trevor Lummis and Jan Marsh, *The woman's domain: women and the English country house* (London, 1990); Arthur Elton, Brett Harrison and Keith Wark, *Researching the country house: a guide for local historians* (London, 1992); Amanda Vickery, *The gentleman's daughter: women's lives in Georgian England* (New Haven, 1998); Dana Arnold, *The Georgian country house: architecture, landscape and society* (Stroud, 1998), pp 79–99; Rosemary Baird, *Mistress of the house: great ladies and grand houses, 1670–1830* (London, 2004); R.M. Larsen (ed.), *Maids and mistresses: celebrating 300 years of women and the Yorkshire country house* (York, 2004); Margot Finn, Helen Clifford, Kate Smith and Ellen Filor, *The East India Company at home, 1757–1857* (2014); http://blogs.ucl.ac.uk/eicah/ [accessed 3 Sept. 2016]; Jon Stobart and Andrew Hann (eds), *The country house: material culture and consumption* (Swindon, 2016). 2 A useful summary of recent publications is provided in Amy Harris, *Siblinghood and social relations in Georgian England* (Manchester, 2012), pp 1–20. 3 A notable exception is Stella Tillyard, *Aristocrats: Caroline, Emily, Louisa and Sarah Lennox, 1750–1832* (London, 1994), in this case made possible by voluminous correspondence and other material preserved in the papers of the families into which they married as well as that of the dukes of Richmond. Had the Lennox sisters not married, it is

invisible to their siblings, on whom their 'financial, emotional, social, and material success' frequently depended.[4] As Amy Harris has noted in her recent study:

> Prescriptive literature enjoined, and children expected, equal affection from parents to help them foster the unity, equality, and solidarity expected of siblinghood. In the contradictory space between sharing equally their parents' affections and being destined for decidedly unequal futures [based on gender and order of birth], young siblings had to learn both their social and their familial niche.[5]

Some found this negotiation more difficult than others. In the case of the Winn family, who have resided at Nostell Priory, West Yorkshire, since the seventeenth century, the actions of aunts, sisters and daughters had consequences extending over three generations.

Contrary to the family tree provided in recent Nostell guidebooks, the early eighteenth-century Winns had large families and a remarkable number of the children survived into adulthood (fig. 2.1). However, perhaps as a result of the demographic shift that 'hit landowners throughout the British Isles during the first half of the … century' and resulted in the birth of fewer sons,[6] many of the Winn women did not find husbands and therefore had only one ancestral home on which to focus (fig. 2.2). Our knowledge of their life-long interest in Nostell may be skewed by the nature of the documents that survive – they certainly reveal much more about the women's relationship with the main branch of the family than they do about the women as independent agents – but the fact remains that aunts and sisters were keenly aware of (and worried by) events taking place at Nostell during the tenure of Sir Rowland Winn, 5th Baronet, and collectively sought to address what they perceived to be problems significant enough to threaten their financial well-being and social standing in the county.

The lives of the 5th Baronet and his wife are reasonably well known but a brief synopsis here will assist in understanding the wider sororal context (fig. 2.3).[7] Rowland (1739–85) was the seventh of nine children born to Sir Rowland Winn, 4th Baronet, and Susannah Henshaw.[8] After attending school in

debatable whether as much archival material would have survived.   **4** Harris, *Siblinghood and social relations*, p. 27.   **5** Ibid.   **6** David Cannadine, *Aspects of aristocracy* (London, 1994), p. 11.   **7** Christopher Todd, 'A Swiss Milady in Yorkshire: Sabine Winn of Nostell Priory', *Yorkshire Archaeological Journal*, 77 (2005), 205–24; Sophie Raikes and Tim Knox, *Nostell Priory and parkland* (Swindon, 2009), pp 54–8.   **8** Because names such as Susannah, Ann, Mary, Katherine and Letitia appear throughout the generations, I have taken the decision to call each Winn sister by the name the extended family used during an individual's lifetime. While acknowledging that this may leave my subjects in a perpetual state of immaturity, the aim is to eliminate confusion for twenty-first century readers. Sir Rowland Winn, 5th Baronet, inherited the family estates in Yorkshire and north Lincolnshire when his father died on 23 August 1765. Before this date, the Sir Rowland to which I refer is the 4th Baronet. After this date, it is the 5th Baronet. The 5th Baronet died on 19 February 1785, after which time his son became the next Sir Rowland.

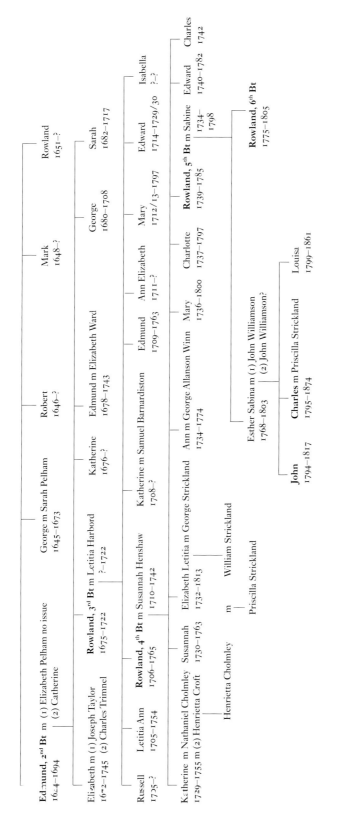

2.1 Family tree of the Winns.

2.2 Nostell Priory, West Yorkshire; photo: author.

Wakefield, he was sent to finish his education in Lausanne where he embedded himself in the Huguenot community and fell in love with Sabine, estranged wife of Gabriel May and daughter of Jacques Philippe d'Herwart, baron de Saint-Légier, governor of the district of Vevey. After Colonel May died in March 1759, Rowland left Lausanne to be in his widow's company. When marriage was mooted, Sir Rowland wrote to his son to warn of the dangers of marrying an older woman unfamiliar with 'the language, customs and manners of the English nation' and urged him to choose a well-connected English wife who could sit at the head of the table and converse with guests without a husband at her side to translate, but it was to no avail.[9]

Negotiations stalled for two years as the 4th Baronet tried to secure some of the d'Herwart inheritance for any younger children born of the marriage and make arrangements for the remainder of d'Herwart's £48,000 fortune. In return,

9 Sir Rowland Winn to Rowland Winn Jr. [1759] (West Yorkshire Archive Service (Wakefield), Winn papers, WYW1352/1/4/3/7). [Hereafter the Winn papers will be cited as WYW1352].

2.3 Hugh Douglas Hamilton, *Sir Rowland and Lady Winn in the library at Nostell Priory*, *c.*1769 © National Trust Images/John Hammond (81285).

the baron offered a dowry of only £10,000, refused to provide for younger children and sought ways to avoid paying the *traite foraine* (a 10 per cent tax on money taken out of the state of Bern).[10] Eventually Sir Rowland travelled to Vevey to conduct matters in person[11] and the couple were married in December 1761. They returned to England via Paris where a waiting letter from the 4th Baronet's unmarried daughters revealed deep concern that they would be unable to communicate with their francophone sister-in-law, especially as Sabine's father had requested that the newly-married couple reside with them at Nostell.[12]

---

10 George Winn to Rowland Winn, 21 Dec. 1760 (WYW1352/1/4/48/15); Rowland Winn unknown, 20 Jan. 1761 (WYW1352/1/4/48/43); Rowland Winn to Sir Rowland Winn, [Feb. 1761] (WYW1352/1/4/48/13); Rowland Winn to Sir Rowland Winn, [?] Apr. 1761 (WYW1352/1/4/48/7). **11** Rowland Winn to Sir Rowland Winn, 19 June [1761] (WYW1352/1/4/48/33); Notebook and Account book, 1755–61 (WYW1352/1/1/4/41). **12** The reasons for this request are unknown; Susannah, Ann, Mary and Charlotte Winn to Sir Rowland Winn, 28 Nov. [1761] (WYW1352/1/1/4/15).

Unfortunately there were considerable delays in the payment of Sabine's dowry and numerous letters and sheets of calculations attest to the difficulties the Winns had receiving her inheritance after the baron died in 1764.[13] The legal wrangling might not have mattered so much if Sabine had proved to be what her new husband believed she was: 'of so distinguish'd a merit in every respect that one cannot say too much in her Behalf '.[14] Instead, the Winn sisters discovered insurmountable obstacles to developing the amicable relationship normally expected with a sister-in-law as Sabine was slow to learn English, saw little reason to assume her place in county society, and inevitably took her husband's side in their many disputes over money.[15]

Although it is difficult to estimate the 5th Baronet's wealth when he inherited in 1765, schedules from 1767 reveal his Yorkshire income to have been £1657 10s. 1d. and from Lincolnshire £1012 4s. 6d.[16] Added to this was income from collieries, rentals in Cornwall and Kent and the substantial sums that Sabine inherited from her father in 1764 and mother in 1779.[17] An annual income of well over £3,000 should have allowed Sir Rowland and Lady Winn to live in comfort. Instead, nearly £20,000 was spent on an abortive political career; a London townhouse seldom used after 1775 when Sabine withdrew into self-imposed isolation at Nostell; and the 5th Baronet also lost a great deal of money when his bank collapsed in 1783.[18] After he died in 1785, his daughter eloped with the Nostell baker, his son drifted, and the collected Winns rallied against his widow, accusing her of mismanaging the family estates and failing to educate and socialize her children.

13 See the folder of papers dealing with financial matters relating to Sabine's inheritance from her father, the 5th Baronet's attempts to settle his mother-in-law's estate, and letters from the Van Necks (WYW1352/1/1/5/17); see also Gerard and Joshua Van Neck to Sir Rowland Winn, 14 Sept. 1764 (WYW1352/1/4/2/57).   14 Rowland Winn to Sir Rowland Winn, n.d. (WYW1352/1/4/48/13).   15 See, for example, Ann Elizabeth Winn to Rowland Winn, 21 July 1762 (WYW1352/1/1/5/7); Ann Elizabeth Winn to Rowland Winn, [July 1763] (WYW1352/1/4/10/5); and Mary Cappe (ed.), *Memoirs of the life of the late Mrs. Catharine Cappe, written by herself* (London, 1822), pp 97–8. Catharine Cappe, née Harrison, was the granddaughter of Edmund Winn of Ackton, younger brother of Sir Rowland Winn, 3rd Baronet. On the relationship normally expected with an in-law, Harris notes that siblings-in-law 'could be easily included [in the ties that bound siblings together] because spouses often came from families that were already friends': Harris, *Siblinghood and social relations*, p. 59. 16 Rowland Winn's marriage settlement and two schedules itemizing his income from his Yorkshire and Lincolnshire estates, 19 June 1767 (WYW1352/3/5/4/65).   17 John Graham's accounts, including Wragby colliery accounts 1777–81 (WYW1352/3/3/1/6/28); Rentals in Cornwall 1764–1765 (WYW1352/3/3/6/6/1); Shepley Watson to Sabine Winn, 25 Jan. 1791 (WYW1352/1/4/18/23).   18 Todd, 'A Swiss Milady in Yorkshire', p. 215; Kerry Bristol, 'A tale of two sales: Sir Rowland Winn and No. 11 St James's Square, London, 1766–1787', *History of Retailing and Consumption*, 2:2 (May 2016), 9–24; Sir Rowland Winn to Sabine Winn, 24 May 1783 (WYW1352/1/1/6/3, letter 75).

SISTERS

Because the 4th Baronet did not remarry after the death of his wife, for twenty-three years he was both father and mother to his eight surviving children. Numerous letters attest that theirs was a warm and loving upbringing. He educated his daughters to a higher standard than his own sisters had been, sent his eldest son abroad to complete his education, and ensured that his second son was able to pursue a much-desired army career.

As Sir Rowland's daughters began to marry into prominent Yorkshire families, a pattern of reciprocal visits developed, often including aunts with unmarried nieces in tow.[19] Cousins such as the Harrisons, Harbords and Derings were also included in the social whirl.[20] Sir Edward Dering, 6th Baronet, whose mother Elizabeth was a sister of Susannah Henshaw, was particularly close to Sir Rowland Winn, 5th Baronet. The Derings were also related to the Cholmleys, the family into which the 4th Baronet's eldest daughter Katherine married, further strengthening their ties.

Katherine (Kitty, 1729–55)
Kitty Winn had an amicable relationship with her siblings, writing chatty letters and giving her brothers small presents.[21] She married Nathaniel Cholmley of Whitby and Howsham Hall, North Yorkshire, in June 1750 in a match much approved of by her family.[22] After Kitty died in childbirth, Cholmley married Henrietta Croft of Stillington and then Anne Smelt of Langton, both in North Yorkshire. This inspired no rancour amongst the Winns,[23] perhaps because he kept in close contact with them all. Henrietta, the eldest child from his second marriage, went on to marry William, the son of Sir George Strickland and Elizabeth Letitia Winn (for whom, see below).

The financial arrangements that existed between Nathaniel Cholmley and his father-in-law were always handled cordially,[24] but that situation did not continue under the 5th Baronet. When the latter was in London in 1774, he informed his wife Sabine that his solicitor 'must go speak to Cholmley tomorrow because you told me that I would not want to see him after the unworthy letters he had

19 Nathaniel Cholmley to Sir Rowland Winn, 3 Aug. 1762 (WYW1352/1/1/4/17); Sabine Winn to Rowland Winn, 20 Mar. 1763 (WYW1352/1/1/5/9). **20** Nathaniel Cholmley to Sir Rowland Winn, 3 Aug. 1760 (WYW1352/1/4/3/16); Nathaniel Cholmley to Sir Rowland Winn, 3 Aug. 1762 (WYW1352/1/1/4/17); Edward Winn to Sir Rowland Winn, 16 June 1765 (WYW1352/1/4/1/8); Sir Rowland Winn to Sabine Winn, 25 Jan. 1769 (WYW1352/1/1/6/3); Sir Rowland Winn to Sabine Winn, 12 Apr. 1777 (WYW1352/1/1/6/3); Sir Rowland Winn to Sabine Winn, 27 May 1781 (WYW1352/1/1/6/3); Sir Rowland Winn to Sabine Winn, 7 June 1784 (WYW1352/1/1/6/3). **21** Katherine Cholmley to Edward Winn, n.d. (WYW1352/1/1/5/4). **22** Mary Winn to Sir Rowland Winn, 27 Mar. 1749 (WYW1352/1/4/1/64); Katherine Barnardiston to Sir Rowland Winn, 17 Apr. 1750 (WYW1352/1/4/1/63). **23** Rowland Winn to Sir Rowland Winn, [1757] (WYW1352/1/4/29/21). **24** Nathaniel Cholmley to Sir Rowland Winn, 3 Aug. 1762 (WYW1352/1/1/4/17).

written me'.[25] A few days later, he claimed exhaustion because 'I have been here at Messrs. Allen and Atkinson's since four o'clock … and I must stay for two or three hours more for this damnable affair of Cholmley'.[26] The root of the problem was probably financial as the 5th Baronet's account book records a contemporary payment to Cholmley of £338.[27]

Susannah (Sukey, 1730–63)
The character of the 4th Baronet's second daughter is elusive as she died unmarried at the age of thirty-three, still living with her father at Nostell.[28] Her aunt, Ann Elizabeth Winn, was quick to assert her belief that the future 5th Baronet would gladly have given Sukey his share of their uncle Edmund's estate when it was discovered that an ambiguity in the phrasing of his will had disinherited her, but it took two years for the surviving siblings to agree a settlement.[29] What amounted to no more than several hundred pounds per legatee caused deep divisions, particularly between Rowland and his third sister, Elizabeth Letitia.

Elizabeth Letitia (Betsy, 1732–1813)
Much like Kitty, Betsy had teased her brothers when they were young and had joined with her sister in playing practical jokes.[30] She married George, the eldest son of her father's friend, Sir William Strickland of Boynton Hall, East Yorkshire (fig. 2.4). Prior family connections existed here as Betsy's aunt Katherine Henshaw had married William Strickland, the second son of Walter Strickland of Beverley, himself a younger son of Sir Thomas Strickland, 2nd Baronet, of Boynton.[31] Aware that the Stricklands' eldest son would inherit estates with an annual income of over £3000, her father ensured that £4000 was provided for any younger children born to the marriage,[32] an arrangement that

25 Sir Rowland Winn to Sabine Winn, 28 Apr. 1774 (WYW1352/1/1/6/3).   26 Sir Rowland Winn to Sabine Winn, 10 May 1774 (WYW1352/1/1/6/3).   27 Account book, 1773–5 with Robert Mayne & Co. (WYW1352/1/4/67/4).   28 Jacques Philippe d'Herwart to Sir Rowland Winn, 20 Mar. 1763 (WYW1352/1/1/4/28); Katherine Barnardiston to Sir Rowland Winn, 17 Apr. 1750 (WYW1352/1/4/1/63); Mary Winn to Sir Rowland Winn, n.d. (WYW1352/1/4/11/14).   29 'Mem: of the Sums of Money to be Pay'd to My Aunts Brother and Sisters from the Divn of the Late Colnls Estate in all amounting to £2332=3=8 to be Divided into Six Parts' (WYW1352/1/1/5/3); Ann Elizabeth Winn to Rowland Winn, 26 May 1763 (WYW1352/1/1/5/7/2); Ann Elizabeth Winn to Rowland Winn, 18 June 1763 (WYW1352/1/1/5/7/2); George Winn to Sir Rowland Winn, 30 Aug. 1766 (WYW1352/1/4/2/35); Ann Elizabeth Winn to Rowland Winn, [July 1763] (WYW1352/1/4/10/5); Rowland Winn to Ann Elizabeth Winn, 2 July 1763 (WYW1352/1/4/10/20); Administration (with will dated 1746 annexed) of Colonel Edmund Winn, 1763 (WYW1352/3/5/4/48).   30 Elizabeth Letitia Winn to Rowland Winn, 22 Mar. [?] (WYW1352/1/1/5/3).   31 Daniel Lysons, 'Eltham' in *The environs of London: vol. 4, Counties of Herts, Essex and Kent* (London, 1796), pp 394–421, *British History Online* http://www.british-history.ac.uk/london-environs/vol4/pp394–421 [accessed 3 June 2016]; http://www.historyofparliament online.org/volume/1715–1754/member/strickland-william-1714–88 [accessed 7 Apr. 2016].   32 Papers and rentals belonging to Sir George Strickland's estate as given in before his

2.4 Arthur Devis, *Sir George and Lady Strickland in the grounds of Boynton Hall*, 1751, collection Ferens Art Gallery, Hull.

evidently meant a great deal to him as he later tried to achieve something similar for Rowland and Sabine.

George Strickland viewed his wife's father with great respect,[33] but the same did not hold true for her brother, and the latter's failure to pay what was owed to the Stricklands from the 4th Baronet's estate destroyed their relationship. Betsy's younger siblings Mary, Charlotte and Edward and George Winn (on behalf of his wife Ann) received their money relatively promptly, but payment to the Stricklands is conspicuous by its absence.[34]

marriage with Elizabeth Winn (WYW1352/1/1/12/39); Marriage settlement of Sir George Strickland and Elizabeth Letitia Winn, 23 Nov. 1751 (WYW1352/3/5/4/34). **33** See, for example, Sir George Strickland to Sir Rowland Winn, 10 June 1763 (WYW1352/1/1/4/16). **34** Item 34 (which suggests that *c.*£1762 was owed) (WYW1352/1/1/5/18); Elizabeth Letitia Strickland to Sir Rowland Winn, 30 Sept. 1768 (WYW1352/1/1/5/3); Rowland Winn to George Winn, 17 Nov. 1766 (WYW1352/1/4/2/34); Sir Rowland Winn to Mary Winn, 14 Aug. 1766 (WYW1352/1/4/2/39).

Oppressed by demands for money that he could not raise, in 1770 the 5th Baronet informed his wife: 'What you told me about looking out for the Stricklands doesn't surprise me, I look at them as on the rest of the family ... as people who do not deserve our attention ... and I can assure you that I ... have looked at these and others for a while as people who are nothing to us'.[35] In 1775 Betsy sent her brother a note of congratulation on the birth of Rowland, the future 6th Baronet, but concluded: 'Sir George desires to be remember'd to you, & hopes (as you are now in Town) you will settle his Affairs with your Agents ... & flatters himself you will not think it an unreasonable request after the expiration of Ten Years'.[36] Sir Rowland made fresh notes on the sums owed, but was having great difficulty in getting power of attorney over his mother-in-law's estate and could not access the money that must have been his only means of payment. In receipt of an abusive letter from Lady Winn, Sir George responded by threatening legal action, stating that if her husband 'means to pay the money at the time he has appointed it can be no inconvenience to him or to your Ladyship for him to give me a security for doing so therefore if he refuses I shall look upon his promise as only given to gain time'; and went on to suggest that Sabine was 'too much secluded from the world' to know who her true friends were.[37]

Then the floodgates opened. After numerous broken promises and a delay of 'about sixteen years in order to oblige you', Sir George demanded that the money be paid to his banker by the end of May 1781.[38] Sir Rowland could do nothing but delay, prompting further Strickland outrage.[39] The respite that occurred when he finally received Mme d'Herwart's fortune was soon followed by financial disaster when his bank Mayne & Graham collapsed.[40] With no money to pay the Stricklands what was rightfully theirs, there was never a resumption of an amicable relationship.

Ann (Nanny, 1734–74)

The fourth Winn daughter was Ann. After the marriages of Kitty and Betsy and the death of Sukey, Nanny kept house for her father. On a visit to Nostell, the Winns' cousin Catharine Harrison was quick to notice that Rowland complained continually about his father and sister 'for no other reason than that Nostel was not immediately resigned to him, on his return from Switzerland ... and that his sister still occupied her seat at the head of the table'.[41] Since Sabine spoke only

---

35 Sir Rowland Winn to Sabine Winn, 27 July 1770 (WYW1352/1/1/6/3).   **36** Elizabeth Letitia Strickland to Sir Rowland Winn, 11 June 1775 (WYW1352/1/4/50/4).   **37** Sir George Strickland to Sabine Winn, 17 Oct. 1780 (WYW1352/1/1/5/3).   **38** Sir George Strickland to Sir Rowland Winn, 22 May 1781 (WYW1352/1/1/5/3).   **39** Sir George Strickland to Sir Rowland Winn, 29 July 1781 and a copy of Rowland's answer of 4 Aug. 1781 (WYW1352/1/4/2/26).   **40** Sir Rowland Winn to Sabine Winn, 24 May 1783 (WYW1352/1/1/6/3, letter 75).   **41** Cappe, *Memoirs*, pp 86–7; on the role of elder sisters as surrogate matriarchs, see Harris, *Siblinghood and social relations*, p. 31.

broken English and had no experience of household management, Rowland's expectations were wildly unrealistic, but only the couple's departure for London brought respite.[42] One can imagine the collective sigh of relief when they moved to a house in Badsworth loaned by the 4th Baronet's close friend Charles Watson-Wentworth, second marquess of Rockingham, which Nathaniel Cholmley thought the marquess 'very polite to offer'.[43]

Nanny married George, the grandson of Sarah Pelham and George Winn, a younger brother of Sir Edmund Winn, 2nd Baronet (of Nostell), who had married Sarah Pelham's sister Elizabeth. Although George Winn was a successful barrister appointed baron of the Court of Exchequer in Scotland 1761–76, he was not a wealthy man and it was only after he inherited the Little Warley estate in Essex that he was allowed to marry his cousin.[44] Given the multiple family connections, however, he was a frequent visitor to Nostell during the 4th Baronet's lifetime and travelled with him in 1761 to assist in the arrangements for the marriage of the future 5th Baronet to Sabine.

After Nanny's marriage in 1765, there was a temporary rapprochement with her brother and the George Winns were recipients of Nostell game; birthday wishes were sent and by 1766 Sabine was conversant enough in English to be able to write to her sister-in-law.[45] The couples became godparents to each other's children, although Rowland was less than kind about his niece Georgiana,[46] and cracks had begun to appear in George's relationship with the extended family before Nanny's death in childbirth in 1774.[47] In the face of their petty jealousy when he was created a baronet in 1776 and succeeded to the Bramham Biggin estate in 1777 (when he adopted the surname of Allanson), and their appalling behaviour after his marriage in 1783 to Jane Blennerhassett of Ballyseedy, Co. Kerry (apparently an Irish wife was considered only a marginal improvement on a Swiss one), it is understandable that he drifted out of their ambit and only returned when his legal advice was required.[48]

42 Cappe, *Memoirs*, p. 90.   **43** Nathaniel Cholmley to Sir Rowland Winn, 8 Dec. 1763 (WYW1352/1/4/11/9).   **44** http://www.cracroftspeerage.co.uk/online/content/headley 1797.htm [accessed 21 Mar. 2016]; see also Ed. Burrows to Sir Rowland Winn, 22 Apr. 1765 (WYW1352/1/4/1/38); Cappe, *Memoirs*, pp 93–4.   **45** Sir Rowland Winn to George Winn, 17 Nov. 1766 (WYW1352/1/4/2/34); Ann Winn to Sir Rowland Winn, 6 Nov. 1767 (WYW1352/1/4/2/73); Ann Winn to Sir Rowland Winn, 16 Mar. 1768 (WYW1352/1/4/2/52).   **46** Sir Rowland Winn to Sabine Winn, 25 Feb. 1773 (WYW1352/1/1/6/3); see also George Winn to Sir Rowland Winn, 19 May 1769 and draft reply dated 22 May 1769 (WYW1352/1/4/3/37); Mary Winn to Sir Rowland Winn, 19 Sept. 1769 (WYW1352/1/4/3/14); Sir Rowland Winn to Sabine Winn, 20 Feb. 1773 (WYW1352/1/1/6/3).   **47** In Charlotte Winn to Sir Rowland Winn, 8 Dec. 1772 (WYW1352/1/4/3/18), George Winn is referred to as 'the great Mr Baron Winn', suggesting that Charlotte (and by implication her brother) thought he was puffed up with his own self-importance.   **48** Charlotte Winn to Sir Rowland Winn, 17 Oct. 1775 (WYW1352/1/4/3/21); Charlotte Winn to Sir Rowland Winn, 15 July 1783 (WYW1352/1/4/37/3); Charlotte Winn to Sir Rowland Winn, 4 Sept. 1783 (WYW1352/1/4/1/43); Charlotte Winn to Sir Rowland Winn, 14 Oct. 1783 (WYW1352/1/4/37/5).

Mary (Molly, 1736–1800)

If Rowland and Sabine's relationship with the Stricklands grew acrimonious and they felt little love for George and Nanny Winn, this was nothing compared to the battle they waged against his fifth sister, Molly, who struggled to survive on the modest annuity of just over £200 per annum left by her father to each of his unmarried daughters.

Of all the Winn women, Molly is the least enigmatic and what emerges from the archive is an independent-minded pragmatist trapped in an era when few women could make financial decisions for themselves. She was the most practical of the Winns and the 4th Baronet had left her in charge of managing the workmen building Nostell when he visited his Lincolnshire estates in 1765.[49] This was precisely the sort of action guaranteed to rouse her brother's ire as, according to their aunt Ann Elizabeth, Rowland habitually put 'ye Worst Construction on Every triffeling Sircumstance' when dealing with Molly.[50] Unwelcome at Nostell after the death of her father, she moved to London and thereafter lived a peripatetic existence visiting her married sisters, and staying in their London townhouses in their absence when she had no lodgings of her own.[51]

Absence never made the heart grow fonder but when Molly visited Spa in the company of George and Nanny Winn in 1766, she assured Sabine that she was making efforts to improve her French.[52] Shortly thereafter she wrote to acknowledge receipt of £20 from her brother and to ask for more so that she could repay George Winn as he had been 'so obliging to pay all my expenses abroad'.[53] Although Rowland's response has not survived, her next letter reveals that he had asked for an account of how much money she had received from him already.[54] Rowland stalled and Molly was forced to raise the subject again as her rent was due, she had nearly £60 of outstanding bills, and she still owed money to George Winn and to her aunts, none of which could be covered by the £40 she had received in the past ten months.[55] Rowland obliged with £100 but sent it to the wrong address and in a form that was neither easy nor cheap to convert into cash. Fortunately George Winn had returned to London at just the right moment and, by endorsing Sir Rowland's draught himself, was able to convince the bank of Child & Co. to translate it into ready cash. With more than a hint of exasperation, Molly suggested:

49 Charlotte Winn to Sir Rowland Winn, 23 May 1765 (WYW1352/1/1/4/18); Mary Winn to Sir Rowland Winn, 23 May 1765 (WYW1352/1/4/1/36).   50 Ann Elizabeth Winn to Sir Rowland Winn [10 Nov. 1765] (WYW1352/1/4/109/5).   51 Mary Winn to Sir Rowland Winn, 9 Oct. 1770 (WYW1352/1/4/2/2); Charlotte Winn to Sir Rowland Winn, 16 Nov. 1782 (WYW1352/1/4/3/13).   52 Mary Winn to Sabine Winn, 7 June 1766 (WYW1352/1/4/2/33).   53 Mary Winn to Sir Rowland Winn, 11 July 1766 (WYW1352/1/4/2/41). 54 Mary Winn to Sir Rowland Winn, 30 Aug. 1766 (WYW1352/1/4/2/60).   55 Mary Winn to Sir Rowland Winn, 25 Sept. 1766 (WYW1352/1/4/2/38).

I am sure it wou'd have been much better for us both, if you had sent to
Mr Milnes at Wakefield for Bills, and am certain he wou'd have let you
have any you desired, for it is very Awkward for a Woman to be sending all
over the City to find out a person who has a [correspondence] in Yorkshire,
especially as I am not acquainted with any of the Merchants, & besides
when one is in a Hurry for the Money, it makes the time so long before one
can receive, according to your desire the Note is at Ten days sight, and
dated the same day as this Letter, so hope you will be so good to Answer
it …[56]

For reasons of his own, Sir Rowland did not write to his sister but to George
Winn with a curt 'Pray tell Moll that I have recd her Letter & draught which I
have paid'.[57] In the end, Molly's brother-in-law loaned her enough money to pay
her creditors while she waited for her brother's bill to be accepted, but she was
still sorely in need of cash, not least because she had been forced to pay
'5 Shillings Pr Cent, for all the Money I receive in that manner, which is more
than I can afford, and I dare say you, yourself think it is hard for me to pay for
my own Money'.[58] Putting off several new creditors to give Sir Rowland time to
raise the money, she asked that another £100 be sent after Christmas. Eventually
he sent a bank bill and promised to settle her affairs when next in London.[59]

The theme of money returned to Molly's correspondence in late 1767 when
she needed to pay her landlord before moving to new accommodation and
visiting the Winns at Little Warley in April 1768, when she needed her half-
year's annuity to pay the rent, and again in 1769 when she had returned to
Warley and was worried that her possessions would be seized if she did not pay
her overdue rent.[60] In each case, she was only asking for £25.

Unsurprisingly, money was a constant refrain in Molly's correspondence
with Sir Rowland throughout the 1770s, when she was either ignored or
reprimanded.[61] One letter was written in such a fury that, although factually
correct in stating when her annuity was due and in what amount, it was hardly
conducive to coaxing money out of her recalcitrant brother:

I receiv'd your Letter dated ye 7th instant, which I must confess I thought
a very extraordinary one from a Brother to a Sister, saying you had for <u>once</u>

56 Mary Winn to Sir Rowland Winn, 28 Oct. 1766 (WYW1352/1/4/2/37).   **57** Sir Rowland
Winn to George Winn, 17 Nov. 1766 (WYW1352/1/4/2/34).   **58** Mary Winn to Sir
Rowland Winn, 2 Dec. 1766 (WYW1352/1/4/2/42).   **59** Ibid.; Mary Winn to Sir Rowland
Winn, 30 Dec. 1766, and draft response of 11 Jan. 1767 (WYW1352/1/4/2/40).   **60** Mary
Winn to Sir Rowland Winn, 17 Sept. 1767 (WYW1352/1/4/2/74); Mary Winn to Sir
Rowland Winn, 6 Apr. 1768 (WYW1352/1/4/2/46); Mary Winn to Sir Rowland Winn, 19
Sept. 1769 (WYW1352/1/4/3/14).   **61** Mary Winn to Sir Rowland Winn, 9 Oct. 1770
(WYW1352/1/4/2/27); Mary Winn to Sir Rowland Winn, 23 Jan. 1773 (WYW1352/
1/4/3/30); Mary Winn to Sir Rowland Winn, 7 Mar. 1773 (WYW1352/1/4/2/16); Mary

paid my draught <u>to save my Credit</u>, tho you distress'd yourself greatly by so doing. Pray dont you think your Credit was as much at Stake as mine could be, and if you only calmly consider what my income is how much more distressing must it be to me not to have that Sum paid, then it possibly can be to you to pay it, for I have as much to do with my Money in the way that I live, as you can have in yours, therefore I cannot do without it, and tho what I receive from you is only an Annuity, I fancy you will find yourself mistaken in respect to the paying it but yearly … as that always depends in what manner it is expressed in the deeds, and if you will be so good to give yourself the trouble to look at the Copy of my deeds, you will there see it is worded in very strong terms, to be paid every quarter, and the days of the month particularized … you say we are a set of people who calls ourselves your relations, who are always pestring you for Money, I can answer to myself that I never either demanded or received from you any thing but what was my due, and dont look on that as any indulgence, <u>as you term it</u>, and as we are the offspring of the same parents, it will not be a very easy matter to shake off the relationship however desirous you may be off it, and am sure no one action of my life has ever been such that any relation I have, need wish to disown me, and cant accuse myself of ever distressing you in any respect, so you do me injustice to lay it to my charge.[62]

A serious rupture then took place for Molly refused an invitation to visit Nostell shortly after their brother Edward's death in 1782 because Sir Rowland had insulted her by 'once forbidding her the house'.[63] She also avoided contact with the 5th Baronet when their visits to Bath overlapped in the summer of 1784[64] and described herself to Rowland's daughter as one 'of those who were not allowed to approach the House at Nostell' while the latter's parents were alive.[65]

Charlotte (1737–97)

If Molly never learned how to speak softly, the youngest Winn sister was a master of the art. The tone of Charlotte's letters to her brother suggests that she was inherently kind, but even she had to admit that relatives were 'sometimes … the best at a distance'.[66] The 5th Baronet dined frequently with her in London, and she assisted him in selecting household goods for Nostell, but he was not a faithful correspondent and could be out of contact for six or more months at a

Winn to Sir Rowland Winn, 4 June 1774 (WYW1352/1/4/3/29).   **62** Mary Winn to Sir Rowland Winn, 13 June 1774 (WYW1352/1/1/5/5).   **63** Charlotte Winn to Sir Rowland Winn, 16 Nov. 1782 (WYW1352/1/4/3/13).   **64** Charlotte Winn to Sir Rowland Winn, 1 July [1784] (WYW1352/1/1/5/6); Sir Rowland Winn to Sabine Winn, 17 Aug. 1784 (WYW1352/1/1/6/3).   **65** Mary Winn to Esther Williamson, 23 May 1797 (WYW1352/1/4/36/2).   **66** Charlotte Winn to Sir Rowland Winn, 16 Nov. 1777 (WYW1352/1/1/5/6).

time.[67] In spite of this, she considered him 'the best of my Relations',[68] and, as the Stricklands, the Cholmleys, the George Winns and Molly formed an alliance against Rowland and Sabine, Charlotte chose the opposite corner. Disappointingly for one so loyal, however, her financial problems echo those of Molly and were compounded by expensive medical bills as Charlotte suffered from epilepsy and debilitating pain.[69] Rowland responded more readily to her pleas for money and he sent game, cheese and other foodstuffs from Nostell, but he was invariably late paying her annuity.[70] In some letters her desperation is palpable and her comment that 'few of my Relations gives me any assistance' suggests that Charlotte could not rely on her sisters in the way that Molly did.[71]

AFTERMATH

The death of Sir Rowland in a coach accident on 19 February 1785 threw his family into financial chaos. Exactly what he owed cannot be determined because the 'particular account of Sir Rowlands Debts which carry Interest & the Rental of the Estate' mentioned by the barrister Fairfax Fearnley does not survive,[72] but the sum must have been substantial as land and the London townhouse were sold quickly to raise money. Although some £14,000 had been paid off by 1791, the 6th Baronet faced substantial debt for most of his adult life.[73]

---

67 Sir Rowland Winn to Sabine Winn, 8 Feb. 1773 (WYW1352/1/1/6/3); Sir Rowland Winn to Sabine Winn, 18 Feb. 1773 (WYW1352/1/1/6/3); Sir Rowland Winn to Sabine Winn, 28 Apr. 1774 (WYW1352/1/1/6/3); Sir Rowland Winn to Sabine Winn, 25 May 1774 (WYW1352/1/1/6/3); Sir Rowland Winn to Sabine Winn, 14 Apr. 1777 (WYW1352/1/1/6/3); Charlotte Winn to Sir Rowland Winn, 1 Feb. 1781 (WYW1352/1/4/3/19); Charlotte Winn to Sir Rowland Winn, 23 Mar. 1782 (WYW1352/1/1/5/6); Sir Rowland Winn to Sabine Winn, 12 May 1783 (WYW1352/1/1/6/3); Sir Rowland Winn to Sabine Winn, 17 May 1783 (WYW1352/1/1/6/3).   **68** Charlotte Winn to Sir Rowland Winn, 15 July 1783 (WYW1352/1/4/37/3).   **69** Katherine Barnardiston to Sir Rowland Winn, 17 Apr. 1750 (WYW1352/1/4/1/63); Katherine Barnardiston to Sir Rowland Winn, 4 May 1751 (WYW1352/1/4/10/10); Memorandum from Dr Shaw, 24 Oct. 1753 (WYW1352/3/4/7/7/2); Charlotte Winn to Sir Rowland Winn, 28 Jan. 1763 (WYW1352/1/4/11/7); Ann Elizabeth Winn to Sir Rowland Winn, 12 Nov. 1763 (WYW1352/1/4/87/26); Culinary recipes and medical prescriptions (WYW1352/3/4/7/3).   **70** Charlotte Winn to Sir Rowland Winn 25 Feb. 1766 (WYW1352/1/1/5/6); Charlotte Winn to Sir Rowland Winn, 26 June 1773 (WYW1352/1/4/3/28); Charlotte Winn to Sir Rowland Winn, 17 Oct. 1775 (WYW1352/1/4/3/21); Charlotte Winn to Sir Rowland Winn, 23 Nov. 1775 (WYW1352/1/1/5/6); Charlotte Winn to Sir Rowland Winn, 1 Feb. 1781 (WYW1352/1/4/3/19); Sir Rowland Winn to Sabine Winn, 12 May 1783 (WYW1352/1/1/6/3); Sir Rowland Winn to Sabine Winn, 17 May 1783 (WYW1352/1/1/6/3); Sir Rowland Winn to Sabine Winn, 26 May 1783 (WYW1352/1/1/6/3); Charlotte Winn to Sir Rowland Winn, 20 Sept. 1783 (WYW1352/1/4/3/25); Charlotte Winn to Sabine Winn, [2 Feb. 1786] (WYW1352/1/4/11/1). **71** Charlotte Winn to Sir Rowland Winn, 23 Apr. 1782 (WYW1352/1/4/2/75).   **72** Fairfax Fearnley to Sabine Winn, 16 Apr. 1785 (WYW1352/1/4/32/4).   **73** Winn Bart v Winn, 18 May 1791 (TNA, C12/1093/21).

The letters of condolence that Sabine received in the days following her husband's death fall into two camps: sympathetic ones from friends, her sister-in-law Charlotte Winn, and relatives with smaller financial interests in the family such as the Derings and Mark Winn of Ackton, and circumspect offers of assistance from Sir George Strickland and Sir George Allanson Winn.[74] Molly Winn's suggestion of a visit to Nostell was answered with the curt response that Sabine was not seeing company at present.[75] Betsy Strickland brushed aside years of animosity and wrote to her sister-in-law several times, but she too was rebuffed.[76]

Had Lady Winn been blessed with foresight, she would have been more wary of Sir George Strickland's enquiry after her children Esther Sabina (1768–1803) and Rowland (1775–1805). The wording is simple – 'I have long lamented the loss of the acquaintance begun on your first arrival in England and have since been much concerned by being deprivd from cultivating a friendship with your children'[77] – but the Stricklands' concern for Rowland and Sabina went far beyond friendship. The lawsuit they masterminded ventured into the realms of the education and social skills necessary to assume one's place in society, their firm belief that kinship ties were vital in supporting more than one generation, and financial responsibility to those family members who were dependent or partly dependent upon the profitability of the Winn estates.

The 5th Baronet's will was approved in York on 14 December 1785. Naming his wife as sole executrix, it stipulated that the maintenance and education of the children were Lady Winn's responsibility unless she remarried. Sabina's education was left entirely to Lady Winn while, between the ages of seven and fifteen, Rowland was to study with a tutor lodged at Nostell who would stay with him until the age of twenty-one, then attend public school for a year before spending two years at Cambridge University, and visiting Lausanne and 'such other places and Countrys as my … Trustees shall advise'.[78]

The first indication that the Stricklands, Molly, Charlotte and Sir George Allanson Winn were taking legal action comes in a letter to Lady Winn from the barrister Fairfax Fearnley. It reveals that Sir George Allanson Winn had queried the identity of Sir Rowland's executor, perhaps with 'an Eye to [the 6th Baronet's] … Education which if neglected or he is suffered to misspend his Time, on an Application to the Lord Chancellor who is the Guardian of all Infant[s] he will make an Order that Sir Rowland be taken from Nostel & sent to some public Schools'.[79] This was followed by a letter Reverend Thomas Leech wrote in March 1785 to a Mr Leadbetter requesting that he visit the 6th

74 Letters concerning the death of Sir Rowland Winn in 1785 (WYW1352/1/1/6/10). **75** Sabine Winn to Charlotte Winn, 25 May 1785 (WYW1352/1/1/6/10). **76** Elizabeth Letitia Strickland to Sabine Winn, 4 Mar. 1785 (WYW1352/1/1/5/3). **77** Sir George Strickland to Sabine Winn, 4 Mar. 1785 (WYW1352/1/1/6/10). **78** Will of Sir Rowland Winn, 5th Baronet, 12 June 1779 (WYW1352/3/5/4/72). **79** Fairfax Fearnley to Sabine Winn, n.d. (WYW1352/1/4/88/29).

Baronet's great aunt Mary to ask whether it was proper to send Sir George a mourning ring and to inform her of 'what has transpired betwixt Lady Strickland and herself'.[80] As Mrs Nicholson packed away Sabine's possessions in London, she informed her former mistress that Leadbetter had been reminded 'of his solemn vows he made when I was at Nostel to stand by your Ladyship and see everything righted if any Accident happend', noting that 'I have explained the just Caracter of both the Streakline Famely and Sir George Allansons which I am no stranger to their Crueltys'.[81]

Lady Winn's first response to the case brought against her is dated 3 September 1789.[82] This makes clear that she did not know where her husband's deeds were kept. Understandably, the estates were languishing and Sabine could say little in her own defence. The children were a different matter and Sabine countered the allegations of neglect and social isolation by asserting that Thomas Leech had been tutor to young Rowland before his father's death and he had remained in post until his own recent death.[83] Rowland had never been allowed to keep 'low or mean Company' nor had he 'contracted habits of Excess of Drinking and prophane swearing'.[84] Sabina had had several governesses and masters and not 'been left wholly to the care of and to associate with the Common domestic servants'.[85] Lady Winn also stated that she had received guests, although the fact that only two visitors were named confirmed everyone's suspicions that the children had little contact with 'society'.[86]

Lady Winn's solicitor, the Wakefield-based Shepley Watson, visited London around this time, ostensibly to consult with Jos. and Jo. Allen, legal colleagues at Furnival's Inn, and he seems to have been in almost constant contact with them thereafter. Their opinion was that Lady Winn's response would be found insufficient unless she could produce documents itemizing her husband's legal relationship with his estates and that, although Sabina had come of age, her mother would still be compelled to respond to the allegations made against her unless Miss Winn did not wish this part of the case to proceed.[87]

As the Allens had predicted, Lady Winn was required to make a further answer to the allegations. On 29 April 1790, it was recorded once again that she had not located her husband's papers and was unable to say more about her son's education beyond noting that (at the age of fifteen) he could 'read English intelligibly and write legibly and has made some Proficiency in Music'.[88]

In her distress, Lady Winn sought advice from her late husband's friend, the barrister Charles Mellish, at that time (unsuccessfully) contesting an election at Pontefract.[89] The complaint about Sabina's education he dismissed on the

80 Thomas Leech to Mr Leadbetter, 29 Mar. 1785 (WYW1352/1/1/6/10). 81 E. Nicholson to Sabine Winn, 1 Apr. 1785 (WYW1352/1/1/6/10). 82 Winn Bart v Winn, 3 Sept. 1789 (TNA, C12/1087/26). 83 Ibid. 84 Ibid. 85 Ibid. 86 Ibid. 87 Shepley Watson to Sabine Winn, 24 Mar. 1790 with an enclosed letter from Jos. and Jo. Allen dated 22 Mar. 1790 (WYW1352/1/4/25/1). 88 Winn v Winn, 29 Apr. 1790 (TNA, C12/1090/29). 89 http://www.historyofparliamentonline.org/volume/1754–1790/member/mellish-charles-

grounds that she had all the education a woman of her rank needed; however, he had an awkward interview with the 6th Baronet during which it emerged that nothing had been done to further the baronet's education since the death of his tutor, Leech, because Lady Winn was waiting to see if the lord chancellor stepped in and made him a ward of court. Mellish had 'much Trouble' devising a plan to progress matters because Lady Winn was determined that her son remain at Nostell under the tutelage of the newly appointed Reverend John Simpson.[90] Mellish feared that Sir George Allanson Winn would 'compel an Account' and that the case would have to be 'thoroughly contested' although he was uncertain whether the family's request to have the 6th Baronet's estates put in the hands of a receiver would be accepted by the lord chancellor.[91] This time Shepley Watson had the thankless task of informing his employer that further procrastination might result in her imprisonment.[92] Several days later, Mellish suggested that Lady Winn employ Fairfax Fearnley directly to deal with the case and he urged her to 'send Mr Watson over to us with every proper Paper'.[93] After Fearnley, Watson and Mellish had met, Mellish informed Lady Winn that he was prepared to write to Sir George Allanson Winn, and he reminded her yet again to prepare the necessary schedules.[94] Watson had also brought with him a letter from Mr Allen informing Lady Winn that 'The great point is gain'd You will have the Appointment of the Tutor', although it was unlikely that Sir George would agree to Sir Rowland being educated at Nostell.[95]

In January 1791, after Fearnley had waited on various Winns in London, Watson drafted a letter to Molly stressing that the 5th Baronet's will had left Lady Winn to make the decisions about her son's education and that any trustees appointed in her stead would still have to abide by the terms of the will.[96] In other words, the best the extended Winns could hope for was that Rowland would attend a public school for a few months before he turned sixteen, at which time the will stipulated that he must go to college. Had the 5th Baronet been alive, 'in the present Circumstances, [he] would never have thought of a public Education; but would have had a Gentleman of Ability Honour & Learning his private Tutor at Nostell in Order to prepare him for the University'.[97] This was the action that Sabine intended to take, hoping that the family would suspend all legal action.

Lady Winn was mistaken and Watson's exhaustion is laid bare in letters he wrote to and received from her in March 1791. Not only had she made him

1736–96 [accessed 8 May 2017].   90 Charles Mellish to John Madocks, 30 June 1790 (WYW1352/1/4/32/3); see also anonymous draft note (WYW1352/1/4/32/7); and Charles Mellish to Sabine Winn, 30 June 1790 (WYW1352/1/4/25/4).   91 Charles Mellish to an unnamed recipient, 1 Sept. 1790 (WYW1352/1/4/25/6).   92 Shepley Watson to Sabine Winn, 5 Nov. 1790 (WYW1352/1/4/25/7).   93 Charles Mellish to Sabine Winn, 9 Nov. 1790 (WYW1352/1/4/25/9).   94 Charles Mellish to Sabine Winn, 9 Nov. 1790 (WYW1352/1/4/25/8).   95 Ibid.   96 Sabine Winn to Mrs Winn and Shepley Watson's note to Sabine Winn of 17 Jan. 1791 (WYW1352/1/1/9/13).   97 Ibid.

promise to visit each of the signatories to the suit,[98] he was exhorted to stress Simpson's appropriateness as tutor, to oppose any suggestion that the young Sir Rowland leave Nostell, and, above all, to work on Molly, 'because it occurs to My Fancy that Something may be done with her, I build upon the Affection She professes to have for S[r] Rowl[d] … If she could by any means be induced to Withdraw her Name from the Bill, I am persuaded it would be a great Point gained'.[99] One can imagine Watson's trepidation when he had to inform her that his emissary Daniel Ecoffay had visited both Sir George Allanson Winn and Charlotte Winn but they were each resolute in separating the 6th Baronet from his mother.[100]

As the time was fast approaching for Lady Winn to submit her formal deposition, Simpson lamented Watson's temporary absence because he feared any delay would be injurious to her cause: the serjeant at law, William Cockell, was due to arrive in Pontefract at the end of the month.[101] This was followed by a warning from Watson himself that he had written to Messrs Taylor and Hepworth in order to invite them to fix a date to take Lady Winn's deposition as, if this did not happen soon, 'an Attachment [a legal seizure of her property] will certainly issue'.[102] Worse news followed, for Cockell advised that the collected Winns' case was likely to succeed if it came to court.[103] Sabine collapsed, although Watson did not give up hope of a positive outcome as he awaited an audience with (the future lord chancellor) Thomas Erskine.[104] He also sought the advice of a Mr West who was to provide evidence against Sir George Strickland.[105] After the much-anticipated audience with Erskine took place, Watson was dismayed: 'it don't give the least Incouragement!'[106]

As the melodrama gathered pace, both the 6th Baronet and Reverend Simpson wrote to Molly Winn. The former's letters do not survive, but her response does. Refusing to communicate with Simpson on the grounds that she did 'not hold it necessary … to answer the Letter of every Person who presumes to write to me upon the Subject', she suggested that the contents of Sir Rowland's letter had been dictated by someone else.[107] Affection for her nephew was not going to stand in the way of her acting in his best interests. The following day Sir Rowland wrote to Shepley Watson, blaming the extended family for twisting his

98 Shepley Watson to Sabine Winn, 16 Mar. 1791 (WYW1352/1/4/25/12). 99 Sabine Winn to Shepley Watson, 23 Mar. 1791 (WYW1352/1/1/9/13). 100 Ibid.; Shepley Watson to Sabine Winn, 31 Mar. 1791 (WYW1352/1/4/25/14). 101 John Simpson to Sabine Winn, 14 Apr. 1791 (WYW1352/1/4/25/15); serjeants-at-law were the highest-ranking barristers, acting as advocates in the court of common pleas, judges were chosen from among their ranks; see http://www.innertemplearchives.org.uk/legal_profession.html [accessed 15 June 2016]. 102 Shepley Watson to Sabine Winn, 20 Apr. 1791 (WYW1352/1/4/25/19). 103 Shepley Watson to Sabine Winn, 27 Apr. 1791 (WYW1352/1/4/25/16). 104 Shepley Watson to Sabine Winn, 4 May 1791 (WYW1352/1/4/25/18). 105 Shepley Watson to Sabine Winn, 6 May 1791 (WYW1352/1/4/25/19). 106 Shepley Watson to Sabine Winn, 7 May 1791 (WYW1352/1/4/25/16). 107 Mary Winn to Sir Rowland Winn, 9 May 1791 (WYW1352/1/1/9/13, letter 3).

aunt's opinion of him.[108] His letter was enclosed in one from his sister Sabina requesting that Watson show the young Rowland's letter to their aunt 'but not to leave it with her to be Scrutinized by the Whole Family'.[109] Evidently the idea of a spell in the Fleet prison had not appealed to Lady Winn as Sabina's letter included welcome news; Hepworth and Taylor had taken Lady Winn's deposition. Documents intended to remind West of Lady Strickland's conduct were also in the post. Watson did show Molly Winn the letter he had received from the 6th Baronet, but could not 'prevail on her to do any Thing but what Sir George agrees to; she appears full as inflexible as he against Sir Rowland's continuing at Nostell'.[110] He hoped that the Winns would accept Simpson as the 6th Baronet's tutor providing it was 'at a Distance from Nostell', but urged Lady Winn to come to an out-of-court agreement with her relations.[111]

Lady Winn's deposition is dated 18 May 1791 and adds no new information to the affair, nor do the remaining letters from Watson.[112] She appears to have remained in control of the estates until her son came of age, but where he was educated after 1791 is unknown. Did a later generation dispose of his correspondence or are we to accept the comment written on the back of his letter to Watson mentioned above: 'N.B. This Letter written by Sir Rowld at the Age of 16 is about the only one he ever wrote except the one to his Aunt … named in this Letter'?[113] The lacuna is only partly filled by cryptic comments that the duke of Norfolk was instrumental in his appointment as deputy lieutenant in 1793,[114] but that the duke had 'not succeeded according to his Wishes for Sir Rowland to continue in the Regiment'.[115] The 6th Baronet became sheriff for the county in 1799–1800, a role he seems to have fulfilled in spite of Molly's misgivings,[116] but he remained aloof from his relatives. He died intestate on 13 October 1805, when the title passed to Edmund Mark Winn of Ackton. As next of kin, the much-maligned Betsy Strickland was appointed administrator of his estate.[117]

If Lady Winn was the dominant figure in the 6th Baronet's life, the same was also true for his sister albeit with very different results. Sabina had once described her immediate family as 'much oppressed & injured' by the collective Winns' actions,[118] but this palled in comparison with the way she was treated by her own mother.

108 Sir Rowland Winn to Shepley Watson, 10 May 1791 (WYW1352/1/1/9/13). 109 Sabina Winn to Shepley Watson, 10 May 1791 (WYW1352/1/1/8/4). 110 Shepley Watson to Sabine Winn, 14 May 1791 (WYW1352/1/4/25/24). 111 Ibid. 112 Winn Bart v Winn, 18 May 1791 (TNA, C12/1093/21); Shepley Watson to Sabine Winn, 29 May 1791 (WYW1352/1/4/45/16); Shepley Watson to Sabine Winn, 10 Sept. 1791 (WYW1352/1/4/18/4). 113 Sir Rowland Winn to Shepley Watson, 10 May 1791 (WYW1352/1/1/9/13). 114 Shepley Watson to Sir Rowland Winn, 22 June 1793 (WYW1352/1/4/32/6); see also Sabine Winn to Shepley Watson, 13 Oct. 1793 (WYW1352/1/1/11/1) and Sir Rowland Winn to the duke of Norfolk, 13 Jan. 1794 (WYW1352/1/1/11). 115 Shepley Watson to Sabine Winn, 4 Apr. 1794 (WYW1352/1/4/32/15). 116 Mary Winn to Esther Williamson, 23 June 1799 (WYW1352/1/4/36/17). 117 Will of Sabine Winn (TNA, PROB 11/1321); Extract of Sabine Winn's will and administration, 3 Aug. 1807 (WYW1352/3/5/4/82). 118 Sabina Winn to Shepley Watson, 10 May 1791 (WYW1352/1/1/8/4).

Letters dating to her childhood reveal that Sabina wrote well and spelled correctly, but that she may have been prone to tantrums.[119] Her father dismissed the allegations made by the husband of a former servant that Lady Winn 'neglected your little girl, and that she was so sensitive to the way you acted with her that she was miserable and only cried from morning to evening. That nothing was good enough for your boy but your girl misses everything, even food';[120] but it is difficult to discover the truth here as there is no corroborating evidence. Caution must also be exercised because of the vitriol Lady Winn directed at Sabina after she eloped with the Nostell baker John Williamson in 1792. Deciding to use her other Christian name, Sabina Winn became Esther Williamson. There was to be no reconciliation with Lady Winn, nor public rehabilitation similar to that experienced by the marquess of Rockingham's sister Harriet Watson-Wentworth after she married her Irish footman. Cut dead by her mother, and deprived of contact with her brother, Esther and her husband settled in Manchester and lived on an annuity handled by Shepley Watson, whose communications were invariably requests for signatures on documents relating to the sale of land to pay off the 5th Baronet's debts.[121]

Esther became fond of her husband's family, which may be why Williamson sought a house near where his mother lived in Lincolnshire.[122] He seems also to have been interested in relocating to Hull if he could find a house that came with enough land,[123] or York, which would have brought Esther closer to 'your cousen Winn's that Lives near York' and Lady Strickland who 'likewise oft inquires after you'.[124] However, unaware of her place of residence, they had no contact with Esther until after Charlotte's death in 1797 when Molly sought out her niece to ensure that she received a small legacy. As Molly expected her stay in London settling Charlotte's affairs to be brief, she requested that her niece respond with the name of a carrier by return of post 'under Cover to Sir George Allanson Winn',[125] whose support she subsequently guaranteed.[126]

A meeting between aunt and niece took place in Manchester in July 1798, when it must have been obvious that the Williamsons were not well off.[127]

---

119 Sabina Winn to Sir Rowland Winn, n.d. (WYW1352/1/1/5/11); Sabina Winn to Sir Rowland Winn, 9 Jan. 1780 (WYW1352/1/1/5/11); Sabina Winn to Sir Rowland Winn, 25 Feb. 1782 (WYW1352/1/1/5/11); see also Sabine Winn to Sir Rowland Winn, 4 July 1776 (WYW1352/1/4/29/12).　　120 Sir Rowland Winn to Sabine Winn, 12 Apr. 1777 (WYW1352/1/1/6/3).　　121 Shepley Watson to Esther Williamson, 1 June 1793 (WYW1352/1/4/39/28); Shepley Watson to Esther Williamson, 26 May 1796 (WYW1352/1/4/39/39).　　122 Esther Williamson to John Williamson, 17 July 1794 (WYW1352/1/4/50/9); John Williamson to Esther Williamson, 23 July [1794] (WYW1352/1/4/50/9).　　123 John Williamson to Esther Williamson, 13 July 1796 (WYW1352/1/4/50/15).　　124 John Williamson to Esther Williamson, 7 July [1796] (WYW1352/1/4/50/1).　　125 Mary Winn to Esther Williamson, 3 May 1797 (WYW1352/1/4/36/14).　　126 Mary Winn to Esther Williamson, 3 Dec. [1797] (WYW1352/1/4/36/6).　　127 Mary Winn to Esther Williamson, 22 June [1798] (WYW1352/1/4/36/16); Mary Winn to Esther Williamson, n.d. (WYW1352/1/4/36/15).

Subsequently staying with the Cholmleys, Molly expressed the hope that 'you have got your Money from Nostell, with all the Arrears'.[128] She then moved on to stay with the Stricklands. This was fortuitous as Sir George was the only surviving trustee of the 4th Baronet's estate, and, through Molly, he warned the Williamsons to be on their guard should Sir Rowland request their signatures on any documents; Watson had recently tried to trick him into agreeing to the sale of the Lincolnshire estates on which Esther's fortune was secured, claiming that the Williamsons had already received the £10,000 agreed in her parents' marriage settlement and that they had acquiesced to the sale.[129]

Shortly thereafter, Lady Winn died. Incensed that the 6th Baronet had left the family to find out via the newspapers, Molly made a point of sealing her letters with red (not black) wax and declared that 'none of us put on Mourning'.[130] Esther Williamson was again warned to be wary of any document emanating from either Sir Rowland or Watson and it was suggested that she write to her brother a condolence letter as a means of re-establishing contact.[131] Instead, Esther wrote to his solicitor. Driven by suspense, Molly contacted her niece to discover if they had been reconciled. They had not, perhaps because (as Molly believed) Watson had never raised the matter with Sir Rowland.[132] Molly also sought legal advice from her nephew William Strickland as Sir Rowland's delay in proving Lady Winn's will meant he was withholding money that was rightfully his sister's.[133]

The will was proved in York on 14 March 1799. Its terms were simple as Sabine's personal fortune had come to her through her mother Mme d'Herwart and she had stipulated that everything was to pass to Esther unless she married 'against the liking and will of her mother'.[134] At a stroke, Esther was disinherited and the last of the d'Herwart wealth went to her brother the 6th Baronet.

Molly Winn died in April 1800 and John Williamson the following month. With their deaths, Esther lost their support and steadiness and she soon contemplated remarriage. One Manchester friend expressed alarm at her choice, apparently another man named John Williamson,[135] and urged her to think again as 'You have <u>once</u> you know acted against the advice of those <u>nearest</u> related to you'.[136] Surely the best course of action was to reconcile with Sir Rowland, avoid

128 Mary Winn to Esther Williamson, 8 July [1798] (WYW1352/1/4/36/10). 129 Mary Winn to Esther Williamson, 19 Sept. 1798 (WYW1352/1/4/36/3). 130 Mary Winn to Esther Williamson, 7 Oct. [1798] (WYW1352/1/4/36/4). 131 Mary Winn to Esther Williamson, 7 Oct. [1798] (WYW1352/1/4/36/4). 132 Mary Winn to Esther Williamson, 15 Dec. [1798] (WYW1352/1/4/36/18). 133 Mary Winn to Esther Williamson, 3 Feb. 1799 (WYW1352/1/4/36/11). 134 Will of Sabine Winn (TNA, PROB 11/1321). Copy of the will of Jeanne Esther d'Herwart of Vevey, 20 Apr. 1779 (WYW1352/1/1/6/11/7). It was more common for women to leave money to other female members of the family; see Harris, *Siblinghood and social relations*, pp 33, 148. 135 Marriage settlement dated 25 July 1802 (WYW1352/1/4/51/20); there is considerable work still to be done untangling the identity of Esther's second husband. 136 Mrs Gould to Esther Williamson, 8 Dec. 1800 (WYW1352/1/4/50/7).

fortune hunters interested in what the 6th Baronet might subsequently settle on his sister and desist from sinking once again 'so <u>much</u> below your <u>natural right in society</u>'?[137] Alas, Sir Rowland continued to keep his sister at arm's length and did little to help beyond paying her annuity.[138] She died on 6 December 1803 and was buried in the parish church of St John the Baptist, Morton, Lincolnshire.[139] Her son John died on his Grand Tour in Rome in 1817 and was succeeded by his brother Charles who married Priscilla, daughter of Sir William Strickland and Henrietta Cholmley and granddaughter of Sir George Strickland and Elizabeth Letitia Winn. Through Charles and Priscilla's marriage, the Winns had come full circle.

CONCLUSION

A reading of the Winn archive suggests conclusions that might be masked in broader histories of aristocratic women. The first, rather obvious, conclusion is that the eighteenth-century custom of leaving women reliant upon men to manage their financial affairs could have unintended consequences. Although the 4th Baronet had made provision for his daughters, the unmarried status and concomitant lack of a dowry in the cases of Molly and Charlotte left them dependent upon their brother to pay their annuities. Both sisters knew where every penny went, but their lives were made unnecessarily difficult by the 5th Baronet's inability to restrain his own spending and his inflated sense of entitlement. Rowland spent his sisters' money on items he could not afford and then blamed them when their requests for money developed an inconvenient urgency. In the end, even Charlotte turned against his memory when she participated in the lawsuit against his widow.

A second conclusion is that marginalizing sisters and aunts by omitting them from the family tree distorts the contexts in which country houses were built, estates were run and future marriages made. How can one understand the significance of the marriage between Charles Williamson Winn and Priscilla Strickland if one is unaware that her grandmother was a Winn and her mother the product of the second marriage of a Winn in-law?

A third conclusion is that women could retain strong feelings of loyalty to their family lineage and ancestral home even when their relationship with the current incumbent had soured. There is no doubt that the Winn women paid close attention to developments at Nostell and, through the husbands of those who married, acted collectively in the face of perceived threats to family status and financial survival. Having barristers in the family helped, as did membership

---

137 Ibid.   **138** Shepley Watson to Esther Williamson, 21 Aug. 1802 (WYW1352/1/4/39/4). **139** Note on the church monument to the Williamsons at Morton, Lincolnshire (WYW1352/1/1/5/11, item 3).

of a close-knit county elite who understood how local society operated. While one might sympathize with Sabine Winn's predicament, her first step should have been to learn English as quickly as possible and her second to accept that, in marrying Sir Rowland, she had also married his extended family. They could never be 'people who are nothing to us'.

Five women of Monksgrange

PHILIP BULL

For nearly a century-and-a-half, from the 1820s to the 1960s, five interesting women presided, in one capacity or another, over the fortunes of the Grange estate (later Monksgrange) lying just below Blackstairs Mountain in Co. Wexford, between the villages of Killann and Rathnure. In the mid-nineteenth century, prior to the land purchase acts, the estate comprised approximately 2,000 acres, the greater part of it let out to tenant farmers. The construction of the house had been completed in 1769 by Goddard Richards – a descendant of the Cromwellian governor of Wexford, Solomon Richards – in a family distribution of inherited land. On his death in 1795 it passed to his son the Reverend John Richards who, with his whole family, left Ireland for England in the midst of the 1798 troubles, when Grange was threatened by the rebel forces, and remained away for the following twenty years, during which time the house and property was badly neglected.

I

It was on the death of the Reverend John Richards in 1827 that the property passed to his son Goddard Hewetson Richards, who in 1823 had married Dorothea Arabella Moore (1799–1886), the first of the women who constitute the subject of this chapter. Her family had been the owners of Mooresfort in Co. Tipperary, sold in 1852 to another family by the name of Moore.[1] Only two years after acquiring Grange her husband succumbed to a severe and unidentified illness and died,[2] leaving her with two small sons aged five and three. Responsibility for the house and estate now largely passed into her hands, although she was assisted in its administration by her brother William Moore who, although he lived in Waterford, took responsibility for overseeing the collection of rents on the estate, advising her on financial matters, and other duties. After 1837 when her other brother, the Reverend Edward Moore, became

The research on this article was made possible by a funded associate research fellowship from the Centre for the Study of Historic Irish Houses and Estates at Maynooth University.
1 Connaught and Munster landed estates database, Moore Institute, NUI Galway, Mooresfort (H4118).   2 Thirty-seven page document annotated by Edward Moore Richards, 'An account of my father's last illness written by my mother a year afterwards' (Monksgrange Archives [hereafter MGA, in private possession] I/F(1)).

the rector of the local parish of Killann, she also had the benefit of his proximity to the house and estate.

In 1838, nearly ten years after the death of her first husband, Dorothea married again, to the Waterford merchant Richard Sargent. Within a short time she was the mother of two more sons but still responsible ultimately for the Grange estate until her older son, John Francis Richards, reached maturity in 1845. Whatever the domestic arrangements during this time there were obviously great challenges for her, living in Waterford with a husband and small children, still responsible for two teenage boys, and regularly visiting the estate at Killann, checking on employees, ensuring that the house was being properly maintained, and supervising planting and care of the gardens. Moreover, her marriage to Richard Sargent had led to her alienation from her own mother as well as from her late husband's family, which affected the extended family environment in which her sons spent their childhood.

While John Francis was eventually to assume his responsibilities as landlord there remained substantial problems in the management of the estate. The new landlord lacked both a practical bent and capacity in financial matters, and was also not good at getting on with people and prone to lose his temper both with employees and his mother. He also suffered from poor health. Dorothea thus continued to carry a substantial burden for the house and estate,[3] including advising him on various financial arrangements. Her letters to John during this period show that she remained on top of all the issues affecting Grange estate and house.[4] Moreover, shortly after her older son had reached maturity the younger son, Edward Moore Richards, to whom she was more deeply attached and from whom she had greater hopes, embarked on a venture that took him to North America for most of the next two decades. Whereas John seemed heavily dependent on her, Edward was fiercely independent and intent on carving out his own life and fortune in the United States. Deeply distressed at what she considered his imprudent marriage there, Dorothea reconciled herself to his wife and their small son in 1852 while they were on an extended visit to Ireland, but continued to hope that he would return permanently with them. This did not happen. Most distressingly for her was that even when in 1860, in close succession, Edward's wife Sarah and his brother John both died, he still did not return. This she now urged on him with even greater vigour, not least because with his brother's death Edward was now the landlord of Grange. Apart from a short visit in 1861 what responsibility he now took had to be exercised from America, with the long delays occasioned by the slowness of the trans-Atlantic post. Dorothea, still having to divide her time between Grange and Waterford, was thus left to make most of the immediate decisions and handle the day-to-day

---

3 Dorothea Sargent to John Francis Richards, 15 Dec. 1845 and another n.d. ['Monday'], MGA/I/C(2). 4 Letters of Dorothea Sargent and Richard Sargent to John Francis Richards, 15 Dec. 1845 and n.d. 'Monday', MGA/I/C(2).

3.1 Portrait of Dorothea Arabella Sargent (1799–1886), artist
unknown; by kind permission of Jeremy Hill.

running of the house and property. During this period, to take one example, she
supervised the cutting down of a beech grove, the subsequent sale of the timber
and the replanting of trees in another field. On another occasion she 'got a great
<u>drenching</u>' in the rain and 'a lecture' from the estate manager's wife 'for staying
out in such weather'.[5] But, as she told Edward, 'You know I am "in my glory"
when planting trees or shrubs'.[6] During this period Edward was deeply
depressed and disoriented by the deaths in quick succession of his wife and two
of his children – his son John from scarlet fever and his wife and infant daughter
from diphtheria – and was adjusting to being the sole parent of his only
remaining child Adela. No doubt because of this his letters to his mother were
often ill-tempered, or at least lacking in grace, impatient of her constant urgings
to come home, and determined still to fulfil his aspiration to become a farmer on
the Kansas frontier.

5 Dorothea Sargent to Edward Moore Richards, 14 Mar. 1862, MGA/I/I(2).   6 Ibid.

However, by 1868 Edward and his twelve-year-old daughter Adela had returned to Grange. Dorothea now provided much of the backbone to domestic arrangements, made easier by the fact that her second husband had by then died and she was able to live permanently at Grange. She created the cultured, sociable and educationally conducive environment for the young Adela whose life so far had been spent mostly in the wild terrain of Kansas. After their return to Ireland, Dorothea introduced Adela to London, took her to the Paris Exhibition of 1867 and enrolled her in a Parisian school for an academic year during which she became fluent in French. The cultural and social transition from Kansas was very difficult for a twelve-year-old but it was her grandmother more than anyone who helped her adjust to the strangeness of people and of situations in Ireland. As Adela later wrote, Dorothea, 'who was sixty-seven years old, was more nearly my age than any one else. We liked the same things and loved dogs ... No one loved the dogs as we did'.[7]

Dorothea Sargent's portrait hangs today in place of honour on the staircase at Monksgrange. Her contribution to the history and survival of the house took two major forms. Through the difficult decades that followed the death of her first husband, while the inheritor of the property was a minor, then through the period of his less-than-effective management of it, his illness and death, and the absence of her other son in America, she had provided the ballast that kept the house and estate afloat. Her second great contribution was her influence on the granddaughter whose motherless upbringing had been so unconventional and who was now inducted into the life of the house and of Ireland in ways that must have added significantly to her eventual commitment to its future. Dorothea died in 1886, alert to the end and having exercised her influence in the house for over sixty years: as lady of the house; as regent-landlord for her older son; as support for him during the difficult times of his occupancy; as de facto manager of the estate during her second son's absence in America; and then as major influence on the young woman who was eventually to inherit. It would be hard to overestimate the major role that this highly intelligent, very capable and well-educated woman played in ensuring that the house and property continued to operate effectively and to survive into the future.

II

With the deaths of his wife, Sarah, and two of his children, Edward Moore Richards assumed the role of sole parent to his daughter Adela resulting in an exceptional relationship between father and daughter, later described by Adela:

---

7 Adela Orpen, *Memories of the old emigrant days in Kansas, 1862–1865, and also of a visit to Paris in 1867* (Edinburgh and London, 1926), pp 261–2.

3.2 Ellen Elizabeth Richards (1851–1944), dressed according to rational dress principles of Edward Richards; by kind permission of Jeremy Hill.

... the bond between us [was] extraordinarily close. Father, mother, playmate, friend, he always was to me, especially during those Kansas years, when my need was greatest; and the influence of his training has remained strong throughout my life.[8]

Two proposals of marriage by Edward, one to Adelia Gates, the governess who had helped bring up Adela in Kansas, and the other to a Swedish woman, Jenny Hansen, whom he had met on his travels, were rejected. In both cases the closeness of his relationship with Adela may well have contributed to this; in the case of the Swedish woman he referred to her as being 'timid' at the thought of entering that family context.[9]

It is significant, therefore, that no sooner had his daughter Adela married in 1880 that Edward himself married. Ellen Aird (1851–1944), his cousin once-removed, had been living at Grange as 'companion to, & caretaker of' Edward's

8 Ibid., p. [vii].   **9** See, for example, Edward Moore Richards to Adela Richards, 6 June 1870, MGA/I/J(2).

mother Dorothea, her mother's aunt, as well as acting as private secretary to Edward himself.[10] As his wife, Ellen was to provide a strong and happy context for the final thirty years of Edward's life, stabilizing the personal life of a man who had been troubled and distressed by aspects of his own character, his obsession with his health, and by the massive personal tragedy of the loss in America of his whole family except for Adela. Ellen was extremely popular and liked by everyone with whom she came in contact, thus providing a strong social framework at Grange, during this time renamed Monksgrange as a romantic whim of Edward's to capture the medieval association with the Cistercian monks at Graigue na Managh. She also became an anchor for the next two generations, much loved and admired by Adela, her husband and their children. Although after Edward's death in 1911 she lived variously in England and Wales nearer to her own family, she maintained until her death in 1944 a regular and intimate correspondence with the next generations of Monksgrange occupants.

It is difficult to put a precise definition on the contribution Ellen Richards made to Monksgrange but there is no doubt that she provided stability and a sense of continuity. Some detailed information about Ellen's role is contained in the diary she kept, but this survives only for the years 1883 to 1886. It gives, however, a sense of the importance of her support for Edward. For example, in February 1883 when Edward was too ill to attend the land court in Enniscorthy where cases from his estate were to be dealt with, she went in his place.[11] In 1886 in the lead-up to the home rule election of that year Edward was asked by the recently formed unionist Irish Loyal and Patriotic Union to undertake a tour of rural districts in England to speak against home rule. He crossed to England on 30 March 1886 and, apart from a short break back at Grange, he continued there until the end of the election campaign in July. From May onwards Ellen accompanied him and, as well as being part of the associated social activities, often assisted in more active ways by handing out leaflets and no doubt discussing widely the relevant political issues with people, both sympathizers and opponents.[12]

III

In 1900, Edward Moore Richards transferred the ownership of Monksgrange to his daughter Adela (1855–1927) rather than have her wait to inherit it after his death. This was partly because of his wish to spend his final years with his wife Ellen away from the burdens of the property but also in the hope, not in the event realized, of taxation benefit. This was not altogether good news to Adela.

---

10 Ellen E. Richards [hereafter EER diary], Introduction to her diary, MGA/I/BB(10); this diary was donated to the Monksgrange Archive by Mrs Anne Wood-Row.   11 EER diary, 13 Feb. 1883.   12 Ibid., various entries, Mar.–July 1886.

In 1880, she had married Goddard Orpen, a London barrister, and they had established a pleasant and rewarding life in the avant garde precinct of London's Bedford Park, where they were bringing up their two children. Although her husband did not enjoy his legal career, Adela had established herself as a writer, having published three novels[13] and many journal articles and short stories. This she now abandoned to become the proprietor of Monksgrange, with a role very different from any of her predecessors. Deeply committed to the house and its history – one of her novels had been based on the experiences of the house in 1798 – she now devoted her life to its survival through difficulties she could never have foreseen. Some of these difficulties derived from the Land War and what that had done to the economic viability of the estate.

Although Adela's father had commenced the process of transferring ownership of farms on the estate to the tenant occupiers this was a task Adela now had to complete under the terms of the Wyndham Land Act of 1903. But the end of landlordism also raised new challenges as to the continued economic viability and role of the property. She unstintingly threw herself into the management of the home farm, supervising labourers, attending to hens, pigs and cattle, growing vegetables, managing the diminishing number of household staff and seeking to be a modernizing and economically efficient agriculturist. On the eve of taking charge of Monksgrange she wrote to the agricultural reformer, Horace Plunkett, to get his views on how she could best 'found a poultry farm on modern ideas'. More generally she wrote of her aspirations:

> I want to introduce new stock, and to have for sale reliable eggs early in the season, and to fatten what is wanted by the consumer when he wants it, and also to show the cottagers how they can grow their best feeding stuffs, instead of importing the wrong food from America.

Plunkett's reply assured her of support from the Irish Agricultural Organization Society. Significantly, she had introduced herself to him not as a landlord but 'in the character of an Irish farmer'.[14] She was indeed embarking on a life sharply in contrast to that in Bedford Park, marking the end of any opportunity to pursue the writing that had been the passion of her life, but also as the proprietor of an Irish country estate on terms very different from that of the traditional landlord.

While Adela sought to protect her husband, Goddard, from the menial physical tasks that she now faced, he appears to have given her considerable

---

13 Two of these novels were based in Kansas: *Perfection city* (London & New York, 1897), and *The jay-hawkers: a story of free soil and border ruffian days* (New York, 1900), and one set at the time of the 1798 Rebellion in Ireland: *Corrageen in '98: a story of the Irish rebellion* (London, 1898). **14** Adela Orpen to Horace Plunkett, 26 Dec. 1899 (copy); Horace Plunkett to Adela Orpen, 29 Dec. 1899, MGA/I/AA(1c).

3.3 Adela Orpen
feeding hens; by
kind permission of
Jeremy Hill.

support in these areas. But these were years of enormous creativity for him,
undertaking the research and writing leading up to the publication between 1911
and 1920 of his four-volume *Ireland under the Normans*, an achievement that only
now is being fully appreciated for its insights, its scholarship and research and
its importance as a formative work in the area of Irish medieval history.[15]
Monksgrange was the setting that made this remarkably creative achievement
possible, and in this he was strongly supported by Adela. But for Adela the story
was a different one. She almost certainly regretted the abandonment of her
writing career and the task of making profitable the Monksgrange farm proved
a heavy burden to her. Periodically she received support and assistance from her
son Edward, but as he lived principally with his wife Margaret in London this
was occasional and while serving in the British army in France from 1916 non-
existent, except for a period of agricultural leave he secured in 1917–18.

15 Sean Duffy, 'Goddard Henry Orpen, *Ireland under the Normans, 1169–1333* (1911–20)',
Irish Historical Studies, 32:126 (Nov. 2000), 246–59; also idem, 'Introduction' to Goddard
Orpen, *Ireland under the Normans, 1169–1333* (Dublin, 2005).

In 1907, a serious fire in the house had caused considerable damage and the stress and labour associated with repairs and pursuit of insurance claims appears to have caused a minor breakdown for Adela from which her health and vigour seem never to have fully recovered. After 1911 it was also a time of disillusionment for her as political developments took a course that deeply distressed her. In the 1890s she had campaigned vigorously against home rule, making speeches in many parts of Great Britain, but now, with her capacity to contribute more limited,[16] she viewed with increasing alarm the developments that occurred, especially after 1916.

The Civil War was to bring more direct challenges for Adela but she rose admirably to them, conducting herself brilliantly on three occasions in 1922 and 1923 when she came face to face with anti-treatyites seeking to raid the house. Keeping calm, and ensuring that the men of the family were kept out of sight, on one occasion she and her daughter-in-law Margaret talked armed men demanding access to the house to requisition petrol and in search of her son Edward (recently an officer in the British army) into a civil mode of behaviour which led to their departure on amicable terms.[17] In the two subsequent raids she was assisted in protecting the house by one of the leading rebels, Myles Fenlon,[18] an employee of the house who played a role in dissuading his colleagues from any intent to set fire to the house as they had done to a number of others. In this she was aware of a precedent; it was believed that in 1798 the rebel James Kelly, 'The boy from Killanne', later hanged on Wexford Bridge, had diverted his followers away from their intention to burn the house. Adela's appreciation of history, sensitivity to the local society and culture, and shrewd sense of how to disarm the intruders secured the house physically for the future. The threat she faced was a very real one with many houses burnt, including nearby Castleboro.[19] Adela may not have had a smooth occupancy of Monksgrange but right up to her death in 1927 she was driven by a passionate commitment to its survival and continuance under the son who was to inherit from her.

Adela's deep depression at the course of political events in Ireland was a significant factor in the decline in her morale. Her adolescent memories of being introduced to the wider culture and history of Europe, of which Ireland and England together formed so significant a part in her worldview, had been shattered by the early 1920s. Her husband Goddard later captured the deeper dimensions of this loss in writing of 'the separation from the greatest civilization the world has yet seen'.[20] For Adela the continued civilization of Ireland as she

16 She did address a meeting in Enniscorthy protesting against home rule on 18 June 1912: *Daily Express*, 19 June 1912. I am indebted to Ruairí Cullen for this reference. **17** Goddard Orpen journal entry, 6 July 1922, MGA/BB(7d). **18** Iris Orpen, diary, 10 Nov. 1922, MGA/VI/C(18) and 2 Apr. 1923, MGA/VI/C(20). **19** For further information on the burning of houses by the anti-treatyites see Terence Dooley, *The decline of the big house in Ireland: a study of Irish landed families* (Dublin, 2001), pp 187–92. **20** Goddard Orpen, Review of Eleanor Hull, *A history of Ireland and her people*, vol. 2, *English Historical Review*,

3.4 Three subjects of this chapter: *l to r*, Adela Orpen, Iris Orpen and Ellen Richards, with
Goddard Orpen and Edward Richards behind, 1890s; by kind permission of Jeremy Hill.

perceived it depended on the link with England. So deeply embittered was she
that in 1922, when Goddard's brother Thomas, to whom they were both devoted,
invited them to visit Cambridge she refused because she could not face having
to meet English people as she 'would find it hard to keep to the ordinary
practices of polite society' because of her 'bitter, scorching hatred of their
treachery towards us'.[21] Political disillusion was compounded by the difficult
struggle she had endured for two decades in attempting to turn to profitability
and success the farm on which she saw the future of Monksgrange depending.

47:185 (Jan. 1932), 119–20. I am indebted to Ruairí Cullen for this reference.   **21** Adela
Orpen to Thomas Herbert Orpen, 27 May 1922, MGA/I/X(3).

IV

Adela Orpen's daughter, Lilian Iris Orpen (1883–1944), known by her second name Iris and nicknamed 'Wig' because of her glorious head of hair, was quite different from the other four women under discussion. Unlike them she was neither a landlord nor the wife of one, and in temperament and personality she was much more inclined to artistic endeavours. Born in 1883 and brought up with her brother Edward in Bedford Park, she was imbued with the ethos of the Arts and Crafts movement. After her mother assumed the proprietorship of the property in 1900 Iris set herself the task of redesigning and reconstructing the gardens. In line with the Arts and Crafts principles she removed the fussy garden beds from the front of the house, replacing them with a sweep of grass held back by a stone retaining wall built by her brother. The gardens to the rear of the house she completely redesigned according to the dictum of Gertrude Jekyll: 'When the eye is trained to perceive pictorial effect, it is frequently struck by something – some combination of grouping, lighting and colour – that is seen to have that complete aspect of unity and beauty that to the artist's eye forms a picture. Such are the impressions that the artist-gardener endeavours to produce in every portion of the garden'.[22] This transformation she made parallel to her brother's building of the missing western sweep of the house, also with features characteristic of the Arts and Crafts movement. Thus Adela's two children contributed significantly to the house and garden we can observe today, building on their childhood aesthetic influences from Bedford Park and expressing their own deep desire to make a contribution to Monksgrange's evolving history. Iris, with her anchorage at Monksgrange, lived a creative wider life as a distinguished professional violinist and an active figure in musical activities in Ireland and England. She also followed assiduously the archaeological and historical interests in which her father had been involved. In addition she achieved some distinction as an artist; in a 1943 exhibition review Thomas McGreevy, later director of the National Gallery of Ireland, identified her as one of a group of women artists whose names are 'guarantees of fine work'.[23] Her circle of talented friends was extensive, one of them the distinguished scholar and archaeologist R.A.S. Macalister, who had sought at one time to marry her and who remained a close confidant up until her death in 1944; neither Iris nor he ever married. Her numerous diaries also provide penetrating insights into the condition of Ireland, usually from a strong anti-nationalist perspective; they chronicle life at Monksgrange including evocative accounts of raids on the house by anti-treatyites during the Civil War.[24]

22 Tom Turner, *Garden history reference encyclopaedia*, https://books.google.ie/books?id= 2q98CAAAQBAJ [accessed 20 Oct. 2016].   **23** Thomas McGreevy, 'A lively exhibition', *Irish Times*, 30 Mar. 1943.   **24** See especially Iris Orpen diary, 10 Nov. 1922, MGA/VI/C(18); 2 Apr. 1923, MGA/VI/C(20).

3.5 Lilian Iris Orpen (1883–1944) in the garden she created; by kind permission of Jeremy Hill.

Iris' monument is the garden to the rear of the house, which remains today one of the distinguishing features of Monksgrange and a major attraction for visitors to the property, including garden experts and amateur gardening enthusiasts. It was the product of painstaking research and labour. Iris' natural artistic temperament as well as the influences from her Bedford Park days equipped her to grasp the essence of the new garden culture promulgated by advanced artists such as William Morris. She had an ideal working situation for meeting the Arts and Crafts vision of joining the house to the garden, and the garden to woodland. The site she had to work on reached between the walled house garden and the wild beech forest to the rear, with Blackstairs Mountain providing a dramatic backdrop. The natural spring on the hill behind the house was the means of creating appropriate streams through the garden and Iris exploited this opportunity with brilliance. Large numbers of flat stones and rocks were introduced to create paths and rock gardens appropriate to the concept of the new garden.

Two features particularly mark out the character of her work. The use of asymmetry on the apron of a wide fanned set of steps, which then led into a path from the top step in a curve rather than a straight line, is characteristic of the work of Sir Edwin Lutyens who had worked with Gertrude Jekyll in many of England's gardens. One of the characteristics of the latter's designs was a sunken garden, and there is a striking example of this at Monksgrange. A mark of Iris' skill is the extent to which she managed to foresee how the plants she introduced would look in maturity and the ways in which they would then relate to other trees and shrubs, allowing the garden to develop to this day in ways that have never required significant redesign.[25]

V

The woman who had the longest continuous association with Monksgrange, apart from Dorothea, was Margaret Richards-Orpen (1886–1963), the wife of Adela's son Edward. She was the daughter of Lewis Tomalin, the founder of the Jaeger Clothing Company, and of his wife Klara, of the German Hessenberg family. She and Edward had married in 1914 but their relocation from London to Monksgrange was delayed by his war service in France between 1917 and early 1919. Her contribution to the house encompassed many different dimensions, but her powerful and forceful presence epitomized Monksgrange from the 1920s to her death in 1963. As with Adela in 1900 she left a world in London that represented excitement and interest, as she had been part of a privileged family in a cultured and cosmopolitan city at the height of its importance and international significance. Much later she explained to the Fine Gael politician and close friend, James Dillon, that while they lived in England, and despite Edward's great attachment to life there, she 'soon realized that Ireland was tugging [at him] all the time'.[26] Earlier she had written to Edward of her absolute

---

25 I am indebted to Jeremy Hill for his advice on the garden and the principles that underpinned it.   26 Margaret Richards-Orpen [hereafter MR-O] to [James Dillon], rough draft [*c*.15 Mar. 1944], MGA/VII/C(6a).

3.6 Margaret August Louise Richards-Orpen (1886–1963), *c.*1916, photograph by
Ethel Barker, Putney; by kind permission of Jeremy Hill.

commitment to Monksgrange. That commitment arose, as one of her friends
explained, from Margaret's sense of duty, to be understood not as a negative but
in positive terms as giving a life satisfaction and 'developing [one's] character'.[27]
That commitment was pivotal to the survival of the house into the present time.

The transition for Margaret from London to Monksgrange proved traumatic,
and her arrival was equally so for Adela. The conflict that ensued reveals much
about the two women as well as illustrating problems that may often have
occurred as the generations overlapped in houses such as this. The plan as
mapped out from the time of Margaret and Edward's marriage was that Edward
would rebuild the western sweep of the house, which had been demolished in the
1820s, as a residence for himself and his wife and, in due course, their children.
It was characteristic of Edward that he saw that in meeting a practical need he

27 Elizabeth Budgen to MR-O, 23 Jan. [?1927 or 1928], MGA/VII/C(4a).

could also fulfil other aspirations dear to his aesthetic and cultural disposition, such as restoring the integrity of his ancestral home and satisfying his intellectual and practical abilities by designing and building the new addition and doing so in a way that embodied aspects of the Arts and Crafts principles dear to him. His father later described the arrangement they had hoped for, namely that he and his household would live at Monksgrange and that he would help to work the farm.[28]

This never happened for reasons that go to the heart of the relationship between Adela and Margaret. During part of the time of Edward's military service in France, Margaret's attempt to live at Monksgrange with their children, while the new wing was still not habitable, proved problematic, as can be gauged from a letter Edward sent his mother:

> The first thing to realize is, that every married woman requires a house of her own, where she rules, and arranges things to her way of thinking, etc.
>
> Secondly that no two people have the same ideas of how things should be done, its not a question of the right or wrong way.
>
> Thirdly that it is out of the question expecting people to be able to accomodate [sic] themselves so as not to interfere with others.[29]

As she braced herself to living at Monksgrange after Edward's demobilization, Margaret threw further light on the issue, admitting that 'it will be kill or cure as regards your mother & me – but if I can stick it out with <u>no</u> housekeeping of mine to annoy her with, it might be cure'.[30]

Attempts to alleviate the situation merely aggravated the tensions. Living at Monksgrange was doomed unless the new wing could be completed but this was dependent on where Edward lived; attempts to find alternative accommodation close to Monksgrange were unsuccessful. In a fatal misjudgement Edward attempted to resolve the impasse by suggesting that his parents should move out temporarily while he completed the building work, thus causing such offence that the suggestion that Adela should 'leave her ancestral home' still rankled with his father several years later.[31] While in February 1927 (shortly before her death) one of Adela's friends referred to the relationship with her son's family having improved,[32] a friend of Margaret's at much the same time was referring to how 'inexcusable' Adela's conduct had been towards Edward and his family.[33] Thus the transition from one generation to another had been seriously compromised. Also caught up in this conflict was Edward's sister Iris and the relationship

28 Goddard Orpen to Edward Richards-Orpen [hereafter ERR-O], 17 Oct. 1924 (copy and damaged original), MGA/I/U(7f). 29 ERR-O to Adela Orpen, 23 Jan. 1919, MGA/I/U(7c). 30 MR-O to ERR-O, 20 Feb. [1919], MGA/VII/A(4n). 31 Goddard Orpen to ERR-O, 17 Oct. 1924, MGA/I/U(7f). 32 Celestia Wattles to Adela Orpen, 3 Feb. 1927, MGA/I/S(6). 33 Elizabeth Budgen to MR-O, 23 Jan. [?1927 or 1928], MGA/VII/C(4a).

between her and Margaret was strained until Iris moved out after the death of her father in 1932.

There was a difference between Adela and Margaret in a more significant area. In January 1919, the Irish Unionist Alliance, of which Adela was an active member, split over the attempt by its president, the earl of Midleton, to shift the organization to support a form of dominion home rule, this as part of belated attempts to avert partition. Adela, long an active campaigner against home rule, was unmoved by new circumstances and spoke so strongly and effectively against Midleton that, following his departure and that of his supporters to form a unionist anti-partition league, she was co-opted to the organization's executive council.[34] Ironically she advised Edward of her new role[35] at much the same time as he was being urged by Margaret to follow Midleton on the grounds 'that the game is up for the die-hards' and 'what good can you do yourself or Ireland or Monksgrange or your family by sticking to it'.[36] It is not evident whether Adela was aware of how far apart politically she was from Margaret, and by extension from her son, but it unquestionably affected Margaret's attitude to her mother-in-law, as did the fact that Edward was hamstrung in trying to establish the farm at Monksgrange on a more viable footing by fundamental disagreements with his mother on how to manage it.

Neither Edward nor Margaret had lived for significant periods in Ireland until after the First World War and then at first only briefly. But in that time Ireland had changed significantly and Margaret in particular, with her English perceptions and, perhaps not least, that upper-middle-class English disdain for the landed elite, may have seen Irish affairs in a clearer light than Edward did. Even earlier Margaret had become very annoyed at what she saw as Adela's sensationalist over-reaction to events in Ireland, most notably to an agricultural labourers' strike in 1918, Margaret describing Adela's letter about this as that of a 'mad woman'.[37] Such differences of perspective on public affairs can only have deepened the other problems that emerged when they attempted to live together.

Once Edward and Margaret returned to live permanently at Monksgrange in the late 1920s following Adela's death there was no doubt about their political allegiance in strongly supporting the Free State and, in due course, the Fine Gael party. Edward quickly established himself as a brilliant innovative thinker in the area of economics and, more particularly, agriculture, becoming a regular columnist for the *Irish Independent* and a prolific writer on Irish affairs. He was a significant contributor to the development of Fine Gael as a political force and in particular to its policies on agriculture. The culmination of this work was his appointment as a senator in 1948. His and Margaret's papers reveal, however, the extent to which his career was a product of their shared endeavours. Many of

34 *Irish Times*, 25 Jan. 1919.   35 Adela Orpen to ERR-O, 15 Feb. 1919, MGA/I/U(7c). 36 MR-O to ERR-O, 23 Feb. [1919], MGA/VII/A(4n).   37 MR-O to ERR-O, 10 Aug.[1918]; ibid., 12 Aug. [1918]; also ERR-O to MR-O, [15 Aug. 1918], MGA/VII/A(4k).

the drafts of his articles and speeches are annotated with Margaret's suggestions and her correspondence, especially with James Dillon, reveal her assiduous devotion to supporting and contributing to his public role. This was particularly significant as Edward, notwithstanding his intellectual prowess and deep commitments, was inefficient and disorganized and her involvement was thus crucial to his effectiveness in the public arena. Her role in this regard was also reinforced by her excellence as a hostess presiding over a regime of hospitality that ensured that Monksgrange became a centre of sociability for their many friends in Ireland and Britain as well as for many of those involved in Irish public life.

Tennis parties, occurring about once a week in the summer holidays according to Margaret's daughter Charmian, were an important feature of Monksgrange life. Anything between two or three dozen visitors might attend, the number unknown beforehand:

> Mum kept a store of porter cakes to supplement the usual afternoon tea. These were rich fruit cakes softened with stout which, if kept in tins, improved with age so could be kept for any length of time. To slake the thirst when playing tennis she provided raspberry vinegar, a much pleasanter drink than the name suggests which we made during the raspberry season to keep in store for the rest of the year.[38]

While Margaret was an active participant in every area of Edward's life, she was also a very busy manager of a household. She took seriously the training of staff; for example, daughters of one of the principal men employed in the house she trained as housemaids and to wait on tables.[39] As a general rule she 'fed at least ten people every day and many more during the summer when the house would be full of visitors'.[40] The poor returns from farming meant that Edward and Margaret had to be very inventive in finding supplementary sources of income and in the 1930s they participated in the 'Europe on wheels' scheme, which enabled wealthy Americans to stay in prestigious homes while they travelled. While Margaret took on the responsibility of providing for them in the house, Edward acted as chauffeur, introducing them to historic and other sites around Ireland: 'They really did get their taste of family life because meals were eaten with us and consisted of good fresh country food with no extra frills',[41] as Charmian later recalled. This scheme was brought to an end by the outbreak of war in 1939 but Edward and Margaret revived the concept in the 1950s with the Monksgrange private guest house venture.[42]

---

38 Charmian Hill, Unpublished reminiscences of her childhood, MGA/VII/D(19), p. 12.
39 Ibid.   40 Ibid., p. 11.   41 Ibid., p. 12; MGA/VII/H(29a-k).   42 MGA/VII/H(29j).

VI

Three of the women who profoundly influenced the future of Monksgrange in the second half of the nineteenth century had to operate within the parameters set by an unusual, often very irritable, in many ways emotionally troubled, but highly talented landlord – Edward Moore Richards. Obsessed with problems of his own health, many of which appear to have been largely imagined, he could make life difficult for the women around him, even though he was devoted to them and held attitudes towards women far more advanced than was usual at the time. He was a lifelong campaigner for reform of women's dress, not only because of the damage he believed that clothing such as stays did to their physical health but also because he saw these modes of dress as symbolizing the subordination of women and the restriction of their capacity to lead full and rewarding lives. His ideas had been consolidated while in America but he later joined the Western Rational Dress Club and subsequently had correspondence and an article published in the *Rational Dress Gazette*.[43] His mother Dorothea, his daughter, Adela, and his second wife, Ellen, were greatly attached to him and any difficulties they had to endure were met with sympathy and devotion, but also with a firmness and determination that ensured that their own interests and their distinctive contributions were protected. Margaret Richards-Orpen for her part committed herself to uncompromising support of a husband whose talents she admired but who in a multitude of ways made life difficult by fecklessness, particularly in the early years of their marriage, and incorrigible forgetfulness and inefficiency, especially in financial matters. His mother Adela had also suffered from many of these attributes of her son, often left in the dark as to his intentions. In one respect Adela was perhaps the most fortunate of the women in enjoying a husband endowed with a combination of outstanding intellect and skills, deep commitment to his wife and family, and an exceptional capacity for support and devotion to those around him.

Each of the women discussed in this chapter made significant contributions to the history of this Co. Wexford house and estate and exercised different but important influences on the individual family members who lived with them or followed them in subsequent years. In some cases, they did this by their strong support of their male counterparts, this being particularly so of Dorothea Sargent, Ellen Richards and Margaret Richards-Orpen, but even in those cases ensuring their own independence of action. Iris Orpen's contribution was a very substantial and lasting physical one in the form of an exquisite garden that

---

43 *Rational Dress Gazette: Organ of the Rational Dress League*, no. 7 (Apr. 1899); no. 15 (Dec. 1899); and no. 16 (Jan. 1900); Minutes of the Western Rational Dress Club, 1897 (I am indebted to Don Chapman for this reference). For further comment on Edward Moore Richards' views on rational dress see Don Chapman, *Wearing the trousers: fashion, freedom and the rise of the modern woman* (Stroud, 2017), pp 202–3, 240.

remains one of the glories of Monksgrange. Adela Orpen, the one woman who presided over the property in her own right as its proprietor, displayed a high level of commitment in steering the enterprise through critical years in which the place of such properties within the wider Irish polity was significantly altered and in some respects threatened.

All these women displayed attributes of courage, imagination, intelligence and character and exemplified qualities of toughness and flexibility. They played major roles in enabling the property and its occupants to weather significant storms and challenges and to operate as a site of considerable creativity and inventiveness across several generations. All of them were crucial in the development and survival of this property into the present time.

Declaring loyalty to the Union: the women of Ulster's country houses and the organization of Ulster Day

JONATHAN CHERRY & ARLENE CRAMPSIE

INTRODUCTION

Across Ireland the waning power of the landed elite was clearly evident by the turn of the twentieth century. A combination of increased centralized state control of local government, the expansion of the franchise, the introduction of the secret ballot, discontent over land reform and the growth of grassroots political organizations all ensured a revolution in traditional power structures. For much of Ireland this was evidenced by the almost total usurpation of local and national power by nationalist candidates in the later part of the nineteenth century. Ulster on the other hand, as in so much of its history, was a case apart. While the slow speed of land reform initially drove a wedge between landlords and tenants there, the realization of the significant threat posed by home rule to the sanctity of the union with Great Britain helped to stem the rift somewhat. However, by the onset of the third home rule crisis, and despite being united through the unionist cause, it was clear that the pendulum of power had swung away from landed society. Establishing an endpoint for the significant political influence of the male landed elite has generated much academic debate, yet little similar consideration has been given to the females of the class. This chapter seeks partly to address this issue by offering an examination of the influence exerted by the women of Ulster's country houses in organizing the signing of the female equivalent of the Ulster Solemn League and Covenant, known as the Declaration, in September 1912.

As the largest single mobilizing event of grassroots Ulster unionism, Ulster Day offers a unique lens through which to examine the political activity of all socio-economic groups across the entire unionist spectrum during the third home rule crisis. On 28 September 1912, almost half a million Ulster men and women pledged their allegiance to the campaign to maintain the union with Great Britain. The administrative and organizational logistics of such a large-scale, widespread event necessitated the assistance of a team of 1,546 organizing agents across 1,028 different signing centres in Ulster. In attempting to chart the role of the women of Ulster's country houses in this event, this chapter draws on primary research from an ongoing digital humanities project to investigate the geographies of Ulster Day. A comprehensive database of organizing agents and signing locations has been compiled through a detailed search and comparison of two separate, online and freely available digitized archival sources – the digital database of the Ulster Covenant hosted by the Public Records Office of Northern Ireland (PRONI) and the 1911 Census Returns hosted by the National Archives of Ireland (NAI). This has facilitated an in-depth examination of the extensive and varied gender, socio-economic and religious profiles of these grassroots leaders.

For the purposes of this chapter the women of Ulster's country houses have been defined as the female relatives of the male aristocracy and landed gentry of the nine counties of Ulster. This was largely due to practicalities with the 1911 Census where, as might be expected considering contemporary social norms, the majority of women from the upper and middle classes returned 'none stated' for their occupation. Thus, in order to identify those of the landed elite a referencing back to the occupation of their nearest male relative on the census, usually listed as head of household, was necessary. This identified a total of twenty-nine female agents whose male relatives self-identified as landowners. However, it was apparent that a number of male landed agents[1] had also identified themselves variously as magistrates, large farmers, and even simply farmers. A second examination of the remaining female agents was therefore undertaken, cross checking their names and that of their male relatives against [Richard] Griffith's Valuation, the 1906 Return of Untenanted Lands (Ireland), *Burke's landed gentry of Ireland* (1912 edition) and *Burke's peerage* (1914 edition).[2] From this a further twenty-seven female agents from the landed class were identified, bringing the total number of women from Ulster's country houses to fifty-six. While every attempt was made to identify all female landed agents, it is possible that a number may remain unaccounted for – illegible handwriting, poor record keeping in some signing centres and agents who did not provide an address or first name proved difficult to definitively identify. Of the total 483 female agents listed across Ulster, seventy-one, or 14.7 per cent, could not be located on the census.

Both authors contributed jointly to the writing of this paper: Dr Jonathan Cherry, School of History and Geography, Dublin City University, and Dr Arlene Crampsie, School of Geography, University College Dublin.   1 The terms 'organizing agent' or 'agent' used throughout this essay reflects the term 'Agent in Charge' as listed on the outside of the folders used to compile the completed Covenant and Declaration signing sheets. The term 'landed agent' is used here *specifically* to refer to those agents identified as being members of Ulster's landed class and occupants of the province's country houses. These should not be confused with the occupation of a land agent (that is, the person charged with daily estate administration).   2 *The general valuation of tenements in Ireland* (Dublin, 1848–64); *Return of untenanted lands in rural districts, distinguishing demesnes on which there is a mansion, showing rural district and electoral division, townland, area in statute acres, valuation (Poor Law) and names of occupiers as in valuation lists*, HC 1906, c.177; Bernard Burke, *A genealogical and heraldic history of the landed gentry of Ireland* (London, 1912); idem, *A genealogical and heraldic history of the peerage and baronetage* (London, 1914).

DECLINING LANDED POLITICAL INFLUENCE?

Before embarking on an examination of the findings it is important to situate these women in their contemporary political landscape. As alluded to at the outset, the first two home rule crises in the late nineteenth century went some way to healing the wounds that had arisen as a result of land reform between unionist landlords and tenants in Ulster. The value of the landed elite to the emerging unionist movement, through their extensive connections to the political elite in Westminster, as well as their significant leadership contribution within the Orange Order, ensured that their social standing and support was actively sought. However, it was no longer as the sole or even dominant power brokers.

Throughout Ulster the unionist leadership encompassed not just the landed elite, but increasingly industrialists, professionals and business leaders. The second home rule crisis saw the organization of the 1892 Ulster Unionist Convention, which attracted 12,000 delegates to a mass anti-home rule demonstration in Belfast. Although the landed elite were instrumental in the organization of this event, it was 'deliberately and carefully planned to accord equal weight to landed, family, business and labouring classes',[3] reflecting the increasing role played by the middle and indeed lower classes in popular politics.[4] Gailey argues that after the successful defeat of this second home rule bill 'the hold of the landed elites on local politics declined sharply in the face of widespread popular discontent'.[5] While he attributes this decline to a range of factors including a renewal of discontent over land reform and growing disillusionment with the Conservative government in the aftermath of the devolution crisis (1904–5), it is clear that the increasing democratization of local government also had a role to play.

Local government reform, through the Local Government (Ireland) Act, 1898, introduced democratically elected county, urban district and rural district councils, which as Fleming suggests empowered the rural middle classes.[6]

---

3 Olwen Purdue, *The big house in the north of Ireland* (Dublin, 2009), p. 171.   **4** See Gordon Lucy, *The great convention, the Ulster Unionist Convention of 1892* (Lurgan, 1995); David Burnett, 'The modernization of unionism, 1892–1914?' in Richard English and Graham Walker (eds), *Unionism in modern Ireland* (Dublin, 1996), pp 41–62; and N.C. Fleming, 'The landed elite, power and Ulster unionism' in D. George Boyce and Alan O'Day (eds), *The Ulster crisis* (London, 2006), pp 86–104. For details on the various roles played by Liberal and Conservative Unionists in 1892 and in unionism more generally see: Graham Walker, 'Thomas Sinclair: Presbyterian Liberal Unionist' in English and Walker (eds), *Unionism in modern Ireland*, pp 19–40; Ian Cawood, 'The persistence of liberal unionism in Irish politics, 1886–1912' in Gabriel Doherty (ed.), *Cork studies in the Irish revolution: the home rule crisis, 1912–1922* (Cork, 2014), pp 333–52.   **5** Andrew Gailey, 'King Carson: an essay on the invention of leadership', *Irish Historical Studies*, 30:117 (May 1996), 66–87 at 70.   **6** N.C. Fleming, 'Leadership, the middle classes and Ulster unionism since the late nineteenth century' in Fintan Lane (ed.), *Politics, society and the middle class in modern Ireland* (Basingstoke, 2010), pp 212–29.

Practically, however, it went much further. Based on a broadened ratepayer franchise and offering the first tentative steps towards meaningful female suffrage, all occupiers regardless of property value or gender became entitled to vote. Furthermore all male and female occupiers could stand for election to the district councils, empowering and enabling all classes to participate fully in local self-government, thereby creating a new, more politically aware, self-sufficient and engaged citizenship.[7]

This engagement was reflected in the rapid growth of numerous political organizations, both nationalist and unionist, in the early twentieth century, which attracted widespread popular support. Chief amongst these for the unionist community was the establishment in 1905 of the Ulster Unionist Council (UUC), designed to unite the various unionist associations across the province, improve linkages between unionists and their MPs and to further advance the unionist cause.[8] Although landed influence was still clearly identifiable, the composition of the UUC reflected the continuing popularization of unionist politics. Half of the 200-strong council were nominated by local unionist associations, 50 were selected from the ranks of the Orange Order, while the remaining 50 would comprise 'distinguished unionists' including the gentry.[9] As a body this council was too large to be effective, necessitating the creation of a standing committee of 66 to oversee the daily workings. This committee further reflected 'the bourgeois predominance which had been developing within Unionism from the 1880s', drawing two-thirds of its members from the middle classes.[10] Only the final third remained the preserve of the landed gentry, peers and sons of peers. This declining influence was perhaps even more clearly identifiable when consideration is given to the role of the landed elite in national politics, where the number of MPs from landed backgrounds had dropped to just five in 1906 and three by December 1910.[11] Thus, while the support and social influence of landlords was still actively sought, their political activity increasingly was not.

This is in stark contrast to the patterns emerging in female political circles by the end of the first decade of the twentieth century, where landed women retained key political roles. Of course women of any class were still relative

---

7 It was 1911, however, before women were entitled to stand for election to county councils. For more see Arlene Crampsie, 'Creating citizens from colonial subjects: reforming local government in early twentieth century Ireland', *Historical Geography*, 42 (2014), 208–28. 8 Although meetings were held discussing the council's formation in 1904, it was 1905 before the name was officially used; F.S.L. Lyons, 'The Irish Unionist Party and the devolution crisis of 1904–5', *Irish Historical Studies*, 6:21 (1948), 1–22; Alvin Jackson, *The Ulster Party, Irish Unionists in the House of Commons, 1884–1911* (Oxford, 1989); Graham Walker, *A history of the Ulster Unionist Party: protest pragmatism and pessimism* (Manchester, 2004), pp 22–5; and Thomas Kennedy, 'War, patriotism and the Ulster Unionist Council, 1914–1918', *Éire-Ireland*, 40:3 & 4 (2005), 189–211. 9 Kennedy, 'War, patriotism and the Ulster Unionist Council', p. 191. 10 Jackson, *The Ulster Party*, p. 239. 11 Fleming, 'The landed elite, power and Ulster unionism', p. 100.

newcomers to political involvement. The latter half of the nineteenth century had witnessed a steady growth in female political involvement as increasing education levels and philanthropic activities created a more socially and politically aware gender cohort.[12] Through petitioning, fundraising, canvassing and demonstrating women began to carve out political roles, which over time fuelled the female suffrage movement. However, it was the increasingly tense political situation in Ireland that benefited most from the growing politicization of women, to the detriment of the suffrage movement, particularly in Ulster.[13]

While female ancillary organizations were established by both nationalists and unionists it is apparent that unionist women were much better organized and structured than their nationalist counterparts.[14] Women had been prominent in the anti-home rule campaign from the outset and had readily demonstrated their ability to mobilize large numbers to their cause. In 1893, a memorial sent to Queen Victoria reportedly contained 103,000 female signatures, while a petition from Ulster women in the same year contained 145,000 signatures.[15] The enfranchisement of women in 1898 for local election purposes further fuelled female political activity, culminating in the establishment of the Ulster Women's Unionist Council (UWUC) in 1911. Founded with the aim of complementing the work of male unionists in pursuit of the common goal of the protection of the union and defeat of home rule, the UWUC operated as an independent but ancillary body. The council's explicitly political focus prevented business engaging with the divisive topic of female suffrage, which was still anathema to many leading male and female unionists.[16] The new council expanded rapidly during its early months and by the end of 1911 thirty-two branches had been formed with a collective membership of 40,000–50,000. By 1913, this number is believed to have reached 115,000–200,000.[17]

While these numbers suggest mass popular support and membership of the UWUC it is clear that here the key power brokers were drawn largely from the landed classes. The first presidents of the council were the 2nd duchess of Abercorn; the 6th marchioness of Londonderry; the 3rd duchess of Abercorn and, from 1923 to 1942, Lady Cecil Craig. Between 1911 and 1939 only one of the ten vice-presidents did not have a title.[18] The list of names included in the

12 For more see Maria Luddy, *Women and philanthropy in nineteenth-century Ireland* (Cambridge, 1995).   13 Only a few months after Ulster Day the Irish Women's Suffrage Society bemoaned the fact that in Belfast 'nothing will be entertained but home rule struggling with Unionism': *Irish Citizen*, 17 May 1913, cited by Diane Urquhart, *Women in Ulster politics, 1890–1940: a history not yet told* (Dublin, 2000), p. 21.   14 For an in-depth discussion of the political involvement of nationalist women in this period see Senia Pašeta, *Irish nationalist women, 1900–1918* (Cambridge, 2013).   15 Anon., 1893 cited in Maria Luddy, 'Women and politics in nineteenth century Ireland' in Alan Hayes and Diane Urquhart (eds), *The Irish women's history reader* (London, 2001), p. 34.   16 Including Edward Carson and the dowager marchioness of Abercorn, vice-president of the UWUC from 1914 to 1919; Urquhart, *Women in Ulster politics*, p. 23.   17 Diane Urquhart (ed.), *The minutes of the Ulster Women's Unionist Council and executive committee, 1911–40* (Dublin, 2001), pp xiii–xv.   18 Idem,

minutes of the early meetings of the council read as a roll call of the most influential in society. After a year of operation, this had not waned. At a meeting on 4 January 1912 the office bearers and provincial representatives were selected: president: duchess of Abercorn; vice-president: marchioness of Londonderry; provincial representatives: Lady Bruce, Lady Heygate, countess of Dartrey, countess of Kilmorey, dowager marchioness of Dufferin and Ava, marchioness of Ely, countess of Erne, Lady Ewart, countess of Gosford, dowager Lady Smiley, Lady Stronge, Mrs Talbot, countess of Leitrim, countess of Ranfurly, countess of Rossmore, Mrs Saunderson, countess of Shaftesbury, marchioness of Hamilton, Lady Dunleath and Lady Clanmorris.[19]

That the leadership of this organization was drawn mainly from the upper and middle classes should come as no surprise, considering contemporary societal norms. However, given the trend towards a lessening influence of the male landed elite, the extent of influence exerted by the females of the class within the council is all the more significant. Indeed it is likely that this is less a result of a gendered split in political attitudes to the landed classes and more a direct result of societal attitudes to female political involvement. As newcomers to the political table, the involvement of high-standing, influential, respectable women lent an important level of credibility to an association that otherwise may have struggled to be taken seriously. Further, although political activity among all classes was increasing, only women of a certain standing had the considerable amount of time and economic liberty to devote to such a substantial political undertaking.

The UWUC quickly proved that, regardless of class, female unionists were an organizational force to be reckoned with. In January 1912, they launched a petition against both the *Ne Temere* papal decree and home rule, which comprised 104,301 signatures when it was presented to parliament in June. A further anti-home rule petition with 100,000 signatures was also forwarded to parliament in May 1912.[20] Thus, the UWUC had amassed a significant degree of experience in advance of the Ulster Day signings of the women's Declaration. Perhaps this is why the organization of the signing events generated so little interest at the foregoing meetings of the UWUC. As Jacobs notes, the Declaration does not appear 'to have been an exceptional aspect of their business' as they 'almost casually' and unanimously passed the wording of the Declaration that had been prepared by an advisory committee.[21] As a subordinate of the UUC it might be expected that the UUC would have dictated all the

' "The female of the species is more deadlier than the male"? The Ulster Women's Unionist Council, 1911–40' in Janet Holmes and Diane Urquhart (eds), *Coming into the light – the work, politics and religion of women in Ulster, 1840–1940* (Belfast, 1994), p. 97.   **19** Urquhart (ed.), *The minutes of the Ulster Women's Unionist Council*, pp 41–2.   **20** Urquhart, 'The Ulster Women's Unionist Council', pp 99–100.   **21** Turner Jacobs, '"To associate ourselves with the men of Ulster": a gendered history of Ulster's Solemn League and Covenant and the Ulster Women's Declaration, 1910–1920', *Voces Novae: Chapman University Historical Review*, 3:1

arrangements for the UWUC's engagement with Ulster Day, but that does not appear to have been entirely the case. The only extant documentary evidence of negotiations between the two bodies comes from a letter sent by Edith Wheeler on behalf of the UWUC's Ulster Day sub-committee to R. Dawson Bates of the Ulster Day Committee.[22] While it is clear that the UUC were in charge of the overall plans for the day and did dictate who was eligible to sign the Declaration – 'only Ulster women or women domiciled in Ulster' – the UWUC were given 'sole responsibility' for the signing event in the Old Town Hall, Belfast, the second-largest signing centre in the province.[23] In addition, this correspondence evidences the autonomy the UWUC were afforded in relation to the wording of the aforementioned Declaration. While a suggested text was prepared by Captain Craig and Mr Sinclair and sent to the UWUC, Dawson Bates was at pains to emphasize that the UWUC 'are, of course, responsible for settling that [sic] Declaration they wish to issue, and the men have nothing to say in regard to it beyond offering their help'.[24]

The ensuing events of Ulster Day 28 September 1912 represented the single largest, simultaneous public display of anti-home rule sentiment expressed across the province; an occasion that David Fitzpatrick describes as 'a matchless triumph of Irish political mobilization'.[25] The remainder of this chapter will focus on examining the actual contribution made by the female landed elite in the gathering of the 219,928[26] female signatures appended to the Declaration and the geographic variations that become apparent across the province.

A ROLE FOR THE WOMEN OF THE COUNTRY HOUSES

Unlike the Ulster Solemn League and Covenant, which pledged the men of Ulster to use all means necessary to preserve the union with Great Britain, the women's Declaration merely associated the women of Ulster with the men's opposition to home rule. Yet, while evidently still perceived as the more delicate sex, there was little difference made in the arrangements for the signing of these two gender specific documents on Ulster Day.[27] Although the majority of media

(2012), 145–68 at 150.   **22** Records of the Ulster Women's Unionist Council (PRONI, D1098/2/3).   **23** Ibid.   **24** Ibid.   **25** David Fitzpatrick, *Descendancy: Irish protestant histories since 1795* (Cambridge, 2014), p. 110.   **26** There is some discrepancy over the total male and female signatures collected. The figure quoted here, and which will be used in the remainder of the paper, is drawn from our research on the number of female signatures gathered in Ulster and available to research on the PRONI website. PRONI quotes an overall figure of 228,991 female signatories, but this excludes signatures gathered outside of Ulster. The most likely accurate and official figure is the 234,046 quoted in the minutes of the UWUC on 16 January 1913; Urquhart (ed.), *The minutes of the Ulster Women's Unionist Council*, p. 68 and also published in Ulster Day Committee, *Ulster Day 1912* (Belfast, 1912) accessed in Unionist papers, PRONI, D1545/6. However, it is likely that a number of sheets have been lost or misplaced over time and prior to digitization.   **27** For more on the gendered dimensions of this event see Jacobs, 'To associate and images surrounding the event depict the largest male Covenant signing event in Belfast's City Hall, the scenes played out there in full symbolic grandeur were replicated on a smaller scale across the nine counties of Ulster.[28] The day began with religious services in the Protestant churches, and thereafter the people processed or in some instances were paraded to local signing centres. The finer details of local arrangements, such as which religious denomination would host the service, who would act as local organizing secretary and where the signing(s) would take place, were left to the discretion of local organizing committees. These events then offer a unique lens through which to view the operation of grassroots popular unionism at a local level and to analyse the social networks and power structures at work in local communities across Ulster in this period. It is remarkable that this rich source has remained underutilized for so long.[29]

Of the 1,028 signing locations identified, 135 were for male signatories only and 168 were female only, leaving 725 or 70.5 per cent of signing centres where both documents were signed simultaneously. The single-gender locations account for a relatively small proportion (just 12 per cent) of the overall signatures collected, despite comprising 29.5 per cent of centres. Thus, despite a gendered approach to the creation of the documents there was less emphasis on securing gendered signing centres, a further reference to the spirit of unionist unity that the day espoused. This also suggests, however, that while the landed-controlled UWUC had played a role in the creation of the Declaration, it did not attempt to stamp its autonomy on local Ulster Day events. This theory is lent further credence when considered in light of the relative absence of discussion about Ulster Day in the UWUC minutes and raises questions about attributing the large number of female signatures collected solely to the work of the UWUC.[30]

In fact, the only obvious gender bias that has been identified in this research is in the relationship between the gender of the organizing agent and the gender

ourselves with the men of Ulster'.   **28** Some images of these do appear in Gordon Lucy, *The Ulster Covenant: a pictorial history of the 1912 home rule crisis* (Belfast, 1989).   **29** A number of academics have successfully used the signing to examine the role played by the various religious denominations and clergy in Ulster unionism, including Andrew Scholes, *The Church of Ireland and the third home rule bill* (Dublin, 2010); N.K. Morris, 'Traitors to their faith?: Protestant clergy and the Ulster Covenant of 1912', *New Hibernia Review*, 15:3 (2011), 16–35; Andrew Scholes, '"Neither Whigs, Tories, nor party politicians"? The Church of Ireland and the Ulster crisis, 1910–1914' in Doherty (ed.), *Home rule crisis*, pp 210–40; Laurence Kirkpatrick, 'Irish Presbyterians and the Ulster Covenant' in Doherty (ed.), *Home rule crisis*, pp 241–75; Fitzpatrick, *Descendancy*, pp 113–35. Beyond these the focus has been on Ulster Day as part of the anti-home rule campaign and a masterstroke of propaganda used by Craig to increase the cult of 'King Carson'. See Gailey, 'King Carson: an essay on the invention of leadership' and Alvin Jackson, 'Unionist myths 1912–1985', *Past and Present*, 136 (1992), 164–85.   **30** This is borne out by the surviving minutes of the Ballycastle branch of the North Antrim Women's Unionist Association which show that the association suggested plans for the day and sent them to the men's committee for approval. These minutes also clearly outline that signing went on well after 28 September as plans were approved for agents of signatures collected. In some signing centres multiple organizing agents collected signatures as an organizing team: in these instances the natural pattern was for male agents to concentrate on the collection of Covenant signatures, while the female agents collected Declaration signatures. In smaller centres where only one or two agents were present it was the norm to find male agents collecting both Covenant and Declaration signatures; however, female agents were significantly less likely to collect male signatures. In the rare cases where women did cross this invisible gender divide, they were disproportionately from the upper classes of society, suggesting that their status allowed them to transcend traditional gender norms more easily.

Despite then the slightly larger number of female-only signing centres, there was a much higher prevalence of male than female agents across the province, with males outnumbering females by a ratio of two to one. Within the female agent cohort, the women of Ulster's country houses were similarly, but even more powerfully, eclipsed. Purdue has suggested that Ulster Day marked 'the political swansong'[31] for the landed elite of Ulster in terms of their leadership role. However, an examination of the number of organizing agents drawn from the female landed elite and their influence in terms of signatures collected, suggests that even in female society the majority had already succumbed to the symbolic role of figurehead rather than active political leaders.[32]

The fifty-six female landed agents identified represent just 11.6 per cent of all female agents, while the 12,805 signatures they collected account for only 5.8 per cent of total signatories. Even considering that the landed elite comprised only a small proportion of the overall population, their status as traditional leaders, their relative liberty and economic freedom, their political linkages and dominance within the leadership of the UWUC, suggest that a relatively large proportion would have actively facilitated the Declaration signing. To put that number in context, Purdue's research identified 110 landed families in the six counties of modern Northern Ireland with estates larger than 2,500 acres.[33] When consideration is given to the number of smaller estates, the numbers of landed families in the remaining three counties and the numbers of females in each family, it is clear that these fifty-six are not close to being even a majority of their own cohort. Furthermore, it would be expected that, given the social status of the female landed agents, that their respective influence in encouraging signings locally would have garnered significant levels of support, yet here too they were comparatively ineffective.

to superintend signings on the Tuesday following: Ulster Women's Unionist Council papers (PRONI, D2866/5/1).   **31** Purdue, *The big house*, p. 179.   **32** This is not to suggest that women of this class had not always assumed symbolic roles; they had, and this is well documented (for example, see Luddy, *Women and philanthropy*), but what it does clearly indicate is that their level of active local involvement is much less than what their provincial level activities (particularly in relation to the UWUC) would indicate.   **33** Purdue, *The big house*, p. 18.

4.1 Women signing the Ulster covenant at Sion Mills, Co. Tyrone.

Source: PRONI, D1422/B/13/34, with the permission of the Deputy Keeper of Records, Public Record Office of Northern Ireland.

4.2 The countess of Kilmorey, seated second from the right with Sir Edward Carson, Captain James Craig and Lord Londonderry among others. It appears to have been taken during Ulster Week, 1913 – the first anniversary of the signing of the covenant – at Craigavon House, Belfast.

Source: PRONI, D1415/D/9, with the permission of the Deputy Keeper of Records, Public Record Office of Northern Ireland.

Before embarking on a detailed analysis of these landed agents and their efficacy during Ulster Day, it is important to note who these agents were and where they were located. Down records the highest number of landed agents with eleven, Antrim and Cavan record eight each, Monaghan seven, Londonderry six, Donegal and Tyrone tied with five and the lowest figure of three is recorded in both Armagh and Fermanagh. These landed women represented a broad sample of their class from the highest levels of Ulster society to those with relatively small estates. However, when compared with the membership of the UWUC it is immediately clear that the representatives of the top echelons of nobility were most notable by their absence. Of exception are the four titled landed organizing agents: the countess of Kilmorey[34] and Viscountess Jocelyn[35] both from Down, Lady Farnham of Cavan[36] and Lady Stronge of Armagh.[37] The remaining fifty-two agents were comprised not only of women from across the range of the lesser gentry, but also those from other long-standing Ulster landed families as well as members of families who had more recently acquired land and its status from the profits of their industrial, professional and even military enterprises.[38]

Unfortunately with such a small sample size and wide range it is impossible to draw meaningful conclusions about the relative efficacy of the women from these backgrounds, but it is possible to suggest some general characteristics of the cohort. The ages of these women varied considerably from fifteen to seventy-two; however, more than half (57 per cent) were in their forties or fifties, with an average age of forty-five.[39] Almost two-thirds were either married or widowed (63 per cent), 57 per cent were Ulster-born and all except six were members of the Church of Ireland.[40] Thus, while it is clear that neither age, religion, marital status nor birthplace was a barrier to assuming an organizational role on Ulster Day, the above figures do illustrate a higher prevalence of mature, married women who were unquestionably 'Ulster women'. The importance of marital status is also confirmed when comparing the average number of signatures

34 Ellen Constance Needham, countess of Kilmorey, wife of Francis Charles Needham, 3rd earl of Kilmorey of Mourne Park, Newry, Co. Down. She was one of the provincial representatives of the UWUC in 1912. See footnote 20 above.   35 Elinor Jessie Jocelyn, Viscountess Jocelyn, wife of Robert Soame Jocelyn, later 8th earl of Roden of Tollymore Park, Bryansford, Co. Down.   36 Aileen Selina Maxwell, Lady Farnham, wife of Arthur Kenlis Maxwell, Lord Farnham of Farnham House, Co. Cavan. Lord Farnham was the main spokesman for Cavan unionists.   37 Ethel Margaret Stronge, Lady Stronge, wife of Sir James Stronge of Tynan Abbey, Co. Armagh. She was one of the provincial representatives of the UWUC in 1912; see footnote 20 above.   38 Cross checking our list of agents from the six counties of modern-day Northern Ireland with Purdue's list of estates of over 2,500 acres uncovers a total of thirteen agents in this grouping (including the four aforementioned titled agents) or 36 per cent of the total agents in those counties. The remaining almost two-thirds were from the lesser landed classes.   39 These figures are calculated using the age of the women as listed on the 1911 census and increasing it by one year to give their 1912 age. We have only been able to identify ages for forty-nine of the fifty-six agents.   40 The remaining six were all Presbyterians.

collected by married/widowed agents with those by single agents. It is clear that married/widowed agents were much more successful with an average of 264 signatures per agent compared with just 187 per single agent. The same, however, does not hold true when considering the relative efficacy of Ulster-born agents. Examining the female landed agents according to place of birth reveals a substantial difference between those from Ulster, the rest of Ireland (outside of Ulster), Great Britain and the rest of the world. While Ulster-born agents were numerically dominant, they collected on average just 193 signatures per agent, which compares relatively unfavourably with the 375 signatures per agent collected by those born in one of the other twenty-three Irish counties and the 255 per agent from Great Britain.[41] These statistics do certainly suggest that landed agents born in either southern Ireland or Great Britain, while fewer in number, were much more effective than their Ulster-born colleagues. This may be indicative of a heightened awareness of the possibilities of life in a nationalist-dominated, home rule Ireland on the part of southern unionists and a more personally informed desire to maintain the links with family and homeland on the part of those from Great Britain.

However, it is in moving beyond the personal attributes of these landed agents themselves to a broader analysis of their Ulster Day activities that a real sense of their role in Ulster Day and Ulster unionist society more widely begins to emerge. In order to fully analyse these localized idiosyncrasies, it is necessary to understand some of the geographic patterns identifiable in the general results of Ulster Day. Unsurprisingly there is an obvious correlation for the most part between the size of the population eligible to sign the Covenant and Declaration, and the number of agents in each county (Table 4.1).[42] The only exceptions to this pattern are Armagh and Monaghan. In Armagh a combination of a number of large signing centres staffed by few agents and a small team of agents coordinating a number of different centres resulted in a substantially reduced agent population. In Monaghan, the wider geographical distribution of the eligible population presumably required a larger number of agents than in Fermanagh. The largest number of agents are recorded in the three most highly urbanized and therefore most densely populated counties – Antrim, Down and Londonderry – which together account for 64 per cent of the total organizing agents across the province and 74 per cent of the eligible population.

---

41 The one female landed agent from the rest of the world (Canada) collected just forty signatures.   42 All men and women over the age of sixteen were eligible to sign the Covenant and Declaration on Ulster Day. However, for the purposes of this project we have calculated the non-Roman Catholic population of each county, who were over the age of fifteen on the 1911 Census, reflecting the clear links that were then being made between Protestantism and unionism.

Table 4.1: Distribution of the eligible population and organizing agents by county

County	Eligible	Total agents	Female agents	% of Female agents
Antrim	244,810	434	192	44.2
Down	153,469	338	129	38.2
Londonderry	52,730	212	64	30.2
Tyrone	45,599	152	17	11.2
Armagh	45,290	96	20	20.8
Donegal	25,406	103	17	16.5
Fermanagh	18,385	76	7	9.2
Monaghan	13,084	79	22	27.8
Cavan	11,900	56	15	26.8
Total	610,673	1,546	483	31.2

Source: Compiled by the authors from the digital archive of the Ulster Covenant and the online Census of Ireland, 1911.

Throughout Ulster, female agents composed just 31 per cent of all agents, but this masks quite stark regional variations, with overall female agent numbers ranging from a high of 44 per cent in Antrim to a low of just 9 per cent in Fermanagh. Here again urbanization appears to be the defining explanatory factor, with the largest proportions of female agents identified in Antrim, Down and Londonderry where they composed more than 30 per cent of all agents. This is further reinforced in the context of Belfast where the majority of agents (59 per cent) were women, although this is at least partially explained by the fact that only four male agents took charge of City Hall where 41,332 male signatures were collected. The more southerly counties of Armagh, Monaghan and Cavan had female agent participation rates of between 20 and 30 per cent, while the westerly counties show significantly lower proportions. This is perhaps reflective of the slower speed at which gender roles were changing in more rural and isolated communities and is suggestive of the fact that local organizing committees in urban areas were more progressive in their attitudes to female political activism. However, it is also likely that female activism was simply more acceptable in the context of the larger signing centres more prevalent in urban areas, where they could operate as part of a team of agents, rather than as the lead organizer.

While such considerations might apply to the middle- and lower-class female agents who were taking possibly their first steps towards political engagement, it

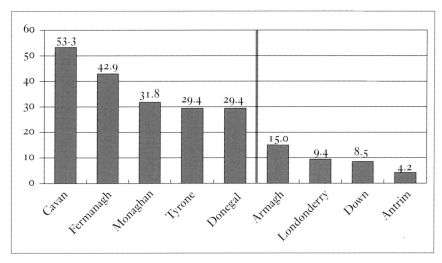

4.3 The percentage of agents drawn from the landed elite as a proportion of total female agents. Compiled by the authors from the digital archive of the Ulster Covenant.

is unlikely that such constraints would have applied to the female agents from the upper classes in general and the landed elite in particular. Regularly involved in political, social and charitable causes these women were no strangers to leadership roles among both genders in rural and urban settings.[43] As the traditional leaders of rural society, a greater involvement by these women might be expected across the more rural counties, suggesting that a more even spread of the fifty-six, or 11.6 per cent, of female agents from the landed classes would be found across the province. This is indeed the case when the number of female landed agents are examined; however, when these agents are viewed as a percentage of the total female agent numbers at a county level a very different pattern emerges. Rather than an even spread, the proportions of female landed agents range from a high of 53.3 per cent in Cavan to a low of 4.2 per cent in Antrim (fig. 4.3). An urban–rural divide is clearly evident, and in this instance the lowest proportion of agents are drawn from the three most urbanized counties (Antrim, Down and Londonderry), while the four least urbanized counties (Cavan, Fermanagh, Monaghan and Donegal) have the largest

43 This trend was reflected in the key leaders of nationalist society: see Pašeta, *Irish nationalist women*. Theresa, marchioness of Londonderry, offers an excellent example of just how extensive the influence of landed women could be. Renowned as a hostess and confidante, Theresa counted among her friends and regular visitors two kings and their queens, as well Edward Carson. Under her lead, Londonderry House became a key centre for political discussion, decision-making and socializing, in which she played an active and influential part: see R.E. Finley-Bowman, 'An ideal unionist: the political career of Theresa, marchioness of Londonderry, 1911–1919', *Journal of International Women's Studies*, 4:3 (2003), 15–29; Diane Urquhart, *The ladies of Londonderry: women and political patronage* (London, 2007).

proportions. What is perhaps more significant, however, is the inverse relationship between the proportion of female agents from the landed elite and the eligible population resident in a given county. Thus Antrim, with only 4.2 per cent of female landed agents, has the highest eligible population in the province while Cavan, with the lowest eligible population, drew more than half of all female agents from the landed class. Although caution must be exercised, given the small numbers involved, this clear correlation between the levels of activity among the female landed elite and the size of the unionist community does point to some interesting spatial variations in the role of the landed elite across Ulster.

While provincial-wide figures suggest that the role of the landed elite had declined to quite insignificant proportions, it appears that in the rural west and north-west, where unionist populations were the minority, the landed elite retained their traditional role as active leaders of the community as late as 1912. This continued deference on the part of small local communities can be explained through both a lack of alternative leadership and a conscious decision to retain the status quo in the interests of preserving community unity and furthering the unionist cause. However, the figures here are also suggestive of the fact that where the perceived threats from home rule were greatest, the landed elite were most zealous in their unionist activity. Thus, in the four counties with large unionist populations the landed elite were either content to trust in others to do the work or were simply surplus to requirements in light of the newly emerging popular political activism, mirroring the experience of their male counterparts. There they maintained their figurehead role by acting as the first signatories in local communities, but this was symbolic, not practical. In contrast, in the counties where unionists were a minority, living in dispersed communities where the fears of life under a home rule government were heightened, it would appear that collective action was deemed more necessary.

There is, of course, a considerable difference between those engaged in organizational activity and their efficacy as agents. It would be easy to assume given their relative standing in the community that the female landed elite would be in a position to exert more influence than other agents to encourage people to sign on Ulster Day. Nevertheless these agents were less than successful across the province, garnering only 5.8 per cent of signatures. Again, however, local idiosyncrasies give rise to unique geographies in the number of signatures collected by these country house women. Across the province 72 per cent of the total eligible population signed the Ulster Covenant and Declaration. The number of Declaration signatures in each county is broadly in line with the eligible population figures, with rates of female signings as a percentage of the total population varying only between 31 and 45 per cent.[44] Yet the percentage of

44 Calculated by the authors from the eligible population outlined above and the Covenant and Declaration signatures recorded in the nine counties of Ulster from the PRONI online database.

signatures collected by the landed women varies from 31.4 per cent in Cavan to just 1.6 per cent in Fermanagh, the county which had the second highest proportion of agents from the landed class (Table 4.2).

Table 4.2: Activity of female landed agents on Ulster Day

County	Total declaration signatures	Collected by female landed agents	Female signatures collected by landed agents (%)	Female landed agents (%)
Antrim	84,008	1,956	2.3	4.2
Down	52,576	5,138	9.8	8.5
Londonderry	20,384	864	4.2	9.4
Armagh	20,328	770	3.8	15.0
Tyrone	18,544	906	4.9	29.4
Donegal	8,361	734	8.8	29.4
Fermanagh	6,886	110	1.6	42.9
Monaghan	5,082	1,145	22.5	31.8
Cavan	3,759	1,182	31.4	53.3
Total	219,928	12,805	5.8	11.6

Source: Compiled by the authors from the digital archive of the Ulster Covenant and the online Census of Ireland, 1911.

In terms of actual numbers, the eleven landed agents in Down were responsible for the largest contribution to overall signatures, adding 5,138 to the county total. Within this group, Mrs Jeannie Ferguson[45] of Edenderry House collected 1,100 signatures at the Temperance Hall in Banbridge, the largest single total collected by a female landed agent, eclipsing the combined effort of this cohort of agents in Donegal and Fermanagh and far surpassing the work of her socially superior county colleagues, the Countess Kilmorey and Viscountess Jocelyn.[46] The countess may, however, have been otherwise engaged as her work as an agent was in addition to the Ulster Day garden party she held at her home

---

45 Mrs Jeannie Ferguson was the Cork-born wife of Howard Ferguson, owner of the linen manufacturing company Messrs Thomas Ferguson & Co. For more on the family and their home, Edenderry House, see Kathleen Rankin, *The linen houses of the Bann Valley: the stories of their families* (Belfast, 2007), p. 61.   **46** They collected 100 and 105 signatures respectively.

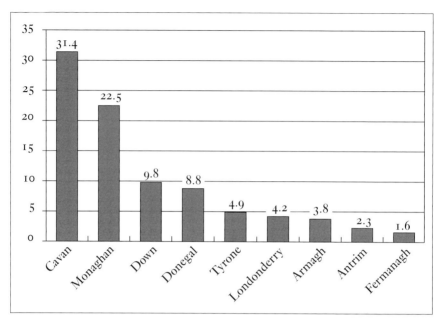

4.4 The percentage of Declaration signatures collected by the female landed agents as a proportion of all Declaration signatures. Compiled by the authors from the digital archive of the Ulster Covenant.

in Mourne Park, to which key figures of Ulster unionism and a number of her fellow organizing agents were invited.[47] The smallest actual contribution came from the landed female agents in Fermanagh where only 110 Declaration signatures were gathered by the three agents – Elizabeth Archdale[48] of Castle Archdale; Georgina Irvine,[49] Manor House, Killadeas, and Isabel Madden[50] of Roslea Manor. These numbers are slightly skewed by the fact that Isabel Madden did not actually collect any Declaration signatures, instead opting to improve Covenant returns by gathering forty-three male signatures. Given that these three were all drawn from significant landed families in the county, a greater degree of influence would have been expected.

In examining the proportion of signatures gathered by female landed agents across Ulster an identifiable geography in relation to their levels of efficacy produces a more complicated picture (fig. 4.4). In only one county did female landed agents outperform their numerical strength – in Down they collected 9.8 per cent of signatures while comprising just 8.5 per cent of total female agents.

47 *Newry Telegraph*, 28 Sept. 1912.   **48** Elizabeth Archdale, wife of the Rt Hon. Edward Archdale of Castle Archdale, Co. Fermanagh.   **49** Georgina Irvine, wife of John Irvine of Killadeas, Co. Fermanagh. She was a daughter of Captain Mervyn Archdale MP of Castle Archdale, and cousin of the Rt Hon. Edward Archdale.   **50** Isabel Madden, daughter of John Madden of Roslea Manor. By 1911 she was living in Aghafin House located between Clones, Co. Monaghan, and Roslea, Co. Fermanagh.

In the remainder of the counties their collecting rate fell substantially below their physical presence. Only in Cavan and Monaghan is it possible to suggest that the women from the landed elite had a significant impact on overall Declaration numbers at just under one-third and one-quarter of signatures respectively, albeit still well below their numerical weight. In both counties the efforts of the female landed agents were spearheaded by key unionist personages. In Cavan, Lady Farnham led the way, collecting a total of 267 signatures for the Declaration in Cavan town, ably assisted by Gertrude Clements[51] who collected 259 signatures in the quieter surrounds of Ashfield demesne. In Monaghan, the combined work of sisters Mary Isabella Murray-Ker[52] of Newbliss House and Mrs Sarah Irwin[53] of Beech Hill collectively accounted for 686 of the 1,145 signatures gathered by the seven Monaghan landed female agents.[54] Undoubtedly, the reality of the threats to the unionist community posed by home rule loomed large for these women living on the southernmost border of Ulster. In their lifetimes they had watched the pendulum swing from unionist to nationalist political dominance in both national and local politics.[55] As two counties with minority unionist populations this sense of urgency was undoubtedly magnified, perhaps adding an impetus to the efficacy of the female landed agents not present to such a significant degree in other counties. In the other counties it would appear that activity levels were dependent on the individual and the level of exertion they were willing to commit.

CONCLUSION

This chapter has attempted to interrogate the political influence of the women of Ulster's country houses during the third home rule crisis through an examination of their role in organizing the Ulster Day Declaration signings. While varied academic opinion exists as to the status of the landed elite in this period, the foregoing discussion has illustrated the importance of engaging with

---

51 Gertrude Clements, wife of Henry Theophilus Clements of Ashfield Lodge, who had died in 1904. He had inherited the extensive estates of his second cousin the 3rd earl of Leitrim following his murder in April 1878.   52 Mary Isabella Murray-Ker was the daughter of Andre Allen Murray-Ker of Newbliss House, Co. Monaghan. She became owner of the estate in 1900 following the death of her mother. She was an active member of the UWUC: see Urquhart (ed.), *The minutes of the Ulster Women's Unionist Council*.   53 Sarah Irwin was the sister of Mary Isabella Murray-Ker. She married Fitzjohn Robert Irwin of Kilkeel in 1880, but he died in 1882. She later returned to reside at Beech Hill, another of the Murray-Ker properties on the outskirts of Monaghan town.   54 For more on the Murray-Ker family and their involvement see Natasha Martin and Stuart McConkey, *The Ulster Covenant and the people of Monaghan* (Monaghan, 2013), available at http://www.monaghanpeace.ie/wp-content/uploads/2013/03/The-Ulster-Covenant-and-County-Monaghan.pdf [accessed 24 Mar. 2016].   55 For more detail on Monaghan attitudes to home rule, see Terence Dooley, *Monaghan: the Irish Revolution, 1912–23* (Dublin, 2017), pp 1–32.

the oftentimes forgotten local geographies within Ulster rather than applying provincial-wide generalizations. The weak political influence exerted by the female landed elite at this landmark event is evident in the urbanized, unionist-dominated counties of Antrim, Down, Armagh and Londonderry. Yet, the more rural counties, with their significantly lower and dispersed unionist populations, show sustained and significant landed engagement and influence. These findings do, however, come with one significant caveat: that activity and efficacy are very different issues. Thus, while the women of Ulster's country houses may have engaged in Ulster Day organization and administration, many could be accused of merely paying lip service to their office given the small numbers of signatures collected compared with the figures achieved by other agents. The major exception to this was in the southern counties of Cavan and Monaghan where participation in Ulster Day events was not so much about resuming or retaining influence and power among the unionist community, as it was a campaign to protect their very way of life. A similar examination of the activity and efficacy of the male landed elite is now required in order to assess whether these patterns are replicated across both gender cohorts.

The research has also raised questions about the role of the UWUC in the administration of the Ulster Day Declaration signings. While involved in the wording of the Declaration, the small number of female-only signing centres combined with the small proportions of signatures collected suggests that the role of the UWUC was limited. It is likely therefore that for the most part members of the UWUC acted on local organizing committees, making arrangements for the signings of both documents, rather than as sole organizers. Furthermore, the number of female signing centres administered by men raises implications for attributing the entire female signature total to the efforts of the UWUC. Further research will be required to explore these place-specific aspects. Any attempt to understand the evolving nature of Ulster unionism in the early twentieth century must look beyond the landed elite and begin to interrogate the geographies of grassroots unionism and its newly emerging local leaders.

Madeline Wyndham of Clouds and Mabel Morrison of Fonthill

CAROLINE DAKERS

Madeline Wyndham (1835–1920) was the daughter of Sir Guy Campbell, a career soldier who had fought in the Peninsular War. He died in 1849 at Kingstown, Dublin, where he was stationed as colonel of the 3rd West India Regiment, when Madeline was only fourteen. On her mother's side, she was descended from the French and Irish aristocracy. Pamela, Lady Campbell was the daughter of the United Irishman Lord Edward FitzGerald (son of the duke of Leinster), who died in prison from wounds inflicted by his captors in 1798, and 'La Belle Pamela', presumed daughter of Louis-Philippe, Duc D'Orleans. Madeline had no fortune but was regarded as strikingly beautiful. She married the Hon. Percy Wyndham (1835–1911) in 1860. He was the grandson of the 3rd earl of Egremont, famous for being the patron of Turner, and he had grown up at Petworth in Sussex. The newly married couple took a lease on 44 Belgrave Square in London; their country homes were temporary until Percy bought the Clouds estate in Wiltshire in 1876 and commissioned a brand-new house.

Mabel Morrison (1847–1933) had a very different parentage. Her father Dr Chermside was rector of Wilton in Wiltshire and her mother Emma Dawson was the daughter of a London merchant with Jamaican plantations. However, the living at Wilton was one of the most desirable in the country, under the patronage of the earls of Pembroke. And Mabel spent part of her childhood in Paris staying with her grandfather, the distinguished doctor Sir Robert Chermside, whose patients included Lady Hertford. Mabel's marriage in 1866 to Alfred Morrison (1821–97) was surprising for two reasons, their disparate ages and financial positions. She was only nineteen, while Alfred was forty-five, an age gap of twenty-six years (Madeline and Percy Wyndham were the same age). Like Madeline Wyndham, she had no fortune of her own, but Alfred was very rich indeed (richer than Percy Wyndham). He was the second son of James Morrison, self-made millionaire haberdasher, Whig MP, merchant banker and landowner, the richest commoner in the nineteenth century. When Alfred married Mabel he already owned a country estate at Fonthill in Wiltshire and a large collection of porcelain, paintings and *objets d'art*.[1]

[1] For further published material on the Wyndhams of Clouds and the Morrisons see Caroline Dakers, *Clouds* (New Haven and London, 1993); *The Holland Park circle* (New Haven, 1999);

Madeline and Mabel knew one another in London society and became close neighbours in Wiltshire though they were never friends. Under the public gaze in town and in the country, the women performed their roles and responsibilities as the wives of wealthy landowners with apparent diligence. They appear in memoirs, biographies and histories of the country house as wives and mothers, hostesses of country-house weekends and organisers of parties for servants and tenants, supporters of their local schools and churches, subjects for artists and engaged in their own artistic activities. They were included in an uncritical and deeply nostalgic book, *Four Victorian ladies of Wiltshire*, written by Edith Olivier during the Second World War and published in 1945. Olivier, who lived in nearby Wilton (her father was also rector of Wilton), got to know them well from the 1890s onwards. She was in her twenties; they, however, were some thirty and forty years older. Her tone is one of uncritical, unmitigated praise. Mabel 'had always her own splendour' while Madeline's 'overflowing love' 'reached its climax in her passionate mother love'.[2] Both are bathed in a golden glow.

Surviving letters and diaries and more recent publications provide rather different pictures of the women.[3] Madeline had an affair with a cousin of her husband, she developed friendships outside his obvious circle, she practised art to a semi-professional level and once she was established at Clouds she exercised increasing power within the home, over both her daughters and their choice of husbands, and as the 'curator' of country-house weekends. Henry James was among the guests, using Madeline as one of the models for Mrs Gereth, the deeply cultured and manipulative widow in *The spoils of Poynton*. All her life, Madeline collected autographs, sketches, letters and snatches of poems and sermons, which she turned into commonplace books. Edith Olivier called them 'diaries of the mind'. They now present us with her selective *curated* view of her own, her children's and grandchildren's lives;[4] between the covers she attempted to organize and re-present her version of the past. However, she was powerless to stop the wave of deaths that engulfed her and her family, losing her husband and eldest son just before the First World War. She then lost five grandsons, killed in France and Egypt.

During Alfred Morrison's lifetime, Mabel's position was most often defined either in relation to his collection or the ill-health she endured after giving birth to five children in just seven years. She appears to have been powerless, merely another (much loved) object within his collection. However, at the age of fifty, she became a wealthy widow, establishing a new life for herself in her own country house. She not only developed eccentric habits that bewildered her

A genius for money: business, art and the Morrisons (New Haven, 2011). Also see Claudia Renton, *Those wild Wyndhams* (London, 2014).   **2** Edith Olivier, *Four Victorian ladies of Wiltshire* (London, 1945), p. 96.   **3** See Renton, *Those wild Wyndhams* and Dakers, *A genius for money*.   **4** Some of Madeline Wyndham's commonplace books are in the Petworth House Archives, which can be viewed at the West Sussex History Centre, Chichester.

children and neighbours but she also sold off very large quantities of Alfred's collection (paintings, textiles, porcelain, armour, furniture, gems) and probably destroyed personal correspondence. Unlike Madeline, she wanted to be free of the objects and houses associated with her husband.

PART ONE: MADELINE WYNDHAM

Though Madeline Campbell brought only £50 a year to her marriage with Percy Wyndham, his father, Lord Leconfield provided her marriage settlement of £22,500, which generated a personal annual income of £900. They were married on 16 October 1860; they were both twenty-five years old.

Percy took a long lease on 44 Belgrave Square where all their five children were born, apparently without incident. The first, Mary, was born in 1862, two years after their marriage; George, the son and heir, was born a year later; Guy, the 'spare' heir, two years later; Madeline four years later and Pamela three years later. Madeline was thirty-six in 1871, when their last child was born, physically unaffected by the comfortably spaced births though prone to 'low spirits' and bleak moods.[5]

Percy and Madeline were united in their passion for art, Percy providing the financial means to commission and collect works and, after he inherited a fortune from his father, to build a new country house. It was Madeline, however, who developed close relationships with a number of artists and designers as well as producing her own work. Both selecting and making art gave her an element of power within their marriage. Percy paid for the art while she collected the artists.

Percy persuaded G.F. Watts to paint Madeline in 1865 (Frederic Leighton painted his portrait), but the sittings did not begin until the spring of 1867. Watts made a number of sketches before completing the portrait in 1874 (see fig. 5.1). The price agreed when the commission was accepted was £600, but Watts later asked for and received £1000. He explained to Percy: 'I should have taken the original price without a word of dissatisfaction though of course as the picture has not really been neglected but constantly worked upon for so many years the matter is a little removed from ordinary conditions.'[6] Perhaps Percy was convinced of the painting's worth when he, presumably, read the review in *Galaxy* by Henry James of the opening of the Grosvenor Gallery in 1877. It was a 'sumptuous' picture. 'The lady looks as if she had thirty thousand a year … the very handsome person whom the painter has depicted is dressed in a fashion which will never be wearisome; a simple yet splendid robe, in the taste of no particular period – of all periods.'[7]

---

5 Renton, *Those wild Wyndhams*, p. 10.   **6** G.F. Watts to Percy Wyndham (Courtauld Institute, Correspondence of G.F. Watts, fiche 27 [hereafter, Courtauld, fiche 27]).   **7** Henry James, 'The picture season in London, *Galaxy*, August 1877' in John L. Sweeney (ed.), *The painter's eye: notes and essays on the pictoral arts* (Wisconsin, 1989), pp 142–3.

5.1 G.F. Watts,
*Portrait of the Hon.
Mrs Percy Wyndham*,
1874, private
collection.

The prolonged sittings led to a friendship forming between artist and model. Madeline herself appears to have negotiated with Watts the price of *Orpheus and Eurydice* for which she modelled Eurydice's arms. Watts wrote to her 'when can you come? … Remember you offered to sit for arms for me, I shall not let you off.'[8] 200 guineas was the agreed price, or, as Watts explained, 'two hundred and ten pounds (like Doctors we always work for the guineas).'[9] Madeline also agreed it would be publicly exhibited. Later she persuaded Watts to paint quick portraits of her sons before they went abroad with their regiments, George to Egypt in 1884 and Guy to India in 1890. Watts wrote consoling letters to her, in case her sons failed to return; artist and patron enjoyed sharing their belief in life after death. 'How can I do more than tell you how much I sympathize with you? As to Death, my friend Death! You know also what I feel about it, the great power always walks by my side with full consciousness on my part, inevitable but not terrible.'[10]

The philandering poet and Arabist, Wilfrid Scawen Blunt, visited Watts' studio while he was painting Madeline, and they conducted an affair early in the 1870s. Blunt found her 'a tall strong woman, such as are the fashion now; no porcelain figure like the beauties of the last century, nor yet the dull classic marble our fathers loved'.[11] But when she broke off the relationship, Blunt attacked her: 'a pottery goddess … I do not think her beautiful, or wise, or good. Her beauty is a little too refined, her wisdom too fantastic, her goodness too selfish.'[12] She was choosing husband and family and she would later warn her daughters about the dangers of drifting from their husbands. She advised Pamela, for example, who was unable to marry the man she loved, that the power 'not to fret over spilt milk is a great faculty it almost amounts to wisdom.'[13] She was well aware that affairs could also lead to pregnancy. Her friend Georgiana Sumner and her eldest daughter Mary Lady Elcho both had a child by Blunt. Even when illegitimate babies were accepted by the cuckolded husbands there could be unpleasant consequences. Mary had accepted her husband's long affair with Hermione, duchess of Leinster, commiserating with him when the duchess died of tuberculosis. But when she revealed she was having Blunt's child, Lord Elcho apparently said, 'I shall forgive you, but I shall be nasty to you'.[14]

Clouds, the country house built for the Wyndhams, was a joint project. Philip Webb was commissioned in 1876 and the house was completed in 1885 (see fig. 5.2). Webb was the architect to the circle of artists with which Madeline related in London: he had designed the Red House for William Morris, and Sandroyd for G.F. Watts' pupil John Roddam Spencer Stanhope. His only other aristocratic patron was George Howard, also a friend of the Wyndhams; Clouds was his grandest commission, and dubbed 'the house of the age'.

8 G.F. Watts to Madeline Wyndham, Courtauld, fiche 27.   9 Ibid.   10 G.F. Watts to Madeline Wyndham, 4 April 1885, Watts papers, Tate Archives.   11 Elizabeth Longford, *A pilgrimage of passion* (London, 1979), p. 102.   12 Ibid.   13 Madeline Wyndham to Pamela Tennant, 1 June 1896 (National Records of Scotland, Glenconner papers, GD510/1/30).   14 Wilfred Scawen

5.2 Photograph of Clouds House, from Madeline Wyndham's commonplace books, from the Petworth House Archives, and viewed at West Sussex History Centre, Chichester.

Percy provided the money but Madeline was making decisions throughout the design phase and actual building. It was she who decided against Webb's first sketch design in 1877 and he agreed to produce another 'as I am not to live in the house and you and Mrs Wyndham will'.[15] Once building was underway Percy fussed over the stables while Madeline focused on the offices and the gardens; the interior decorations and furnishings, mostly from Morris & Co., were also in her hands. A letter from Webb to Madeline, written on 24 January 1882, is typical: 'I send you the engineer's re-arrangement of the cooking and other apparatuses to the kitchen-scullery, still-room etc. based, according to my directions, on the amendments and suggestions made by you on the former.'[16] In November the following year they were engaged in an animated correspondence concerning bells, speaking tubes, cupboards and lifts.

After they moved in, Madeline took up a position centre stage, as hostess to politicians, writers and artists. Webb's biographer described the house as if it had

Blunt, 'Secret memoirs', xvii, 16 August 1895 (Fitzwilliam Museum, Cambridge). **15** Dakers, *Clouds*, p. 52.   **16** Ibid., p. 65.

'been imagined by its gifted hostess as a palace of weekending.'[17] But it was no ordinary country house. Madeline brought together a beguiling mix of famous guests and family, children and dogs, for conversation, games of tennis, billiards, theatricals, parties for the tenants, sketching and reading. Edith Olivier thought Madeline made her guests living members of the world in which she lived and moved. In twenty-first century terminology she was the *curator* of Clouds.

Madeline literally placed herself at the centre, sitting at a desk in the drawing room, which she called her 'scrattle' table, where she drew and painted. A grand-daughter recalled 'behind a long table … sat Gan Gan with all her artistic paraphernalia, and there we congregated to enjoy ourselves with the paints. But we must make no noise.'[18] She took lessons from the enamellist, Alexander Fisher, and created designs for enamels, which she fired in a small stove. She persuaded artists to help with designs for her enamelling; Philip Webb, for example, drew peacocks. Edward Poynter researched in the South Kensington Library for designs for a garden maze, writing to her in 1888, 'there were plans of various sorts of mazes which were enough to shew me that ours would work out all right.'[19] She was an artist of considerable skills; the limitations to her productions were as much to do with her social position as her gender, but through her artistic activities she achieved a sort of equality with her creative guests. Her watercolours, including a series of the interior of Petworth House, her embroidery and her enamelling could have been developed to professional levels. She was a founder member of the Royal School of Art Needlework (1872), she gave Alexander Fisher support, including a one-man show in her London house, and he dedicated his *The art of enamelling upon metal* (1906) to her 'for her patronage and help in reviving the Art of Enamelling'.

Henry James gave Mrs Gereth, the chatelaine of Poynton, the genius that turned her house into a 'complete work of art … that would appeal so to those who were really informed.'[20] Like Mrs Gereth, Madeline undoubtedly aimed to make Clouds a work of art. Clouds was her 'psychologically, socially, artistically and even politically satisfying home'.[21] As Deborah Cohen has noted, her role coincided with a more general acquisition of power in the home by women. From the 1880s women of some means were able to be the 'innovative and industrious creators of the House Beautiful' without criticism, and Madeline led the way.[22]

Edith Olivier, in *Four Victorian ladies of Wiltshire*, was effusive in her description of Madeline's operations at Clouds: 'From the moment when her guests stepped over her threshold to be taken to her heart and to be made free of her circle, they were no more stray individuals, but living members of the world

17 W.R. Lethaby, *Philip Webb and his work* (London, 1979), p. 99.   **18** Memoirs of Pamela Adeane, granddaughter of Madeline Wyndham (private collection).   **19** From one of Madeline Wyndham's commonplace books, acquired at the sale of Wilsford by Christopher Gibb.   **20** Henry James, *The spoils of Poynton* (London, 1964; first published 1897), p. 11.   **21** Stefan Muthesius, *The poetic home* (London, 2009), p. 12.   **22** Deborah Cohen, *Household gods: the British and their possessions* (New Haven, 2006), p. 114.

in which she lived and moved.'[23] However, her position at the centre of Clouds was not entirely benign. Not everyone was welcome, or rather, they were only welcome on her terms. She had 'sweetness and social charm' but also an 'underlying steel'.[24] She made it perfectly clear, for example, to the young artist Philip Burne-Jones (son of Edward) that his interest in her eldest daughter Mary was inappropriate, and 'practically shut her doors' on him. She took to her bed when a younger daughter expressed a preference for a Cambridgeshire landowner with a relatively small rental income and no title.[25]

John Singer Sargent's grand portrait of her three daughters, *The Wyndham sisters* (fig. 5.3), was painted in the drawing room of 44 Belgrave Square in 1899 and exhibited in 1900 at the Royal Academy to general acclaim. Sargent included in the background Watts' portrait of Madeline that hung on the wall. Madeline is thus forever fixed looking down on her daughters, exerting control from inside the painting just as she exerted control from behind her 'scrattle table' in the drawing room at Clouds. And she continued to exert her influence over her daughters after they left their parental home. Pamela, the second youngest, had been forbidden to marry the man she loved, and struggled to cope with the forbidding home of her new Scottish father-in-law Sir Charles Tennant. However, rather than criticise her mother, she found comfort through trying to re-create Madeline's effects: 'in my little sitting room I am going to get the Clouds drawing room chintz – and a pattern of an armchair at home – and in time get Mamma's sketches on the walls … and it will look like Clouds.'[26] Mary, unhappily married to the philandering and gambling Lord Elcho, stayed for prolonged periods at Clouds, her stays often coinciding with visits by her intimate friend Arthur Balfour. Her mother's house remained her true home: 'I feel I have … transplanted <u>very</u> badly and am always lean & hungry for want of the soil I am accustomed to – <u>everywhere</u> except at home, I feel like a mangy fir tree with a bald top.'[27] Her youngest daughter Madeline – as the new chatelaine of Babraham in Cambridgeshire – simply confessed, 'all I do is a feeble imitation of you'.[28]

Percy Wyndham died in 1911 in his bedroom at Clouds. Though he had professed little religious faith during his life, Madeline was convinced he found God on his deathbed, writing to her old lover Wilfrid Scawen Blunt: 'God <u>revealed</u> himself to Percy & gave him such a vision OF LOVE & HAPPINESS & glory that I can never forget it.'[29] Madeline was left a lifetime interest in their London house plus £1000 and an annuity of £3100, also Percy's horses,

23 Olivier, *Four Victorian ladies*, p. 95.   24 Cynthia Asquith, *Haply I may remember* (London, 1950), p. 42.   25 Renton, *Those wild Wyndhams*, pp 110–11.   26 Simon Blow, *Broken blood* (London, 1987), pp 115–16.   27 Mary Elcho to Madeline Wyndham, 6 Jan. 1886 (Stanway, earl of Wemyss and March papers, uncatalogued).   28 Madeline Adeane to Madeline Wyndham, 17 July 1889 (Adeane papers, private collection).   29 Madeline Wyndham to Wilfrid Scawen Blunt, 6 Dec. 1918, quoted in Renton, *Those wild Wyndhams*, p. 278.

5.3 John Singer Sargent, *The Wyndham sisters*, 1899, Catharine Lorillard Wolfe Collection, Wolfe Fund 1927, Metropolitan Museum of Art, New York.

carriages, personal effects and 'consumable stores'. Their eldest son, George, inherited the Clouds estate so, when not in London, Madeline divided her time between all her children's country houses – Clouds, Stanway, Babraham and Wilsford. George's wife, Lady Sibell Grosvenor, was now the chatelaine of Clouds.

Madeline had been first *fixed* by G.F. Watts, in the portrait commissioned by her husband; she was fixed, again, by Sargent, forever watching over her daughters from her place hanging on the wall inside Watts' frame. She, in turn, fixed people, literally, in the numerous albums, commonplace books or scrapbooks that she created throughout her married life. In her widowhood, this now became her strategy for ordering her life and events around her, of managing disappointment and loss. Cutting and sticking, juxtaposing image and text, photographs, newspaper cuttings, sketches, remembered snatches of verse, she assembled the 'chaos of memories' defined by Walter Benjamin in his essay 'Unpacking my library'.[30]

However, she could not control the effects of disease, of physical and spiritual collapse and of world events. Two years after Percy's death, her eldest son George, aged forty-nine, was dead of a heart attack, probably in the arms of either a Parisian prostitute or his mistress. Neither his marriage nor his career as Irish secretary had been successful. His only son, Percy Lyulph, known as Perf, inherited the Clouds estate and £20,000 death duties, but the following year, 1914, Britain declared war on Germany. As a professional soldier, a lieutenant in the Coldstream Guards, Perf was immediately deployed to the Western Front where he was shot. Four more of Madeline's grandsons were killed during the war. Edith Olivier understood the presence of death in Madeline's commonplace books: 'these books reveal that the thought of death … was never far away. She had no fear of it. On the contrary, the memory of death gave to the passing hours their supreme value for her.'[31]

Madeline placed a plaque in the church at East Knoyle in memory of her five dead grandsons; they were buried where they fell in France and Egypt. She never lost her faith; her daughter Mary described spending two nights holding her hands, 'talking of people long since dead and roaming with her through strange realms of phantasy and delirium in what seemed a death chamber, or birth into another world.'[32] She died on 8 March 1920 at Babraham and her ashes were buried in the family plot at East Knoyle next to Percy.

30 Walter Benjamin, *Illuminations* (London, 1977), p. 66. Benjamin inherited two albums of his mother's containing stick-in pictures she pasted in as a child. He described them as 'book like creations from fringe areas'.   **31** Olivier, *Four Victoiran ladies*, p. 92.   **32** Mary Elcho to Arthur Balfour, 10 Oct. 1919, quoted in Renton, *Those wild Wyndhams*, p. 351.

PART TWO: MABEL MORRISON

Mabel Morrison's experience was very different to Madeline Wyndham's. When Mabel Chermside married Alfred Morrison on 11 April 1866 she was nineteen, twenty-six years younger than her husband (fig. 5.4). Although Mabel could expect no money from Dr Chermside she had received a sophisticated upbringing in Paris, staying with her grandfather Sir Robert Chermside. The Chermsides were also friends with the Herberts of Wilton, their neighbours and patrons of the living. The difference in wealth between Mabel and Alfred was extreme. Alfred had inherited a country house, land, investments and works of art from his father, who died in 1857. Fonthill House in Wiltshire was the surviving wing of Alderman Beckford's Fonthill 'Splendens', demolished by the Alderman's son William Beckford when he built the Gothic Fonthill Abbey.

Since inheriting the estate, Alfred had been building up his own large collection of engravings, Chinese Imperial porcelain, autograph letters and contemporary art. He had bought 16 Carlton House Terrace, a very large town house in London, and commissioned Owen Jones to design the decorations, furniture and fittings in London and at Fonthill. He consequently provided Mabel with town and country houses already complete. This was very different to the joint partnership in home-building enjoyed by the Wyndhams. He also provided Mabel with a generous marriage settlement, which included £50,000 worth of consolidated stock of the East India Railway, but the income of £2000 per annum was to be hers only after his death.

The gap in age between Mabel and Alfred would have been considered large even for the Victorians; Alfred was three years older than his father-in-law, Dr Chermside. Mabel's father expressed anxiety about the marriage in a handful of surviving letters: 'I remember how young my child is, and how much discipline of life it takes to form character and to clothe it with true grace, no less than to train it into noble force.'[33] It is impossible to know whether Dr Chermside was seriously concerned his daughter was marrying a man who was so much older than she. But already very ill, he could offer her little support and was unable to conduct her wedding ceremony; he died a year later aged only forty-four.

After a honeymoon in the south of France, Mabel and Alfred moved into 2 Harley Street while the decorations in Carlton House Terrace were completed. An aristocratic neighbour in Wiltshire met Mabel for the first time in September 1866. They were attending church in Fonthill, Gifford. The diary entry is barbed: Mabel was 'very young very cheerful, invincibly goodnatured & quite as if she had had £50,000 a year all her life'.[34] Mabel's first child, Rachel, was born early in 1867 but died aged ten months. Mabel was pregnant again by the time

33 Dr Chermside to Ellen Morrison, 9 Feb. 1866 (Fonthill Estate Archives, Ellen Morrison papers, J/01).   34 Diary of Lady Theodora Grosvenor, 2 Sept. 1866 (private collection).

5.4 Galbraith, detail of
Mabel Morrison, 1867,
private collection.

Rachel died and a drawing by John Brett, completed a month before the next baby was due, presents her as serious, wistful, anxious.[35] Hugh, the heir, was born with no apparent complications, but photographs taken of Mabel with her new baby show her in 'double' mourning, for both her daughter and her father. Katharine was born in 1869, fourteen months after Hugh, but the attendance of two doctors were required a month before the birth. Dorothy was born in 1871, Archie in 1873. Mabel collapsed soon after. Her symptoms suggest that she was suffering from a prolapsed uterus (womb), a condition brought about by long and difficult labours. She was only twenty-six years old. Edith Olivier explained:

35 The drawing is illustrated in Christiana Payne and Ann Sumner, *Objects of affection: pre-Raphaelite portraits by John Brett* (Bristol, 2010), p. 104.

'for twelve years after the birth of her last child … she endured very great pain from an internal illness, and was condemned to be nearly always on her back'.[36] The choice of activities appropriate for a young invalid was limited; her physical position was very different to that of Madeline Wyndham.

Mabel Morrison played no part, at least initially, in the decoration of her husband's town and country houses, or the content of his collections. Alfred had been addicted to collecting for over a decade before his marriage. His approach was to focus on a particular object, artist or designer, then collect as much as he could afford: 2000 pieces of porcelain from the Summer Palace in Pekin; thousands of manuscripts and autographs; 3000 portrait engravings of famous men and women, including works by Rembrandt and Hogarth; the work of a select number of Royal Academicians; unique commissions by French enamellists and goldsmiths. As a final touch his initials were added to new pieces, furniture and fittings, clocks, tables and vases, even estate cottages. Contemporaries found him competitive, arrogant, fanatical and obsessed. It is tempting to relate him to the fastidious and hyper-critical Gilbert Osmond in Henry James' *The portrait of a lady*, first published in 1881. Was Mabel part of Alfred's collection – with the addition year on year of their children – just as Isobel Armstrong and her step-daughter Pansy were part of Osmond's collection? James describes Osmond occupying 'a sorted, sifted, arranged world, thinking about art and beauty and history. He had consulted his taste in everything – his taste alone perhaps.'[37] The description could easily be applied to Alfred. Intending a compliment, Edith Olivier wrote: 'Mabel's independent mind was an unfailing delight to her husband, in whose eyes she remained the most unique among all the treasures he had collected.'[38] But Jean Baudrillard's powerful image of the collector comes to mind, the 'master of a secret seraglio'. 'There is something of the harem about collecting, for the whole attraction may be summed up as that of an intimate series (one term of which is at any given time the favourite) combined with serial intimacy'.[39]

Percy Wyndham commissioned portraits of Madeline and later his three daughters that were sumptuous, in the grand manner, by famous artists (G.F. Watts and John Singer Sargent; see figs 5.1 & 5.3) and shown to the public at the Grosvenor Gallery and the Royal Academy. The Wyndhams also lent their painting of Westminster Bridge, Whistler's *Nocturne in blue and gold*, to the Grosvenor in 1877. The painting had been bought by Percy at the Dudley Gallery in 1875, but the lender to the Grosvenor was named as Mrs Percy Wyndham.[40] She was defined both by her portrait and by her artistic taste.

Alfred's approach to showing off his young wife in paintings or in the flesh appears to have been rather different. He began buying the work of John Brett

36 Olivier, *Four Victorian ladies*, p. 54.   **37** Henry James, *The portrait of a lady* (London, 1986), p. 312.   **38** Olivier, *Four Victorian ladies*, p. 60.   **39** Jean Baudrillard, *The system of objects* (London, 2005), p. 94.   **40** Christopher Newall, *The Grosvenor Gallery exhibitions* (Cambridge, 1995), p. 17.

5.5 Photograph of Mabel Morrison, her children and Miss Willis at the Ranche, Fonthill, Fonthill Estate Archives.

before he was married, at the Royal Academy and directly from Brett's studio. Brett drew and painted Mabel four times in 1868 but only one drawing, kept by Brett himself, has been located. None were publicly displayed, neither was Brett's chalk drawing of Alfred.[41] The portrait signed 'Galbraith 1867' remains a mystery (see fig. 5.4), as no artist called Galbraith has been identified.

Two miniatures on enamel of Mabel were lent by Alfred to the 1867 Exposition Universelle, though described only as 'two miniatures of an English lady'. These were made by the French enamellist Charles Lepec, another of Alfred's closest artist-friends, honoured by having a bedroom named after him

---

41 On John Brett see Christiana Payne, *John Bret, pre-Raphaelite landscape painter* (New Haven and London, 2010).

at Fonthill. Lepec completed the tiny portraits in 1866, the year of the Morrisons' marriage; one was for Alfred and the other for Mabel's father.[42] Mabel's public viewing is anonymous and on a very small scale; she has been transformed into an exquisite *objet d'art*.

Ill-health limited her activities. In 1872, just before her major collapse, she joined Madeline Wyndham and other aristocratic women in the founding of the School of Art Needlework. The motive was to supply 'suitable employment for gentlewomen' and to 'restore ornamental needlework to the high place it once held among the decorative arts.'[43] In 1875 the Queen became patron, and the school became 'Royal'. Unlike Madeline, however, Mabel appears not to have worked embroideries designed by the artists (Burne-Jones, William Morris) who supported the initiative. Nor did she attend committee meetings or sales of work.

Alfred was not unthoughtful towards his young wife. He paid £3000 for the Ranche, a luxurious cabin, to be built in the Great Ridge Woods at Fonthill. Here Mabel retired for days at a time, with her children. But the photograph of her lying on her day-bed, a diminutive figure surrounded by children and servants, suggests that even here she was contained and controlled by her poor health (fig. 5.5). The woman standing to the right is Caroline Willis, devoted life-long servant of the Morrisons. It is she who draws our attention, a rival to the group on the steps and veranda. Presumably as a reward for a life-time of service Miss Willis was provided with an expensive gravestone in Fonthill Gifford, and Alfred's chest tomb was erected immediately adjacent to it. Alfred's descendants wonder, not surprisingly, whether the relationship between them was more than master and servant.

In the mid-1880s Mabel literally rose from her sick bed and began to enjoy a normal life as country house hostess. She had been attended by Dr James Watt Black, a distinguished obstetrics physician and lecturer on midwifery at the Charing Cross Hospital. Without surviving medical evidence, the assumption must be that her condition was relieved by the use of a pessary to hold the uterus in place, or surgery (if, indeed, she was suffering from a prolapsed uterus). By the end of the century, 'repairs could be safely made, because of the development of anaesthesia and antisepsis'.[44] She could have undergone a hysterectomy.

The contrast between Mabel's age and Alfred's was now extreme: in 1887 she was only forty; Alfred was sixty-six and their children almost grown-up. She copied her neighbour Madeline Wyndham, who was by this time established at Clouds, throwing her own memorable parties at Fonthill. There were private

42 On Charles Lepec see Olivier Hurstel and Martin Levy, 'Charles Lepec and the patronage of Alfred Morrison', *Metropolitan Journal*, 50 (2015), 194–223.   **43** For further information on the Royal School of Art Needlework see Barbara Morris, *Victorian embroidery* (London, 1962); see also Winifride Jackson and Elizabeth Pettifer, *The Royal School of Needlework yesterday and to-day* (Leicester, 1986).   **44** Mabel Collins Donnelly, *The American Victorian woman: the myth and the reality* (New York, 1986), p. 58.

musical recitals for select friends from London and aristocratic neighbours, children's parties and annual garden parties. The Wyndhams attended a party in 1885, their daughter Madeline writing to her elder sister, Mary, on 22 October:

> I suppose you know that the Morrisons live only about 6 miles from here [Clouds]. Mrs Morrison is very pretty and very delicate. She is always very smart, and you have never heard anyone talk so much, one flow of conversation … Last Saturday they gave a party to which we all went. There was most beautiful music given in the picture gallery. Henry Holmes played the violin, Mrs Hutchinson sang, quite beautifully, and Madame Haas played the piano.[45]

Mabel was coming alive as Alfred grew old.

The death of Alfred in 1897, aged seventy-six, dramatically changed Mabel's life. She stepped outside the exquisite frame in which she had been contained, exercising the power of a wealthy widow of fifty. Alfred had not altered his will since his marriage, to the dismay of their eldest son Hugh. Mabel consequently inherited a lifetime interest in Fonthill House and 300 acres of parkland, the London house, the household effects in London and the country, and stables in Duke Street. Her marriage settlement produced an income of £2000 per annum and she received an additional annuity of £150,000, yielding an income of £6000, hers to keep even if she married again. Hugh had married Lady Mary Leveson-Gower five years before, but the young couple were now faced with the prospect of not inheriting Fonthill for thirty years or more. In the end Mabel lived until she was eighty-six, outliving her eldest son by two years.

Alfred had attempted to safeguard part of his collection by requesting in his will that a list of heirlooms should be drawn up by Christie's, 'having regard to their artistic and intrinsic value or merit and their suitability in their surroundings.' However, pieces of 'no art value, or which, in [Christie's] opinion, were of but trifling intrinsic value and of small or no artistic merit' were to be excluded.[46] The list finally included most of Alfred's Old Master paintings, a selection of engravings, his collection of medals and most of the Imperial porcelain, and the fittings designed for Fonthill by Owen Jones, but the list omitted many contemporary paintings, autograph letters, small items such as rings, embroideries, Greek vases, also a number of pieces commissioned by Alfred from French and Spanish craftsmen. It was consequently easy for Mabel to raise the £10,000 required in death duties from just three sales conducted by Christies in 1898.

However, Mabel continued to sell: seven sales in 1899 alone (porcelain, embroideries, pictures), and a further seven between 1901 and 1906, the latter

45 Madeline Wyndham (daughter) to Mary Lady Elcho, 22 Oct. 1885 (Stanway, Wemyss and March papers).   **46** *The Times*, 22 June 1900.

all from Alfred's enormous collection of engravings. She sold most of his contemporary art collection, including the entire collection of works by John Brett apart from Alfred's portrait. Brett's drawings of her are missing possibly destroyed, also virtually all the personal correspondence between her, Alfred and their children. The house in Carlton House Terrace, with a remaining sixty-three-year lease, was valued for probate at £20,650. Mabel immediately sold it, together with all the fittings and furniture designed by Owen Jones, and moved to a smaller house in Bruton Street.

There was some economic sense in moving house in London, though she only reduced the number of servants from sixteen to thirteen, but Mabel's disposal, year on year, of her husband's extraordinary and unique collection suggests another motive. She was disposing of objects that had surrounded her since the beginning of her married life, objects that mattered enormously to her husband; it was as if she was also disposing of him, bit by bit, through the auction houses. She did, however, like some of his Old Master paintings, which had been included in the list of heirlooms, and took a number to her new house in Bruton Street. The Morrisons had to take her to the High Court before she would return the items.

She also appears to have been greedy. Alfred's collection of autograph letters was of international significance and Mabel sold part in 1900 including the correspondence between Emma Hamilton and Lord Nelson. In 1902, Sotheby's offered her the very large sum of £200,000 if she would sell through them the rest of the collection in its entirety to J. Pierpoint Morgan. Mabel asked for £250,000. Pierpoint Morgan withdrew and the sale collapsed. When she finally disposed of the collection during the First World War she received just over £53,000.

Mabel continued to run Fonthill House as her country home but the situation there was far from comfortable. Her eldest son Hugh and his wife were guests in the house that would eventually be theirs; Katharine and Dorothy were unmarried so still living with their mother. Only Archie had moved away. Then in 1902, Hugh made the decision to build a brand-new house on the Fonthill estate called Little Ridge so that he could be independent of his mother, and three years later Katharine married the retired chief justice of Gibraltar Sir Stephen Gatty. She was thirty-six years old; he was fifty-six, a friend of the Morrisons and a widower. In 1909, with only Dorothy still on her hands, Mabel decided to leave Fonthill.

Her motivation appears to have been financial, again. Her husband's elder brother Charles, a bachelor and multi-millionaire financier, died in 1909, leaving his vast wealth to all his extended family. Mabel, however, was disappointed that she received a legacy of only £20,000 (a considerable sum at the time). Her daughter-in-law Lady Mary thought she was 'really rather childish … I rather wonder whether she may have some rather big debt which she had always counted on being able to pay off when she came in for her share of the money she expected.'[47] Mabel, however, was clear she could no longer cope with the expense and responsibility of Fonthill. She wrote a bitter rambling letter to Hugh on 6 June 1909:

> I write to warn you that my present intention is to give up Fonthill Jan 1st 1910. I should hand you over the house the heirlooms etc & then you will of course deal with them as you think fit – I shall warn Squarey [the land agent managing the estate] & all the people in my employment will be given notice some time before & I shall make them a present on leaving … This is no sudden resolve it has been my firm intention to do this had Dorothy married or as is now the case on your inheriting from your Uncle [Charles] – I hope with all my heart you will pull the house I live in down – You have of course a perfect right to build yr house on any corner of the estate & I also never dispute yr right to prefer say the Jacobean style [a reference to Little Ridge] to the classical architecture – But I do grieve at two big houses within sight of each other. Then two gardens etc the spoiling of Fonthill which I love & the appalling waste of money. For years I have lived on the margins of debt & of debt incurred through [no] fault of my own but by my being placed in a position too large for my income – I tried to hide from Katharine & Dorothy how distasteful the life was to me but the bitterest thought was the uselessness of my sacrifice & the positively sinful waste of money! When I think of the thousands of pounds wasted, electric light, water supply galleries etc etc I wring my hands in sheer despair. You will I hope pull down the house & build a fine stone building across the Lake & make a drive under the wood in the deer park right up to Little Ridge. If you make a real bridge <u>&</u> a good road then you could … I shall sell Lennox Gardens [another London house] & if I have a house at all I shall have some tiny little inexpensive house which will require very few servants.[48]

The letter reads as if written by someone fearful of poverty rather than by a wealthy widow in control of her own inheritance and with sufficient means to maintain Fonthill House. Mabel then asked her son to give her the £10,000 she had paid in death duties, the money for her to use 'during my life', presumably to buy the 'tiny little inexpensive house'. There may have been an element of greed to Mabel's actions, but it appears more likely she wanted to free herself from all of her husband's property, his collections, his house in London and now his country estate.

---

47 Lady Mary Morrison to Hugh, 3 June 1909 (Fonthill Estate Archive, Lady Mary Morrison papers).   **48** Mabel Morrison to Hugh Morrison, 6 June 1909 (ibid.).

5.6 Mathilde de Cordoba, *Mabel Morrison*, 1912, reproduced in Edith Olivier, *The quest of joy* (London, 1937), opposite page 44.

After much fussing over different properties, Mabel finally moved away in 1912, at the same time as Dorothy (now forty-one) married Stafford Northcote Viscount Saint Cyres, only son of the earl of Iddesleigh. Shawford Place near Winchester was hardly 'some tiny little inexpensive house' but rather a sizeable country house, built in 1685 for Sir Henry Mildmay, with ninety acres of land including the home farm. The library was forty feet long; the 'great room or music room' was 'about 54ft by 21ft with domed ceiling. Above the 2ft wainscoted dado the entire walls and ceiling are decoratively painted on canvas like the celebrated painted room in Garrick's Villa ... The open fireplace is fitted with marble surround, hearth and curb, and is surmounted by a finely carved pine chimneypiece, late XVIIth century, removed from a house in Great Pulteney Street [Bath], partly supported by Caryatides and ornamented by Acanthus leaves and other carved enrichments.'[49]

Mabel was in her element. She was painted by Mathilde de Cordoba (see fig. 5.6) soon after the move. This is a very different image to the exquisite

49 Sale particulars, 9 Oct. 1923 (Fonthill Estate Archives, 9/1/1202).

miniatures produced by Charles Lepec, or the anxious face drawn by John Brett and painted by Galbraith, or even the drawing by Charles Gere, completed in 1909. She exudes confidence; she is in control. And she commissions a new wing by Harry Herbert Jewell for Shawford Place.

Edith Olivier describes Mabel's idiosyncratic and increasingly eccentric life at Shawford:

> Old age was Mrs Morrison's supreme and ultimate achievement. Most old ladies are deemed to have fulfilled their vocation if they succeed in growing old gracefully. This means that they must find contentment in receding into the background, and becoming with the years an ever fainter shadow of what they were in their prime ... they should welcome visitors with gentle pleasure, and should be ready, when invited, to relate their early memories, though at not too great a length. Mrs Morrison did nothing of the sort. She grew old in her own way.[50]

She wore her white hair like a French lady at the court of Louis XVI and dressed in the fashion of a Gainsborough picture. During the First World War she provided accommodation for soldiers (Shawford's proximity to Winchester was ideal) and was delighted to receive government pay for her efforts. She kept unconventional hours, and delighted in moving pieces of furniture from room to room with the assistance of obliging men sent from Christie's auction house.

Mabel moved for the last time, in 1923, aged seventy-six, to Littleden at Highcliffe-on-Sea, but she was still a long way from her 'tiny' house. There were three reception rooms, eight bedrooms, three bathrooms and domestic offices, plus a garage for two cars and quarters for the chauffeur above.

She died in 1933, leaving generous bequests to all her servants including her dairyman at Shawford and £250 each to the sons of her architect. She left Littleden and virtually all its contents plus £14,000 to a nephew on her Chermside side of the family; her own children and grand-children received only minor bequests. Her final resting place was not beside her husband or eldest son in Fonthill. She chose a relatively simple grave in the churchyard of St Michael and All Angels, Hinton, Hampshire.

CONCLUSION

Unlike Mabel Morrison, Madeline Wyndham had been able to exercise power during her marriage; Clouds and the life led within it was her creation. She was rendered powerless as a widow; she no longer had a home in the country and was reliant on the hospitality of her children. However, she could relive the past as

---

50 Olivier, *Four Victorian ladies*, p. 63.

the curator of her commonplace books, her 'diaries of the mind', sorting and assembling, remembering the dead. Mabel, trapped for twenty years by childbirth and the painful after effects, emerged in widowhood and re-invented herself, selling as much as she could of her husband's collections, almost as if she was disposing of Alfred bit by bit through the auction houses.

Clouds, and the unswerving support of her husband, provided Madeline with power; Mabel found freedom only as a widow. Madeline planned the burial ground at East Knoyle, commissioning the enamellist Alexander Fisher (her teacher) to design graves side by side for Percy and herself. Mabel chose *not* to be buried at Fonthill next to Alfred and their devoted servant Miss Willis.

Catherine Maria Bury of Charleville Castle, Co. Offaly, and the design of the country house, 1800–12

JUDITH HILL

Charleville Castle, a Gothic revival castle, built between 1800 and 1812 in King's County (Co. Offaly), Ireland, reflected contemporary English thinking about Gothic architecture and domestic comfort.[1] It was designed by Francis Johnston (1760–1829) who, two years before the Charleville commission, had completed Townley Hall, Co. Louth, and was earning a reputation as a designer of classical houses.[2] But, as befitted a talented and ambitious architect of the period, Johnston had an interest in Gothic architecture, and experience designing in a Gothic idiom. His surviving journal, written during a tour he made in Wales and southern England in 1796, together with his library catalogue, reveal that he had a critical interest in medieval and contemporary Gothic architecture, a picturesque sensibility and an awareness of antiquarian scholarship.[3] But it is also clear from these documents that he was not familiar with the most advanced works of antiquarian scholarship and that his perception of Gothic was heavily influenced by the classicism in which he had been trained. His particular understanding of, and feeling for, Gothic is evident in the battlemented gateway he designed for William Burton Conyngham at Slane Castle, Co. Meath, in *c*.1795, which is medieval in motif rather than spirit, but projects a picturesque response to the landscape setting.

The design of Charleville Castle represented a significant development in Johnston's Gothic repertoire. This suggests that his patrons had a decisive input into the project. It is evident that this was the case for both Charles William Bury and Catherine Maria Bury (later Lord and Lady Charleville) who were attuned to contemporary Gothic. Charles Bury's 1799 library catalogue, and the short account he wrote of a journey in Wales, reveal an interest in the picturesque and antiquarianism.[4] A terse diary written by Charles Bury at the time Charleville

1 Charleville Castle, its patrons and architects are discussed in Judith Hill, 'Perceptions and uses of Gothic in Irish domestic and ecclesiastical architecture, 1800–1815' (PhD, Trinity College Dublin, 2016), chapters 1–3. 2 See assessment in Christine Casey and Alistair Rowan, *The buildings of Ireland: north Leinster* (London, 1993), pp 503–8; Townley Hall was completed in *c*.1798. 3 Diary of Francis Johnston, 25 Mar.–14 Apr. 1796 (Armagh County Museum, ARMCM.3.1949); Charles Sharpe [Dublin], 'Francis Johnston: sale of architectural library (portion of), 10 May 1843' (Royal Irish Academy, Dublin, private MS copy). 4 'Catalogue of books in the possession of the Rt Hon. Charles William, Lord Tullamore', 1799 (Offaly County Library, Howard Bury papers, P59); R. Warwick Bond (ed.), *The Marlay*

Castle was being constructed, together with letters he wrote to his wife from Charleville, show him looking at contemporary English Gothic buildings and judging Johnston's progress at Charleville.[5] But it is Catherine Bury's letters to Frederick Trench (1746–1836), an antiquarian, Gothic connoisseur, amateur architect and close friend, who created a picturesque demesne in nearby Heywood, Queen's County (now Co. Laois), that reveal the enthusiasm for Gothic inflected by picturesque and romantic sensibility that undoubtedly influenced Johnston.[6] There are also a number of surviving sketches, some signed by Catherine Bury, others attributable to her, which reveal that she played an active role in formulating the initial concept for the castle, developing the design of the structure and providing ideas for the interior scheme.

Women's contributions to architectural design have been greatly underplayed in the work of architectural historians. This is partly because circumstances, expectations and opportunities conspired to make it relatively rare for women to be involved in the building of country houses from the seventeenth to the nineteenth century. Few women were owners of estates, some travelled extensively, but many did not, and women's spheres of activity and influence tended to be confined to the domestic realm and their social circle. But women's activities as designers and builders have also been overlooked by architectural historians, who, until relatively recently, were focused on architects rather than patrons, and, then male rather than female figures. As Ruth Thorpe has observed, the breakthrough did not come until the exhibition, 'Women architects: their work', was shown in London in 1984.[7]

It was another twenty years before architectural historians were purposefully investigating the building activities of Irish aristocratic women, and, through the pioneering work of Finola O'Kane and Ruth Thorpe, we now know of several prominent and influential women who were active and effective as patrons in Ireland in the eighteenth and nineteenth centuries.[8] O'Kane has uncovered Lady Louisa Conolly's role in designing estate buildings, a cottage ornée, and model school at Castletown, Co. Kildare, from 1758 to 1811. O'Kane has noted that the picturesque cottage was considered particularly appropriate for female patron-designers in this period due to its ability to project the purposefully naïve and amateur: '[t]he cottage style proclaimed its owner as an unassuming, modest, sensible, retiring and tasteful individual'.[9] By designing buildings for estate

letters, 1778–1820 (London, 1937), pp 256–7.   **5** Viscount Charleville's diary, 20 July 1802–[6] June 1803 (Westmeath County Library and Archives Service, Howard Bury Collection, P1/25) [hereafter Bury papers]; Letters from C.W. Bury to C. M. Bury, [4 Dec. 1805] – 29 July 1818 (University of Nottingham, Marlay papers, MSS MY 77–96) [hereafter Marlay papers].   **6** For discussion of Trench see Patricia Friel, *Frederick Trench (1746–1836) and Heywood, Queen's County: the creation of a romantic demesne* (Dublin, 2000).   **7** Discussion of the historiography of women's involvement in architecture in Ruth Thorpe, *Women, architecture and building in the east of Ireland, c.1790–1840* (Dublin, 2013), pp 8–10.   **8** Finola O'Kane, 'Design and rule: women in the Irish countryside, 1715–1831', *Eighteenth-Century Ireland*, 19 (2004), 56–74; see also, Thorpe, *Women, architecture and building*.   **9** O'Kane,

workers and their children Conolly was, in some measure, staying within the established parameters of female activity. Thorpe's research has established this theme for the work of other women, who extended traditional occupations – such as drawing – and interests – such as landscape – to architectural projects, and who worked within the socially sanctioned philanthropic sphere. She has also found that women travelled more widely in the nineteenth century than previously, and were encouraged by better-travelled and better-educated husbands or brothers. By investigating personal correspondence, diaries, sketch books and drawings rather than the more traditional architectural historian's approach of consulting correspondence with architects or building accounts, which tend to feature the male players, Thorpe has uncovered a number of active female patrons.[10] Lady Helena Domvile, the daughter of Frederick Trench, was involved with the design of picturesque cottages.[11] Anna Maria Dawson (1770–1820), the sister of Blayney Townley Balfour of Townley Hall, was an 'engaged client' of Francis Johnston, who helped to shape the design of Townley Hall, as well as Galtrim, Co. Meath, and Loughgilly Glebe, Co. Armagh, two smaller houses that she lived in after her marriage.[12] The aim of this chapter is to contribute to the growing understanding of women's active participation in design by investigating the role of Lady Charleville in the realization of a project for a castle that was self-consciously grand, and which engaged with contemporary debate about the use of Gothic in domestic architecture.[13]

LORD AND LADY CHARLEVILLE

The Burys were wealthy and titled, but they had had to actively establish themselves and their family at Charleville, and Charles William Bury (1764–1835) worked hard to obtain his titles. Bury inherited considerable property when he came of age in June 1785: the Bury family estate of Shannongrove, Co. Limerick; the Charleville estate near Tullamore in King's County, which had been inherited by Charles' father, John Bury, from his maternal uncle, Charles Moore (1712–64); property in Dublin; and the Sopwell Hall estate in Tipperary, which Charles inherited from his mother.[14] At 21, Charles Bury had a regular income of over £14,000 per year from his estates, and no substantial debts.[15] John Bury, Charles' father, had died five weeks after his son's birth, and when his widow married Henry Prittie of Kilboy, Co. Tipperary, Charles Bury was

'Design and rule', 66. **10** Thorpe, *Women, architecture and building*, pp 9–10. **11** Ibid., pp 38–49. **12** Ibid., pp 11–27, 30–5, 51–3, 59–60. **13** O'Kane, discussing Lady Charleville's sensibility in a picturesque context, touched on her design activity but did not investigate Lady Charleville's role in relation to Johnston in detail; Finola O'Kane, *Ireland and the picturesque: design, landscape painting and tourism, 1700–1840* (New Haven & London, 2013), pp 174–80. **14** John Lodge, *The peerage of Ireland*, 5 vols (Dublin, 1789), ii, 82–91. **15** 'Particulars of Lord Charleville's estates in Ireland' [mid-1830s] (Bury papers, P1/2).

brought up on his stepfather's estate. Rather than returning to Shannongrove, Charles chose to establish himself at Charleville. Charles Moore had moved to Charleville, then Redwood, in 1740, to live in the house erected there in the early seventeenth century, and this was where Charles Bury lived until Charleville Castle was substantially completed in 1809.[16]

Charles Moore had been created earl of Charleville on 16 September 1758, but the title became extinct on his death. Charles Bury was intent on regaining the earldom. Supported by documents to prove his entitlement to a baronetcy, he was created Baron Tullamore of the second creation in November 1797.[17] Three years later on 29 December 1800 he became Viscount Charleville as a reward for supporting the Union, and, after petitioning the viceroy to elevate him to the peerage by assuming his great-uncle's title, he became earl of Charleville in February 1806.[18]

Charles Bury married Catherine Maria Tisdall (née Dawson) (1762–1851) in June 1798. Catherine Maria, the daughter of Thomas Townley Dawson of Armagh, and the widow of James Tisdall of Bawn, Co. Louth, who had died suddenly in November 1797, was a prudent woman of independent means.[19] Her first husband's estate was indebted and she used her Dawson and Saunders (her mother's family) legacies to pay off the debt so that her son by her first marriage should inherit an unencumbered estate, retaining £600 a year for herself.[20] Worldly, with a carefully calibrated sense of Bury wealth, she joined with her husband in the extravagant enterprise of castle building, but she was careful in her personal expenditure and together they could economize in the running of the household.[21]

Charles William Bury had a gentleman's education; he graduated from Trinity College Dublin in 1785, and spent 1788–9 on a grand tour in Italy.[22] On his return he was elected MP for Kilmallock in 1790 and again in 1792.[23] He made no mark in parliament and supported the Union. On his death he left a large number of manuscripts written in his hand. R. Warwick Bond, who was commissioned by the family in 1912 to edit Lady Charleville's letters,

---

16 C.W. Bury, MS fragment of account of Charleville, n.d.; (Marlay papers, MS MY 1043/1). 17 Six weeks earlier C.W. Bury received the right to bear arms; 'Confirmation of arms to Charles William Bury Oct. 15 1797' (NLI, Genealogical Office, MS 103, p. 153). 18 In November 1805 the viceroy, 3rd earl of Hardwicke, recommended Viscount Charleville's elevation to the peerage in a letter to the home secretary; 3rd earl of Hardwicke to Lord Hawkesbury, 6 Nov. 1805 (TNA, Home Office papers: Ireland, HO 100/130, p. 22). 19 Bond, *Marlay letters*, pp 23–7, 45. 20 Ibid., pp 23–4, 49–50. 21 In 1806, C.W. Bury wrote: 'The Dean has not been so magnificent in his loans, & we shall find it difficult to keep two footmen, without a supply from hence': C.W. Bury to C.M. Bury, 30 Jan. 1809 (University of Nottingham, Marlay papers, MS MY 84). 22 George Dames Burtchaell and Thomas Ulick Sadleir (eds), *Alumni Dublinenses, a register of the students, graduates, professors and provosts of Trinity College in the University of Dublin (1593–1860)* (Dublin, 1935), p. 120; John Ingamells, *A dictionary of British and Irish travellers in Italy, 1701–1800* (New Haven & London, 1997), p. 164. 23 E.M. Johnston-Liik, *History of the Irish parliament, 1692–1800*,

meticulously analysed this large, amorphous collection, discovering that it was largely a disordered copying of extracts from histories, literary and political works, without obvious plan or purpose.[24] It showed he had wide interests, but an unwillingness to discipline his thoughts.

Catherine Maria, on the other hand, intelligent and curious, had direction, force, persistence and a streak of subversiveness. Writing aged eighty-six to her godson, Brinsley Marlay, about her French education she said that what remained to her was 'the satisfactory conviction [that] the study of the exact Sciences produces a habit of keeping the mind directly to the given point and leading one from waste of time on useless divergence.'[25] Her education, though haphazard, was broad for a young woman living in the late eighteenth century. Her parents took her to France, and she spent two summers at the Collège Royal in Toulouse where she was taught mathematics and philology in French.[26] She read Joseph Butler's *Analogy of religion* of 1736, a defence of Christianity against fashionable deism, using empirical rather than rationalist arguments.[27] She had a grounding in the classics, which she displayed in her correspondence with men, and she had an enthusiastic interest in literature; later in life she read the novels of Walter Scott as they appeared, encouraged the young novelist Sydney Owenson, and corresponded with the novelist Maria Edgeworth.[28] Catherine wrote a play, and translated the French correspondence in Charles Fox's seventeenth-century history of England into English.[29]

Despite debilitating rheumatism, Catherine cultivated an impressive social presence, noted by Sydney Owenson, who described her as 'large, stately, and imposing, with magnificent grey eyes, a courtly, formal manner, and a deeply-toned voice, which made her most trifling observations impressive'.[30] She had an intellectual presence, attracting the respect of Richard Marlay, bishop of Waterford, and Dr Thomas Barnard, bishop of Limerick, friend of the great artistic, political and literary figures of the day, Joshua Reynolds, Edmund Burke and Samuel Johnson.[31] Catherine seems to have made great efforts to appear conservative, though her actions betrayed sympathy for more radical ideas. Owenson observed that Lady Charleville felt constrained to act as the great lady, 'reared in the bosom of high Toryism', and that when she engaged with alternative doctrines – which she did as the patron of Owenson and Edgeworth – she affected amazement and bewilderment.[32]

6 vols (Belfast, 2002), iii, 331–2.   24 Bond, *Marlay letters*, pp v, 36.   25 Quoted in ibid., p. 3. 26 Ibid., pp 3–7.   27 Ibid., p. 3.   28 C.M. Bury's grounding in the classics emerged in her correspondence with Frederick Trench, see below. For C.M. Bury's correspondence with female novelists see Bond, *Marlay letters*, pp 299–313, 336–403.   29 C.W. Bury to C.M. Bury, 17 July 1808 (Marlay papers, MS, MY 91); see also Charles Fox, *A history of the early part of the reign of James the second*, 4 vols (London, 1808).   30 *Lady Morgan's memoirs: autobiography, diaries and correspondence*, 2 vols (2nd ed. London, 1863), ii, 68.   31 For C.M. Bury's relationship with Marlay and Barnard see Bond, *Marlay letters*, pp 56–60; Anthony Powell (ed.), *Barnard letters, 1778–1824* (London, 1928), p. 119.   32 *Lady Morgan's memoirs*, ii, 389–90.

This reticence may have been due to an earlier literary scandal. When still married to James Tisdall, Catherine collaborated with Charles Bury on a translation of Voltaire's *La Pucelle*, which was privately and anonymously printed in 1796–7.[33] Voltaire wrote *La Pucelle*, a poem in twenty-one cantos published in 1755, attacking modern writers' rejection of classical epic heroism, with its emphasis on the masculine, aristocratic and humane. He used satire, aping the literary techniques he decried – disordered plots and sentimental writing – and he seemed to revel in the burlesque scenes of rape and bestiality, which his satire required. Although the translation was advertised as being Charles Bury's work, surviving letters reveal that Catherine had been involved, and that her role, only definitely known to her immediate social circle, was the subject of considerable speculation in wider society.[34] Because so much of the poem was deemed to be outside a woman's sphere of knowledge, Catherine's involvement was regarded with embarrassment by some of her close friends, such as Louisa Conolly and her sister Sarah Napier. However, Bishop Barnard, who disapproved of Catherine's involvement with *La Pucelle*, admired her literary skill, and told Sarah Napier, who relayed his judgment to Catherine in a letter a few years later. Quoting the bishop, Sarah wrote: 'no woman should have lent her aid – indeed few women could; and, if you set aside the principle which ought to have prevented it, the verse is to her praise'.[35] Catherine was condemned by some for her involvement; Maria Edgeworth regarded *La Pucelle* as 'a poem which a decent woman cannot read' and recorded that it had prevented people from 'seek[ing] her [Catherine's] acquaintance'.[36] Bury attempted to stem the scandal by vigorously denying her role and destroying many of the copies of the poem.[37] *La Pucelle* is the only literary project associated with Bury that was completed, a fact alone that argues for Catherine's involvement.

Catherine, like most young women of the period, learnt to draw. Skilled and versatile, she mastered a technique for drawing the figure using geometry, which Maria Edgeworth and her father struggled to learn.[38] A surviving drawing of a Tuscan column annotated in Catherine's hand reveals an interest in architectural drawing.[39] A watercolour of Penrhyn Castle attributed to Catherine, which depicts the distant castle between the rugged slopes of the Welsh coast, is romantic in spirit and picturesque in composition, and demonstrates considerable technical ability, especially in the rendering of trees.[40]

Picturesque sensibility, interest in antiquarianism and susceptibility to the sublime were pervasive cultural influences in the late eighteenth century, and

33 *La Pucelle: or, the maid of Orleans: a poem, in XXI cantos. From the French of M. de Voltaire. With the author's preface and original notes*, 2 vols ([London], 1796–7).   **34** Bond, *Marlay letters*, pp 37–40.   **35** Ibid., p. 39.   **36** Quoted in O'Kane, *Ireland and the picturesque*, p. 179.   **37** Even Bond, commissioned by the family in 1911 to edit C.M. Bury's letters, only argued tentatively for her involvement; Bond, *Marlay letters*, pp 40–3.   **38** O'Kane, *Ireland and the picturesque*, pp 178–9.   **39** C.M. Bury (attrib.), 'Notes, sketches and dimensions of a Tuscan portico', n.d. (Marlay papers, MY 969).   **40** C.M. Bury, *Penrhyn Castle, near Bangor,*

prevalent in the Burys' social circle. It was the lens through which they saw medieval architecture. The Bury library contained editions of three of William Gilpin's books based on his tours to the wilder parts of Britain – the Wye valley and South Wales, Cumberland and Westmorland, and the Scottish Highlands – that popularized the picturesque in the 1780s.[41] Although Gothic architecture was not a primary focus of Gilpin's volumes, it had its place, and the books established a landscape context for the appreciation of Gothic architecture. Gilpin defined the role of medieval architecture within the picturesque view, stating categorically in *Observations on the River Wye* that the presence of a castle made a landscape picturesque, that is, a suitable subject for a landscape painter.[42] In *Three essays*, the book he wrote to define the picturesque and published in 1794, Gilpin argued that ruggedness and irregularity were the salient qualities of the picturesque.[43] This idea, applied to both landscape and architecture, was evident in his description of the ruin of Brecknock Castle in *River Wye* in which he described the features that make a good picturesque ruin, and connected the broken coherence of the castle with the disjointed rhythm of the rocky landscape.[44]

Catherine Bury was familiar with these works, but her enthusiasm for Gothic was kindled by the Burys' neighbour at Heywood, Frederick Trench. He added antiquarian knowledge and a vivid sense of the sublime to the picturesque sensibility that inflected his appreciation of Gothic. This compound response to medieval architecture in its contemporary landscape setting was expressed in a letter written in October 1808 about a visit to Fountains Abbey in Yorkshire.[45] Referring to Gilpin, and thus signalling an awareness of the picturesque, Trench began his letter with his concern that the relationship of the abbey ruins to the adjacent park at Studley Royal was too domesticated. Trench wrote that he was keen to find an appropriate image for the abbey, fixing eventually on the view from the north-east in preference to the more commonly illustrated south-west view 'which take[s] in the long range of the ambulatory and the walls of the dormitory over it … giv[ing] an appearance of a castellated not a monkish building'.[46] The following evening he returned to the abbey with his companions

Gwynedd, North Wales, n.d., in Christie's [London], *Glin Castle, A knight in Ireland*, auction catalogue, 7 May 2009, lot 89.   **41** 'Catalogue of books in the possession of the Rt Hon. Charles William, Lord Tullamore' [1799] (Offaly County Library, Howard Bury papers, P59); the books were: William Gilpin, *Observations … lakes of Cumberland, and Westmoreland, relative chiefly to picturesque beauty*, 2 vols (2nd ed. London, 1788); William Gilpin, *Observations on the River Wye and several parts of South Wales etc, relative chiefly to picturesque beauty* (2nd ed. London, 1789); Gilpin, *Observations … the Highlands of Scotland, relative chiefly to picturesque beauty*, 3 vols (London, 1789).   **42** Gilpin, *River Wye* (1789), p. 63. **43** William Gilpin, *Three essays: on picturesque beauty; on picturesque travel; and on sketching landscape* (London, 1794), pp 3–27.   **44** Gilpin, *River Wye* (1789), pp 91–2.   **45** M.F. Trench to Andrew Caldwell, 15 Oct. 1808 (NLI, Domvile papers, MS 11,353); for date, attribution, and the observation that the letter was never sent because of Caldwell's death in July 1808 see O'Kane, *Ireland and the picturesque*, pp 159, 210 fn 95. Trench's full name was Michael Frederick Trench.   **46** M.F. Trench to Andrew Caldwell, 15 Oct. 1808 (NLI, Domvile

to contrive an emotionally charged, romantic encounter with the ruins: '[we] reached [Studley] as the setting sun appeared thro' the steeple Windows, twas Solemn and Majestick – we enjoyed the Twilight, dined by it in the Ambulatory on Benches for Tables'.[47] The next day Trench carefully inspected the ruins, drawing a free-hand plan to scale, observing structural details, noting anomalies, speculating about the builder's intentions and making comparisons between Fountains and other abbeys.

That he transmitted this scholarly and emotional interest in medieval architecture to Catherine Bury and acted as an informal teacher is clear from an acknowledgment that Catherine made in a lively letter she wrote to him in summer 1802, six days after she and Charles Bury had visited the medieval castles at Warwick and Kenilworth: 'I ... assure you I was worthy of your lessons at least on this subject, & equally delighted as you could be, with the entrance & Julius Caesar's Tower etc'.[48] In this letter Catherine, displaying her classical knowledge, used an image from classical mythology to convey to Trench how inspiring she had found Warwick Castle: 'I think the plainest spoken man in England would dream of Apollo, & the muses if he rode over Mount Helicon; whither he got or not upon Pegasus' back; and it were almost as great a sacrilege to pass a day at Warwick without sharing with you the enthusiasm the Castle cannot fail of inspiring all true lovers of Gothic architecture.'[49]

In Greek mythology Mount Helicon was the location of two sacred springs, one of which, released by a kick from the winged horse Pegasus, had become a well-known emblem of poetic inspiration. When she mentioned Apollo and the muses, Catherine Bury was referring to Mount Parnassus, the mythical home of Apollo, to which he brought the nine muses from Mount Helicon, and which was a symbol of earthly paradise.[50] Catherine used the references to articulate in the most poetically emphatic way possible that Warwick Castle was both the fount and the apogee of medievalism for her generation.

To stress inspiration as the primary experience at Warwick Castle was a Romantic gesture. Continuing in a Romantic vein in her letter to Trench, Catherine proceeded to tell him how she had tried to escape the present in order to dream about the past, but was thwarted by the loquacious earl of Warwick who intruded with accounts of his everyday concerns: 'Most unfortunately for our reveries of <u>past times</u> the noble proprietor chose to receive us at the gate & to remain the whole time pressing dinner, beds ... & portfolios of children's drawings on us & ... to give us a minute detail of his progress in agriculture'.[51] Yet, although the earl's talk of present-day life was a barrier to her imaginative

papers, MS 11,353).   **47** Ibid.   **48** C.M. Ch[arleville] to Frederick Trench, 2 Aug. [1802] (NLI, Domvile papers, MS 11,358).   **49** Ibid.   **50** Claudia Lazzaro, *The Italian renaissance garden: from the conventions of planting, design, and ornament to grand gardens of sixteenth-century central Italy* (New Haven & London, 1990), p. 132.   **51** C.M. Ch[arleville] to Frederick Trench, 2 Aug. [1802] (NLI, Domvile papers, MS 11,358).

connection to the past, she did appreciate the continuous tradition of careful proprietorship on the part of the earl, ending the letter: '… I believe it is a little ungrateful to laugh at this right courteous Earl, who is certainly an exceeding fine gentleman.'[52] Warwick, a ruined medieval castle of towered curtain walls, harboured a seventeenth-century hall range on the south side, which gave it the unusual capacity to inspire this contradictory reaction. John Byng, visiting in July 1785, enjoyed both types of experience: from the town bridge in the half-light of dusk he indulged in romantic contemplation of the historic roots of the castle, imagining himself transported back to the middle ages; next morning, having passed through the gates, he critically inspected the building by daylight, considering questions of taste, such as the elegance of the furniture.[53]

A notable aspect of Catherine's social circle was its inclusion of women involved in building projects. When she lived near Leixlip, Co. Kildare, as Mrs Tisdall, Catherine met Louisa Conolly (about nineteen years her senior) and corresponded with her until Louisa's death in 1811.[54] Catherine also knew Florence Balfour, the wife of Blayney Townley Balfour, a talented draftswoman and cut-paper artist who made plans for estate buildings and collaborated with Blayney and his sister, Anna Maria Dawson, on the designs for Townley Hall.[55] Catherine undoubtedly knew Dawson, who entered Catherine's extended family when she married Revd Vesey Dawson, nephew of Viscount Cremorne of Dawson Grove, Co. Monaghan.[56] Catherine Bury almost certainly knew Helena Domvile, the daughter of Frederick Trench.[57]

THE DESIGNING OF CHARLEVILLE CASTLE: EXTERIOR

The Charleville demesne, standing in a flat, boggy landscape to the west of Tullamore, was dominated by a large area of ancient woodland composed of oak and ash rooted in rich limestone soils.[58] To the west was the sinuous, tree-lined river Clodagh. Charles Moore had landscaped the demesne in the Brownian manner in the mid-eighteenth century.[59] When he came of age in 1785, Charles Bury commissioned Thomas Leggett to make proposals to improve the demesne,

52 Ibid.   **53** C. Bruyn Andrews (ed.), *The Torrington diaries containing the tours through England and Wales of the Hon. John Byng between the years 1781 and 1794*, 4 vols (new ed. New York & London, 1970), i, 227, 230.   **54** Bond, *Marlay letters*, pp 26, 94.   **55** Ibid., p. 172; Thorpe, *Women, architecture and building*, pp 11, 23–5.   **56** Thorpe, *Women, architecture and building*, p. 16.   **57** Ibid., p. 38.   **58** Howley Harrington Architects, 'Charleville Forest demesne, Tullamore, Co. Offaly, conservation report' (Nov. 2003). Edward Wakefield described the flat bogs surrounding Charleville, concluding, 'I never saw an instance of so much money expended in erecting a princely mansion in so bad a situation'; Edward Wakefield, *An account of Ireland, statistical and political*, 2 vols (London, 1812), i, 45. **59** Michael Cuddehy, 'A survey of Charleville demesne the seat of Charles William Bury esq, situate in the King's County, containing 924.2.36 plantation measures', 1785 (in private possession).

which included an idea for a large lake to the south, and wooded islands and cascades for the river to increase its picturesque appeal, all of which would be realized.[60] In 1789, while in Rome on the grand tour, Bury engaged James Byres to design a classical house, which was probably intended for the apex of the curved avenue – a house was shown in this position on Leggett's plan – where it would address a vast lawn and the lake proposed by Leggett.[61] This was not realized.

Eight years later Bury commissioned a Gothic castle from the obscure Dublin architect, John Pentland.[62] The proposed house had a U-shaped plan and was connected to a larger U-shaped stable yard by walls fenestrated with blank windows to appear continuous with the house. The resulting ranges had four square corner towers, long symmetrical elevations, and two towered gateways. It was elaborately decorated in a style that recalled mid-eighteenth-century Gothic: arched corbel tables, stepped battlements, cresting and friezes. These included quotations from James Cavanah Murphy's recently published book on the church and the Dominican monastery at Batalha church in Portugal, which were suggested by Bury who incorporated them in his own proposed elevations.[63] It is likely that Bury had chosen Gothic for its associations with dynastic heritage, for in 1797 he been created Baron Tullamore.

Pentland's design was too regular to be picturesque and too elaborate to suggest an authentic medieval castle. Three years later Francis Johnston was working on a design for Charleville Castle that was picturesque in character and siting and more authentic in spirit, and that would be magnificently realized by 1812. On the reverse of one of Pentland's drawings is a rough pencilled elevational sketch with battered corner towers, plain castellations and no extraneous decoration.[64] On the same page is a hesitant, lightly drawn perspective sketch of an irregularly castellated bawn wall punctuated by towers

60 Thomas Leggett, 'Plan of intended improvements at Charleville, the estate of Charles William Bury Esq.', 1786 (in private possession).   61 James Byres (attrib.), 'Photographs of ground floor and first floor plans, elevation, transverse and longitudinal sections of proposal for Mr Bury's house' [1789] (IAA, Misc. drawings, A/4/1–3).   62 John Pentland, 'Seven plans for proposed castle at Charleville' [1797] (IAA, Charleville Forest Drawings Collection, 86/24/10–16); John Pentland (attrib.), 'Photographs of drawings of four elevations for proposed castle at Charleville [1797] (IAA, Miscellaneous drawings, A/6/11–14); C.W. Bury, 'Drawing of proposed north and south elevations for Charleville Castle' [1797] (IAA, Guinness Drawings Collection, 96/68/1–2); C.W. Bury (attrib.), 'Photograph of drawing of south elevation for proposed castle at Charleville' [1797] (IAA, Miscellaneous drawings, A/6/10).   63 James Cavanah Murphy, *Plans, elevations, sections and views of the church of Batalha in the province of Estramadura in Portugal* (London, 1795). Bury included cresting, frieze and arched corbel tables from Murphy's *Batalha* in two proposed south elevations; C.W. Bury (attrib.), 'Photograph of drawing of south elevation for proposed castle at Charleville' [1797] (IAA, Miscellaneous drawings, A/6/10); C.W. Bury (attrib.), 'Drawing of proposed south elevation for Charleville Castle' [1797] (IAA, Guinness Drawings Collection, 96/68/2). 64 C.M. Tisdall (attrib.), 'Sketch of castle elevation and perspective sketch of a bawn' [1797] (IAA, Charleville Forest Drawings Collection, 86/24/5, verso).

and an arched gate. This signalled the new approach, a change of direction that was more than likely due to Catherine.

Her role has been obscured by her own and others' assessments of the building project. In most contemporary accounts of the castle neither patron is mentioned as an instigator of the design.[65] However, it was common to link the castle to its owner, as Sir Richard Colt Hoare, the highly educated and well-travelled owner of Stourhead in Wiltshire who knew Bury from the Society of Dilettanti and visited Charleville in 1806, did, recording in his diary that it was Lord Charleville's seat and that '[it] is now erecting under the superintendence of Johnson [sic] the architect.'[66] It was Catherine Bury herself who broadcast her husband's design involvement in the new castle, for Lady Louisa Conolly wrote to her in November 1800: 'I am very glad to hear that you have begun your Castle for I think there are few occupations more entertaining than Building, & Lord Tullamore I am sure will enjoy it much, having planned it all himself.'[67]

A different story is presented by Judge Robert Day, who visited Charleville in July 1812, and was told that Catherine was the motivator of the design:

> Drive to Tullamore Forest where we are most courteously and kindly received by our noble host and his poor infirm lady, Lord and Lady Charleville. A magnificent castle, and on the cursory view I could take of it, admirably contrived. Does great credit to the taste and munificence of the noble owner, or rather of her ladyship, who I understand projected the whole under the auspices of Johnston, our Irish and very ingenious architect. She is distinguished for very fine taste in the arts, possesses a masculine understanding, and, what is much better, an ardent spirit of charity and benevolence.[68]

His account, in which he grudgingly acknowledged her intellect and understanding of architecture, reveals that he felt uncomfortable with her precedence as patron. He was warmer in his approval of her work financing and erecting a school and supervising the operation of the county infirmary, both in Tullamore, which he went on to describe in more detail. He also engaged more readily with her illness, about which he wrote, 'she fancies to be rheumatism but I fear is paralytic, and w[hi]ch in truth might warrant if not require confinement to the room.'[69] Philanthropy and illness were more readily associated with women than architectural design in the early nineteenth century.

65 Francis Johnston, 'A letter from Francis Johnston', *Quarterly Bulletin of the Irish Georgian Society*, 6:1 (Jan.–Mar. 1963), 1–5; Wakefield, *An account of Ireland*, i, pp 44–5; James Norris Brewer, *The beauties of Ireland*, 2 vols (Dublin, 1825–6), ii, 137.   **66** Richard Colt Hoare, *Journal of a tour in Ireland A.D. 1806* (London, 1807), p. 33. The Society of Dilettanti was set up in 1734 for aristocrats and scholars who had been on the grand tour to promote the study and propagation of classical art and architecture.   **67** Lady Louisa Conolly to C.M. Bury, 8 Nov. 1800 (Marlay papers, MY 27/1–2).   **68** Quoted in Gerald O'Carroll (ed.), *Robert Day: the diaries and the addresses to grand juries, 1793–1829* (Tralee, 2004), pp 224–5.   **69** Ibid., p. 225.

6.1 Perspective sketch of proposed castle set in trees with pointed-arch gate set in a wall to east, ink and wash, attributed to C.M. Bury [1800]; RIAI Murray Collection, Irish Architectural Archive.

Even by the mid-twentieth century architectural historians were loathe to credit female initiative. In his account of Charleville in a 1962 *Country Life* article, Mark Girouard was alert to hints in the surviving family correspondence that Catherine had more determination than her husband.[70] Girouard characterized her as the power behind the throne: 'It seems likely that anything that Lord Charleville achieved in his career, including his translations, his peerage and his castle, were the result of hard shoves from his energetic, ambitious and intelligent wife.'[71] True to the spirit of his period, Girouard

---

70 Mark Girouard, 'Charleville Forest, Co. Offaly, Eire', *Country Life* (27 Sept. 1962), 710.
71 Ibid. Discussions of the castle by architectural historians have mainly concentrated on style: Alistair Rowan, 'Georgian castles in Ireland – 1', *Quarterly Bulletin of the Irish Georgian Society*, 7:1 (Jan.–Mar. 1964), 23–5; idem, 'The castle style in British domestic architecture in the eighteenth and early nineteenth centuries' (PhD, University of Cambridge, 1965), pp 240–1; Edward McParland, 'Francis Johnston, architect, 1760–1829', *Quarterly Bulletin of the Irish Georgian Society*, 12 (3 & 4 July–Dec. 1969), 87–93; Douglas Scott Richardson, *Gothic revival architecture in Ireland*, 2 vols (New York and London, 1983), i, 119–23; Ned Pakenham, 'Two castles and a chapel by Francis Johnston (1760–1829)' (MA, Courtauld Institute of Art,

painted the insubstantial husband as the more likable character: 'Yet the impression one gets from his few surviving letters is by no means an unattractive one; one suspects that his wife had the energy, but that he had the charm'.[72]

A number of surviving unsigned perspective sketches and plans strongly suggest that Catherine worked closely with the architect, Francis Johnston, on the new concept for the castle, exploring with him and finally resolving the composition, massing and fenestration. Several sketches can be attributed to Catherine Bury on the grounds that well-executed trees are an integral part of the images. We know that she was adept at representing trees, and their presence suggests that the draftsperson was thinking about the projected castle in association with the forest at Charleville. This is something that Catherine would have more readily embraced than her husband who had commissioned a landscape proposal for the demesne that separated a projected new house from the existing forest. Several of the sketches also made reference to Warwick Castle, which we know was deeply admired by Catherine. It is possible that Catherine brought Johnston to Charleville, having been introduced to him by Florence Balfour or Anna Maria Dawson.

An early tentative sketch attributed to Catherine shows a central tower and two battlemented corner towers that imitated prominent towers at Warwick Castle: one was octagonal and machicolated like Guy's Tower, the other had a clover-leaf plan in imitation of Caesar's Tower (fig. 6.1).[73] Apart from her own enthusiasm for Warwick, Catherine was also following the example of her contemporaries who quarried Warwick's towers for new designs. Guy's tower in particular was admired for its lightness in comparison to heavy Norman towers, for its picturesque qualities and for its associations with baronial residences.[74] It is likely that Frederick Trench had used it as the model for the octagonal tower that was part of his castellated gateway at Heywood.[75] We know that the Burys explicitly wanted Charleville to evoke an 'old British castle', for the phrase was used by Johnston when he later referred to his work at Charleville: 'In the King's Co I planned and erected Charleville Castle and offices, it is a very extensive building imitating as near as modern convenience and comfort would admit an

2005), pp 1–19.   **72** Girouard, 'Charleville Forest', 710.   **73** C.M. Bury (attrib.), 'Perspective sketch of proposed castle at Charleville [1800]' (IAA, RIAI Murray Collection, 92/46.194). **74** James Dallaway, *Observations on English architecture, military, ecclesiastical, and civil* (London, 1806), p. 98. In a letter to Robert Smirke, senior, written from Warwick in 1801, the landscape painter, Joseph Farington (1747–1821), described Warwick Castle as 'a fine specimen of an old Baronial residence and from many points very picturesque'; Joseph Farington to Robert Smirke, 16 Aug. 1801 (RIBA, Drawings and Archives Collections, Smirke Family papers, SMK.1/2). Sanderson Miller based his octagonal castellated tower at Radway, Warwickshire in 1745–7 on Guy's Tower; see James Stevens Curl, *Georgian architecture in the British Isles, 1714–1830* (2nd expanded ed. London, 2011), p. 85. The octagonal tower was a lynch pin of several of John Nash's asymmetric castles including East Cowes (*c*.1798), Luscombe (1799), Lough Cutra (1811), and Ravensworth (begun 1807).   **75** C.M. Bury sent an image of Warwick Castle by John Dees to Trench; C.M. Bury to Frederick Trench, 28 Aug. 1802 (NLI, Domvile papers, MS 11,348/1).

6.2 Perspective sketch of proposed castle from north-east showing single-storey link to chapel to north-west, ink and watercolour, attributed to C.M. Bury [1800]; RIAI Murray Collection, Irish Architectural Archive.

old British castle.'[76] It is more than likely that they were all thinking of that medieval paradigm, Warwick Castle.

In another sketch design for Charleville, Catherine, apparently inspired by Paul Sandby's perspective engraving of Warwick Castle in his book *One hundred and fifty select views*, altered the composition of the towers for Charleville, reproducing the relationship of Guy's and Caesar's towers to each other and with the central gatehouse as seen in the engraving (figs 6.2 & 6.3).[77] The Warwick gatehouse, which appears to be set back in Sandby's drawing, is transposed into the central square tower proposed for Charleville. This composition is reproduced in a plan attributed to Johnston dated to 1800.[78] A variation of this plan, attributed to Catherine, replaces the clover-leaf tower with a circular tower, an idea that would be retained.[79] A perspective sketch, drawn in ink with vigour

76 'A letter from Francis Johnston', 4.   **77** C.M. Bury, 'Perspective sketch of proposed castle at Charleville [1800]' (IAA, Charleville Forest Drawings Collection, 86/24/17); Paul Sandby, *A collection of one hundred and fifty select views, in England, Wales, Scotland and Ireland*, 2 vols (London, 1783), ii, pl. 71. Sandby's book was probably in the Bury's library in 1800; Allen and Townsend [Dublin], *Fine art auction ... to be held at Charleville Castle*, 1–5 Nov. 1948, lot 1218.   **78** Francis Johnston (attrib.), 'Sketch plan of proposed principal floor for Charleville Castle [1800]' (IAA, RIAI Murray Collection, 92/46.195).   **79** C.M. Bury (attrib.), 'Sketch plan of

6.3 'Warwick Castle', Paul Sandby, *c.*1778, from Sandby, *A collection of one hundred and fifty select views in England, Wales, Scotland, and Ireland*, vol. 1 (1783), pl. 71; image courtesy of the National Library of Ireland.

and assurance and attributed to Johnston, graphically demonstrates the potential of this scheme to deliver an integrated collection of robust towers clustered about a strong rectangular keep (fig. 6.4).[80] It presents a romantic object with the jagged skyline and complex three-dimensional form that picturesque sensibility demanded of a castle.[81] Johnston realized this ideal in detailed designs that, surviving drawings reveal, focused on efforts to orchestrate the massing of the elements, simplify the facades, create deep shadow lines and a well-defined skyline.

Another design perspective sketch, attributed to Catherine, showing the side and rear elevations of the proposed castle, together with a towered wall leading away from the octagonal tower to the edge of the drawing, reveals that Charleville

proposed principal floor for Charleville Castle [1800])' in ibid., 92/46.196.   **80** Francis Johnston, 'Perspective sketch of proposal for Charleville Castle [1800]' (IAA, Charleville Forest Drawings Collection, 86/24/18).   **81** See Humphry Repton's advocacy of a castellated design for Luscombe in June 1799: 'a castle which by blending a chaste correctness of proportion with bold irregularity of outline, its deep recesses and projections producing broad masses of light and shadow, while its roof is enriched by turrets, battlements, corbels, and lofty chimneys, has infinitely more picturesque effect than any other stile of building', quoted in John Summerson, *The life and works of John Nash, architect* (London, 1980), p. 38.

6.4 Perspective sketch of proposed castle from north-west, ink on paper, attributed to Francis Johnston [1800]; courtesy of the Irish Architectural Archive.

6.5 Perspective design sketch showing west and south facades of proposed castle, attributed to C.M. Bury [1800–1]; collection of Rolf and Magda Loeber.

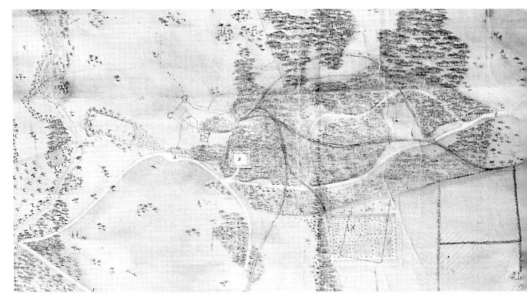

6.6 Demesne proposal for Charleville, Thomas Leggett, 1786, private collection.

was not conceived simply as a keep, but that it would be connected to kitchen and stable courts to form an asymmetric plan (fig 6.5).[82] Catherine based this drawing on Johnston's early detailed design drawings for the final scheme.[83] In Catherine's drawing, Charleville is shown in a forest clearing, and a towered entrance is just visible projecting from the trees behind the house. Pencilled additions to Leggett's scheme for Charleville demesne commissioned by Bury in 1786 depict the proposed plan of the castle as it was being developed in 1800, and locate it in the trees at the edge of the forest, to the north-east of the original proposed location for a new house (fig. 6.6).[84] The new position gave the castle a picturesque setting inspired by literature: the image of the medieval castle appearing above trees was a literary picturesque commonplace, expressed in the much-quoted couplet from Milton's *L'Allegro*: 'Towers, and Battlements it sees/Boosom'd high in tufted Trees'.[85]

Catherine's design proposals were informed by what she knew of recent and contemporary castle architecture. She saw these buildings with her husband, and

82 C.M. Bury (attrib.), 'Perspective sketch of proposal for Charleville Castle [1800–1801]' in the collection of Rolf and Magda Loeber.   **83** For sketches by Johnston which include similar details to C.M. Bury's sketch see Francis Johnston, 'Measured drawing of proposed part of rear (south) façade [1800–1801]' (IAA, RIAI Murray Collection, 92/46.197 recto and verso). **84** Thomas Leggett, 'Plan of intended improvements at Charleville, the estate of Charles William Bury Esq.', 1786 (in private possession).   **85** Quoted in Malcolm Andrews, *The search for the picturesque* (Aldershot, 1989), pp 12–13; Andrews observed that many picturesque tourists would recall these phrases when looking at Welsh or Scottish landscapes, indicating they no doubt assessed them together. Catherine fits into the category of female designers who were encouraged by their husbands: her designs were informed by a shared sensibility; their correspondence reveals that they had a close relationship; and we know from the *La Pucelle* episode that Catherine worked freely within Bury's orbit. Attitudes towards castle building were changing in Britain when Charleville was being designed. By creating a largely symmetrical central block and classically inflected fenestration, Johnston and the Burys were acknowledging conservative Georgian castle design pioneered by the architect Roger Morris (1695–1749) at Clearwell Castle, Gloucestershire, in 1727, and at Inveraray Castle, Argyllshire, in 1745. In Ireland, this trend was reflected in James Wyatt's design for William Burton Conyngham at Slane, Co. Meath, in 1785.[86] But, by proposing a broken skyline and asymmetric extension to the north-west – in the executed castle a chapel with two large square towers projects at an angle from the octagonal tower and forms one side of a kitchen court, beyond which there is a stable court defined by three battlemented gateways – Charleville's designers were responding to the picturesque sensibility, which was now applying the notions of irregularity and asymmetry to castle architecture. Castellar picturesque asymmetry was pioneered by Richard Payne Knight at Downton Castle in 1771–8, to be taken up by John Nash in Hafod, Aberystwyth, in 1794 and Castle House, also in Aberystwyth, in 1795.[87] Nash, in association with Humphry Repton, developed designs for asymmetric castles in the 1790s and 1800s. Charleville's debt to Warwick Castle also owed something to contemporary antiquarianism, which was beginning to promote the use of authentic medieval sources in new buildings.[88] In his later building designs, James Wyatt demonstrated a closer engagement with medieval sources as well as an understanding of the implications of asymmetric design, seen in Fonthill Abbey, Wiltshire (1796–1817), Belvoir Castle, Leicestershire (1801–13), and Norris Castle, Isle of Wight (completed 1799).[89]

Catherine and Charles Bury were critically aware of the castles being erected by Wyatt and Nash. They visited Pennsylvania Castle, Dorset, built by John Penn on Portland Island, an asymmetric composition, with round- and pointed-arched windows, completed in 1800.[90] They knew Fonthill, either from visits or by viewing Wyatt's drawings at the Royal Academy, for Catherine referred to the

that the picturesque sensibility was to a significant degree pre-conditioned by literary knowledge.   86 Mark Odlum, 'Slane Castle, Co. Meath – I, II, III', *Country Life* (17, 24, 31 July 1980), 198–201, 278–81, 382–5.   87 David Watkin, *The English vision: the picturesque in architecture, landscape and garden design* (London, 1982), pp 94–112.   88 For discussion of new castles in the context of antiquarianism, the picturesque and the sublime see: Chris Brooks, *The Gothic revival* (London, 1999), pp 83–104; Hill, 'Perceptions and uses of Gothic', pp 27–52.   89 John Martin Robinson, *James Wyatt, 1746–1813, architect to George III* (New Haven & London, 2012), pp 219–46, 262–70.   90 C.W. Bury visited John Penn on the Isle of Portland two years after Pennsylvania Castle was completed; Viscount Charleville's diary, 2 Oct. 1802 (Bury papers, P1/25).

fenestration at Fonthill in a letter.[91] They were also aware of Wyatt's work at Windsor Castle (1800–13), which transformed the state apartments into a Gothic palace and which Charles Bury used as a design standard for Charleville.[92] There is a strong possibility that they were familiar with Wyatt's work at Belvoir Castle through their connection to the duke and duchess of Rutland, and, because of their prolonged visits to Weymouth for the sake of Catherine's rheumatism, they probably knew Nash's East Cowes Castle, designed for himself *c*.1798, and Luscombe Castle, Dawlish, Devon, designed for Charles Hoare in 1799.[93]

THE DESIGNING OF CHARLEVILLE CASTLE: INTERIOR

Of the seven castles that Johnston designed, only Charleville had a Gothic interior. However, Gothic decoration was more common in contemporary English castles; Wyatt designed Gothic rooms for Lee Priory, Kent; Wilton House, Wiltshire; Fonthill Abbey, Wiltshire; Ashridge Park, Hertfordshire and Windsor Castle, Berkshire. Nash included Gothic details at Corsham Castle, Wiltshire, West Grinstead Park, Sussex and Ravensworth Castle, Tyne and Wear.[94] Surviving sketches and documents reveal that Catherine and Charles brought ideas and models to Johnston to ensure that the design of Charleville related to the mid- to late eighteenth-century Gothic work of Horace Walpole and his circle at Strawberry Hill and to the contemporary work of Nash and Wyatt.

One aspect of Walpole's example at Strawberry Hill was the idea that ecclesiastical medieval models should be used for domestic interiors. In his unfinished description of Charleville, Bury copied the passage in Walpole's *Description of the villa of Mr Horace Walpole* that advocated this idea: 'The view – to exhibit specimens of Gothic architecture, as collected from Cathedrals and Chapel-tombs, and to show how they may be apply'd to Chimney Pieces, Ceilings, windows, balustrades, etc.'[95] It is Catherine, however, who looked purposefully for medieval and sixteenth-century sources for Charleville, evident

91 C.M. Bury to Frederick Trench, 28 Aug. 1802 (NLI, Domvile papers, MS 11,348/1); Wyatt's drawings were exhibited at the Royal Academy summer exhibition in 1797–9; Algernon Graves, *The Royal Academy of Arts: a complete dictionary of contributors and their work from its foundation in 1769 to 1904*, 4 vols (Kingsmead, 1989), iv, 372. **92** C.W. Bury to C.M. Bury, 10 June 1808 (Marlay papers, MY 87). **93** The Charlevilles were linked to Belvoir Castle through Frederick Trench, who advised the 4th duke of Rutland, and through his son, Frederick Trench, who was cultural advisor to the wife of the 5th duke of Rutland. Record of the Burys' visits to Weymouth and surrounding area can be found in Viscount Charleville's diary, 17 Sept.–18 Nov. 1802, 1 Jan.–3 Mar. 1803, 2 Apr.–23 May 1803 (Howard Bury papers, P1/25). **94** Robinson, *James Wyatt*, pp 220–3, 232–9, 241–4, 262–6; Geoffrey Tyack, 'Domestic Gothic' in Geoffrey Tyack (ed.), *John Nash: architect of the picturesque* (Swindon, 2013), pp 35–56. **95** C.W. Bury, 'MS fragment of account of Charleville, n.d.' (Marlay papers, MY 1043/1).

in an observation she made to Trench about a 'fine charming piece of statuary marble gilt dated 1571' which she saw in the gatehouse at Kenilworth Castle and of which she '… took a correct sketch for our eating room'.[96]

One of the most pervasive decorative influences in Charleville Castle is Strawberry Hill itself. Apart from Walpole's book on his villa published in 1784, the Burys knew Strawberry Hill from a visit they made in July 1802.[97] Two alternative sketch designs for the interior of the hall and gallery at Charleville attributed to Catherine show the influence of the main staircase in Strawberry Hill as represented in an engraving of Walpole's *Description of the villa*: the balustrading is similar; the plasterwork wall decoration in Catherine's upper scheme is based on the wall decoration above the arches of the armory at Strawberry Hill; Walpole's idea of presenting armour within niches is reproduced in both of Catherine's sketches.[98] Neither scheme was realized, but, on the evidence of these drawings, Catherine seems to have established the ceiling form for each room – quadripartite vaulting for the hall and fan vaulting for the gallery. The sketches also contrived the character of each room: the hall for the formal display of Charleville ancestry; the gallery to be a more comfortable drawing room. Elements of the scheme appeared elsewhere in Charleville, most notably the eight-leaved figure motif from the Strawberry Hill balustrade was used for the dado in the dining room and as a framework for family crests under the windows in the gallery and on the dining room ceiling.

Catherine's boudoir, located on the main floor in the round tower and accessed from her bed chamber, is a space whose character can be attributed to its occupant.[99] The use of the term 'boudoir' was rare in Ireland; Patricia McCarthy has observed that the earliest use was in drawings for Townley Hall *c.*1794.[100] Catherine may have got the idea from Anna Maria Dawson, who had encountered it on her travels in France and used it in plans for other houses.[101] The decoration of Catherine Bury's boudoir, which had alternate semi-circular and square-shaped recesses and a vault which rises to a golden star, was heavily influenced by the Tribune in Strawberry Hill.

That Catherine was attuned to contemporary Gothic detailing is evident in a sketch she made of the hall doors at Corsham Castle, designed by Nash in *c.*1796–7.[102] Her annotation, which describes where the door was found and how

96 C.M. Ch[arleville] to Frederick Trench, 2 Aug. [1802] (NLI, Domvile papers, MS 11,358). There is no evidence that the design was realized.   97 Viscount Charleville's diary, 21 July 1802 (Bury papers, P1/25).   98 C.M. Bury (attrib.), 'Sections showing alternative decorative schemes for entrance hall and gallery at Charleville Castle [1801–1804]' (IAA, Miscellaneous Drawings, 89/88); Horace Walpole, *A description of the villa of Mr Horace Walpole* (London, 1784), engraving between pp 438–9.   99 The word 'boudoir' was used in a letter written by C.W. Bury to C.M. Bury, 6 Jan. 1805 (Marlay papers, MY 81/1–2).   100 Patricia McCarthy, *Life in the country house in Georgian Ireland* (New Haven & London, 2016), p. 189. 101 Thorpe, *Women, architecture and building*, p. 13.   102 C.M. Bury, 'Sketch of a door in Corsham Court, Wilts [1802]' (IAA, RIAI Murray Collection, 92/46.202).

consistently it was used at Corsham, suggests that she was thinking of applying it to Charleville: 'Pattern of all doors leading to hall at Corsham. The hall door was the same pattern folding door. The cross board plac'd one qr of eith of door'. This drawing was the basis of Johnston's design for the internal drawing room and dining room doors at Charleville.

Charles Bury criticized Johnston's doors (it is not clear which) in a letter to Catherine dated 10 June 1808 for not matching up to Wyatt's work at Windsor: 'What has been done since I was here before is in general well; but I must make him [Johnston] alter the doors which do not open to my mind. And are not finished with the true mouldings notwithstanding all our efforts – there is twice as much work on them, as on those of Windsor & not such effect. Like other things, it can't be helped; & they are still very handsome.'[103] Where Charles accepted that which he found to be unsatisfactory, Catherine was prepared to get a second opinion. This is seen in her pursuit of a satisfactory design for the stained glass intended for the great perpendicular-style window above the entrance door at Charleville. Decorated with the Charleville arms and those of their ancestors, and the window lit the main stair, which rose to the gallery and reception rooms, and was the centerpiece of the castle's decorative scheme. The idea that visitors would savour the grandeur of the Charlevilles as, having left the gallery where Moore and Bury arms decorated the fan vaulted ceiling, they descended the wide stair to be presented with the glowing, coronetted Charleville arms in the great window, was described in a poem commissioned from John Doran, an obscure poet, to celebrate the family's status: 'His dignified arms from their centre glares/ With royal splendour view it from the stairs'.[104]

Catherine was uneasy about the ecclesiastical overtones of the perpendicular style of the window opening. Her hesitation may have derived from reading Humphry Repton's influential book, *Observations on the theory and practice of landscape gardening*, in which he argued that where '*House* Gothic' and '*Castle* Gothic' were appropriate for new houses, '*Church* Gothic' was stylistically inappropriate and meant extra large windows.[105] Consulting Frederick Trench, Catherine compared the proposed design for Charleville with realized windows at Fonthill and Corsham where Nash had ignored Repton's advice:

> I inclose you a sketch of a window the framework of which Lord Charleville fancies violently for his Hall & the decoration of which is beautifully made out by Eginton at Birmingham …You will perhaps think this too Monastical, but tho' it be in that stile, I have seen at Corsham &

103 C.W. Bury to C.M. Bury, 10 June 1808 (Marlay papers, MY 87).   **104** John Doran, *A poem on Charleville and castle, addressed to the Rt Hon. the earl of Charleville* [1809], lines 39 & 40 (Bury papers, P1/33). The heraldic glass has subsequently been replaced.   **105** Humphry Repton, *Observations on the theory and practice of landscape gardening including some remarks on Grecian and Gothic architecture* (London, 1803), p. 190.

the windows for Fonthill, which were more so – If you have any better idea communicate it by return of post directed to Birmingham, as there we shall go to finally agree for the coloured ornaments with Eginton.[106]

Glossing over the fact that Fonthill – an abbey – and Corsham – Nash's response to existing sixteenth-century work – belonged to different categories of Gothic revival from Charleville, Catherine seems to have been less concerned to be true to the castellar character of Charleville than with producing a fashionable building. To approach the glass painter, Francis Eginton, for heraldic glass was in itself a modish thing to do. He had responded to a demand for painted glass by setting up a manufactory in Soho, Birmingham, in 1784, and, largely through the patronage of James Wyatt, his customers included William Beckford of Fonthill, and George III who had commissioned glass depicting the arms of the knights of the Garter for St George's Chapel, Windsor, in 1786.[107] The perpendicular design was retained for Charleville and fitted with armorial glass designed by Eginton. The Burys' aspirations to be lauded as a family of wealth, taste and landed pedigree were realized when the viceroy, 4th duke of Richmond, came with his entourage on a four-day visit in October 1809, and again, in 1826 when the topographer James Brewer wrote in his second volume of *The beauties of Ireland*, '[Charleville Castle] reflect[s] high honour on the good taste, and munificent spirit, of the successive noble owners of this estate.'[108]

Through her contribution to the design of Charleville Castle, a large-scale project intended to project the grandeur and status of the recently ennobled family, Catherine Maria Bury went beyond the confines of what was regarded as the feminine sphere and entered the male realm of architecture. She applied contemporary English taste for Gothic to a pioneering castle design in Ireland and developed the concept with the architect, Francis Johnston. She revealed her knowledge of contemporary debates about Gothic and the work of prominent English architects in her suggestions for the interior design, much, though not all, of which was taken up and developed by Francis Johnston. She was able to have an influence partly because of her own strength of character, but also because of the shared interest and support of a husband who lacked her forcefulness, and because her architect was receptive to the aspirations and ideas of his patrons. Arguably, Catherine Bury had a decisive influence on Johnston. He incorporated picturesque asymmetry into castle designs for St Catherine's Co. Kildare, in 1802, and Pakenham Hall (now Tullynally Castle), Co. Westmeath, in 1806, and conceived the remodeling of Killeen Castle, Co. Meath,

---

106 C.M. Bury to Frederick Trench, 28 Aug. 1802 (NLI, Domville papers, MS 11,348/1). **107** For accounts of Eginton see: [W.R. Eginton and S. Lowe], *Gentleman's Magazine*, 1:75 (1805), 387, 482–3, 606; W.C. Aitken, 'Francis Eginton', *Birmingham and Midland Institute, Archaeological Section, Transactions, Excursions and Reports*, 3 (15 Feb. 1872), 27–43. **108** Cutting from unidentified newspaper, 17 Oct. 1809 (Marlay papers, MY 1130/2); Brewer, *Beauties of Ireland*, ii, 137.

for the 7th earl of Fingall in 1803 in strongly picturesque terms.[109] But none of his subsequent castles, all remodellings, would have the panache of Charleville where Catherine's informed, imaginative involvement established the parameters of the scheme and her discrimination and determination inspired Johnston to produce a bold and impressive design.

109 Francis Johnston, 'Drawing of proposed east elevation for St Catherine's Co. Kildare, Nov. 1802' (IAA, RIAI Murray Collection, 92/46.1079); Francis Johnston, 'Drawing of proposed elevation for Pakenham Hall, Co. Westmeath [31 July 1806] in ibid., 92/46.1202; Francis Johnston, 'Proposals for Killeen Castle, Co. Meath, Feb. 1803', in ibid., 92/46.902–8.

Lady Harriet Kavanagh of Borris House, 1800–85, matriarch and guardian of the future

EDMUND JOYCE

Lady Harriet Le Poer Trench was the daughter of the 2nd earl of Clancarty of Garbally Court, Co. Galway. Her father became British ambassador to the Netherlands in 1813, and she spent her formative years travelling extensively on the Continent with him, mixing and socializing within diplomatic circles amongst the European elite. The skills she acquired would stand her in good stead in her future life in nineteenth-century rural Ireland.

Lady Harriet Kavanagh, *née* Le Poer Trench (fig. 7.1), became a woman of forceful and dynamic character. As the matriarch of her late husband's family for a period of nearly twenty years (1837–*c*.1855), and effectively the manager of the very large Kavanagh estate, she treated her situation as a stewardship and was content to slip away into retirement when her only surviving son married and a new chatelaine took control of Borris House. As the second wife of Thomas Kavanagh of Borris, Co. Carlow, she had found herself in a situation of considerable delicacy. Her new husband was thirty-three years her senior. When she married him in 1825, she inherited a ready-made family of eight stepchildren, one of whom – the only boy – was likely to prevent any son she might bear from succeeding to the estate. She came from a family settled at Ballinasloe in the east of Co. Galway (since the 1630s) and was now married into an ancient Irish family which, since the early eighteenth century, had drawn its marriage partners exclusively from a Kilkenny-based network of Old English Butlers. One of these, Lady Elizabeth Butler, had been Thomas Kavanagh's first wife. Harriet's family, the Le Poer Trenches, who were Evangelical Protestants of Huguenot extraction, had little in common with the Roman Catholic past of the Kavanaghs and Butlers. To surmount any difficulties, Harriet needed considerable resources of tact combined with motherly and conjugal affection, kindness of disposition and honesty of purpose.

Marrying a wife of child-bearing age was not all that unusual for an ageing widower with an existing heir. For example, just a few years earlier the forty-two-year-old widower Charles William Stewart, the future marquess of Londonderry,

Thanks to Morgan and Sara Kavanagh who provided access to the Kavanagh archive at Borris, and to Anthony Malcomson, and Paula Lalor, for reading and commenting on an earlier draft of this chapter.

had married the nineteen-year-old heiress Lady Frances Vane.[1] Despite such precedents, the timing of Harriet's marriage to Thomas Kavanagh, which took place on 28 February 1825, was contentious. His first wife, Elizabeth, had died just over two months previously, on 14 December 1824,[2] after twenty-five years of apparently happy marriage.[3] However, it appears that Lady Elizabeth's family, the Butlers of Kilkenny Castle, marquesses of Ormonde, supported Thomas Kavanagh's precipitate action. Part of the explanation was that James Butler, the then marquess and Elizabeth's brother, was married to Grace Louisa Staples, an aunt of Harriet.[4] The Le Poer Trenches, too, in spite of the diversity of the two family traditions (and of the disparity in the couple's ages), seem to have been content with the arrangement. Though young in comparison to her husband, and a contemporary of the eldest of his surviving daughters, Anne Wandesforde, wife of Henry Bruen of Oakpark, Carlow,[5] Harriet was by the standards of the day not in the first flush of youth and was in danger of holding up the marriages of her younger sisters. This consideration may have held weight with her family. The marriage was solemnized by special licence at Garbally by Harriet's uncle 'the Ven. and Hon. [Charles Le Poer Trench] the Archdeacon of Ardagh …'.[6]

Thomas Kavanagh's plans extended beyond providing a stepmother for his children: he needed to increase his already large family in the hope of securing the male succession to the estate. Kavanagh boys were then scarce and had been scarce for some time. Lady Elizabeth had borne him one son and eight daughters (one of whom, Mary Wandesforde, predeceased her).[7] Thomas Kavanagh's son Walter (named after Thomas' eldest brother) was only twelve, and an Eton schoolboy when his father remarried. Thomas himself had been the youngest of five sons, and at fifty-seven had buried all four of his brothers, the eldest of whom was just 5fifty-eight when he died in 1818. None of his brothers had produced an heir.[8] Thomas Kavanagh's father, also Thomas, was an only son, so there was no collateral branch springing from his generation. This mattered to Thomas Jnr. Although without a title in the British peerage, he was almost certainly determined to reinforce the male line in order to protect the Borris Kavanagh's legitimate claim to the (hereditary) ancient Gaelic title of The MacMurrough. Without a male successor, the title for which his ancestors had

---

1 N.C. Fleming, *The marquess of Londonderry, aristocracy, power and politics in Britain and Ireland* (London, 2005), p. 8.   2 John Ryan, *The history and antiquities of the county of Carlow* (Dublin, 1833), p. 371; see also the wall plaque in former Church of Ireland church of St Mullins, Co. Carlow.   3 Until now it was believed that Lady Elizabeth had died just over two years prior to the second marriage; however, the notice in the newspaper announcing the birth of her daughter, Agnes, in March 1824 (*Freeman's Journal*, 5 Mar. 1824) and the inscription on the wall plaque in St Mullins' church indicates that 14 Dec. 1824 (and not 14 Dec. 1822) is the correct date.   4 John Debrett, *Debrett's peerage of the United Kingdom*, 2 vols (London, 1820), ii, 928.   5 Henry Walford, *The county families of the United Kingdom* (London, 1869), p. 142.   6 *Freeman's Journal*, 9 Mar. 1825.   7 Wall plaque in former Church of Ireland, St Mullins, Co. Carlow.   8 Sir William Betham, *Kavanagh pedigree book*, 1814–18 (Kavanagh Archive, Borris House [hereafter KAB], uncatalogued).

7.1 Lady Harriet Le Poer Trench, *c*.1825 (possibly a self portrait), Borris House collection; reproduced by kind permission of the Kavanagh family.

fought so hard would be lost to a distant branch of the family. (It is likely that child bearing so far into her forties had a major part to play in Elizabeth's untimely death.) Against this background, there was positive advantage in Thomas marrying a much younger woman, and it must have been expected by all parties that the union was likely to produce further children.

Harriet's father, Richard, 2nd earl of Clancarty, rose in the British diplomatic service through a combination of his own ability and his family connection with Lord Castlereagh.[9] Following the liberation of Holland from the French, Clancarty was appointed British ambassador to The Hague.[10] On 11 August 1814, he was named one of the four British plenipotentiaries to the Congress of Vienna, and when Wellington left Vienna for Waterloo in March 1815, Clancarty became the senior British plenipotentiary.[11] Harriet, then in her teens, danced at the duchess of Richmond's famous ball on the eve of the battle of Waterloo in 1815.[12] On 22 May 1816, Clancarty was appointed ambassador to the new kingdom of the Netherlands and held that position until his retirement in 1823. He was honoured by the king of the Netherlands for his service as British ambassador to The Hague with the hereditary title of marquess of Heusden. Harriet spent a great deal of her youth living on the Continent. This exposure to travel so early on helped nurture an intrepid spirit and a love of travel, which became so much a part of her later life.

Harriet brought with her a dowry of £6000.[13] This sum could be considered meagre in light of her father's political status and rank in the peerage, but it was appropriate to the Clancarty family's landed wealth and to the number of the Le Poer Trench younger children. The £6000 certainly appears diminutive when compared to the marriage portion of £11,000 that Lady Elizabeth, Thomas Kavanagh's first wife, had brought with her some twenty-six years earlier.[14] However, in 1822, Anne Wandesforde, Thomas Kavanagh's eldest daughter, had also brought a marriage portion of £6000 when she married Col. Henry Bruen.[15] There were no primogeniture advantages when it came to the allocation of marriage portions and daughters were generally 'treated equally as to level of portion'.[16] Thomas Kavanagh's frugality therefore reflected the fact that at the

9 Clancarty's late mother-in-law was Harriet Staples *née* Conolly of Castletown, Co. Kildare. She was a sister of Castlereagh's mother-in-law, Caroline Hobart *née* Conolly. See John Burke, *A genealogical and heraldic dictionary of the peerage and baronetage of the British empire* (London, 1847), p. 250.   **10** Clancarty to Lady Clancarty, 1 Dec. 1813, quoted in Aideen Ireland (ed.), 'Clancarty correspondence, 1785–1861', *Journal of the Galway Archaeological and Historical Society*, 46 (1994), 197–202.   **11** Eric Anderson Walker, *The Cambridge history of the British empire*, 8 vols (Cambridge, 1963), ii, 211.   **12** Emmet Jackson, 'An Irish woman in Egypt: the travels of Lady Harriet Kavanagh' in Diana Fortenberry (ed.), *Souvenirs and new ideas* (Oxford, 2013), p. 56.   **13** Settlement on the marriage of Thomas Kavanagh and Lady Harriet Le Poer Trench, 25 Feb. 1825 (KAB, A/3).   **14** Document relating to the portions of Thomas Kavanagh's younger children, 23 Apr. 1834 (KAB, A/3.)   **15** Extract from settlement on marriage of Col. Henry Bruen with Miss Anne Kavanagh, 13 Sept. 1822 (KAB, A/3).   **16** Anthony Malcomson, *The pursuit of the heiress: aristocratic marriage in*

time of Anne Wandesforde's marriage (just three years prior to his own second marriage) he had six unmarried daughters all potentially requiring equal portions.[17] Therefore, Harriet's marriage portion was appropriate to Thomas Kavanagh's reasonable expectations, since he already had an heir in the person of his son, Walter. Should Walter reach adulthood and produce a subsequent heir, it was unlikely that any grandchildren of the 2nd earl of Clancarty would ever become heir to the Kavanagh estates. The arrangement was satisfactory to both parties: the Le Poer Trenches had succeeded in marrying the first of their four daughters into an affluent and powerful family, and Thomas Kavanagh now had a well-connected young bride who would, at the very least, become stepmother to his existing family and if all went according to plan would produce yet more children, preferably male.

A less confident young woman, uprooted from the security of home, engrafted on an already established family miles away, and confronted with the running of an extensive household, would have been daunted by the change in her circumstances. Not so Harriet, who assumed her new role with energy and aplomb. The house at Borris had been remodelled between 1813 and 1818 by Thomas Kavanagh's bachelor brother, Walter, who had commissioned for the work the great Irish architects of the era, Sir Richard Morrison and his son, William Vitruvius. The high quality of much of the Morrisons' work stretched the family's finances, and on Walter Kavanagh's sudden death in 1818 it was revealed that Thomas Kavanagh, his heir, had also inherited a considerable debt.[18] The first nineteen years of Thomas and Lady Elizabeth's marriage had been spent at Ballyragget Lodge, Co. Kilkenny, a property that had come into Kavanagh ownership via inheritance from a distant Butler kinsman in 1813. But in 1818 they moved into Borris without delay, which for the first time in many years became a family home crowded with young or youngish children. When Harriet succeeded to the role of chatelaine of Borris in 1825, she declined to live there in the shadow of the recently deceased, Elizabeth, and immediately set about making Borris (fig. 7.2) her own. It is reputed that, on taking up residence, she stripped the chapel attached to the house of all its Catholic effigies, thus asserting that the crypto-Catholicism of the Kavanaghs had now been overtaken by her Le Poer Trench devotion to the Established Church.[19]

Harriet was not inexperienced when it came to the furnishing and laying out a house. She had been exposed to a major building project *c.*1820 when her father had commissioned the English architect, Thomas Cundy, to build the house at Garbally.[20] Marriage often prompted a building project;[21] however, since

---

Ireland, 1740–1840 (Belfast, 2006), p. 32.   **17** Only three of these daughters outlived their father and only two of the six – Susannah and Grace – married.   **18** Edmund Joyce, *Borris House and elite regency patronage* (Dublin, 2013), pp 14–29.   **19** Jackson, 'An Irish woman in Egypt', p. 56.   **20** Mark Bence Jones, *Burke's guide to Irish country houses* (London, 1978), p. 131.   **21** Richard Wilson and Alan Mackey, *The building of the English country house* (London, 2000), p. 270.

much of Borris was then of recent construction and resources were not unlimited, the newly married couple concentrated their efforts on reimagining and decorating existing spaces.[22] The majority of the plate procured during this period (which was engraved with the Kavanagh arms, crest and motto) was for the dining room, indicating that Thomas and Harriet were busy entertaining.[23] This is not surprising as Thomas Kavanagh who had been MP for Co. Kilkenny from 1797 to 1799 was preparing to run as a Conservative candidate for Carlow in the upcoming elections.[24] This rediscovered interest in politics was no doubt spurred on by Harriet.

Over the coming years Harriet exceeded expectations in the matter of child-bearing; she brought Thomas four children: Thomas (Tom) b.1827, Charles b.1829, Harriet (Hoddy) b.1830 and Arthur b.1831 (fig. 7.3). Arthur MacMurrough Kavanagh, Harriet's youngest and most celebrated son, was born on 25 March 1831, and although a very healthy baby, was born without arms or legs. By calling him after his fourteenth-century ancestor, Art, the legendary warrior horseman and king of Leinster, Harriet sought to make her son aware of his heritage and to inspire him to triumph over adversity. In contrast to Honora Edgeworth (d.1780), a stepmother whose philosophy was to educate her own children and 'unruly step-children' at her home in Longford,[25] Harriet sent her younger stepchildren off to school in London. In the eyes of one contemporary her actions suggested indifference to the well-being of her stepchildren. In 1830, Anne O'Brien, a passenger aboard a ship from England to Ireland, made the acquaintance of Agnes, Harriet's six-year-old and youngest stepchild (then on her way back to Ireland after spending the previous two years at boarding school). O'Brien thought Agnes looked 'so very delicate that I am sure she ought to be kept at home and taken great care of', and added peevishly: 'I should think, from what I hear of Lady Harriet, that she is not the sort of person to do so.' She also criticized Lady Ormonde's apparent lack of interest in her grandchild's well-being.[26] This early account runs counter to more explicit evidence of how Harriet treated her only stepson, Walter.

As the only son by Thomas Kavanagh's first marriage, Walter was the stepchild whom Harriet might have been expected to regard as an obstacle or even a threat. But it seems to have been the reverse. As a result of his apparently declining health, it was decided that he should travel to a warmer climate for the winter of 1835–6. Walter, by then 21, was a student at Cambridge University. Drawing on her own travel experience, Harriet arranged a trip to Italy that

22 Joyce, *Borris House*, p. 46.   23 Bill from Fisher, Braithwaite and Jones to Thomas Kavanagh, Oct. 1825 (KAB, J/1–2).   24 Edmund Burke (ed.), *The annual register; or A view of the history of politics and literature of the year 1837* (London, 1838), p. 169.   25 Allison Twells, *British women's history, a documentary history from the Enlightenment to World War I* (London, 2007), p. 51.   26 Anne O'Brien to Mrs James O'Brien, [?] 1830 (PRONI, Kerr papers, D2916/1/C/16).

7.2 Borris House, the seat of the Kavanaghs; photo: author.

7.3 Miniature group portrait. *Back l–r*: Harriet (Hoddy) (b.1830), Thomas (Tom) (b.1827), Agnes (b.1824). *Front l–r*: Charles (b.1829) and Arthur (b.1831). Artist unknown. Borris House collection; reproduced by kind permission of the Kavanagh family.

included her two stepdaughters Grace and Susan.[27] Amanda Vickery has claimed that marriage and childbearing meant that 'women became less mobile and their time for company was radically reduced.'[28] This was not so in Harriet's case; motherhood had provided her with travel companions and had apparently reignited her intrepidness. At this time, her husband Thomas was too preoccupied by politics and his parliamentary responsibilities in London to have time to devote to his children, so this responsibility, not surprisingly, devolved upon their stepmother. Although he did accompany Harriet on at least one continental trip in 1828,[29] he was happy to grant her independence. He sat as a Conservative MP for Co. Carlow from 1826 to 1831 and from 1835 to his death in 1837.[30] Despite the complicated logistics associated with foreign travel, it was not that unusual for aristocratic women to have their children and retinue accompany them.[31] The travels of Lady Charlotte Campbell, one-time lady-in-waiting to Caroline, princess of Wales, are comparable to those of Harriet. In 1814, aged thirty-nine, and then a widow, Lady Charlotte had taken her five children on an extended tour of Italy.[32]

Harriet spent a great deal of time travelling with Walter, and when he was unable to walk, she arranged to have him carried about. Walter's health declined, and as the trip progressed he became increasingly infirm. At one point Harriet referred to how the gout that started in his knees had spread to his arm and shoulder.[33] Within weeks of returning home he died at Borris, aged twenty-one, on 19 June 1836. His obituary stated how 'he only attained his majority in March; and his premature death has cast a gloom on the political interests of that spirited county [of Carlow] …' Thomas Kavanagh, Harriet's eldest son, was now heir to his father Thomas.[34]

In January 1837, Harriet's responsibilities at Borris increased further when her husband of twelve years died. Thomas was just ten years old. Consequently, all responsibilities fell to the widowed Harriet, then aged thirty-seven. Prior to his death, Thomas Snr had appointed Harriet's father and brother as trustees to his estate.[35] A codicil to his will indicates that a portion of her jointure, equating to £1000, should be paid to Harriet 'on the day next after the day of my decease … ', and that Harriet was to own all her 'watches, jewels, ornaments, and … paraphernalia' following his death. He also bequeathed all his carriages and

27 Lady Harriet Kavanagh travel journal, 1835–9 (PRONI, Kavanagh papers, D3235/2/1). 28 Amanda Vickery, *The gentleman's daughter: women's lives in Georgian England* (London, 1998), p. 115. 29 *Finn's Leinster Journal*, 16 Aug. 1828. 30 Edmund Joyce and Sara Kavanagh, *Borris House, the ancestral history of an Irish estate* (Borris, 2015), p. 16. 31 Grand tour women and their children feature repeatedly on the résumé of portraits generated by Pompeo Batoni (1708–87); Rosemary Sweet, *Cities and the Grand Tour: the British in Italy, c.1690–1820* (Cambridge, 2012), p. 63. 32 James Bieri, *Percy Bysshe Shelley, a biography: exile of unfulfilled renown, 1816–1822* (Newark, 2010), p. 109. 33 Lady H. Kavanagh travel journal, 1835–9 (PRONI, Dorothy Kerr papers, D3235/2/1). 34 *Kerry Evening Post*, 3 Sept. 1836. 35 Thomas Kavanagh's last will and testament, 1835 (KAB, F/1).

carriage horses to Harriet and allowed her 'the use during her life time of all [his] plate and … furniture'.[36] It appears, from correspondence of the time, that initially Harriet received much guidance from her father. Letters from Lord Clancarty to Charles Doyne, the long-established agent at Borris,[37] on whom Harriet relied greatly, indicate how the former thought the house and demesne should be managed during his grandson's minority. In a letter dated 17 March 1837 he wrote: 'it is to be regretted that Harriet is for the present in England. Her future residence in the house at Borris is the best means of preventing dilapidation, [and] … would be the best arrangement for the minor'. It appears that finances at this time were somewhat straitened, as he added: 'if she were with us [in Borris], we could at once settle as to the disposal of the extra furniture, wines, etc … [and] it seems to me that the demesne should be let out so long as the minority shall continue'.[38] Despite Lord Clancarty's zealous involvement in affairs at Borris, his influence was short-lived as he died in November of that year, just ten months after the death of Thomas Kavanagh.[39]

Harriet was now left on her own, though she still enjoyed the support of her agent Charles Doyne. She did return to Borris and so fulfilled the wish that the house and establishment should be kept up just as in her husband's lifetime. She also did not flinch from resolving a number of pressing problems. The first was her disabled youngest son, Arthur. Although it was deemed impractical to send him to Eton like his brothers, she was determined that he should have a suitable education; Arthur, she declared, was 'so full of energy and life that he will only wither away if he stays indefinitely at Borris'.[40] Accordingly, she took him abroad with her at every opportunity, and when he was at home, she placed him under the influence of suitable tutors.

The remoteness of many country seats such as Borris meant that 'polite sociability depended upon considerable mobility and long visits'.[41] In 1839, Harriet, in her first major journey overseas since Thomas Kavanagh's death, took her four children and her mother to Italy. On their return to Borris later in the year, Arthur was placed in the care of the Revd Samuel Greer, 'a good clergyman of high scholarly attainments'. He was curate of Celbridge, Co. Kildare, and lived in a house inside the gates of Castletown, the home of Harriet's first cousin,

---

36 Codicil to Thomas Kavanagh's last will and testament, 26 Aug. 1835 (KAB, F/1). **37** Charles Doyne served as agent on the Borris estate for numerous years. He lived at Newtownpark House, Blackrock. In 1857 Charles Doyne (together with Arthur MacMurrough Kavanagh and Denis William Pack-Beresford) was announced as high sheriff for Carlow; *Thom's Irish almanac and official directory for the United Kingdom, for the year 1857* (London, 1857), p. 816. Doyne also served as agent on the Pack-Beresford estate at Fenagh, Co. Carlow; see James Nesbitt et al., *The reign of terror in Carlow* (London, 1841), p. 34. He is buried at St Brigid's Churchyard, Stillorgan. **38** Richard Le Poer Trench to Charles Doyne, 17 Mar. 1837 (KAB, M/42). **39** Edmund Lodge, *The peerage of the British empire* (London, 1846), p. 120. **40** Donald McCormick, *The incredible Mr Kavanagh* (London, 1960), p. 59. **41** Vickery, *The gentleman's daughter*, p. 116.

Col. Edward Conolly. Celbridge was chosen so that Arthur could be within easy reach of the renowned Dublin surgeon Sir Philip Crampton. It was hoped at this early stage that Crampton would be able to devise a set of prosthetic limbs for Arthur. But, despite the manufacture of several prototypes and numerous painful fittings, this plan had to be abandoned.[42]

Harriet also took initiatives in the usually male preserves of estate management and local politics. Unlike many other women who were effectively just caretakers during their sons' minority,[43] Harriet had the power to invest estate income. In 1839, she decided to enlarge the Kavanagh estates by purchasing the Crown estate in Co. Carlow.[44] A newspaper report dated 16 November 1839 announced that 'Lady Harriet has been declared the purchaser of the Crown Estate, formerly the property of Gilbert Fitzgerald esq. …, and [it] will in a short time send forth a considerable number of electors to support the Conservative interests'.[45] Improving and developing the political value of land was part and parcel of good estate management.[46] Although none of her sons was of age to stand for parliament at the general election of 1841, Harriet exerted herself in the Tory cause, spurring on the Kavanagh tenantry 'like Queen Elizabeth going to meet her troops at Tilbury.'[47] Her actions are not unusual in this regard; widowhood with a minor heir meant that many women in a similar position used their patronage to support a worthy political candidate.[48] In 1841, following the election, in which Col. Henry Bruen, who had been married to Harriet's late stepdaughter, Anne Wandesforde (d.1830), topped the poll, Harriet held celebrations at Borris House for some 200 of her tenantry 'in commendation of the victory they so materially contributed to achieve at the last election'.

The celebrations showed that she had a decided gift for publicity and for raising the profile of the Kavanagh family. The field day activities were followed by 'the interesting ceremony of presentation … [and] every one of the tenants … were presented by Mr Charles Doyne to her ladyship'. Later Harriet proceeded to the house where dinner tables were laid out, and she presided over the chief table, with her stepdaughters Susan and Grace at two others. After toasts by the Revd Trench and George Whitney (probably George Boleyn Whitney of New Park, Co. Westmeath), Charles Doyne rose to return thanks and express

---

42 See Sarah Steele, *The right honourable Arthur MacMurrough Kavanagh* (London, 1891).
43 Deborah Wilson, *Women, marriage and property in wealthy landed families in Ireland, 1750–1850* (Manchester, 2009), pp 90–2.   44 Bought by Lady Harriet Kavanagh for *c.*£14,000 (KAB, D1–4).   45 *Leinster Express*, 16 Nov. 1839.   46 Judith S. Lewis, *Sacred to female patriotism: gender, class, and politics in late Georgian Britain* (New York, 2003), p. 14.   47 P.J. Kavanagh, 'Thomas Kavanagh MP (1767–1837) and his political contemporaries', *Carloviana*, 2:28 (1977–8), 4–6.   48 Lewis, *Sacred to female patriotism*, p. 75.

his sorrow that their youthful landlord [Tom Kavanagh] was not present that night to meet them … [and] although in a foreign land pursing his studies, he could ensure the company that he had not forgotten them, and his conduct on a future occasion would testify to the gratitude he felt towards those who nobly stood forward to defend his rights and their own privileges.[49]

As chatelaine of Borris, Harriet soon discovered the need to carry out major repairs to the fabric of the house. Her principal advisers during this time were her brother, the 3rd earl of Clancarty, and Charles Doyne. In 1842, she commissioned the architect John B. Keane (a former apprentice of Sir Richard Morrison) to carry out repairs to the roof and basement of Borris. A letter addressed to Charles Doyne from John B. Keane, 20 November 1842, reveals that the house needed an entire new roof.[50] Once again Harriet was given an opportunity – though hardly a welcome one – to improve on the work done on Borris House by her husband's predecessor.

In the autumn of 1846, Harriet (then 47) made the decision to take her young family on a prolonged tour across the Mediterranean, down into Egypt and across to the Holy Land. Though now middle-aged, she was still an active and intrepid traveller, willing to venture into more arduous and dangerous territories, building on the experiences of her early years when she accompanied her father on his many continental appointments. Accompanied by her children, with the exception of Charles who had recently joined the army, she left Ireland in September 1846. Although travel to the Middle East was not uncommon, it was unusual for a lady accompanied by her children to make such a journey. Traditionally, female travellers tended to journey in parties in the company of men;[51] however, the Kavanaghs remained largely independent and only occasionally would they travel with others.[52] It was expected that this trip might last for up to a year, but as the tour progressed, Harriet's desire to travel further meant that they did not return to Ireland until May 1848. The family's absence shielded the young Tom temporarily from the sights and horrors of the Famine back in Ireland.

Initially it appears that Harriet's primary interest in Egypt was religious and 'lay in the country's biblical connections'. But as the tour progressed, Harriet pursued her interest in antiquity. She became acquainted with established Egyptologists such as Sophia Poole and Harriet Martineau, and intrigued by the ancient surroundings she began accumulating a number of ancient artefacts. It was an age of discovery in Egypt and here an Irish lady was at the fore; her

49 *Leinster Express*, 20 Nov. 1842.   **50** J.B. Keane to Charles Doyne, 20 Nov. 1842 (KAB, M/45).   **51** Deborah Manley (ed.), *Women travellers in Egypt, from the eighteenth to the twenty-first century* (New York, 2012), pp 1–3.   **52** Two-volume journal kept by Lady Harriet of a tour to the Middle East, 1 Oct. 1846–6 May 1847 (KAB, N1).

7.4 Lady Harriet Kavanagh, watercolour, boats on the Nile. Borris House collection;
reproduced by kind permission of the Kavanagh family.

passion and interest were manifested in her sketches and journals, where she documented finds, trips and locations. In Cairo alone she collected sixty-one artefacts. She developed a close relationship with the missionaries John and Alice Lieder, who encouraged her love of Egypt and supported her in her dream to travel to the Holy Land. The Kavanaghs spent many months living aboard two *dahibiyas* on which they sailed the Nile. Living conditions onboard were very rudimentary and at one point the boats had to be sunk in order to evict the rats.[53] Harriet's sketches and journals have survived in pristine condition: a dozen watercolours, and a large sketchbook documenting the tour, exist in the Kavanagh collection at Borris (fig. 7.4). Judging by their contents it appears that Harriet only made entries when travelling.

On returning to Ireland in 1848, the family was exposed to the full horror of the Great Famine. Harriet had maintained close contact with her agent Charles Doyne while travelling, and his correspondence reveals the extent of the relief projects that were underway, including wall-building, drainage schemes and

---

53 Jackson, 'An Irish woman in Egypt', pp 57–9.

repairs to the main street in Borris.[54] Prior to her departure Harriet had initiated a relief scheme. On seeing the rapid decline in the circumstances of her tenants, Harriet devised a solution to alleviate the poverty that was taking hold on her estate. Drawing on her collection of lace, which had been gathered on her many continental trips, she decided that even though the country was in the midst of turmoil, there was a market for such creations among the upper classes. Her desire was to give employment to wives and daughters. The home industry was a major success and in the following decades Borris lace grew from strength to strength. According to Frances, wife of Arthur MacMurrough Kavanagh, writing in 1897, 'the cleverness with which these women and girls copied the stitches of old lace is marvellous'.[55]

Shortly after the family's return from the Middle East in 1848, Tom Kavanagh reached his majority. But this made no difference in practice to Harriet's role as acting head of the family and chatelaine of Borris, especially as on 4 June 1849, Tom and Arthur departed once more on an extended tour to the Far East with the Revd David Wood as a tutor and companion.[56] While engrossed in her charitable work Lady Harriet received an invitation to Dublin Castle, but in a letter to her two sons dated 13 July 1849 she proclaimed she herself had 'neither curiosity nor loyalty enough to go to the expense or trouble to attend' the Queen's drawing room in the capital in August. She conceded that if her daughter Hoddy wished to go, then 'Sarah Clancarty will take her.'[57] But her son Charles was present, as a young officer in the seventh Hussars, escorting the Queen and her party to the levee at Dublin Castle, where he was later presented to her by his uncle, Lord Clancarty.[58]

In mid-December 1851 it was announced in national and local newspapers that 'Thomas Kavanagh esq., of Borris House, will be the high sheriff of the Co. Carlow for the ensuing year. Mr Kavanagh is expected home in a few days, after a tour of India.'[59] Harriet eagerly awaited her son's return to Borris and the delayed assumption of his responsibilities; but, much to her dismay, news arrived that he was ill and that he could not travel immediately. On 31 December 1851, less than two weeks after his appointment as high sheriff had been announced, the *Belfast Newsletter* recorded that 'Lady Harriet Kavanagh proceeded on Saturday, without delay, for England, *en route* to Bombay, partly over land to see … her son; … owing to Mr Kavanagh's unexpected illness [tuberculosis]'.[60]

---

54 Charles Doyne to Lady Harriet Kavanagh, [?] 1846 (KAB, M/47).   **55** Horace Curzon Plunkett, *Irish Homestead special: some Irish industries* (Dublin, 1897), p. 12.   **56** This trip extended 'through Scandinavia, Russia, down the Volga and over the Caspian, to Northern Persia, Kurdistan, and, by the valley of the Tigris and the Persian Gulf, to the Bombay Presidency and the Province of Berar', and in the event lasted – under very altered circumstances – into 1852: see Steele, *Arthur MacMurrough Kavanagh*, p. 30.   **57** Lady Harriet to hers sons Thomas and Arthur, [?] 1850 (NLI, Kavanagh papers, N.6316, P.7157).   **58** Kenneth Kavanagh, *Born without limbs* (Milton Keynes, 1989), p. 53.   **59** *Freeman's Journal*, 18 Dec. 1851.   **60** *Belfast NewsLetter*, 31 Dec. 1851.

Her journey was pointless, as Tom, and David Wood had decided to return home via Australia, apparently in the hope that the extended sea voyage would arrest the progress of Tom's tuberculosis.

Harriet seems to have travelled no further than Corfu, where she stayed with Hoddy and her husband, Col. William Alexander Middleton, deputy adjutant-general in the Royal Artillery, whom she had married in 1851 while he was stationed on the island.[61] Whilst there Harriet made arrangements for Arthur, who had stayed behind in Bombay, to come and join her, so that they could travel back to Ireland together.[62] There must have been some other reason for her decision to return home, since news of the departure of Tom and David Wood for Australia could not possibly have reached her. On her way back and after her arrival at Borris, she received sporadic, and delayed, communications from Wood, which contained misleading and optimistic accounts of Tom's health. Though she waited anxiously for his safe arrival, it was not to be. On 21 August 1852, it was announced in the *Carlow Sentinel* that he had died in January 'on a passage from Sumatra to Australia'.[63] The news of his death and burial at sea some five months earlier had only just reached Borris. In a cruel twist of fate, by the time Wood's tragic letter reached Harriet, he himself had been killed in an accident.[64]

Charles Kavanagh, Harriet's second son (b.1829), now succeeded to the Kavanagh estates, and was appointed a justice of the peace for Co. Carlow in November 1852.[65] His career in the army had been short-lived, as he had been 'compelled … to retire from service' on grounds of ill-health[66] – an ominous sign that Harriet might not yet be relieved from the responsibilities of stewardship. In fact, Charles enjoyed his inheritance for only a few months before meeting with a fatal accident. Apparently suffering from convulsions, he had been placed in the care of a man called Falconer Miles (presumed to be a physician). In the latter's account Charles was in good spirits as he was due to be married on Easter Monday[67] to Annette Georgiana Mary,[68] the eldest daughter of the Revd E.

61 George Dames Burtchaell, *Genealogical memoirs of the members of parliament for the county and city of Kilkenny* (Dublin, 1888), p. 191.   62 Steele, *Arthur MacMurrough Kavanagh*, pp 126–7.   63 Kavanagh, *Born without limbs*, pp 71–2.   64 Steele, *Arthur MacMurrough Kavanagh*, p. 126.   65 *Freeman's Journal*, 1 Dec. 1852.   66 *Kerry Evening Post*, 26 Feb. 1853. 67 Falconer Miles, 'Omissions and Corrections', *The Zoist, a Journal of Cerebral Physiology and Mesmerism*, 12 (1855), 210–11.   68 Annette Georgiana Frances Groome was a niece by marriage of the Borris agent, Charles Doyne. She later married Nathaniel Robert Powell (and their third son was christened Charles Doyne Powell). It appears that Annette Groome was Charles Doyne's heiress. Her mother, Fanny Emily Groome, was a sister to Charles Doyne's wife Helena Sellina. They were daughters of Robert Uniacke of Woodhouse, Co. Waterford, and Anne Constantia Beresford: see Bernard Burke, *A genealogical and heraldic dictionary of the landed gentry of Great Britain and Ireland*, 2 vols (London, 1863), ii, 1562. Fanny Emily Groome is buried in the same grave as Charles Doyne at St Brigid's Cemetery, Stillorgan. In 1805 Anne Constantia Beresford, after her first husband Robert Uniacke died, married Robert Doyne of Wells, Co. Wexford: see John Burke, *A genealogical and heraldic dictionary of the*

7.5 Arthur MacMurrough Kavanagh (1831–89), artist unknown, Borris House collection; reproduced by kind permission of the Kavanagh family.

Groome, rector of Beaulieu, Co. Louth.[69] On the Sunday morning while dressing, it appears that Charles suffered an attack and stumbled into the open hearth. He was badly burnt and he died the following night.[70] The same newspapers that announced his engagement on 19 January 1853 reported his death on 28 February 1853.[71]

peerage and baronetage of the British empire (London, 1839), p. 1080.   **69** *Belfast Newsletter*, 19 Jan. 1853.   **70** *The Zoist*, 210–11.   **71** *Freeman's Journal*, 28 Feb. 1853.

The new owner of Borris was Arthur MacMurrough Kavanagh, the youngest of the three brothers. He had not returned from India until late in 1852, when he had been appointed under-agent for the Kavanagh estates to which he now succeeded. Family finances appear to have been in poor shape in 1853. Unpaid rents and heavy outgoings during the Great Famine had taken their toll. Arthur was intent from the outset on reversing what he saw as a decline, but he seems to have been on the best of terms with his mother and in no hurry to dispense either with her presence at Borris or with her advice. As master of Borris, Arthur was a very eligible bachelor, but his severe disability meant that he needed a wife who would be exceptionally attentive to his needs, and ideally someone with a strong faith and sense of duty. Such a paragon was found in the person of Frances Leathley, the daughter of a clergyman and, significantly, from a family connected to the Le Poer Trenches. The marriage took place on 15 March 1856, and was happy and successful: Arthur and Frances had seven children, four boys and three girls.[72]

Arthur fulfilled all the expectations of his mother and showed that the efforts she had made to inculcate in him self-reliance and a determination to do everything expected of the head of the Kavanagh family, in a period of great challenge to the landlord class. He was a justice of the peace for counties Carlow, Kilkenny and Wexford. He served as high sheriff of Co. Kilkenny in 1856 and of Co. Carlow in 1857. He stood for Wexford in the by-election of 1866 and headed the poll. At the general election of November 1868 he was returned unopposed for Co. Carlow along with his cousin, Henry Bruen of Oak Park. Arthur continued to serve as MP for Co. Carlow until the general election of 1880, when he was defeated. Subsequently his main contribution to public life was as a widely acknowledged expert on the vexed Irish land question. On this subject he was highly respected for his well-informed and moderate views.[73]

Harriet continued to live with Arthur (fig. 7.5) and Frances in Borris House until 1861 when it was announced that 'Mr Kavanagh [of] Borris is making arrangements for fitting up the lodge, Ballyragget, as a permanent residence for his mother, Harriet Kavanagh, and in order that he and Mrs Kavanagh may pay frequent visits to his Ballyragget property.'[74] Ballyragget Lodge, located approximately twenty-eight miles from Borris, had been emptied of family contents which were sold at auction in September 1818 when Thomas Kavanagh and his first wife Elizabeth had moved to Borris.[75] The house had been leased in the intervening years.[76] Considering the extent of the Borris archive it is surprising how few papers relating to Harriet survive dating from her time at

72 Joyce et al., *Borris House*, p. 32.   **73** Steele, *Arthur MacMurrough Kavanagh*, pp 163–83. **74** *Leinster Express*, 17 Aug. 1861.   **75** *Finn's Leinster Journal*, 12 Sept. 1818.   **76** Ballyragget Lodge was leased firstly to a Captain Ball, then to Gerald FitzGerald esq., and finally to Lt Col. Ralph Henry Johnson Walsh: see *Finn's Leinster Journal*, 24 May 1828; *Nenagh Guardian*, 26 Nov. 1853; *Leinster Express*, 20 July 1861.

7.6 Lady Harriet Kavanagh, *c.*1855, Borris House collection, reproduced by kind permission of the Kavanagh family.

Ballyragget.[77] It is known from snippets of information found in correspondence and published sources that Harriet did continue to travel extensively. Newspapers reported her journeying to and from Dublin on a regular basis. Although now married, her daughter Hoddy remained a regular travel companion. On 4 December 1857, Harriet and Hoddy set sail aboard the steamer *Indus* from Southampton to Calcutta.[78] Her son Arthur was a keen yachtsman who travelled extensively,[79] and in December 1860 it was reported that he had left Borris for Corfu, in his handsome yacht accompanied by his mother. The announcement also stated that 'Mrs [Frances] Kavanagh and children will also proceed to Corfu via France'.[80] Harriet was back in Corfu in 1867.[81] But she lost her daughter and travelling companion when Hoddy died in England in 1876.

In the latter years of her life, due to failing health, Harriet (fig. 7.6) was almost entirely confined to her home at Ballyragget Lodge. She died there aged

77 The Kavanagh papers comprise *c.*8,500 documents and volumes (almost entirely the former), 1575–1980.   **78** *Allen's Indian Mail*, 15 Dec. 1857.   **79** See Arthur MacMurrough Kavanagh, *The cruise of the [R.Y.S.] Eva* (Dublin, 1863).   **80** *Freeman's Journal*, 13 Dec. 1860.   **81** Ibid., 4 Feb. 1867.

eighty-five on 14 July 1885 and her remains were brought to Borris for one night before being interred in the family crypt at St Mullins.[82] Drafts of her will indicate that she made adjustments as members of her family predeceased her. In her final will and testament, Hoddy's four daughters were the chief benefactors, each receiving £500. Along with numerous bequests to various Christian charities Harriet did not forget her faithful servants: her butler and a maid received £50 each, her gardener £10 and all her house staff received half a year's wages.[83] Harriet bequeathed her collection of 250 ancient Egyptian and other artefacts to the Kilkenny Archaeological Society to which she had been elected in January 1851. In 1890, it became the Royal Society of Antiquaries of Ireland, and in 1920 the RSAI loaned the Kavanagh collection to the National Museum of Ireland where it has remained ever since as a lasting legacy to one of Ireland's most noteworthy Egyptologists.[84]

   In 1920, her grandson, Walter MacMurrough Kavanagh, wrote an unpublished account of the life of his father, Arthur, Harriet's youngest son, and offered the following reminiscence of his grandmother:

> It was there [at Ballyragget Lodge] that Lady Harriet (or, as the name was pronounced in Ireland in those days, Har-yot) lived her peaceful, charitable life, with her books, her sketching, her dogs, and her old-time memories. A masterful personality; one who was born to command and be obeyed; yet with the kindest, tenderest heart for all in trouble or in need; and with all the charm of manner and the melody of voice which are so particularly the features of an Irish lady – such was the Lady Harriet Kavanagh. Her name and her memory still clings to the place, a link with the past and with a generation whose like Ireland will know no more.[85]

It was a poignant reflection on the death of the matriarch of the Kavanaghs, a widow for forty-eight years, who had outlived all eight of her stepchildren and three of her own four children. Her youngest son, the limbless Arthur MacMurrough, survived her by only four years. It also underlines the key role she played in providing continuity within the Kavanagh family, in surmounting the various tragedies that struck them, and in successfully grooming for succession, against almost insurmountable odds, the most illustrious Kavanagh since his eponymous ancestor, Art.

82 Steele, *Arthur MacMurrough Kavanagh*, p. 261.   83 Versions of and codicils to Lady Harriet's last will and testament, 1854, 1863, 1867, 1884 (KAB, F/1).   84 Jackson, 'An Irish woman in Egypt', p. 65.   85 Walter MacMurrough Kavanagh, Unpublished biography of Arthur MacMurrough Kavanagh, 1920 (KAB, M/70).

Sisterly guidance: elite women, sorority and the life cycle, 1770–1860

RUTH LARSEN

When exploring the experiences of women within elite families, much of the focus has been on them as wives and mothers. Women were vital to a pedigree's dynastic success as they enabled the continuation of the family line and as wives they played important roles as their husband's ally in running the household, estate and the family's political interest.[1] However, it is also important to look at elite women's relationships with other women. The depth of female friendships and the significance of the affection that those relationships provided has been recognized by a number of historians.[2] The nature of these female friendships when they were between elite sisters, whose close relationships were not just based on emotional ties but also on dynastic loyalty too, has not been subject to the same degree of scrutiny. Scholars such as Leonore Davidoff have highlighted the importance of siblings in the eighteenth- and nineteenth-century middle-class family, but although there have been biographies of groups of elite sisters, such as Stella Tillyard's work on the Lennox sisters, there have been surprisingly few studies of the role sisters played in aristocratic networks.[3] As Naomi Tadmor has demonstrated, having strong political friends was crucial to the social politics of the eighteenth and early nineteenth centuries, and aristocratic sisters helped to form and maintain these friendships.[4] Sisters were often the glue that kept aristocratic familial networks together and so were of central importance to the domestic and the dynastic aspects of country house life.

1 See, for example, Katie Barclay, *Love, intimacy and power: marriage and patriarchy in Scotland, 1650–1850* (Manchester, 2011); Elaine Chalus, *Elite women in English political life, c.1754–1790* (Oxford, 2005); J.S. Lewis, *In the family way: childbearing in the British aristocracy, 1760–1860* (New Brunswick, NJ, 1986); K.D. Reynolds, *Aristocratic women and political society in Victorian Britain* (Oxford, 1998); Amanda Vickery (ed.), *Women, privilege, and power: British politics, 1750 to the present* (Stanford, 2001).   2 For example, Betty Rizzo, *Companions without vows: relationships among eighteenth-century British women* (Athens, GA, 1994); Stuart Curran, 'Dynamics of female friendship in the later eighteenth century', *Nineteenth-Century Contexts*, 23:2 (2001), 221–39.   3 Leonore Davidoff, *Thicker than water: siblings and their relations, 1780–1920* (Oxford, 2012); Stella Tillyard, *Aristocrats: Caroline, Emily, Louisa and Sarah Lennox, 1740–1832* (London, 1994). Other recent work on sibling relations has been focused on the American family, including C. Dallett Hemphill, *Siblings: brothers and sisters in American history* (New York & Oxford, 2011) and Lorri Glover, *All our relations: blood ties and emotional bonds among the early South Carolina gentry* (Baltimore, 2000).   4 Naomi Tadmor, *Family and*

In order to explore the importance of sisters this chapter considers the relationships between aristocratic sisters from the late eighteenth century to the mid-nineteenth century. Many of the chosen examples come from sibling networks that had a connection to Castle Howard in Yorkshire, home to the Howard family who held the title earls of Carlisle (Table 8.1). They were well-connected Whigs, having marital connections to the Leveson Gower family, and the 1801 marriage of George, Lord Morpeth, later the 6th earl of Carlisle, to Lady Georgiana Cavendish of Chatsworth in Derbyshire developed these links further; she was the eldest child of the 5th duke and duchess of Devonshire and her mother and grandmother had been central to much Whig electioneering in the previous forty years.[5] This chapter explores the relationship between Georgiana and her sister, Harriet, who married the 1st Earl Granville in 1809. As children, the Cavendish sisters were known as 'Little G' and 'Hary-o' and they formed a close and affectionate bond, and as married women they played an active role not only in each other's lives, but in their nieces' and nephews' affairs too.[6] Georgiana Cavendish, as Lady Morpeth, was the mother of twelve children, and this chapter also explores their sibling relationships. Like their mother and maternal aunt, a number of Georgiana's daughters married important Whig aristocrats and in turn also became mothers, chatelaines and political networkers in their own right. They also drew upon each other for practical and emotional support, especially the four eldest sisters: Caroline (later Lady Lascelles), Georgiana (later Lady Dover), Harriet (later the 2nd duchess of Sutherland), and Blanche (later Countess Burlington).[7] As a network of women these Howard sisters were a notable force, joining together major Whig families, shaping Royal politics through the roles some of them held in Queen Victoria's household and providing one another with practical domestic advice and comfort in times of crisis.

The women of the Howard family were not unusual; many other elite sisters had similar relationships that were both affectionate and dynastic. Christina Rossetti's poem, 'Goblin market' (1862), includes the line 'there is no friend like a sister', a sentiment that would have been recognized by many aristocratic women in the previous century.[8] By using the Cavendish and Howard siblings as

---

friends in eighteenth-century England: household, kinship, and patronage (Cambridge, 2001). **5** See Chalus, *Elite women in English political life*; J.S. Lewis, *Sacred to female patriotism: gender, class, and politics in late Georgian Britain* (London, 2003); idem, '1784 and all that: aristocratic women and electoral politics' in Vickery (ed.), *Women, privilege, and power*, pp 89–122; Amanda Foreman, 'A politician's politician: Georgiana, duchess of Devonshire and the Whig party' in H. Barker and Elaine Chalus (eds), *Gender in eighteenth-century England: roles, representations and responsibilities* (London, 1997), pp 179–204.   **6** Although they held various titles throughout their lives, in this essay they will be known as the Cavendish sisters or Harriet Granville and Georgiana Morpeth.   **7** For clarity these sisters will be called the Howard sisters throughout this essay or Caroline Lascelles, Georgiana Dover, Harriet Sutherland and Blanche Burlington.   **8** Christina Rossetti, 'Goblin market' in *Goblin market and other poems* (2nd ed., London, 1865), p. 30.

Table 8.1: Family tree for the Howard and Cavendish families, adapted

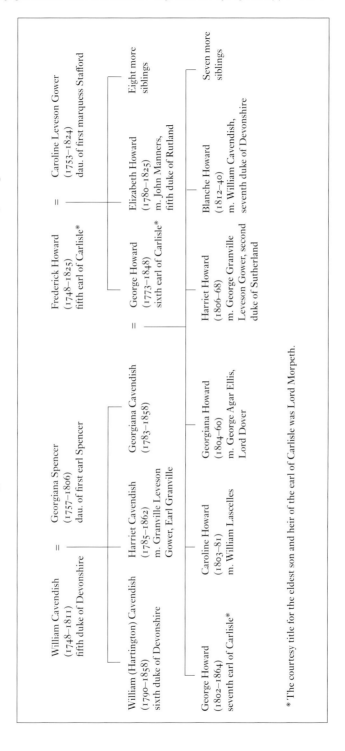

* The courtesy title for the eldest son and heir of the earl of Carlisle was Lord Morpeth.

a case study it is evident that elite sisters worked as a sorority, that is to say a group of women with a shared interest, the family interest.[9] This took two forms: they actively promoted family networks through their marriages, political roles and other connections, and they provided friendship, emotional solace and practical support for one another. In this chapter the connections between women as they progressed through the lifecycle are explored, and the importance of these connections for them as maidens, wives, mothers and chatelaines is considered. Instead of focusing on unmarried women, for whom the position of sister was usually their primary family role, this chapter instead focuses on the sisterly relations of women who married.[10] Marriage and motherhood did not replace sisterhood, but rather sisterhood enhanced and shaped these roles. Being a sister remained an important part of their identity and was central to enabling them to fulfil their roles as aristocratic women.

The very many letters that aristocratic siblings sent to one another reflect how important their relationships with their sisters were to them; many started with addresses such as 'Dearest sister' and often included news about other siblings, joy at their happiness, and concern about their woes.[11] They enjoyed writing to one another and receiving news; one letter to Harriet Granville, which contained very little information at all, was signed off by Georgiana Morpeth with the comment 'Adieu Dearest – I only write that I may not be a day without.'[12] The combination of fervent evangelicalism and secular romanticism of the late eighteenth and early nineteenth centuries encouraged the expression of inhibited feelings and also increased the focus on piety and sentimentality.[13] As Leonore Davidoff has noted, these movements shaped notions of sibling intimacy, as can be seen in the literature and culture of the period, and in turn, these wider cultural influences shaped elite women's letter-writing practices.[14] When separated, the Cavendish sisters wrote to one another regularly, and often the language used was very similar to that used between lovers. In 1813 Harriet wrote to Georgiana Morpeth: 'I do love you so very dearly. I do think you so adorable and such a greater angel than any I know of besides.'[15] Likewise, many of the Howard sisters were often quite intimate in nature: a letter from Georgiana Dover to Harriet Sutherland finished with: 'I ought not to write in this way. Dearest, I love you.'[16] Therefore, many sibling correspondents expected their ideas to remain private; Harriet Granville's letters to her sister often included an insistence that she did not show the contents to Lord Morpeth, as

9 Chalus, *Elite women in English political life*, pp 179–91.   **10** For a discussion of elite single women see Ruth Larsen, '"For want of a good fortune": elite single women's experiences in Yorkshire, 1730–1860', *Women's History Review*, 16:3 (2007), 387–401.   **11** Anne Vernon to Caroline Carlisle, n.d. (Castle Howard, Carlisle papers, MS J15/1/157).   **12** Georgiana Morpeth to Harriet Granville, *c.*1821 (TNA 30/29/17/5/9).   **13** See discussion on elite female piety in Peter Mandler, 'From Almacks to Willis: aristocratic women and politics, 1815–1867' in Vickery (ed.), *Women, privilege, and power*, pp 163–7.   **14** Davidoff, *Thicker than water*, pp 201–3.   **15** Virginia Surtees (ed.), *A second self: the letters of Harriet Granville, 1810–45* (Salisbury, 1990), p. 63.   **16** Georgiana Dover to Harriet Gower, n.d. (Staffordshire

she was embarrassed about the strongly worded emotions that she expressed.[17] Women acted as their sisters' confidantes; as significant elements of many aristocratic women's lives were party to public scrutiny, letters between siblings provided a private space where they could articulate their feelings and their failings. Because there was a strong sense that sisterly relationships were important, those women who did not fulfil the ideals of sisterhood were criticized. Georgiana Morpeth's sister-in-law, Elizabeth, 5th duchess of Rutland, was known as a proud woman, whose abrupt and unfriendly manner to her less well-connected Howard siblings caused her father much sorrow, especially her 'unsister-like coldness' exhibited while he was grieving the loss of his wife, her mother, in 1824.[18] In the nineteenth century the sister was increasingly the model for virtuous femininity and sibling relations were celebrated. An essay published in 1832 noted that sibling relationships contained 'all the sweet confidence of friendship, the winning tenderness of pure love … the consciousness of power, protection and support'.[19] Siblings valued this close connection and therefore lamented when it was not there.

One of the reasons why sisterly relations were so important to elite women can be found by exploring their childhoods. Most young women spent a considerable amount of time with their female relatives when growing up in the country house. An early nineteenth-century letter from Caroline Howard, the eldest daughter of the Morpeths, set out in detail the daily activities of her and her sisters during a stay at Chatsworth, their mother's childhood home:

> We get up at seven and learn our geography, our catechism and grammar and sometimes before breakfast but in general after, then after we write our verbs. Georgiana has finished hers and the verses of the History of France. While I play on the piano, Georgiana writes English and French dialogues and sometimes her Calligraphy.[20]

The letter goes on to give an account of the lesson of her younger sister, but makes no mention of their brothers, who were of a similar age, reflecting how the gendered nature of their upbringing meant that young elite women spent most of their time during childhood with their female siblings. While boys were usually sent to school, where they could develop important connections that could shape their adult relationships, girls were usually home educated.[21] These

Record Office, Sutherland papers, D6579/76/12).   **17** For example, see Surtees, *A second self*, p. 144.   **18** Frederick Carlisle to Elizabeth Rutland, [1824] (Castle Howard, Carlisle papers, MS J14/1/72).   **19** M.A. Hedge, 'On the reciprocal duties of brother and sister' (1832), cited in Davidoff, *Thicker than water*, p. 202.   **20** Caroline Howard to Georgiana Morpeth, n.d. (Castle Howard, Carlisle papers, MS J18/11/16). In another letter from around the same time, written in French, Caroline mentions that Frederick, two years her junior, was struggling with Latin, but indicates that she and her sisters were not party to his lessons: Caroline Howard to Georgiana Morpeth, n.d. (Castle Howard, Carlisle papers, MS J18/11/1). **21** Anthony Fletcher, *Gender, sex and subordination in England, 1500–1800* (New Haven and

childhood experiences meant that they formed close friendships with each other as they often had little company other than their relatives. This can be seen in the childhood letters from Harriet to Georgiana Cavendish, which were not just accounts of her activities but also declarations of her affection for her sibling; she wrote in 1791, when just twelve years old, 'I never knew how much I loved you till I was away from you'.[22] Young sisters were often reliant on one another for companionship and so it is not surprising that bonds formed then often lasted a lifetime.

Despite this close emotional connection with their sisters, the vast majority of elite girls were aware that they were expected to move away from their natal home at some point. While a notable number of elite women never married, the end of most elite girlhoods was marked by the search for a spouse.[23] Although by 1770 arranged marriages were very unusual, and the ideal was for affectionate and companionate unions, dynastic concerns were not wholly dismissed.[24] Because of the importance of maintaining elite status, as it helped aristocrats to remain part of the ruling class, strategic matches remained attractive. This led to some sisters speculating about each other's future husbands; the pool of potential spouses for well-connected aristocrats could be quite small and so young women would be aware of the range of possible suitors. In 1798 the Cavendish girls were aware that the duke of Bedford was a suitable match for Georgiana.[25] Harriet teasingly wrote to her elder sister: 'my dear sister, when you are D-s of B-d, will you invite me to W-n?'.[26] This not only shows that she was well aware of the benefits that she could gain from Georgiana's potential betrothal, but that there was a desire that their close relationship would continue after marriage. For many parents, negotiating the marriage market could be seen as something of a chore, especially for those with large families. Revd Sydney Smith, friend to the Morpeths, wrote to Lady Grey to suggest an easy solution: 'why should not all your sons marry all Morpeth's daughters and all your daughters his sons? It would save a great deal of trouble'.[27] Smith's suggestion was not serious; although sometimes siblings did marry with siblings, this type of arrangement was not favoured by ambitious families as it reduced the number

London, 1995), p. 300; Henry French and Mark Rothery '"Upon your entry into the world": masculine values and the threshold of adulthood among landed elites in England, 1680–1800', *Social History*, 33:4 (2008), 404–7.   **22** G. Leveson Gower and Iris Palmer (eds), *Hary-O: the letters of Lady Harriet Cavendish, 1796–1809* (London, 1940), p. 5.   **23** T.H. Hollingsworth, 'Demography of the British peerage', Supplement to *Population Studies*, 18:2 (1964), 20.   **24** I.H. Tague, 'Love, honour and obedience: fashionable women and the discourse of marriage in the early eighteenth century', *Journal of British Studies* 40 (2001), 76–106; Barclay, *Love, intimacy and power*, pp 70–101; J.R. Gillis, *For better, for worse: British marriages, 1600 to the present* (Oxford, 1985), p. 136; Lewis, *In the family way*, pp 18–20.   **25** Amanda Foreman, *Georgiana, duchess of Devonshire* (London, 1988), p. 333.   **26** Leveson Gower and Palmer (eds), *Hary-O*, p. 4. Miss Cavendish did not marry the duke but instead married George Howard, Lord Morpeth, later the 6th earl of Carlisle.   **27** N.C. Smith (ed.), *The letters of Sydney Smith* (Oxford, 1953), p. 395. One Morpeth child did marry a Grey when Elizabeth Howard married Revd Francis Grey in 1840.

of in-laws and therefore networking opportunities created by marriage.[28] However, interfamilial marriages could have some benefits if they helped to maintain existing links. Of Morpeth's six daughters, two married within the close family network. Harriet's marriage to Earl Gower, later the 2nd duke of Sutherland, was not only advantageous due to his wealth and connections, but he was also already part of the family: his father and her grandmother were siblings.[29] Likewise, Blanche Howard married William, earl of Burlington, the heir of her uncle Hart, the 6th duke of Devonshire; if she had not died prematurely she would have become the duchess of Devonshire, like her grandmother before her. These familial alliances can be seen as helping to maintain the family's position in the heart of the Whig cousindom, which was especially helpful for their eldest brother, later the 7th earl, in his political career.[30]

However, there was also an expectation of a degree of affection within a marriage; it was not all about power. Both Blanche and Harriet Howard's marriages appear to have been companionate and they should not be seen as solely strategic alliances, but rather ones that mixed domestic affection and dynastic ambition. Sisters took a proactive interest in the happiness of their siblings and their siblings' children and so wanted to ensure that a balance of romance and reason was present in any new marriage. It therefore upset Georgiana Morpeth greatly in 1809 that she was not able to see Lord Granville the day before he was due to marry her sister as she had given birth a few days earlier. She wrote:

> I have pined a little at not seeing Ld Granville last night … I like to think that you will know as I do that there is no happiness like that of possessing the affection of a beloved husband.[31]

As a woman who had found love in her own marriage she hoped that her sister was going to enjoy the same degree of happiness. This concern for a relative's happiness could, though, sometimes turn into interference. When Harriet Granville met George Agar Ellis in 1821 she was not impressed with her guest; she wrote: 'he has a great deal of skin deep warmth, and is a spoilt child.'[32]

---

28 For example, Elizabeth Scarburgh married Charles Ingram in 1726; her sister Anne married Henry Ingram in 1728. The two couples lived together in Temple Newsam (near Leeds) and were later joined by a third Scarburgh sister, the widowed Henrietta. For a discussion of 'close marriages' see Davidoff, *Thicker than water*, pp 225–49.   29 Maud Leconfield (ed.) [completed by John Gore], *Three Howard sisters: selections from the writings of Lady Caroline Lascelles, Lady Dover and Countess Gower, 1825 to 1833* (London, 1955), p. 17. 30 David Gent, 'Aristocratic Whig politics in early-Victorian Yorkshire: Lord Morpeth and his world' (PhD, University of York, 2010), pp 36–7; for a discussion of the Whig cousindom see Peter Mandler, *Aristocratic government in the age of reform: Whigs and Liberals, 1830–1852* (Oxford, 1990).   31 Georgiana Morpeth to Harriet Grenville, 25 Dec. 1809 (TNA, PRO 30/29/17/5/6).   32 Surtees, *A second self*, p. 159.

Therefore, when Harriet became aware that Agar Ellis may have wanted to marry her niece, she expressed her concerns. She wrote to her sister that she 'cannot wish it', adding: 'If she falls in love with him we must hope the best, but if she does not for God's sake do not let any consideration lead you to persuade her to it.'[33] They did fall in love, though, leading to Harriet having to accept her new relation:

> Forgive me my beloved sister for having thought nothing good enough for her. I am quite happy now. The mistake of my friends with regard to me, is not finding out that I am a fool, a very great regular fool … Tell Georgiana that I shall look upon her and Agar as my two eldest children – and love and scold them accordingly. I swell like the frog in the fable when I think of the enlarged scale of Auntitude which I have entered upon.[34]

It is interesting to note that she highlighted her sisterly relationship and the notion of friendship in her apology; this dual role appears to have given her some permission to interfere. When sisters became aunts they gained new spheres of influence and, as the children became adults, new connections. Aristocratic family alliances led to multiple and complex relations which were not only sometimes difficult for families to manage but could be especially hard for those on the outside to negotiate; as Sir Robert Peel declared: 'Damn the Whigs, they're all cousins.'[35]

Once their siblings were married they remained concerned about whether the relationship remained happy. Georgiana Dover wrote with great pleasure in 1830 about how happy her younger sister Blanche and her new husband were: 'They do seem (as far as one can judge) the happiest people possible, sufficiently engrossed with each other and their pursuits to prevent them wishing for anything beyond, and sufficiently satisfied to prevent them from having any anxieties.'[36] Therefore, when marriages began to show signs of discord it caused real concern. Elizabeth, 10th countess of Pembroke, was so moved by the marital problems faced by her sister, Lady Diana Beauclerk, that she felt physically unwell. She wrote in 1779: 'I have been almost distracted these ten days with miseries of my poor Sister's … I have a most constant headache at present, from what I have gone through about it all.'[37] This concern, though, was not always about just the emotional well-being of their sister; it could also be tempered with concerns about propriety. The family of Lady Sarah Bunbury, a daughter of the 2nd duke of Richmond, cut off contact with her after she eloped with her lover in 1769. Reinstatement within the family came at a price; she needed to show suitable remorse and live a life of penitence. Her sister Louisa wrote: 'She is very

33 Ibid., pp 161–2.   **34** Ibid., p. 163.   **35** Robert Peel cited in Hugh Cunningham, *The challenge of democracy: Britain, 1832–1918* (London, 2001), p. 40.   **36** Leconfield, *Three Howard sisters*, pp 119–20.   **37** Carola Hicks, *Improper pursuits: the scandalous life of Lady Di Beauclerk* (London, 2001), p. 253.

unhappy, and we who love her cannot wish her otherwise.'[38] The sisterly connections remained, but they were aware of the damage done to her own and her wider family's reputation.

Once married, the new wife had a new set of familial relationships to negotiate, including the presence of new sisters-in-law. These in-laws were often keen to welcome their new sister into the family as it would have meant that not only potential friendships could be formed but also, crucially, networks could be enhanced. Despite the fact that her mother-in-law was one of the leading female supporters of Pitt the Younger, Elizabeth, 5th duchess of Rutland, wanted to keep her connections with the Whigs of her Castle Howard childhood.[39] She was therefore delighted when her brother became engaged to Georgiana Cavendish as it gave her a link to the influential and fashionable Devonshire family. She wrote to congratulate them, noting how 'happy the thoughts of having so amicable a sister made me; allow me, my dear Georgiana, to ask for your friendship'.[40] However, the in-laws could cause real problems. When it was reported in 1783 that the 5th duchess of Devonshire was breast-feeding her baby daughter herself, her sister-in-law was quick to criticize her for putting new maternal fashions before the future of the Devonshire name; she had not yet provided a male heir and breastfeeding was considered to be a contraceptive.[41] Likewise, political concerns could become problematic if the natal and marital families held opposing viewpoints. The Cavendish sisters were caught in a family rift between their two fathers-in-law who had fallen out over a political argument and the Howard sisters also faced similar problems with their in-laws.[42] When Caroline Howard married William Lascelles in 1823 she joined a Tory family and the differing politics did cause some discord, especially when it was rumoured that William's brother might stand for election against one of Caroline's siblings who was MP for the West Riding of Yorkshire. Her mother wrote of this news: 'I am afraid Caro will be annoyed ab[ou]t this opposition as she will know that it is a source of annoyance to us'.[43] As the Howard siblings were very close there was relief when Edwin Lascelles did not stand in the 1835 election. Sibling relationships remained as important to many women as their marital connections, and loyalties to their natal family remained strong even after marriage.

Married aristocratic women not only had to negotiate the tricky relationships between the two families that they were connected with, but they also had the challenges of running a country house. This did not just mean organizing their home, ordering redecorations and managing staff, it was also about being seen as

38 Lady Louise Conolly (1769) cited in Tillyard, *Aristocrats*, p. 286.   **39** For a discussion of the political role of Isabelle, 4th duchess of Rutland, see Lewis, '1784 and all that', pp 103–5. **40** Elizabeth Rutland to Georgiana Morpeth, 18 Jan. [1801] (Castle Howard, Carlisle papers, MS J18/48/6).   **41** Lewis, *In the family way*, p. 211.   **42** Surtees, *A second self*, p. 124. **43** Georgiana Carlisle to Harriet Sutherland, [29 Dec. 1834] (Staffordshire Record Office, Sutherland papers, D6579/75/20). Edwin Lascelles did not stand in the 1835 election.

a good and efficient chatelaine. Domesticity was considered a feminine virtue in this period but aristocratic women needed to fulfil the ideals of their sex without transgressing those of their class; elite women could not work and still be considered as 'ladies', and so the occupations that filled their day could not be construed as labour.[44] The performance of domestic duties was therefore important as it allowed them to demonstrate that they upheld its ideology without damaging their elite credentials.[45] Therefore, many aristocratic women turned to their siblings for advice and guidance about how to fulfil this role. Caroline Lascelles perceived her sister-in-law Louisa, countess of Harewood, to be something of a domestic goddess; they both married into the Lascelles family within a few weeks of each other in 1823, and as their friendship blossomed they exchanged practical advice regarding household management.[46] This source of knowledge was soon shared with other Howard sisters; Harriet Sutherland used her relationship with her sibling to gain access to the 'domestic oracle', asking Caroline to consult Louisa for practical help about running her new household:

> ask her for me if the housekeeper and maids should cut, make and mark the house linen. I also want to know how the curtains are at Goldsbro. Do they draw without concealing the bow?[47]

These enquiries reflect Harriet's anxiety about undertaking her role correctly; when she married George Granville, who was nearly twenty years her senior, there was some concern that Harriet was too young, too lively, and too flirtatious in her demeanour to succeed in her new position.[48] It was therefore important for Harriet to be seen as an effective lady of the house and her sister was seen as the best conduit to gain reliable advice. Siblings could also provide emotional support when a new bride had to negotiate the problems of managing a strange household; for many elite women there was not just one country house to oversee. Being dislocated from the household staff and friendship networks of one's main home could be a cause of anxiety, especially if entertaining guests. Thus, Caroline, 5th countess of Carlisle, was keen to have her own sister's company with her when she went to Naworth Castle in 1770, the Howards' Cumbrian home. She wrote to her stepmother:

> I wish you could find out whether my Sister would like to go into Cumberland with me, and if my father would have no objection to letting her, I am afraid it sounds very unreasonable but if she would go it will be a monstrous comfort to me as Milord will be obliged to be a great deal out

44 Reynolds, *Aristocratic women*, p. 21.   **45** R.M. Larsen, 'Dynastic domesticity: the role of elite women in the Yorkshire country house, 1685–1858' (PhD, University of York, 2003), pp 43–63.   **46** Leconfield, *Three Howard sisters*, p. 53.   **47** Ibid., p. 80.   **48** Ibid., pp 33–5.

and she would help me to entertain all the People, do contrive it for me if you can.[49]

It does seem that Caroline was in desperate need of both help and company, and so was keen to use her sister as an ally. Sisters could be trusted to provide useful practical help and to conceal from others their siblings' anxieties, and so enabled one another to fulfil the ideals of their class and gender.

Due to the importance of dynastic survival, elite women were not only expected to be wives and chatelaines but also mothers. However, to present aristocratic mothers as disinterested incubators of heirs overlooks both the joys and status that many women gained from this role.[50] Becoming a mother, though, was not without its dangers and for many, the process of pregnancy and birth was a cause of real concern. Sisters played a central role in the management of these risks; by sharing their knowledge and experiences of childbirth, sisters provided practical advice for one another. In families where there was a high incidence of miscarriage sisters shared advice with one another during the early stages of their pregnancies.[51] Women often turned to their network of female relatives in order to guide them in their choice of medical staff; for example, Harriet Granville, Georgiana Morpeth and Georgiana's three eldest daughters all used the same nurse for a number of their pregnancies, and a similar pattern of behaviour can be found among the Strangeways sisters.[52] Although by 1780 the tradition of the childbed as a female-only space was in decline, it remained a time when the family came together.[53] Despite the increasing medicalization of childbirth, having a reliable female friend present remained crucial for most women, and in many cases this was a sister as they were able to provide a level of emotional comfort that they could not expect from their paid staff. Siblings were therefore concerned when they could not be present at the childbed, especially when it was the mother's first birth. Harriet Sutherland lamented that she was not going to be with her sister, Blanche, when she faced 'the prospect of the first time before

49 Caroline Carlisle to Lady Gower, [?] 1770 (TNA, PRO 30/29/4/2/66).   **50** See Lawrence Stone, *The family, sex and marriage in England, 1500–1800* (London, 1979), pp 405–48; Randolph Trumbach, *The rise of the egalitarian family: aristocratic kinship and domestic relations in eighteenth-century England* (New York, 1978), pp 187–236; Larsen, 'Dynastic domesticity', pp 144–87; Ellen Ross, 'New thoughts on "the oldest vocation": mothers and motherhood in recent feminists scholarship', *Signs: Journal of Women in Culture and Society* 20 (1995), 397–9; N.J. Miller, 'Mothering others: caregiving as spectrum and spectacle in the early modern period' in N.J. Miller and Naomi Yavneh (eds), *Maternal measures: figuring caregiving in the early modern period* (Aldershot, 2000), p. 7.   **51** See, for example, the case of the Strangeways families in Joanna Martin, *Wives and daughters: women and children in the Georgian country house* (London, 2004), pp 177–8.   **52** Lewis, *In the family way*, pp 164–5; Leconfield, *Three Howard sisters*, p. 252.   **53** L.F. Cody, 'The politics of reproduction: from midwives' alternative public sphere to the public spectacle of man-midwifery', *Eighteenth-Century Studies*, 32 (1999), 477–9; Adrian Wilson, 'The ceremony of childbirth and its interpretation' in V.A. Fildes (ed.), *Women as mothers in pre-Industrial England: essays in memory of Dorothy McLaren* (London, 1990), pp 68–70.

her. It is an epoch that never returns, and I cannot cease to regret not being with her.'[54] Sibling guidance was felt to be especially needed when the expectant mother could not have her own mother with her during the birth. As their mother had died in 1806, Harriet Granville was keen to have Georgiana with her at the birth of her children. She wrote in 1810: 'God bless my own sister. I am grown very big and my child really quite impetuous in his movement. You must not delay.'[55] Likewise, she was keen to be with her sister when Georgiana gave birth, writing in 1812: 'You, my own G., are everything to me every where ... Promise not to lay in without me'.[56] Maternal absence was also felt by the Strangeways sisters, who felt that their father's second wife was not a satisfactory substitute at the childbed for their mother, the 2nd countess of Ilchester. Instead, like the Cavendishes and the Howards, the sisters regularly travelled great distances in order to be with one another when one of them was due to give birth. They preferred the support of their siblings, including their unmarried sisters, to the presence of their stepmother, for although, in the words of Elizabeth Strangeways, they 'would be of no use at the moment' they would be 'a much great comfort ... than anyone'.[57] While the practical knowledge that an experienced mother could bring to the childbed was valued, the comfort of a sister's presence was deemed to be of even greater worth.

The comfort of a sibling was also sought at times of a crisis, and when the family faced a challenge to its reputation or its well-being, sisters often came together. Georgiana, 5th duchess of Devonshire, and her sister Harriet, Countess Bessborough, remained loyal to one another despite the scandals caused by their marital difficulties, gambling problems and the criticisms of their political activities. The duchess was therefore upset when she did not get the same level of support from her husband's sister, who had pronounced that Georgiana was ostracized from the Cavendish family in 1791.[58] For other sisters, while public disgrace could damage relationships at first, the power of kinship ties was often too strong. Jane, Lady Harrington, had ceased to have contact with her sister Seymour, Lady Worsley, following the criminal conversation trial in 1782 where the details of Lady Worsley's multiple affairs had been publicly aired. However, when Seymour fell ill, Jane decided to support her sister, not just by visiting her bedside but by also escorting her to various fashionable seaside resorts, which helped with Lady Worsely's reintroduction into polite society.[59] The Howard and Cavendish sisters did not face such public embarrassments, but at times of illness or bereavement the family did come together to provide emotional or practical support.[60] For example, the extended

---

54 Leconfield, *Three Howard sisters*, p. 216.   **55** Surtees, *A second self*, pp 35–6.   **56** Ibid., p. 47.   **57** Martin, *Wives and daughters*, p. 182.   **58** Foreman, *Georgiana*, p. 254.   **59** Hallie Rubenhold, *Lady Worsley's whim: an eighteenth-century tale of sex, scandal and divorce* (London, 2008), pp 247–8.   **60** See, for example, Georgiana Carlisle to 6th earl of Carlisle, n.d. (Castle Howard, Carlisle papers, MS J18/2/43); Leconfield, *Three Howard sisters*, p. 52.

Howard family came to stay with Georgiana, Lady Dover, when her husband fell seriously ill in 1833. Caroline's detailed account of the subsequent death of her brother-in-law suggests that they were more concerned for Georgiana's well-being than they were for George; as their sister, she was their focus for anxiety.[61] Marriage did not sever a woman's ties with her natal family and those childhood bonds remained strong into later life.

Unsurprisingly, therefore, responses to the death of a sibling reflect the very real affection that most held for one another. In 1860, following the death of Lady Dover, her sister, Harriet Sutherland, wrote to a family friend: 'How can I [hope] to tell you what I have to say is the saddest letter that can be written. I have lost my dearest sister Georgiana.'[62] Sisterly ties were often the longest-lasting relationships that women had, and the sense of loss in many of the resultant letters is palpable. When Georgiana Morpeth died in 1858, her sister Harriet lost her longest-standing companion and epistolary friend. She was left to mark her emotions in a commonplace book rather than a letter, as she did not have Georgiana to send it to, where she wrote: 'Adored sister, may God grant – His will be done'.[63]

Being a sister was a crucially important element of elite women's identity in the late eighteenth- and early nineteenth-century country house. In a letter dated Christmas Day 1809 Georgiana Morpeth wrote to her sister that for her she held 'the feelings of Mother, sister and friend'; the three caring roles were very much intertwined.[64] Being a sister was about providing political connections, pragmatic advice and practical assistance for one's relatives. Crucially, though, it was also about being a central part of the emotional worlds of their siblings, and even those who had happy marriages regularly turned to their sisters for affection and comfort, especially when they needed another woman's advice and knowledge. Throughout their lives, sisterhood was a constant, from the nursery and schoolroom, to being allies in the marriage market, as political friends, birthing partners, and long term confidantes. Elite women worked together with shared interests, and so provided support for one another as they negotiated their twin roles of being a woman and an aristocrat. Sisters did not just do it for themselves, but for their siblings and their natal dynasties too.

61 An edited version of this account appears in Leconfield, *Three Howard sisters*, pp 274–7; John Gore, who completed the book following Lady Leconfield's death, notes that the original narrative was of 'enormous length', and contended there were fewer more detailed descriptions of a death-bed scene than Caroline's description.　62 Harriet Sutherland to Ralph Sneyd, [?] 1860 (Keele University Library, Sneyd papers, MS SC12/151).　63 Betty Askwith, *Piety and wit: a biography of Harriet Countess Granville, 1785–1862* (London, 1982), p. 180.　64 Letter from Georgiana Morpeth to Harriet, Countess Grenville, 25 Dec. 1809 (TNA, 30/29/17/5/6).

'Lasting monuments': Lady Gregory's domesticated landscape and forestry

ANNA PILZ

Books and trees were Lady Gregory's chief charmers: the one nearest her mind, the other nearest her heart. She laboured long and lovingly in the woods of Coole.[1]

'Nearly all my book royalties grow into trees', said Lady Augusta Gregory to Signe Toksvig, one of her visitors at Coole Park in Co. Galway.[2] Reading through Gregory's journals one is struck by the abundance of references to the planting of saplings of ash, beech, birch, larch, larkspur, lime, oak, spruce, sycamore and yew. A keen amateur planter, she held a life-long interest in forestry and an appreciation of the cultural value of the arboreal landscape. This dual regard is articulated in an article on 'Tree planting', one of her early works that was published in the *Irish Homestead* of February 1898.[3] By that time, she had taken charge of her marital home at Coole with an eye to protecting and developing the family's legacy after the death of her husband, Sir William Gregory, in 1892. As custodian of the estate for her son Robert (1881–1918), Lady Gregory understood environmental stewardship as an integral part of estate management, spending both time and a significant proportion of her income on the upkeep of Coole's woodland.

While landownership and silviculture were considered as man's prerogative, Gregory crossed these gender boundaries as custodian and planter. In her perception of nature as both a material reality and a conceptual space, Gregory engaged with and shaped the environs of the country house. As K.D. Reynolds argues, 'the central aristocratic concept in landownership was one of stewardship: land was always held in trust for future generations, and while it was generally expedient for that trust to be executed by and between men, there was no absolute reason for the trust not to be transmitted through women.'[4] Widowed at the age of 40 with a son who had not yet reached his teens, Gregory's approach to woodland management can be understood precisely in

This research was funded by the Irish Research Council. I wish to thank Colin Smythe for his generosity in sharing photographs, and for granting copyright permission. **1** Sean O'Casey, *Inishfallen fare thee well* (London, 1949), p. 148. **2** Signe Toksvig, 'A visit to Lady Gregory', *The North American Review*, 214:789 (1921), 195. **3** Lady Gregory, 'Tree planting', *Irish Forestry – Journal of the Society of Irish Foresters*, 33:2 (1976), 94–8. **4** K.D. Reynolds, *Aristocratic women and political society in Victorian Britain* (Oxford, 1998), p. 44.

terms of stewardship. After her son's death in 1918, her responsibility shifted to her grandson as she remarked that '[t]he machinery of my life has not changed. Last month I was planting for Robert, now I am planting for Richard.'[5] Yet her tree planting activity was not simply one of the ascendancy's duties for posterity nor was her article on the subject a mere piece of instructive journalism.

Gregory's husbandry and conceptualization of arboriculture offers insight into her understanding of self within her marital family's legacy and her agency in creating cultural signs within the demesne landscape. Judith W. Page and Elise L. Smith note that between 1780 and 1870 'the domesticated landscape was central to women's complex negotiation of public and private life'. During this transitional period, they argue, female 'writers and artists used the subject matter of gardens and plants to educate their audience, to enter into political and cultural debates, particularly around issues of gender and class, and to signal moments of intellectual and spiritual insight.'[6] This argument pertaining to the meanings of gardens is instructive when applied to the meanings of trees and woods in Gregory's writing and to her planting practice. She moved beyond the approved (and more comfortable) female space of the kitchen and flower garden in the immediate vicinity of the house to the cultivation of the demesne with its plantations.[7] For her article, she drew on her experience, horticultural texts, and treatises on husbandry, and she combined those with life writing, reflections on improvement, class relations, and cautious political commentary. Coole Park was central to her musings in its dual function as a private home and as a public exemplar of the Irish country house.

The 1890s were a transformative period for Gregory. On a personal level, she was the caretaker of a highly mortgaged estate in the west of Ireland, a task that demanded skilled economizing, and a balancing act of keeping an active social network in London while steadily refocusing on life at Coole. She continued her Irish lessons (begun in the 1880s) and her interest in local Irish folklore deepened. The family seat with its garden, greenhouses, orchard and woods became the centre of Gregory's life. It was the arboreal landscape in particular that fostered an increasing attachment to place; as she remarked in her autobiography, 'that love [for Coole] has grown through the long years of widowed life, when the woods especially became my occupation and delight.'[8] Gregory articulated here the meaning of woods as a site of both pleasure and labour. The act of planting assisted in putting down roots; as Judith Hill comments, 'the planting of trees was a gesture of intent to stay'.[9] On a more

5 Lady Gregory to John Quinn, 10 Feb. 1918 (New York Public Library, Berg Collection) [no reference numbers, hereafter Berg].   6 Judith W. Page and Elise L. Smith, *Women, literature, and the domesticated landscape: England's disciples of flora, 1780–1870* (Cambridge, 2011), p. 1. 7 In 1917, it was noted in the *Irish Monthly* that 'the art of gardening sprung from the patient toil and mothering care of women': see David Houston, 'Gardening by women', *Irish Monthly*, 45:525 (1917), 176.   8 Lady Gregory *Seventy years*, ed. Colin Smythe (New York, 1974), pp 25–6.   9 Judith Hill, *Lady Gregory: an Irish life* (Dublin, 2011), p. 139.

public level, she curated the family's reputation by editing, first her husband's autobiography, and then his grandfather's letters.[10] With these publications, she accentuated the Gregorys' legacy as benevolent landowners while also paying tribute to their contribution to Irish politics in their respective roles as member of parliament and under-secretary for Ireland. Despite her gender, Gregory confidently placed herself within that familial tradition as an active custodian. She became an ardent supporter of Horace Plunkett's co-operative movement and her political opposition to home rule gradually shifted towards Irish nationalism. When, in the summer of 1897, the neighbouring landlord and writer Edward Martyn of Tulira Castle (Co. Galway) visited her with his guest, the young poet W.B. Yeats, she soon became the patron of the Irish literary revival, with Coole as its headquarters.

It was, most likely, in that summer that Gregory started to extend invitations to her contemporaries on the Irish cultural and literary scene to carve their initials into the bark of a magnificent copper beech tree in the grounds of Coole. The first to inscribe their names, we can assume, were Robert Gregory, Douglas Hyde, Æ, Yeats, and Augusta herself.[11] Her decision to include her own initials indicates a desire to link her name to the location, and thereby to situate herself within the Gregory family history. This 'sacred tree of Coole', as Sean O'Casey described it, stands as a monument to *her* legacy.[12] This practice of laying claim to the landscape was based on exclusivity and by invitation only. Rather reproachfully, Gregory noted later: 'But alas! Once or twice country lads doing some work in the orchard, seeing these signatures, thought it natural to add their own, and these unknown to literature, may puzzle some future antiquarian.'[13] This not only betrayed her elitism but also asserted her belief that not everyone was as worthy of remembrance as were she and her colleagues.

In 'Tree planting', such cultural conceptualization of the arboreal world is wedded to its material reality. '[I]f woods, like friendships, are not kept in constant repair,' she warned her readers, 'the day will come when they will be but a memory.'[14] Gregory recalled that 'Ireland, more than other countries, ought to be a country of trees, for the very letters of her alphabet are named after them.' She was explicitly gesturing toward the Gaelic League in musing, 'Perhaps with the revival of her old language they will be better called to mind.'[15]

10 Lady Gregory (ed.), *Sir William Gregory. K.C.M.G., formerly member of parliament and sometime governor of Ceylon: an autobiography* (London, 1894); Lady Gregory (ed.), *Mr Gregory's letter-box, 1813–1830* (London, 1898).   11 No record in diaries or letters could be found that would assist in dating the first inscriptions. My thanks go to James Pethica for a discussion on the most plausible date.   12 O'Casey, *Inishfallen*, p. 148.   13 Lady Gregory, *Coole*, ed. Colin Smythe (Dublin, 1971), p. 103.   14 Gregory, 'Tree planting', p. 94.   15 Ibid. This betrays perhaps a particular ignorance on Gregory's part. The Irish public was reminded of its former woodlands when, for instance, Arthur Griffith's *United Irishman*, 29 Oct. 1904 to 14 Apr. 1906, ran a 68-part series of place-lore titled, 'The woods of Ireland', 'listing the locations and names of vanished woods'. See Maria Tymoczko, *The Irish Ulysses* (Berkeley & Los Angeles, 1997), p. 236.

Appearing in the pages of the *Irish Homestead*, a weekly paper associated with Horace Plunkett's Irish Agricultural Organization Society (IAOS), her article demonstrates her progressive views on agriculture. By linking Plunkett's self-help movement with Hyde's endeavours, Gregory proposed that re-afforestation and language revival went hand in hand.[16] Her interest in his views was suggestive of a more than passing fancy for his initiative; they frequently dined together.[17] Plunkett was central enough to her social circle that in March of 1897, in honour of her recently established acquaintance with Yeats, she invited him to meet the young poet.[18] The gathering, which also included the nationalist Barry O'Brien, pointed to her sense that literary pursuits and national politics were interwoven with agriculture and political economy. Through such dinner parties, Gregory sought intellectual engagement in contemporary debates while testing and developing new ideas on the estate. In an effort to introduce co-operative initiatives at Coole, she had arranged for local farmers to meet with Plunkett in that year, 'but it was a fine day after long rain, & very few came – but he came & talked to them outside the hall door, explaining the methods.'[19] Gregory also assisted the self-help movement by sharing her knowledge of silviculture and her thoughts on the present and future state of Irish forestry.

While it was common for a woman to take part in horticultural pursuits, with gardening magazines and advice books by and for women proliferating during the Victorian era, literature about and the practice of silviculture was very much a male-dominated field.[20] Rather than elaborating in a passive and observant manner on the aesthetic benefits of trees and woods as would have been expected from a female author, her article was instructive, practical and ideological. Gregory entered the arboreal discourse in a remarkably confident tone and she aimed to educate by offering guidance on the best times for planting, what species were most suitable for what purposes, and alerted her readers to trees' needs with regards to different soil types. Such practical knowledge was not

16 Gregory's contribution to the *Irish Homestead* goes unremarked in P.J. Mathew's study, *Revival: the Abbey Theatre, Sinn Féin, the Gaelic League and the co-operative movement* (Cork, 2003). He focuses on Gregory's article 'Ireland, real and ideal' from *The Nineteenth Century: a Monthly Review*, 44:261 (1898), 769–82. Here she pairs again the co-operative movement with the Gaelic League, representing respectively the real and ideal.   17 See, for example, Gregory's diary entry for 16 March 1897 in which she noted: 'After dinner had a talk with Horace Plunkett on Irish co-operation', and for 19 [i.e., 18th] March 1897, 'had a long talk with Horace Plunkett': *Lady Gregory's diaries, 1892–1902*, ed. James Pethica (Gerrards Cross, 1996), pp 133, 134.   18 Entry for 21 Mar. 1897, *Lady Gregory's diaries*, pp 135–7.   19 Entry for 30 Nov. 1897, *Lady Gregory's diaries*, p. 152. Plunkett would two years later become the founding vice-president of the Department of Agriculture and Technical Instruction for Ireland.   20 Sarah Bilston, 'Queens of the garden: Victorian women gardeners and the rise of the gardening advice text', *Victorian Literature and Culture*, 36:1 (2008), 1–19. In the final two decades of the century the professionalization of horticulture gained momentum with the provision of horticultural education opening up to Irish and British women: see Mary Forrest and Valerie Ingram, 'Education for lady gardeners in Ireland', *Garden History*, 27:2 (1999), 207.

altogether unusual among women of the country house. For instance, a century earlier both Katherine Conolly and her daughter-in-law Lady Louisa Conolly considered the demesne's woodland and ornamental plantations at Castletown House as key to the overall landscape design, and both were principally involved in their management and preservation.[21] Indeed, Lady Louisa had solicited 'a short dissertation on planting' from John Walker who 'hopes [that it] will convey almost all the information she may wish for upon the subject', evidencing her scientific interest and hands-on approach to tree planting.[22]

In keeping with the self-help ethos of the *Irish Homestead*, Gregory's husbandry was informed by observation, consultation with relatives and neighbours, and bookish knowledge. In January 1896, she recorded in her diary:

> Have planted about 1400 trees, in nutwood & clump in '45 acres' – larch, spruce – silver – scotch - & some evergreen oaks & new lilacs in nutwood – & Frank has been over today & advised me to get 1000 birch, as a man had been over from England buying them at L. Cutra, for clog soles – anyhow they are very silvery, showing through dark foliage – I have been studying seed potatoes! & wrote to Talbot Power – to ask advice – but he writes back that he is not an agriculturalist – but will send me a ton of 'flourballs'.[23]

Her recommendation to readers to 'note what does best in the neighbourhood' is thus based on her own method of seeking advice from fellow landlords such as Sir John Talbot Power from Wexford and of being observant when visiting gardens and country houses in Ireland and abroad.[24] In the summer of 1882, for instance, she had visited Penshurst in Kent and noted that 'The gardens are laid out with vegetables and flowers mixed, a hedge of roses and rows of carrots, apple trees covered with clematis. The borders herbaceous.'[25] Both passages highlight her attention to aesthetic as well as practical concerns, hinting at mixed motives in her horticultural and forestry pursuits.

Her diary entry further indicates the sheer scale of planting activity at Coole that was driven by a commitment to sustainable woodland management. Gregory approvingly opened 'Tree planting' with reference to an earlier article from the *Irish Homestead* that reported on the fact that 'the number of trees planted in Ireland last year was considerably larger than the number of trees cut down.' Giving a brief list of timber use for building materials and roofing as well as for fuel, she cautioned that such harvesting would result in a fast depletion of

---

21 Finola O'Kane, *Landscape design in eighteenth-century Ireland: mixing foreign trees with the natives* (Cork, 2004), p. 54. By the late eighteenth century, Castletown House had sixty-one acres of woodland.   **22** John Walker, 'Essay on plantations of trees presented to Lady Louisa Conolly' (1809) (NLI, MS 15,397).   **23** Diary entry, 31 Jan. 1896, *Lady Gregory's diaries*, p. 107.   **24** Gregory, 'Tree planting', p. 96.   **25** Lady Gregory's diary entry 5 [Aug. 1882]: Lady Gregory, Diary, Part 1. (Nov. 1881–Feb. 1884), Berg.

woodland if not carefully managed. She recounted that when Robert cut down a tree as a young boy, she promptly 'told him that he must never cut one down without planting two in its place.'[26] Gregory thus raised her son to be aware of the responsibilities of environmental stewardship. This is further apparent in her diary entry for January 1898 when she recorded the joint activity of mother and son: 'Arranging tree planting – R. & I having marked 30 spruce for the people, & to leave gaps for the shooting, I am ordering 300 spruce, 300 larch, 100 silvers to take their place.'[27] A few weeks later, she sent off her article to the *Homestead*.[28]

With 'Tree planting' Gregory contributed to a long tradition of practical literature on husbandry and silviculture that was, however, predominantly written by and for men. At Coole, she had access to a number of classic texts on the topic dating from the sixteenth to the nineteenth century. The holdings in the library gave testimony to the Gregorys' interest in landscape design, gardening, and forestry across generations. These included copies of Richard Payne Knight's *The landscape* (1795), William Marshall's *Planting and rural ornament* (1796), Humphrey Repton's *Observations on the theory and practice of landscape gardening* (1803), Richard Morris' *Essays on landscape gardening, and on uniting picturesque effect with rural scenery* (1825) and John Claudius Loudon's quintessential *An encyclopaedia of gardening* (1825). In addition, there was William Pontey's *Forest pruner* (1805), alongside various volumes of the Board of Agriculture on subjects relating to husbandry and improvement (1797–1808) and the complete first series of the transactions from the Horticultural Society of London (1812–30).[29] Previous generations of the Gregory family consulted and studied these works closely; the copy of Erasmus Darwin's *Phytologia; or, The philosophy of agriculture and gardening* (1800), for instance, comes 'with Richard Gregory's annotations, some on inserted slips'.[30]

Lady Gregory likewise engaged in regular study on the subject as revealed by her knowledge of Thomas Tusser's *Five hundred points of good husbandry*, a volume also held in the Coole library and quoted in the article. This particular sixteenth-century text was considered essential, at least in an Irish context. In the eighteenth century, Robert Molesworth, an ardent planter on his estate at Breckdenston near Swords, asserted that '"Tusser's old Book of Husbandry should be taught to the boys [of Ireland], to read, to copy, and to get by heart."'[31] Gregory's inclusion of some lines from Tusser's volume ('If cattle or coney may enter to crop, / Young oak is in danger of losing his top') provided a firm

---

26 Gregory, 'Tree planting', p. 95.   27 Diary entry, 30 Jan. 1898, *Lady Gregory's diaries*, p. 165. Similarly, in April 1903, she noted that '2,500 little trees just arrived to supplement those we have cut'; see Gregory, *Seventy years*, p. 428.   28 Diary entry, 10 Feb. 1898, *Lady Gregory's diaries*, p. 166.   29 Sotheby & Co., *Catalogue of printed books formerly in the library at Coole* (London, 1972). Dates given are in reference to the respective edition held at Coole. 30 Ibid., p. 21.   31 Robert Southey (ed.), *Select works of the British poets, from Chaucer to Jonson, with biographical sketches* (London, 1831), p. 143.

indication that she knew this georgic intimately, and considered herself among those entitled to study and pursue the type of husbandry that Tusser advocated.[32] In fact, Tusser's work was a great influence on John Evelyn, author of the first treatise entirely devoted to silviculture.

If given the choice of six books from the library of her marital home, Gregory counted Evelyn's *Silva; or, A discourse of forest-trees, and the propagation of timber in his Majesty's dominions* to be one of them, 'with its beautiful coloured plates of larch and "Silver firr"'.[33] First published in 1664 under the auspices of the Royal Society, this is one of the most influential books on forestry. Gregory's reference is to the 1786 edition, edited with extensive notes by A. Hunter and featuring forty coloured plates.[34] Considering that Gregory held this book in such high regard, we can surmise that it was a constant companion, frequently consulted and re-read. Evelyn's lasting success was due to his comprehensive approach and to his incorporation of poetry and classical texts, including the story of Ulysses. For Gregory, it was this title that prompted her to recognize how planting trees was a means of connecting past, present and future as well as a way to insert herself within the family's legacy. She quotes from Evelyn's book:

> When Ulysses, after a ten years' absence, was returned from Troy, and coming home found his aged father in the field planting of trees, he asked him, 'Why, being now so advanced in years, he would put himself to the fatigue and labour of planting that of which he was never likely to enjoy the fruits?' The old man, taking him for a stranger, gently replied, 'I plant against my son Ulysses comes home'.[35]

As the passage indicates, the educational task of environmental stewardship was traditionally framed along paternal lines. Yet Gregory clearly associated herself in imaginative and practical terms with the father planting for his son's return and, irrespective of her gender, she considered it to be perfectly natural to take on that role.

With subtlety, she draws on Evelyn's authority to argue for woman's equal (if not even superior) role in environmental stewardship. '"Men seldom plant trees till they begin to be wise", says Evelyn'; having drawn attention to her conscientious tree planting and role as educator, Gregory – with the insertion of this quotation – proclaimed her own wisdom.[36] In confirming her intellectual and practical abilities, she simultaneously asserted her right to take on the duties expected of the landed class. In Evelyn's *Silva*, the above passage is included on the same page as the following:

32 Gregory, 'Tree planting', p. 96.   33 Gregory, *Coole*, p. 20.   34 *Catalogue of printed books.*   35 Gregory, 'Tree planting', p. 95; for the direct quotation see John Evelyn, *Silva; or, A discourse of forest-trees, and the propagation of timber in his majesty's dominions*, 2 vols (York, 1801 [3rd ed.]), i, 32.   36 Gregory, 'Tree planting', p. 96.

It is what all persons who are owners of land may contribute to, and with infinite delight, as well as profit, who are touched with that laudable ambition of imitating their illustrious ancestors, and of worthily serving their generation. To these my earnest and humble advice should be; that at their first coming to their estates, and as soon as they get children, they would seriously think of this work of propagation.[37]

Here, Evelyn's vision of planting for posterity is seen to be reliant on the efforts of England's landowners. Yet, while Gregory's own planting ethos was similar, her uncomplicated inclusion of Evelyn's treatise is a curious one within the context of Ireland's colonial history.

His call for re-afforestation pointed towards the consequences of human interaction with the natural environment, specifically via an extractive economy that might result in both a crisis of prosperity and a detrimental mark on the landscape. Commissioned by the Royal Navy, *Silva* was a response to the rapid decline in England's woodland during the Civil War. The Royal Navy's constant need for timber was, according to Irish nationalist narratives and scholarship, one of the driving forces for England's exploitation of Ireland's rich woodlands as the nearest and cheapest resource in the seventeenth and eighteenth centuries.[38] James Joyce directly linked the island's limited woodlands to colonization when he proclaimed that 'the moral debt of the English government for not having seen to the reforestation of this disease-ridden swamp for over an entire century amounts to over 500 million francs.'[39]

This environmental history has recently come under scrutiny, however. Nigel Everett argues that 'far from carelessly wrecking a great arboreal patrimony, the English conquest and the rising ascendancy introduced conservative standards of forest management until then neglected'.[40] Everett draws attention to the pivotal role played by the landed class in environmental stewardship, a narrative that was not entirely alien to Gregory and her contemporaries. In 1915, Archibald E. Moeran observed in his article on 'Irish Demesnes' in *Irish Gardening* that

37 Evelyn, *Silva*, p. 32.   **38** Patrick Duffy, for instance, argues that Ireland's plentiful supply of oak 'was as much a driving force for British colonization as other economic or political considerations,' leading to the destruction of 'the most extensive woodlands': see Patrick J. Duffy, *Exploring the history and heritage of Irish landscapes* (Dublin, 2007), p. 37.   **39** James Joyce, 'Home rule comes of age' in Kevin Barry (ed.), *Occasional, critical and political writing* (Oxford, 2000), p. 144.   **40** Nigel Everett, *The woods of Ireland: a history, 700–1800* (Dublin, 2014), p. 15.

one branch of our modern history ... is already so forgotten, or overlooked, that its story is little likely ever to be written, and for this I am sorry, for it is the story of the great planting revolution – bloodless and non-political – which, beginning in the latter half of the eighteenth century and lasting up to, say, 1830 or 1840, gave employment to tens of thousands of Irishmen at home, and which re-clothed her hills and valleys with some, at any rate, of the woods which centuries of war and waste had swept almost utterly away. ... Of course it was at the same time that the great majority of our country houses were built.[41]

Gregory recognized the transforming potential of human agency in altering and shaping the natural environment. Such recognition carried a 'bloodless and non-political' vision 'of the great planting revolution' into the twentieth century.

Like Evelyn's, Gregory's argument is situated within a national framework. She called for a nation-wide revolution of tree planting that would unite the oppositional groups of those who supported Ireland's constitutional status as per the Act of Union of 1800 and those who campaigned for either home rule or separation. In the very year in which Irish nationalists were marking the centenary of the 1798 Rebellion, she overtly expressed her wish 'that every Nationalist would plant at least one tree in this year of '98, and every Unionist in 1900, and every waverer or indifferent person in the year that separates them'.[42] For Gregory, environmental stewardship and ecological thought had thus the power to sidestep political division. Not only did she concern herself with the increase in Ireland's woodland cover but also advocated diversity in agricultural crops. Appropriately at the time, she referred her readers to the leader of the United Irishmen: 'When Wolfe Tone was in France, a hundred years ago, he noticed how the people there planted orchards, and their children looked after them, and he wished the example might be followed in Ireland.'[43]

Whereas she appealed to farmers irrespective of the size of their holdings to join in a collaborative task of all classes, we are quickly reminded that the beautification of the country as well as its environmental stewardship should be spearheaded by the landed class: 'We can't all have woods,' she notes at one point, 'nor is it to be wished that pasture or tillage fields should be turned into forests.'[44] Through the use of this inclusive 'we', Lady Gregory placed her own husbandry within a familiar and, until that point, patrimonial ascendancy tradition that had started with Robert Gregory in the eighteenth century. As evidence that she was aware of this tradition and the importance of continuing

41 A.E. Moeran, 'Irish demesnes', *Irish Gardening: a Journal Devoted to the Advancement of Horticulture and Arboriculture in Ireland*, 10:107 (Jan. 1915), 3. For a more recent discussion on the topic see Terence Reeves-Smyth, 'The natural history of demesnes' in John Wilson Foster (ed.), *Nature in Ireland: a scientific and cultural history* (Dublin, 1997), pp 549–72. 42 Gregory, 'Tree planting', p. 95. 43 Ibid. 44 Ibid.

it, she noted in her journals that Arthur Young, who toured Ireland in the 1770s, complimented her husband's ancestors' "'noble nursery, the plantations for which would change the face of the district'", adding proudly that 'those woods still remain'.[45] Sir William inherited the estate in 1847 and Coole demesne is listed with 1355 acres in Griffith's valuation.[46] In the 1850s, he experimented with exotic tree species, spending large sums of money (despite increasing gambling debts) on the importation of conifers to plant a pinetum at Coole.[47] In 'Tree planting', Gregory highlighted Sir William's mixed motives in forestry: 'My husband planted rare pines that now tower skywards, and many larch and spruce, for he believed in the future of home-grown timber.'[48] The pinetum in particular points toward aesthetic concerns and a reinforcement of status alongside an acknowledgement of trees' commercial value as a long-term cash crop.

In order to justify her continuation of Coole's planting tradition Gregory was sensitive to female predecessors within the family. She fondly referred to 'an avenue of ilex trees planted by my husband's mother ... about forty years ago'. The trees evoke their planter: 'we think gratefully of her as we note their evergreen compactness and their silvery upper shoots shining against the sky.'[49] For Gregory, woods and trees act as commemorations of human endeavour, and she consistently establishes the connection between plantation and planter in her writings on the subject: 'a childless member of the family, wishing to have his wife kept in remembrance, planted a wood in her name – the "Isabella Wood". So when descendants of the people whose friend she had been pass near it, or ask for timber from it, her name is on their lips.'[50] The act of naming these living things after her effectively renders the trees her progeny.

Whereas trees and woods enabled Gregory's entry into the established order, they equally offered the opportunity to negotiate class boundaries. After all, tree planting was a collaborative enterprise. Gregory acknowledged in *Coole* that she had not managed the woods on her own:

> my companion and best helper an old man, now passed away. Many a time in winter snow we have gone out together with tar and brush to make the bark distasteful to hungry rabbits, or in summer time, he with slasher, I with spud, to free our nurselings from the choking of brambles or of grass. He was an old master of the business, had loved it through his lifetime.[51]

The old man was Gregory's wood-cutter, John Farrell. Having worked on the Coole estate for Sir William previously, Farrell was intimately acquainted with

45 Lady Gregory's diary entry, 23 Apr. 1920, *Lady Gregory's journals*, ed. Daniel J. Murphy (Gerrards Cross, 1978), i, 148.   **46** http://www.askaboutireland.ie/griffithvaluation/index. xml?action=doNameSearch&PlaceID=540179&county=Galway&barony=Kiltartan&parish= Kiltartan&townland=%3Cb%3ECoole%20demesne%3C/b%3E [accessed 1 Oct. 2016]. **47** Gregory, *Sir William Gregory*, p. 154.   **48** Gregory, 'Tree planting', p. 95.   **49** Ibid. **50** Ibid.   **51** Gregory, *Coole*, p. 94.

the demesne woods. He was listed as a 'farm servant' on the census for 1901, aged seventy-nine at that time.[52] Gregory's description of Farrell proposes an ambivalent cross-class relation. On the one hand, he is seen as a 'companion' with whom – despite his lower social order – she is engaging in the same work; remarkably, she expresses no apparent class-consciousness with regard to the physical labour. Equipped with a spud and appropriately attired with 'galoshes over her shoes, cotton gardening gloves over her mittens', Gregory engaged freely in planting and protecting the young saplings.[53] On the other hand, although she acknowledged his contribution as 'master of the business', he is perceived as a 'helper', a term that would suggest her superior position and supervisory role. It is she who has the final word as to which trees are to be cut and which are to be ordered as she indicated in her diary entries. Yet woodland management was not their only collaborative work.

In addition to looking after Coole's woods, Farrell also contributed to their mythologization. He offered up folklore to both Gregory and Yeats, being, as he was, witness to 'an unearthly sight in the woods'.[54] This vision occurred to him while cutting timber in Inchy Wood at Coole; he thus channelled both the natural and supernatural of the arboreal environment. His stories were included in Yeats and Gregory's publications, including an essay on 'The enchanted woods' and *Visions and beliefs in the west of Ireland*.[55] But despite his service to woodland management at Coole and to the literary revival through his folklore of the 'Seven woods', his name is not inscribed in the 'autograph tree'; nor is any tree planted in his memory. His name, therefore, does not cling to the arboreal landscape as do the names of others.

Gregory's deeply felt connection to that arboreal landscape is articulated in what is perhaps the most expressive passage in 'Tree planting', when she evoked a familiar bond with trees and woods in romantic terms but with clear cultural and political connotations:

> we find the little seedlings we had put down in faith are over our heads, and acting as our protectors. And even if we do not live to sit under their shade, yet none the less 'they will grow while we are sleeping' that long sleep in which we may so easily be forgotten, and we are not likely to have more lasting monuments put over us, and we cannot have more gracious ones than the living, rustling trees that we had planted and that we had loved.[56]

52 http://www.census.nationalarchives.ie/pages/1901/Galway/Kiltartan/Coole_Demesne/ 1384414/ [accessed 29 Sept. 2016]. Note that, under 'Education', the census records that John Farrell 'Cannot Read'.   **53** Anne Gregory, *Me and Nu: childhood at Coole* (Gerrards Cross, 1970), p. 93.   **54** W.B. Yeats, *The Celtic twilight* (London, 1902), p. 103.   **55** Lady Gregory, *Visions and beliefs in the west of Ireland collected and arranged by Lady Gregory: with two essays and notes by W.B. Yeats* (New York & London, 1920); Yeats, *The Celtic twilight*, pp 101–3. I wish to express my warmest thanks to John Farrell's great-great-granddaughter, Louise Stone, for drawing my attention to John's life and work.   **56** Gregory, 'Tree planting', p. 94.

9.1 Lady Gregory under the catalpa tree at Coole, 1927; courtesy Colin Smythe.

The politics of this passage can be understood via her three central metaphors: trees as 'protectors' of status and power; trees as 'lasting monuments' of tradition and family legacy, a living inheritance; and 'gracious' trees as the aesthetic value of a place. Gregory implies that it is through her continuance of the family tradition of planting and through the works and writings of the revivalists that the Gregory name will be forever linked to the woods of Coole. Thereby, Gregory's legacy is transcending the confines of the domesticated landscape of the demesne to encompass both the literary and the natural landscape, the private and the public.

Yet by the 1920s, Gregory was no longer able to afford the upkeep of house and woods. A large extent of the property was sold in early 1921, leaving 'a little demesne about 350 acres, wooded and romantic and beautiful.'[57] In 1927, house, demesne and wood were sold to the government, with the woods bringing in the highest profit.[58] Gregory at that point became merely a tenant at Coole. During the sale negotiations, she repeatedly lobbied for the Forestry Department to secure 'the maintenance and improvement of the woods' which she argued 'would give employment and be for the good and dignity of the country'.[59] She was relieved when one of the forest inspectors, 'Young Gaynor', assured her that they 'will always spare the fine or exotic trees' and delighted in the fact that 'the woods will take on a new vigour & not fade away' (the Forestry Service would, in fact, manage the land until 1987).[60] Although she was no longer directly involved in planting, her interest in the topic remained. Late in 1928, as she was reading the latest work by a principal advocate of Irish forestry, John Mackay's *Trodden gold*, Gregory wrote:

> The facts he gives about our poverty of trees in Ireland are heart-rending – to me … For myself I did my utmost, from the time I began to earn £50 or so in the year, I spent it in planting little patches, a few acres, at a time, in the poorer parts of our woods … And although I had to stop when I took over all the expenses of Coole, my plantings make a good show for their age. And I am happy, very happy, that the Forestry Department has become the owner – 'God prosper it'.[61]

A month later, she was happy to report on the progress of the foresters who 'will plant great spaces, in comparison with my few acres at a time', adding a comment that this was work she 'had been forced to abandon'.[62]

---

57 Diary entry, 14 Jan. 1921, *Lady Gregory's journals*, ed. Murphy, i, 218.   58 Diary entry, 2 Feb. 1927, *Lady Gregory's journals*, ed. Daniel J. Murphy (Gerrards' Cross, 1987), ii, 165. Gregory noted that the Forestry Department 'will only give £4000, that is, Woods £1908, Land £1600, House £500'. The Agreement was signed in November: see diary entry for 7 Nov. 1927, ibid., ii, 213.   59 Diary entry, 20 Oct. 1927, ibid., ii, 208.   60 Diary entry, 14 June 1928, ibid., 275.   61 Diary entry, 16 Nov. 1928, ibid., 339–40.   62 Diary entry, 13 Dec. 1928, ibid., 361.

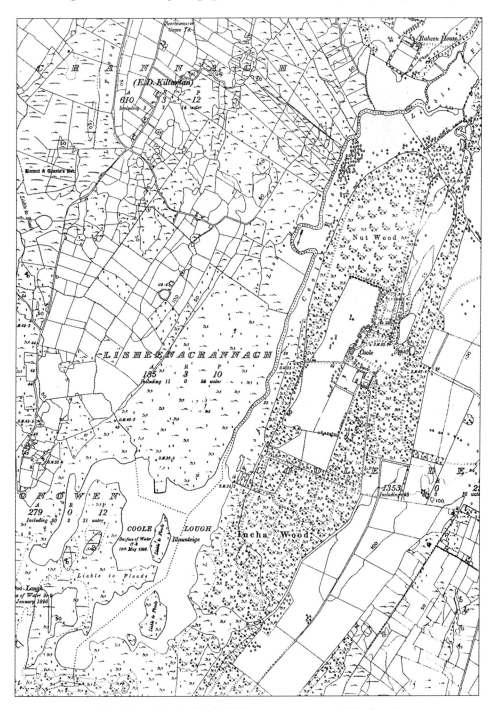

9.2 Coole's woodlands, 6-inch OSI map, 1922; courtesy Colin Smythe.

While family inheritances, collections, and houses can decay to the point of no return, the natural landscape is always full of regenerative possibilities. In the end, it was through its natural environment that Coole became part of the infrastructure of the new Irish state. When Gregory enquired whether the Forestry Department would use the house at Coole after her death, she was

> asked if someone of my family would not keep it, but I said that is very unlikely … But as a hive of industry, the woods increasing and flourishing around it, there would be no degradation, it would have the dignity of a centre of the Forestry that will hold pride as well as future profit for the countryside.[63]

What remains unmentioned, but is implied, is the continuity of a tradition that would – at least in name – be associated with the Gregorys. The thriving arboreal landscape offers an alternative to the common narrative of the decline of the country house, and at Coole the transfer to the Forestry Service was considered as 'no degradation'.

She closely observed the work done by the Forestry Department, approvingly but also with a little condescension:

> such a joy to see the work going on *en gros*, that I had done *en Detail*. They have cleared twenty acres there [in Pairc-na-Tarav] and are about to plant it, as well as Raheen strip and Pond Field, – chiefly with larch spruce, a little beech which he says helps to protect the larch. They will be regularly employing about twenty men, more while planting is going on. Such a help to the neighbourhood, as well as keeping up the tradition and increasing the welfare of the 'Seven Woods'![64]

Among Gregory's last journal entries there is also a hint of that elitism that had often surfaced in her writings and actions, that preference for aesthetics over economics: 'And glad as I am that our woods are in the hands of the Forestry Department – their quiet & beauty is being of necessity spoiled – for the sake of more profitable future – & present – planting.'[65] Yet her love of the woods was widely known and it was to the act of planting that those wishing to celebrate her life turned when seeking ways of commemorating her immediately after her death in 1932. The *Connacht Tribune* reported on her funeral procession: 'In tribute to her great love of nature, Mr Michael O'Beirne, of the Forestry Department, planted a tree outside Coole Park last evening, and local people intend to plant a number of trees in her memory'.[66] Surely, she would have been delighted had she known. Yet her remark regarding the Irish government's eye

63 Diary entry, 13 July 1930, ibid., 538.   64 Diary entry, 23 Jan. 1929, ibid., 381.   65 Diary entry, 30 Mar. 1931, ibid., 601–2.   66 'Lady Gregory's death', *Connacht Tribune*, 28 May 1932.

to a 'more profitable future' was prophetic. In the years after her death, numerous trees, among them rare pines, were cut and replaced with common conifers.[67] These would, in their turn, also be used for commercial timber. Coole house was demolished in 1941, and subsequently the focus shifted from neglect and depreciation of the built environment to a nurturing one of the natural environment. From 1987 onwards the National Parks and Wildlife Service managed the woodland Gregory had so carefully nurtured. Since 2014, commercial timber species have been removed to foster the regeneration of native species.[68]

Today's visitors continue to marvel at the autograph tree; it stands encircled with a fence to protect the bark (and, no doubt, to prevent additional inscriptions). The presence of the woods, with their associated names and stories, form a counterpart to the absence of the house. Here Gregory had inaugurated a literary landscape, and fostered and protected what is now a nature reserve. She regarded the demesne's trees and woods as a space where human intervention imbued nature with meaning, and in which gender distinctions could be negotiated and class boundaries fortified. While she was part of a tradition of landed women who actively shaped the landscape of the country house, her public contribution to the discourse of the country's re-afforestation via a piece of practical literature on silviculture was a more unusual if not to say bold endeavour for a woman. Her planting practice and conceptualization of it highlight the interplay of private and public landscapes. With the house gone, the woods remain as her 'lasting monument'.

67 Lionel Pilkington, 'Coole Park: from big house to people's park', *Irish Arts Review*, 20:3 (2003), 104.   68 http://www.coolepark.ie/history/timeline [accessed 1 Oct. 2016].

'I serve my God, and I fear not man': the Rebecca Riots and a female landowner's response to Welsh rural protest, 1843–4

LOWRI ANN REES

Among the collection of Home Office correspondence, held at the National Archives in London, is a series of letters written by a female landowner from south-west Wales. She is writing at the height of the Rebecca Riots (1839–43) following an attack upon her home, Glanmedeni, a modest late-Georgian country house in south Cardiganshire.[1] Highly detailed, forceful and often stinging in their criticisms, these letters present a unique insight into a turbulent era in Welsh history. It is all the more significant that they were written by a woman, who was determined to defend her home, and her position within society, at a time of rural unrest. While it was not very common to be a female landowner in Wales, it is notable that the 1873 return of owners of land revealed that of the 164 great landowners in Wales (defined by owning estates encompassing more than 3,000 acres, and generating rentals greater than £3,000), eleven were women.[2] Russell Davies suggests this figure would have been greater were it not for the fact that during the previous decade or so, the property rights of ten landed women had been transferred to their husbands on marriage.[3]

Perhaps one of the key literary representations of the Rebecca Riots by a woman is the novel by Amy Dillwyn (1845–1935), *The Rebecca rioter*, published in 1880. However, the author did not live through the riots; it is a work of fiction that takes inspiration from her father's involvement, in his capacity as a magistrate, in suppressing the riots.[4] Conversely, the account of the riots forwarded by Miss Jane Walters of Glanmedeni was that of an elite woman who had witnessed the unrest at first hand. This chapter will first place the Rebecca Riots in context and introduce the woman under focus. It will then analyse the

1 Lowri Ann Rees, '"The wail of Miss Jane": the Rebecca Riots and Jane Walters of Glanmedeni, 1843–44', *Ceredigion*, 15:3 (2007), 37–68. 2 Brian Ll. James, 'The great landowners of Wales in 1873', *National Library of Wales Journal*, 14:3 (Summer 1966), 301. 3 Russell Davies, *Hope and heartbreak: a social history of Wales and the Welsh, 1776–1871* (Cardiff, 2005), p. 94. 4 Handwritten account by Lewis Llewelyn Dillwyn of his encounter with Rebecca Rioters at the Pontarddulais Turnpike Gate, 10 Sept. 1843 (Richard Burton Archives (RBA), Swansea University, LAC/26/D/82); Katie Gramich, 'Introduction' in Amy Dillwyn, *The Rebecca rioter: a story of Killay life* (South Glamorgan, 2008), pp xii–xiii.

correspondence, considering landed perceptions of Welsh rural protest, the prejudices displayed, and the perceived role and obligations of the elite. In conclusion, Jane's response to attack will be considered in relation to her position as an unmarried, elite woman.

A series of largely rural disturbances that took place in south-west Wales during the late 1830s and early 1840s came to be known as the Rebecca Riots. The riots stemmed from the dire socio-economic conditions of the 1830s, when the rural economy was rocked by a number of poor harvests. During economic downturns, rental levels rose with prices, but rarely fell with them. Demands were made of landlords to reduce their rents, sometimes by as much as 20 to 30 per cent. In addition to the various rates and taxes, another burden was the payment of tolls to use the roads, administered by the Turnpike Trusts. The money collected was to be used to maintain the turnpike roads; however, the tolls were poorly administered, and there were numerous instances of extortionately high rates charged. In addition, there was very little regulation as to the number of tollgates and bars, with junctions on busy roads, near market towns and limekilns being particularly profitable places to erect gates.[5]

The Rebecca Riots form a striking chapter in the history of Wales, striking due to the method of disguise adopted by the protestors, as they carried out their nocturnal attacks wearing women's clothing. The feminine imagery was further reinforced by the female figure of Rebecca, who led her 'daughters' in their attacks. Feminine disguise was effective as a mask, but also as a means of disarming the response of the authorities. The punishment on being caught rioting was harsh, and of the number of rioters captured, some were imprisoned, while others were sentenced to transportation to the penal colonies in Van Diemen's Land.[6] There are several examples of protestors adopting feminine attire in other eighteenth- and nineteenth-century protests, suggesting the methods of Rebecca and her daughters were not distinctive or singular.[7] Through these rituals of protest, a confounding of gender stereotypes took place, exhibiting complicated forms of transgression.[8] It is probable that the name of the movement stems from a literal interpretation of Genesis 24:60: 'And they blessed Rebecca, and said unto her, "Thou art our sister; be thou the mother of thousands of millions, and let thy seed possess the gates of those which hate them"'. Those who partook in the riots were largely farmers, labourers and farm servants, and predominantly young men in their teens and early twenties.[9]

5 For more on the Rebecca Riots, see Rhian E. Jones, *Petticoat heroes: gender, culture and popular protest in the Rebecca Riots* (Cardiff, 2015); David J.V. Jones, *Rebecca's children: a study of rural society, crime and protest* (Cardiff, 1989); David W. Howell, 'The Rebecca Riots' in Trevor Herbert and Gareth Elwyn Jones (eds), *People and protest: Wales, 1815–1880* (Cardiff, 1988); David Williams, *The Rebecca riots: a study in agrarian discontent* (Cardiff, 1955). **6** Known as Tasmania from 1856. **7** For examples and discussion of cross-dressing as part of social protest, see Natalie Zemon Davis, *Society and culture in early modern France: eight essays* (London, 1965). **8** For analysis of cross-dressing and the influence of community ritual and festival on the Rebecca riots, see Jones, *Petticoat heroes*, pp 59–80. **9** Jones,

The first recorded appearance of a Rebecca attack was on 13 May 1839 at Efail Wen, on the border between Carmarthenshire and Pembrokeshire. Under cover of night, a band of men, disguised in women's clothing, descended on the new tollgate that had been erected there, and swiftly demolished it. The riots were, however, at their height during 1843, when the rural economy was under particular strain. While the tollgates were the principal target of the riots, during the summer of 1843 attacks on private property intensified. Indeed, nearly half of the 530 attacks carried out in Rebecca's name between 1839 and 1843 were unrelated to the tollgates.[10] During this time, the property of the landed interest became a target for the rioters. Such attacks proved a challenge to the paternalistic authority of the elite. There was a real fear that the unrest and violence could escalate, therefore the propertied class called for the authorities to act swiftly and sharply to quash the riots.[11] Some chose to flee, becoming absentee landlords. However, others chose to resist, taking measures to bring those who had dared challenge or intimidate them to justice – Jane was one such example.

Jane Walters was born on 22 October 1792, the youngest of the three surviving children of a prosperous farming family.[12] The Walters family had farmed Perthcereint in Cardiganshire over several generations, and watched it flourish and grow into a profitable enterprise. They were socially ambitious, and with their newly acquired fortunes were able to provide for their children. Both Jane and her elder sister, Frances, were well-educated, Jane having spent three years at a Miss Swift's boarding school in Worcester. From there, Jane returned home to Perthcereint where she settled into a comfortable, county elite lifestyle. Along with her mother and sister, she undertook the usual social round of visits, dinners and parties. They spent summers at the Welsh seaside resort of Aberystwyth and the spa towns of Llanwrtyd and Llandrindod Wells, where they socialized with the local gentry and people of fashion. Jane and Frances had therefore enjoyed a comfortable upbringing. Later in 1836, the sisters and their widowed father moved to their newly built home of Glanmedeni. Five years later, Abel Walters passed away on 2 April 1841, leaving his two unmarried daughters as custodians of Glanmedeni.[13] Their father had made provisions for them in his will, bequeathing £1000 to each daughter, along with his personal estate.[14]

Rebecca's children, pp 242–3.   **10** David J.V. Jones, 'Rebecca, crime and policing: a turning-point in nineteenth-century attitudes', *Transactions of the Honourable Society of Cymmrodorion* (1990), 104.   **11** For more on attacks on the property of the landed elite, see Lowri Ann Rees, 'Paternalism and rural protest: the Rebecca riots and the landed interest of south-west Wales', *Agricultural History Review*, 59:1 (2011), 36–60.   **12** A daughter and a son, Jane and Thomas, who had died in infancy, were followed by Frances (1786–1851), John (1788–1865), and Jane (1792–1881).   **13** Background on the Walters family from Francis Jones, 'Walters of Perthcereint', *Ceredigion*, 6:2 (1969), 171–5.   **14** Abel Walters Esq, Glanmedenii [*sic*], Betws Ifan, Cardigan, 1841 (National Library of Wales (NLW) St David's Probate Records, 1556–1858 9933041602419) (http://hdl.handle.net/10107/520371, accessed 19 May 2017).

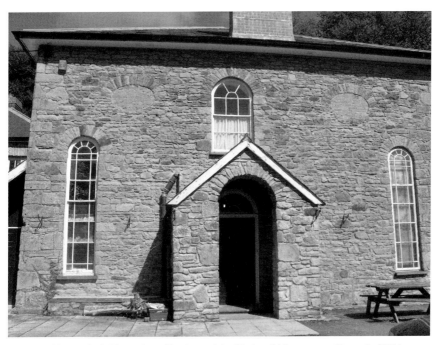

10.1 Glanmedeni. From the collections of the National Monuments Record of Wales
© Michael Tree/O'r casgliadau o Gofnod Henebion Cenedlaethol Cymru
© Hawlfraint: Michael Tree.

Jane was clearly a strong personality. Deeply religious, her personal letters display a strong Christian conviction. She was also cultured, writing poetry and competing in literary contests at Eisteddfodau.[15] An avid correspondent, letter-writing had been important to her from a young age. One of her regular correspondents was her maternal grandfather, who imparted guidance and advice on spelling, grammar and handwriting. The improvement of her handwriting was not his sole concern however, as he wrote to Jane that 'this is the time of life for you to improve yourself in that as well as in all other things'.[16] The importance Jane placed on correspondence in adulthood may well be explained by the advice she received from her grandfather as a 13-year-old:

> You ought to keep every letter you received from every body you correspond with, and keep a copy of all yours, that will make count in all your correspondence and know what you had said and done.[17]

---

15 An Eisteddfod is a Welsh festival of poetry, literary and musical competitions.   **16** Thomas Phillips to Jane Walters, 14 Jan. 1807 (Carmarthenshire Record Office (CRO) Aberglasney 4: 24/565).   **17** Thomas Phillips to Jane Walters, 22 July 1806 (CRO Aberglasney 4: 24/565).

It is curious to note that the elder sister, Frances, is less visible in the events that followed. It is clear that Jane took it upon herself to represent both sisters, as shall become evident.

Two separate incidents involving the Walters sisters and their family might have attracted the attention of Rebecca and her daughters. The first incident had occurred around 1838, when the two sisters had crossed paths with a group of youths leaving the celebrations following a wedding near the town of Cardigan. One of the young men was urged by his companions to rush forward and kiss one of the sisters. Driven by the promise of a reward of half a crown, the young man, named 'Davy' in the press report of the incident, 'ran up to one of them, threw his arms round her neck and attempted the tender infliction'. Jane was the unsuspecting target of the kiss, which was 'most resolutely resisted'. It was noted in the piece that while the young man won his half crown, he was later fined £1. The report concluded that the subsequent attack upon Glanmedeni by Rebecca's daughters was driven by the desire to seek compensation for an unfair punishment of youthful folly.[18]

The second occurrence was of a more long-standing nature. In early September 1843, a letter addressed to Jane arrived at Glanmedeni. It was signed 'Rebecca'. Jane was accused of neglecting to pay a portion of the wages of a former servant, Dina Davies of Rhydypentre. The sum of £1 had remained unpaid for twenty years. Rebecca demanded she pay the debt and the interest accrued over the previous twenty years. The letter ended with the threat that payment of the debt 'will save me and my daughters the trouble of recovering the same'.[19] Even though Jane was the younger sister, it was she who received the letter demanding payment. This suggests her role as acknowledged mistress of Glanmedeni, the letter writer having identified her as the head of the household. The sending of anonymous threatening letters, signed 'Rebecca', was a tactic employed by the rioters to relate grievances and, crucially, to intimidate. Threatening letters were used to unsettle the recipient, with little danger of the sender being identified. Landlords received letters demanding they lower their rents, or reimburse tenants who had paid too much rent. There were also instances of letters demanding the redress of a perceived moral wrongdoing or injustice, as in this example.

In addition to the threatening letter to Frances, Jane also received two anonymous poems. One was entitled 'The wail of Miss Jane', the other was an ode sung to the air of 'Old English gentlemen'. Both have been censored, presumably by Jane herself, with lines heavily marked out in ink or the edges of the paper torn away. They are derogatory in nature, and in addition to containing unflattering personal comments, portray the Walters family as snobbish and gaudy *nouveau riche* upstarts.[20]

---

18 *The Welshman*, 15 Sept. 1843.   19 'Rebecca' to Jane Walters, 1 Sept. 1843 CRO Aberglasney: 4 24/570a).   20 Two anonymous notes to Jane Walters, 'There was a fine old

The threatening letter of 1 September that arrived at Glanmedeni was followed by a visit on Monday 4 September from, as Jane described in her first letter to the Home Office, a 'party of Rebeccaites' and a 'multitude of masked female attired nightly assailants'. They descended on Glanmedeni, capturing three of the male servants. Meanwhile Jane, Frances and a female servant swiftly retreated upstairs. With the crowd gathered outside, taunting and jeering, Jane addressed them from an upstairs window. She spoke in Welsh, asking why she and her sister had been targeted in this way. When ordered to hand over money, Jane declared there was none in the house, the sisters having not received their rents, and not wanting to pressurise their tenants to pay during an economically difficult time. Her response angered the crowd, and a reply was heard: 'a house such as this cannot be empty of money you are not to disceive [*sic*]'. They reminded Jane that they had written to her, ordering the reimbursement of the former servant, Dina Davies. Jane acknowledged that the sisters had indeed received a letter, but one which ordered them to send their men servants and labourers to join the Rebeccaites in demolishing a local tollgate. Seeing they would not receive payment that evening, a deadline was imposed: 'provide by next Friday at your peril the money', to which Jane defiantly declared, 'I serve my God, and I fear not man.' Three shots were subsequently fired and a window broken.[21] Jane, rather worryingly, had also heard a cry of 'Fire! Fire!' from the crowd.[22] Rebecca and her daughters had on a number of occasions during the summer of 1843 resorted to incendiary attacks. However, in this instance, Glanmedeni was spared the torch. Instead, the crowd moved away from the house and turned their attention to the surrounding gardens. In protest they cut down eighteen trees.[23] As it would take several years and additional finances to replant and cultivate these trees, damaging plantations was, in the words of Carl J. Griffin, 'an important tool of rural terror'.[24] The rioters also broke a rustic seat and threatened to tear down the lodge with the inhabitant within. The rioters had a message for the lodge keeper to pass on to the Walters sisters: they had until the following Monday night at the very latest to pay, and non-payment would result in Rebecca and her daughters razing Glandmedeni House to the ground.[25] Such threats to the property of the landed interest elicited real fear, and several landlords in south-west Wales lost agricultural produce and received menacing visitations from bands of protestors. After the crowd who had surrounded Glandmedeni had disappeared, a length of rope with a noose tied at the end was

Welshwoman' and 'The wail of Miss Jane ...', no date (CRO, Aberglasney 4:24/570a). 21 Jane Walters to the Home Office, 5 Sept. 1843 (The National Archives (TNA), Home Office Letters and Papers (HO) 45/454).   22 Jane Walters to the Home Office, 13 Oct. 1843 (TNA, HO 45/454).   23 Jane Walters to the Home Office, 5 Sept. 1843 (TNA, HO 45/454). 24 Carl J. Griffin, '"Cut down by some cowardly miscreants": plant maiming, or the malicious cutting of flora, as an act of protest in eighteenth- and nineteenth-century rural England', *Rural History*, 19 (2008), 45.   25 Jane Walters to the Home Office, 5 Sept. 1843 (TNA, HO 45/454).

discovered to have been left behind, a crude and sinister warning to the Walters sisters of the potential consequences of non-payment of the debt.[26]

Following the attack, and an unsurprisingly sleepless night, the following morning Jane wrote to the Home Office, describing 'this unprovoked assault on private property'.[27] What followed were a series of detailed letters, revealing Jane's perceptions of the riots, her opinion of the rioters, the way the movement was organized, and suggestions on how it could be suppressed. Jane firmly believed that only martial law would quell the violent disturbances. She predicted that if they were not stopped within six weeks the rioters would be out of control.[28] While she praised the efforts of the Royal Marines stationed in the area, she feared the rioters were eluding the authorities via a system of 'secret communications'.[29]

The response from the Home Office to her first letter, outlining the attack on Glanmedeni, was favourable. The home secretary, Sir James Graham (1792–1861), was prepared to offer an award and look into the possibility of granting a pardon from the Queen to any accomplices who came forward with information.[30] Coincidentally, a month later, in October, due to the Queen's growing concern for the state of the country, a royal proclamation was declared promising the granting of substantial rewards for information on violent attacks and instances of arson.[31] The Home Office had also been in contact with the lord lieutenant of Cardiganshire, Colonel William Edward Powell (1788–1854) of Nanteos, informing him of the attack upon Glanmedeni, as relayed in Jane's letter, and the offer of a reward.[32]

Jane wrote how, with their health in a fragile state, the sisters decided to gather their valuables and leave Glanmedeni, staying for a short while at a friend's house before taking up lease of a house at the nearby town of Newcastle Emlyn, some three miles from Glanmedeni. They vowed to stay away, and only return once the district had become safer. Jane lamented leaving Glanmedeni, and felt that she had been driven away from the land her forefathers had farmed. However, the sisters had by no means abandoned the house. Jane and Frances proposed to visit as often as they could, and were employing men to guard the property around the clock, sleeping there at night in case they needed to defend the house from further attack.[33] A week after the attack of 4 September, Jane wrote to the Home Office, having learnt of a sighting of 'a large company of them [rioters] assembled'. A scene of violence ensued, with 'dozens flying over the hedges'. The crowd however disappeared shortly before the troops arrived. Jane

---

26 Jane Walters to the Home Office, 13 Oct. 1843 (TNA, HO 45/454).   **27** Jane Walters to the Home Office, 5 Sept. 1843 (TNA, HO 45/454).   **28** Ibid.   **29** Jane Walters to the Home Office, 20 Sept. 1843 (TNA, HO 45/454).   **30** Secretary of state's office to Jane Walters, 11 Sept. 1843 (CRO, Aberglasney, 4:24/570a).   **31** Jones, *Rebecca's children*, p. 258.   **32** W.E. Powell to Jane Walters, 18 Sept. 1843 (CRO, Aberglasney, 4:24/570a). Colonel W.E. Powell was also the member of parliament for the county from 1816 until his death in 1854.   **33** Jane Walters to the Home Office, 20 Sept. 1843 (TNA, HO 45/454).

commented how the district had since been relatively quiet, but suspected the rioters were planning 'future mischief'. However, there had been threats to set alight nine farm houses in the locality following their occupants refusing to join Rebecca.[34] Jane wrote of other homes being targeted, the rioters similarly demanding money from their inhabitants, concluding that 'In short the threatening letters which they receive reminds them that their lives, their families and their property is in danger every moment'.[35]

In describing the rioters, Jane was very particular in her assessment of their identity. She did not believe they were farmers, reckoning them instead to be the rural working classes and 'idle persons who live on killing game'. Of these people, she claimed there were plenty in the Newcastle Emlyn area.[36] She later described them as ranging in age from 12 to 25 years, being farmers' sons, servants and labourers. Jane judged them to be discontent, driven by the belief they had suffered at the hands of the landlords and their masters. She identified the dissatisfaction with the elite, but apart from a later reference to the tithes, did not offer a possible explanation as to why the rural populace might feel such resentment. She believed the rioters met at markets, fairs, meeting houses, and what she perceived as most dangerous of all, night meetings, in order 'to plot, plan redress'.[37] On the threats of the latter, Jane remarked: 'until the night meetings are stopped nothing can be done'.[38] She believed the rioters had scouts hiding in the hedges, watching the movements of the authorities and relaying messages. When the military were called to the scene of an attack, Jane lamented how they were always ten minutes too late. She also wrote of local 'boys' who kept watch over gentry houses, observing messengers coming and going.[39]

Sharing a commonly held belief, Jane was convinced the rioters were being led by persuasive leaders, who were alert to local grievances and discontent, and inflamed the rioters 'to madness'.[40] Jane even went as far as suggesting these figures were being paid by an unidentified individual to write the threatening letters signed 'Rebecca'. She believed these leaders listened to the grievances of the people and 'in general prejudice them against *the very characters* in the neighbourhood which are the most probable *to hold the link of social connection in the community* by useful charitable and exemplary example in their circle of influence'.[41] It is clear that Jane believed the rioters were intentionally targeting the elite. As her letters suggest, she could not understand the reason for attacking the people responsible for maintaining the social equilibrium through

34 Ibid.   35 Jane Walters to the Home Office, 20 Sept. 1843 (TNA, HO 45/454).   36 Jane Walters to the Home Office, 5 Sept. 1843 (TNA, HO 45/454).   37 Jane Walters to the Home Office, undated, received 4 Oct. 1843 (TNA, HO 45/454).   38 Jane Walters to the Home Office, undated, received 2 Oct. 1843 (TNA, HO 45/454).   39 Jane Walters to the Home Office, undated, received 4 Oct. 1843 (TNA, HO 45/454).   40 Ibid.; Jones, *Rebecca's children*, pp 244–8. Several of the landed interest did not believe that the Welsh were capable of organizing such an uprising, believing they were being influenced by outsiders from beyond the local community, such as incoming Englishmen.   41 Ibid. Emphasis in original.

the mechanisms of paternalism and philanthropy. She believed these outside influences were manipulating the local men, telling them that if they eradicated the authority of the landed class and magistrates, they would find themselves paying next to no rent and no longer expected to pay tithes. Jane clearly saw the rioters as susceptible and easily influenced, lured by wild and unrealistic promises. She did not place much faith in their ability to think for themselves, rather they were led on by the outside elements she mentioned. This becomes apparent as she describes the rioters as 'poor deluded creatures'.[42]

In addition to describing the rioters as gullible followers, Jane cast an equally critical eye towards those charged with upholding law and order locally – the magistrates. Ironically, this was an opinion she shared with the rioters, the corruption of magistrates being one of their grievances. While she believed the threat of punishment at the hands of magistrates did help in deterring further attacks, she also believed they had largely failed to respond to the riots.[43] The high sheriff of Cardiganshire, the solicitor and heir to more than 1000 acres, Edward Crompton Lloyd Hall, believed 'that the further you go westward in this district the more incompetent the magistrates appear to be'.[44] Lloyd Hall was another avid writer to the Home Office during the riots. As David J.V. Jones states, his letters provided the government with an insight into the state of rural communities, and the problems that plagued them. Lloyd Hall was critical of Rebecca, seeing the riots as symptomatic of the discontent in rural communities. He was also a strong believer in the role and position of the landed interest.[45] Jane believed that by releasing apprehended suspects shortly after their capture, magistrates were conveying the wrong messages. There was little threat of punishment, which she feared could lead to more people joining the movement, resulting in Rebecca and her daughters becoming more powerful.[46] Jane felt there had been too many cases of magistrates abusing their powers in the locality. The example she cited was of a farming family struggling to pay the tithe, suffering the confiscation of the family Bible, a precious household item. She therefore felt that she had to speak out against the negligent approach the magistrates took to their duties. She believed that only through appointing stipendiary magistrates, who were supported by a strong military force, would the unrest be quashed.[47] She had long believed that 'the trials by jury have for years in this country been corrupt'. Listing a sample of such offences that had occurred in the locality, she promised there were many more, asking 'but where has the evil began?'[48] She did not, however, attempt to answer this question, and there is no real sense that she had considered the root causes of the disturbances beyond the burden of the tithes. The number of tollgates and bars in the area

42 Ibid.   43 Ibid.   44 Edward Crompton Lloyd Hall to Sir James Graham, 8 Sept. 1843 (TNA, HO 45/454).   45 Jones, *Rebecca's children*, pp 45, 77.   46 Jane Walters to the Home Office, undated, received 2 Oct. 1843 (TNA, HO 45/454).   47 Jane Walters to the Home Office, 20 Sept. 1843 (TNA, HO 45/454).   48 Jane Walters to the Home Office, undated,

were not as dense as other parts of south-west Wales, and it was her belief that the tithes were the principal cause of unease in the area.[49]

The issue of high rental levels does not appear in Jane's letters. She placed the blame firmly on the negligent execution of authority, in particular when it came to severe cases of law breaking. She claimed there were clear examples of personal interest clouding the judgement of the magistrates, citing cases relating to the game laws and Turnpike Trusts. It is worth noting that the systems of government and administration in Wales during the nineteenth century had not developed to accommodate a growing population and evolving social structure. Therefore, Jane's criticisms of the magisterial system hold some significance.[50]

Nonetheless, there may have been a more personal interest driving Jane's criticisms. The Walters sisters had fallen foul of local magistrates themselves when they built a private road to allow access to Glanmedeni. Men were dispatched by the magistrates to Glanmedeni under cover of night to pull down the fences the sisters had erected in a somewhat similar invasion of their private space by Rebecca and her daughters. The sisters were aware that they would have to suffer a long drawn out and expensive law suit in order to defend their right to maintain the road as a private right of way. At the time, their father was ill, and his death in 1841 left them alone, the only inhabitants of Glanmedeni house.[51] Perhaps this incident coloured Jane's opinion of the role of the magistrate, encouraging her to be more vocal in her condemnation of lax or corrupt magistrates.

Meanwhile, it had been hoped that the offer of a reward would entice informants to come forward following the attack on Glanmedeni, but there was a real fear that informers could be punished for betraying Rebecca, Jane suspecting they would be murdered before giving evidence. One of the men in the sisters' employment had confided in Jane: 'I had need have one leg on board ship and the other rising off the land before I could venture to say any thing even if I knew at present'.[52] By the end of September, on behalf of the sisters, Jane had drafted a notice in both English and Welsh. They were to offer a £50 reward (which the government would also match) for information leading to the apprehension of those involved in the attack. Jane was determined that the culprits should be brought to justice. Accomplices who came forward with information would be offered a pardon and a reward on the conviction of the main culprits.[53] By 13 October, the sum had increased, and there were up to five rewards of £100 for the apprehension of the guilty parties and ringleaders of the attack. Jane was convinced that if the notices were printed in Whitehall, rather

received 4 Oct. 1843 (TNA, HO 45/454). **49** Jane Walters to the Home Office, 13 Oct. 1843 (TNA, HO 45/454). **50** Williams, *The Rebecca riots*, p. viii. **51** Jane Walters to the Home Office, undated, received 4 Oct. 1843 (TNA, HO 45/454). **52** Jane Walters to the Home Office, 20 Sept. 1843 (TNA, HO 45/454). **53** Jane Walters to the Home Office, undated, received 2 Oct. 1843 (TNA, HO 45/454); Home Office to Jane Walters, 2 Oct. 1843 (CRO,

than in Wales, they would hold more weight, and strike greater fear in the hearts of the rioters. They would, she also hoped, provide a powerful deterrent to any future unrest.[54]

After her letter of 13 October to the Home Office, there was no further correspondence until the following March. While instances of unrest were few and far between by then, the disturbances having died down during the winter months of 1843–4, Jane felt that the threat from Rebecca had not subsided, and outlined her fears in a letter: 'To enter into fact will require a volume not a letter, but a sense of duty impels me under experience of the past, and a *clear view of the future*: to say that this country *is not in a state of safety*.'[55] In this letter Jane was writing to then prime minister, Sir Robert Peel, and to the master-general of the Ordnance, Sir George Murray, to offer three acres of land for the building of a barracks to accommodate a large number of soldiers, ready to deal with any outbreak of unrest or rioting.[56] The sisters must have felt in need of further protection. In the same letter she praised the efforts of the lord lieutenant of Carmarthenshire, George Rice Trevor (1795–1869), for his part in quelling the riots. Colonel Trevor was single-minded in his response to the riots. He rallied the troops of the 4th Light Dragoons and 73rd Infantry Regiment, and assured magistrates in Newcastle Emlyn during the summer of 1843 that he had no reservations in ordering the troops to turn their guns on the rioters.[57] Without Colonel Trevor's input, Jane pondered, what would have been the fate of the gentlemen of Cardiganshire, Carmarthenshire and Pembrokeshire, the three counties of south-west Wales affected by the riots. However, despite her glowing appraisal of leading figures in the vicinity, she maintained her belief that there was no justice for the victims of the attacks waged in Cardiganshire.[58] Whether she counted herself among the former group is unclear. Her use of the word 'gentlemen' suggests not, but she certainly saw herself as a member of the latter. This last correspondence was particularly significant as it was the first and only time that she wrote directly to the prime minister. Prior to March 1844, she had been addressing the home secretary. Here was an untitled lady, unmarried, and therefore not connected into other elite families, who was very much at the fringes of the gentry, situated in what would have been perceived by the recipient of her letters as remote, rural west Wales. Nonetheless, she was able, out of the blue, to address the head of the British government. She clearly had confidence in her ability to write and put forward her case. While this might demonstrate a

Aberglasney, 4:24/570a).   **54** Jane Walters to the Home Office, 13 Oct. 1843 (TNA, HO 45/454).   **55** Jane Walters to the Home Office, 23 Mar. 1844 (TNA, HO 45/454). Emphasis in original.   **56** Home Office to Jane Walters, 11 Mar. 1844 (CRO Aberglasney 4:24/570a); Jane Walters to the Home Office, 23 Mar. 1844 (TNA, HO 45/454).   **57** Matthew Cragoe, 'Trevor, George Rice Rice-, fourth Baron Dynevor (1795–1869)', *Oxford dictionary of national biography* (Oxford, 2004), www.oxforddnb.com/view/article/46662, accessed 19 May 2017. **58** Jane Walters to the Home Office, 23 Mar. 1844 (TNA, HO 45/454).

strong personality, it might also signify that she felt she had no other recourse, being unmarried and holding little faith in the power of the local magistracy.

To all intents and purposes, Jane appeared the very model of an elite woman, a veritable Lady Bountiful.[59] She was also supportive of the Welsh language and the nation's culture, and her Christian zeal saw her raise money for missionary societies. She wrote to the Home Office with descriptions of charitable work undertaken, which included donating coal to her tenants and the poor of the area, adding: 'I mention these things not from egotism but to enable you to form some idea of the country amidst all this.'[60] What is apparent is her confusion as to why a charitable and benevolent woman had fallen victim of redress at the hands of the rioters. She believed that she had been living her life according to paternalistic ideals, therefore why was she being punished? Perhaps she was seen as an easy target because she was a woman? Crucially, many a Lady Bountiful was deferential towards their father or husband, the landlord. As independent women, and property and land owners in their own right, Jane and Frances were neither. One possible answer, which Jane herself suggests, is that the unexpected attack waged by the rioters of 4 September 1843 was driven by financial motives, concluding that 'the object was to get money'.[61] Jane was inclined to think that these sums of money taken by Rebecca and her daughters were to buy guns and other weapons utilized in attacks.[62]

Jane believed that because she and her sister spoke Welsh, they understood the state of the country and grievances of the people better than the magistrates, some of whom faced communication barriers by not being able to speak the language. It is telling that the notice Jane and Frances issued was first written in Welsh, and then translated as closely as possible into English. This shows how anxious they were to appeal to the local people for information. Jane herself believed that the Welsh notice read much better than the English, and had taken the step to request a clergyman read through it to check for any mistakes.[63]

Having remained at Newcastle Emlyn since September 1843, Jane finally returned to Glanmedeni in 1851, after her sister passed away on 21 July of that year, having left her everything. Jane never married, and remained as head of the household until her death on 7 February 1881 at the age of 88. She left Glanmedeni house and a number of farms and cottages in the surrounding parishes, the annual rental amounting to £309 10s. 0d. Her belongings, money, investments and stocks came to £2529 18s. 7d. These were bequeathed to her niece, Elizabeth Frances Lloyd-Philipps, the youngest daughter and only surviving child of her late brother, John Walters Philipps. Her remains were laid

---

59 Defined by the *Oxford English dictionary* as 'a woman who engages in ostentatious acts of charity to impress others'; Jessica Gerard, 'Lady Bountiful: women and the landed classes and rural philanthropy', *Victorian Studies*, 30:2 (Winter 1987), 183–210.   **60** Jane Walters to the Home Office, undated, received 4 Oct. 1843 (TNA, HO 45/454).   **61** Ibid.   **62** Ibid. **63** Jane Walters to the Home Office, 13 Oct. 1843 (TNA HO 45/454).

10.2 The Methodist Watch Tower chapel built near Glanmedeni © Crown copyright: Royal Commission on the Ancient and Historical Monuments of Wales / © Hawlfraint y Goron: Comisiwn Brenhinol Henebion Cymru.

to rest in the grounds of the Methodist Watch Tower chapel she had erected on her land.[64] A sense of the grandeur of Glanmedeni and its contents is given in an advertisement for its sale in *The Welshman* newspaper in 1895, which outlines the sale of 'all of the valuable Household Furniture and other effects, comprising very handsome drawing and dining-room suites; the contents of several bedrooms, entrance hall, kitchen and pantry, and dairy utensils; carriages, pony trap, and harness; garden tools etc'.[65]

How characteristic of an elite woman was Jane's response to the Rebecca attack on her home? She chose to write directly to the Home Office, and did not use an intermediary such as a local magistrate (which, given her general opinion of them, would have been unlikely) or even the lord lieutenant of the county. Instead, she took it upon herself to address the home secretary, and even wrote directly to the prime minister, to report the attacks upon her property and request assistance. However, these were not begging letters. Jane was far from a helpless victim. Although feeling beleaguered and let down, there is no sense of feminine passivity in her letters. Perhaps her unmarried status informed this

64 Jones, 'Walters of Perthcereint', 190–1.   65 *The Welshman*, 28 June 1895.

more active stance, having to act on behalf of her sister and herself in the absence of a patriarchal figure. The tone is very determined as she put forward her case, offering solutions, advancing money for rewards and even proposing a donation of land to establish barracks in the vicinity. She held strong opinions, and was not afraid to share them, in particular her condemnation of the system of local law and order. Her perceptions of the rioters reveal the prejudices of her class. There is a strong sense of disbelief at the audacity of the rioters targeting an upstanding and benevolent member of the community, and was firmly of the belief that she was doing all in her power to live according to paternalistic ideals. She was also keen to emphasize the impact of the attack upon her home: 'As a deep sufferer in every point of view from the shock which I had to sustain *on the night of the 4th of September last* in the attack made by the Rebeccaites on my *Life* and *Property* never having since *slept* in the County of Cardigan'.[66] Indeed, following the riots the government gave attention to strengthening of law and order in south-west Wales to prevent any further unrest.[67]

By the time Jane wrote her last letter to the Home Office in March 1844, there were very few instances of unrest. In the aftermath of the riots a report was published by a commission sent to south Wales to investigate the operation of the Turnpike Trusts. The report was published on 6 March 1844, recommending the consolidation of the various trusts. The subsequent South Wales Turnpike Trust Amendment Bill (1844) resulted in a uniform system of tolls, regulated by the County and District Roads Boards.[68] It is interesting to note that the report was published two weeks before her letter to the Home Office on 23 March. She may very well have read, or discussed the content of the report, and seen that it might offer a solution to the grievances concerning the tolls.

Jane's letters provide an insight into her views and opinions, as someone who felt they had suffered at the hands of the rioters. She wrote of the shocking nature of the attack, and how 'shaken' she and her sister were. They had lost confidence in their fellow countrymen, and felt that they had been driven away from living among them.[69] The letters also convey the perceptions of a member of the landed class of the riots. Her disbelief at being targeted, after all her philanthropic deeds, is apparent. While displaying much of the prejudices of her class, beyond identifying the tithes as a possible grievance, there is little attempt at understanding what was compelling the rioters to act. Nonetheless, this particular case study is quite unique. Here is the voice of a woman caught up in the riots. Perhaps it can be seen as rather ironic that a protest movement symbolized by a female figure chose to target another woman. However, in the battle between the real and the symbolic woman, Jane was not willing to yield to Rebecca.

66 Newcastle Emlyn, where Jane and Frances had resided since the attack on Glanmedeni on 4 September 1844, was just over the county border in Carmarthenshire. Jane Walters to the Home Office, 23 Mar. 1844 (TNA, HO 45/454). Emphasis in original. **67** Jones, *Rebecca's children*, p. 347. **68** Ibid. **69** Jane Walters to the Home Office, 23 Mar. 1844 (TNA, HO 45/454).

The country house and the Great Famine: Mildred Darby's novel, *The hunger*

CIARÁN REILLY

On the night of 30 July 1922, a party of anti-treaty IRA, numbering between twenty to thirty men, burned Leap Castle, the home of the Darby family, located near Parsonstown, King's County (now Birr, Co. Offaly), in the Irish midlands. The following day, as the local community scavenged through the castle, it was clear that only a portion had been burned and that half the castle remained intact. Realizing that they had not succeeded, the IRA returned later that night and once more set fire to Leap. While a number of reasons were suggested as to why Leap had fallen victim to the house-burning mania that swept the country (it was one of eighteen houses in Offaly burnt during the revolutionary years, 1920–3), the fervent unionism of its owner, Jonathon Darby, was seen as the most obvious.[1] In the months that followed, Offaly County Council received a claim for compensation of £40,000. This claim included the loss of many fine paintings, furniture, jewellery and other family heirlooms. However, perhaps of most sentimental value were the numerous manuscripts, novels and short stories written by Mildred Darby (1867–1932), and among them one which had been recently sold to the American film company, Metro-Goldwyn for £2000.[2]

Born in Brighton, England, in 1867, Mildred Darby was the daughter of Richard, a medical doctor, and Augusta Caroline Dill, daughter of Sir Charles Wale, a lieutenant general in the British army and sometime governor of Martinique. In 1889 Mildred Dill married Jonathon Darby, owner of a 4000 acre estate in King's County.[3] Today she is best remembered for her writings on what she called the 'elemental' or the 'thing', a reference to the apparitions and hauntings which she witnessed during her years at Leap Castle.[4] A prolific writer, using the pseudonym Andrew Merry, her novels included *An April fool* (1898), *The green country* (1902) and *Anthropoid apes* (1908).[5] However, it was the novel,

---

1 *Midland Tribune*, 5 Aug. 1922. See also Mildred H. Darby to Mr Carroll, 7 Aug. 1922 (NLI, Darby papers, MS 17,877).   2 Donald Harman Akenson, *Discovering the end of time: Irish evangelicals in the age of Daniel O'Connell* (Montreal, 2016), p. 98.   3 For details of the marriage see *King's County Chronicle*, 14 Nov. 1889.   4 Andrew Tierncy, 'The Gothic and the Gaelic: exploring the place of castles in Ireland's Celtic revival', *International Journal of Historical Archaeology*, 8:3 (Sept. 2004), 185–98.   5 Her pseudonym, Andrew Merry, was likely to have been taken from the term a 'Merry Andrew', which is a person who entertains others by means of comedy, effectively a clown. To what extent Darby took herself seriously remains uncertain.

11.1 Mildred's husband, Jonathon C. Darby, courtesy of Offaly Historical Society.

The hunger: being realties of the famine years in Ireland, 1845 to 1848, which proved most successful.[6] Although the book was first published in 1910, many of the chapters had appeared as early as September 1908 in the *Weekly Freeman* and were described as 'a must for every Irish home'.[7] The subsequent publication of the book in 1910 was greeted with critical acclaim. A reviewer in the *Irish*

---

6 I am grateful to Christopher Cusack for his comments on this chapter.   **7** *Freeman's Journal*, 2 Sept. 1908.

Independent believed that her account gave 'food for poignant thought',[8] while the *Freeman's Journal* was even more complimentary stating that it was

> the most impressive work on the subject that we have read to this one, although it is in the form of fiction based on first-hand knowledge, gleaned from the survivors of the catastrophe ... many people have written about the terrible Irish famine, but we question if anyone has given such a memorable picture of it.[9]

Likewise, the *Irish Book Lover* believed that it was 'faithfully and graphically sketched by a practiced pen' and that it was 'a book that will live'.[10]

However, although she had successfully published a number of books using the pseudonym, 'Andrew Merry', Mildred's identity was revealed shortly after the publication of *The hunger*. Indeed, at least two publications – the *Irish Book Lover* and the *Review of Reviews* – referred to her as the 'gifted and public-spirited English lady who married into an Irish family'.[11] Following the publication of the book Jonathon Darby forbade his wife from writing again, an indication of the control he exerted (or attempted to exert) in the marriage.[12] It was, according to Tierney, something which left her 'perplexed and, no doubt, frustrated'.[13] The early years of the twentieth century witnessed a decline in marital happiness between husband and wife, made all the more difficult by their difference of opinion in relation to the 'haunting' or the 'elemental' at Leap.[14] In 1897, during renovations at the castle, a huge haul of bones was discovered by workmen, believed to have dated to the sixteenth century.[15] This incident is regularly cited as the reason why Mildred became interested in supernatural doings at Leap, although ghostly apparitions had been recorded as early as 1851.[16] The bones were said to reflect the savagery of the O'Carrolls, the Gaelic Irish clan who formerly occupied the castle. Perhaps as husband and wife bickered over the supernatural doings at Leap, *The hunger* provided the means of reminding Jonathon, and the class he belonged to, that there were more recent ghosts that they could not escape.[17]

For Jonathon Darby, the publication of *The hunger* had caused great personal embarrassment and among the King's County gentry there was general displeasure with the contents of the book. It was not, however, the first time that Mildred Darby had courted controversy in her married life. In 1897, she caused outrage in King's County when Samuel Hemphill, rector of Birr, refused to grant permission for the staging of a burlesque play she had written.[18] Despite

8 *Irish Independent*, 9 May 1910. 9 *Freeman's Journal*, 28 May 1910. 10 *Irish Book Lover* (June 1910), p. 150. 11 See *Irish Book Lover*, i (May 1910), p. 133 and *The Review of Reviews*, 41 (1910), 473. 12 Quoted in Tierney, 'The Gothic and the Gaelic', p. 197. 13 Ibid. 14 Ibid., p. 196. 15 See, for example, *Evening Herald*, 20 Mar. 1894. 16 See Tierney, 'The Gothic and the Gaelic', p. 195. 17 Ibid., p. 196. 18 *Freeman's Journal*, 12 Feb. 1897.

11.2 Leap Castle, *c.*1900, courtesy of Offaly Historical Society.

this, Darby continued to enjoy the trappings of landed society in King's County and was a frequent guest at Birr Castle and other country houses in the south of the county, which included Sharavogue, Corolanty, Glasshouse, Milltown, Cangort and Gloster.[19] Although it has been suggested that she suffered from 'colonial guilt' and resented the world she had married into, Mildred was content to partake in the varied trappings of ascendancy life.[20] Tierney claims that she was unhappy with her position as 'lady of the castle' and was aware of the growing dissension towards the landed class as the century drew to a close.[21] However, an examination of her social world and activity would suggest otherwise. Indeed, within a short time of her arrival at Leap, Mildred Darby had established a ladies' cricket team which she called the 'Leapers', competing against neighbouring gentry families.[22] In 1897, for example, the Queen's jubilee was celebrated with great aplomb at Leap where Mildred presented jubilee medals to the children of the nearby school at Aghancon.[23] She also took an active role in the organization of the Orange ball, held annually at Leap in June, and in the King's County and Ormond hunt and its associated activities.[24]

19 For an insight into the social world of some country houses in King's County see *Nenagh Guardian*, 3 Sept. 1892; *Leinster Express*, 31 Dec. 1892; 28 Apr. 1894 & 8 Dec. 1900. 20 Tierney, 'The Gothic and the Gaelic', p. 194. 21 Ibid., p. 192. 22 *Kildare Observer*, 28 Sept. 1890. 23 *King's County Chronicle*, 8 July 1897. 24 Ibid., 11 June 1912.

At the same time she had also integrated with the local community and as a result was said to be acutely aware of the legacy of the Great Famine.[25] She was aware that there was lingering resentment towards the landlord class. Such resentment would be made evident in time; for example, those who burned Castlebernard (sometimes Kinnitty Castle) in July 1922 claimed that it was retribution for the evictions carried out by 'Black' Thomas Bernard in 1852.[26] Interestingly, in *The hunger*, Darby portrays the absentee and feckless landlord to be a man named 'Buck' Bernard of Bernardstown. Other central characters in the book, including 'Lord Torrabegh', bore a striking resemblance to some of Jonathon Darby's ancestors, while neighbouring gentry could be easily identified by name, habit and more importantly their conduct during the Famine. It was little wonder then that Jonathon Darby took umbrage at the contents of his wife's novel, which she stated in the introduction was based on fact.

The publication should not have come as a surprise to her husband because he was aware that she had been researching the Famine, for as she noted in the introduction, she had widely consulted with public and private sources in neighbouring country houses. These were testing times and their estate, and King's County in general, was engulfed in agrarian outrage during the so-called 'ranch war' of the opening decade of the twentieth century.[27]

From her arrival at Leap in 1889 Mildred Darby appears to have been extremely interested in the history of the castle, of its previous owners, 'the warlike O'Carrolls' and the 'vanquished' Gaelic Irish of the county. She was so well versed in the history of the castle that she often helped those who wished to write newspaper features and books on the house, then considered to be one of the most haunted houses in Ireland.[28] Moreover, when her children were born they were christened as 'O'Carroll-Darby', another indication of her interest in the castle's history. Mildred alone was not responsible for cultivating this Gaelic ancestry, which appears to have begun almost twenty years before her arrival in Leap.[29]

Whereas her earlier stories and books were sympathetic to both landlord and tenant in Ireland, in writing *The hunger*, Mildred was determined to tell 'both

---

25 The social memory of the family suggests that Mildred was largely sympathetic to the plight of the peasantry. See, for example, *Midland Tribune*, 12 Jan. 1991.   **26** *Freeman's Journal*, 28 Dec. 1922. In other instances, 'Famine kindness' was said to have been the reason why a house was spared the fate of burning. At Glasshouse, Shinrone in King's County, owned by the Rolleston family, and who included among them the celebrated nationalist T.W. Rolleston, Henry Rolleston was informed that his house would be spared the fate of being burned or raided because his father some fifty years previous had defended a local tenant, Mike Finnegan, who had been convicted of murder. See Noel McMahon, *In the shadow of the Fairy Hill: a history of Shinrone* (Birr, 1998), p. 76.   **27** For an account of the ranch war in King's County see John Noel McEvoy, 'A study of the United Irish League in the King's County, 1899–1918' (MA thesis, St Patrick's College, Maynooth, 1992).   **28** *Irish Times*, 16 Mar. 1901.   **29** Tierney, 'The Gothic and the Gaelic', p. 192, quotes J. Godkin and J.A. Walker, *The new handbook of Ireland* (Dublin, 1870), pp 243–4.

11.3 Title page of Mildred Darby's novel, *The hunger*, courtesy of Offaly Historical Society.

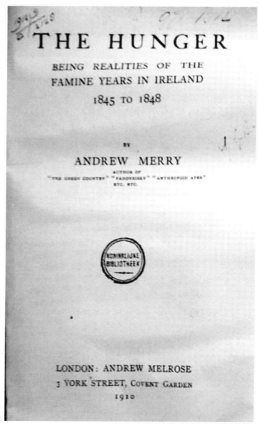

THE HUNGER

BEING REALITIES OF THE
FAMINE YEARS IN IRELAND
1845 TO 1848

BY

ANDREW MERRY

AUTHOR OF
"THE GREEN COUNTRY" "PADDYRISKY" "ANTHROPOID APES"
ETC. ETC.

LONDON: ANDREW MELROSE
3 YORK STREET, COVENT GARDEN
1910

sides and all versions of the same tale'.[30] She was meticulous in her research and consulted newspapers, parliamentary reports and private correspondence. The consultation of material in private possession was evident in the content of the novel, which drew heavily on real events in King's County. She spoke with the local community and those who had survived the Famine, although Darby was aware of the 'silence' that pervaded in certain quarters. Nonetheless, this recording of the 'social memory' of the Famine was important, given that it predated by more than thirty years the work undertaken by the Folklore Commission of the 1940s.

Much of the perceived harmony on the Darby estate was believed to have stemmed from the benevolence of Jonathan's predecessors, particularly during the Famine years of the 1840s. The Darbys had emerged from the Famine with a reputation for generosity and providing relief work, while they were also hailed as progressive farmers.[31] In the 1890s the family were praised for the fact that for several generations they had been 'resident' landlords.[32] There appears to have

30 Merry, *The hunger*, p. 3.　**31** *Irish Times*, 23 Oct. 1869.　**32** *Evening Herald*, 20 Mar. 1894.

been a level of truth to these claims and in 1847, Horatio Darby, the land agent
and brother of the owner William, was singled out for the fact that:

> his benevolence was a pure and inexhaustible fountain; but now it is
> overflowing bringing life and comfort home to many sorrow-stricken and
> sinking spirits. This philanthropic gentleman has given seed not only to the
> tenants of his brother, W.H. Darby, whose estate he manages, but he has
> also furnished many distressed persons in the Anaghcon district. He
> procured a large supply of Indian meal, which he gave to the tenantry at
> cost price; and he has also furnished them with employment on the
> property, at an increased rate of wages.[33]

Throughout the course of the Famine, William Darby urged others to follow his
example. Addressing the Parsonstown Agricultural Society in October 1846,
Darby called for more employment, planting and growing of grain and asked
members to practise 'self-denial' and to 'pull together by giving as much
employment as possible'.[34] He was also widely praised for his efforts in uniting
fellow landowners to contribute to a fund in order to put the 'able bodied' poor
to work.[35] On another occasion he was praised for the fact that he had not
charged the poor rate for the parish of Ettagh in order to alleviate the effects of
hunger.[36] Darby also took a personal interest in the tenants who were applying
for relief.[37] By 1849 it was alleged that not a single person on the Darby estate
received relief.[38] However, this was probably due to the fact that in that same year
over a hundred people were assisted in emigrating to America. Unlike other
schemes of assisted emigration that incurred popular criticism, the Darbys were
widely praised for their efforts. And so it was little wonder then that by the end
of the century, although Irish landlords were blamed for inaction during the
Famine years, the Darbys could look back with pride on their own efforts during
the crisis.

Mildred Darby's reading of the Famine crisis was erudite, displaying an in-
depth knowledge of the various layers of society and how each was affected. In
The hunger, her central characters include the landlord, the middleman, the
priest, the parson and the peasant. She also highlighted the role of women
during the Famine, championing the 'gentle women of all classes' who 'for the
love of their god and their fellow creatures, walked boldly amongst the fever
stricken'.[39] She successfully portrayed the complexities of the Famine. This is
best exemplified in her treatment of the middleman, Denis O'Flaherty, and the
absentee landlord, Lord Torrabegh, who both exploited the practice of

---

33 *Dublin Evening Packet and Correspondent*, 10 Apr. 1847.   34 *King's County Chronicle*, 21
Oct. 1846. See also *Leinster Express*, 24 Oct. 1846.   35 See *Athlone Sentinel*, 6 Dec. 1848.
36 *Anglo-Celt*, 1 June 1849.   37 *Tipperary Vindicator*, 14 Nov. 1846.   38 *Dublin Evening
Mail*, 12 Nov. 1849.   39 Merry, *The hunger*, pp 16–17.

subdivision in the years prior to the Famine. Of the middleman, O'Flaherty, she wrote that he 'found himself rather isolated – no one exhibiting any keen desire to sit next him'. Indeed, even O'Flaherty's wife was particularly uncomfortable with all that they possessed. Middlemen, or tiarnaí beaga ('little lords') as they were known, were generally denounced in their attempts to lord it over their social inferiors, especially the cottier class.[40] Etching out an existence on tiny plots of land (usually no more than an acre), Darby's description of this class who were 'divided into three degrees of misery' further displayed a thorough understanding of the period.[41] Likewise, her ridiculing of Lord Torrabegh for his inaction and absenteeism mirrored the prevailing attitudes of the 1840s. For example, those who had endeavoured in 1846 and 1847 to grant abatements and forgo the collection of rent soon changed their attitudes and looked to alternative ways of managing their tenants in crisis. Here Darby perhaps drew on the then recently published memoirs of William O'Connor Morris, in which the King's County landlord stressed the pressures placed on the family as the Famine wore on.[42]

While a number of Darby's other novels were set in various locations across the country, *The hunger* drew on events that had occurred in the immediate world of Leap. For example, Darby's inclusion of the 'Fishcurers Assurance Company' is almost certainly a reference to the so-called 'Kilcloncouse affair', near Kinnitty, where tenants on crown estates were evicted in 1852 and shipped to America.[43] These evictions left a lasting bitterness among the local population. There was also resentment towards the inadequacies and abuses that were prevalent in the relief schemes throughout the country.[44] This was best characterized by the petty squabbling of the relief committees, again something that was a major problem in the King's County of the 1840s. *The hunger* also captures the changing attitudes towards the poor as the Famine wore on. A weary relief committee official declares: 'Let the people go elsewhere if they can't get food here. If there are no men belongin' to them fit to labour, what good are they to themselves or any other person'.[45] Such apathy towards the plight of the poor mirrored what Perrse Grome had to say in 1848 when he thundered at a meeting of the Parsonstown board of guardians that:

> it was truly ridiculous to be wasting so much of their valuable time in talking over so much unimportant matters. It was all sympathy for paupers and beggars, brats and in what way they were to be made comfortable, as if they had not been used to cabins and hovels of the meanest and filthiest kind from their birth; such talk was really monstrous and absurd and while

40 Maura Cronin, *Agrarian protest in Ireland, 1750–1960* (Dundalk, 2012), p. 61.   41 Merry, *The hunger*, p. 8.   42 See William O'Connor Morris, *Memories and thoughts of a life* (London, 1895).   43 See Eilish Ellis, 'State aided emigration schemes from crown estates in Ireland, c.1850', *Analecta Hibernica*, 22 (1960), 383.   44 Merry, *The hunger*, p. 242.   45 Ibid., p. 249.

all the pity was for the beggars, there was no sympathy for the landlords
and gentlemen of the country, at whose expense these persons were to be
fed sumptuously.[46]

One of the striking features of the novel is the emphasis the author places on
the charitable work of the 'Goodbody' family and the Quaker community in
general.[47] The Quakers were 'the friends of everyone, the enemies of none' she
declared.[48] Undoubtedly, the heroine of the story is Barbara Goodbody, almost
certainly modelled on the exploits of the charitable Lydia Goodbody of Clara in
King's County some thirty miles from Leap.[49] Throughout the novel the
generosity and unfailing compassion of Barbara Goodbody, the 'Quakeress', is
shown in her visits to the homes of the peasantry, and nursing the children of the
sick and dying. A devout Protestant and wary of the Quaker religion, Jonathon
Darby's ire at *The hunger* may have been partly as a result of the glowing tributes
to the Society of Friends.[50] These included comments such as 'Musha, but them
Goodbodys at the Mount are the real gentry – God knows the half of the parish
owe their lives to the Quakers'[51] and 'we would not be living now but in our grave
… but for them Goodbodys.'[52] Likewise, Fr Spain, the Roman Catholic priest of
the fictional 'Torrabegh', is praised for his endeavours to help his parishioners
in their time of want. This character was almost certainly based on his namesake,
Fr John Spain of nearby Parsonstown, who succumbed to Famine fever in 1848,
having laboured to relieve the plight of his parishioners.[53]

In general, *The hunger* stresses that the landed class had failed in their duties
during the Famine years. This is made quite clear with the inclusion of a chapter
titled 'Feasting and famine'. One gathering is described as follows:

> Hosts and guests had discussed the potato blight, and speculated over its
> cause, with their soup and fish; they had commented with many head-
> shakings upon the prevailing scarcity of food, while great dishes filled by
> smoking joints and artistic entrees provided them with a pleasant contrast
> to their topic of conversation.

Others were accused of 'feastings and junketings in the city of London', as
the Famine took hold in Ireland.[54] Darby related how social events such as

---

46 'Parsonstown Board of Guardians, minute book, 1848': quoted in Sandra Robinson (ed.), *The
diary of an Offaly schoolboy, 1858–59: William Davis* (Tullamore, 2010), p. xxx.   **47** Merry, *The
hunger*, p. 29.   **48** Ibid., p. 244.   **49** The diaries of Lydia Goodbody (in private possession)
highlight her efforts at relieving the plight of the people of Clara and the wider area.
50 Jonathon Darby's wedding party wore orange and shamrock in his honour: see *King's County
Chronicle*, 14 Nov. 1889. A member of the King's County branch of the Irish Unionist Alliance,
he was described by contemporaries as 'a very militant Orangeman': see John E. Walsh to W.J.H.
Tyrrell, 23 July 1918 (in private possession), and Freeman-Attwood, *Leap*, pp 136–7.   **51** Merry,
The hunger, p. 32.   **52** Ibid., p. 214.   **53** Ibid., p. 29.   **54** Ibid., p. 243.

hunting, racing, cricket and archery continued unabated during the Famine, noting that it was 'a sorrowful season for any jollification'.[55] However, she did concede that 'the excitement of the racing was forgotten. From all parts of the course the ill-clad beggars and the respectable poor alike flocked to the tent where the food and drink were to be given out.'[56] For Jonathon Darby this negative portrayal of the landlord class was unfair and overlooked the important contribution his own family had made during the Famine years.[57] In helping tenants to emigrate Horatio Darby was widely lauded; he was one of a few King's County landlords who did so during the Famine. It is interesting that Mildred Darby derided those who later posed as 'philanthropists' for doing so. She wrote: 'Thousands of destitute men, women and children were shipped off with nothing they could call their own but the rags they stood up in, and dumped down upon a foreign strand.'[58]

***

Following the publication of *The hunger* in 1910, Jonathon Darby was outraged that his wife had depicted the landlord class in such a way.[59] It remains unclear what motives lay behind Mildred Darby's decision to write about the Great Famine, apart from her desire, as she stated in the introduction, to present the true facts. She may have tried to understand the peasantry, but that is not to say that she sympathized with them any more than other members of her class did. The description of survivors of the Famine as being somewhat 'soft in the head' did not reflect an innate sympathy for the peasantry. Moreover, while castigating the inaction of some Irish landlords, Darby also highlighted the fact that others were themselves adversely affected by the Famine. It was evident that 'mansion house and mud-cabin alike paid toll to the gaunt spectre stalking over the land',[60] that the Famine had a disastrous effect on the landed class and that 'it too swept families and all before them', a reference to the impact of the Encumbered Estates Court.[61]

The hunger presents an informed account of the Famine. As a novelist, Darby displayed the skills of a historian. Her treatment and assessment of a number of issues relating to the Famine have only recently been addressed by scholars. Her novel raised the question of culpability – who was responsible for, or who

55 Merry, *The hunger*, p. 32. **56** Ibid., p. 65. For a contemporary account see *Nenagh Guardian*, 10 Mar. 1849. **57** Tierney, 'The Gothic and the Gaelic', pp 195–6. **58** Merry, *The hunger*, p. 86. **59** According to Tierney, following the publication 'her husband would forbid her ever to publish again, something which left her perplexed and, no doubt, frustrated'. See Tierney, 'Gothic and the Gaelic', p. 197. **60** Merry, *The hunger*, p. 17. **61** The Encumbered Estates Court was designed to expedite the sale of encumbered property by making the legal process less complicated, and oversaw the largest transfer of land in Ireland since the 1650s. See P.H. Fitzgerald, *The story of the Encumbered Estates Court* (London, 1862).

exacerbated, the Famine crisis. However, Mildred Darby remained at odds with herself as to whether she had accurately portrayed the enormity of the situation. Mildred Darby left Leap in 1922 after months of intimidation directed towards the family and their servants. When the house was burned in July she refused to return to Leap and lamented the plight of the 'unfortunate southern loyal, law abiding minority, now homeless penniless wanderers'.[62] Awaiting compensation for the burning of Leap, the family moved to live with their daughter at Doory Hall, near Ballymahon in Co. Longford. By 1925, she was described as being in 'bad health' and had left Longford and removed to London, where she died in January 1932 aged sixty-four.[63]

62 Mildred Darby to Lady Anderson, Belfast, 4 Jan. 1923 (PRONI, T/2858/3/2).   63 *Belfast Newsletter*, 12 Feb. 1925.

Rosalind Howard, the contradictory countess of Carlisle

CHRISTOPHER RIDGWAY

Rosalind Howard (née Stanley) was born at Alderley Park, Cheshire, in 1845 (fig. 12.1). Her father Edward, 2nd Baron Stanley of Alderley, came from the radical wing of the Whig party, and sat as an MP from 1831 to 1848, occupying a succession of political offices.[1] His wife Henrietta Maria (1807–1895), eldest daughter of the 13th Viscount Dillon of Co. Mayo, played the role of political hostess, presiding over a salon in London, and in 1872 she was a founder member of Girton College, Cambridge.[2] Rosalind grew up in an intensely political family, she was well educated, accustomed to the cut and thrust of political debate, and through her parents encountered politicians, writers and thinkers. Along with several of her siblings she became committed to various public causes. Among those she especially espoused were the Liberal party, temperance, women's suffrage, and home rule for Ireland; she would remain steadfastly committed to these until her death in 1921.

After her marriage to George Howard in 1864, heir to the 78,000-acre estates in the north of England, Rosalind was not content with the life of a chatelaine at the two family seats, Castle Howard in Yorkshire and Naworth Castle in Cumbria.[3] Before their wedding she had written to her fiancé declaring, 'It would

[1] Edward John Stanley (1802–69) served in the administrations of Lords Melbourne, Russell and Palmerston variously as under-secretary of state for foreign affairs, president of the Board of Trade, and postmaster-general. He was known as 'Benjamin Backbite' on account of his satirical wit. In 1832, he voted in favour of the Irish Reform Bill. See his entry in *The history of parliament online*, the entries for him and his wife Henrietta Maria in the *ODNB*, and also Nancy Mitford (ed.), *The Stanleys of Alderley* (London, 1939). [2] Henry Augustus Dillon Lee (1777–1832), 13th Viscount Dillon, was MP for Harwich in Essex from 1799 to 1802, and then sat for Co. Mayo from 1802 to 1814; see his entries in *The history of parliament online*, and the *ODNB*. In 1807, he married Henrietta Browne (d.1862) who was descended from the 1st earl of Altamont of Westport House, Co. Mayo. Viscount Dillon was an Irish peerage created in 1622, and the family seats were Loughglynn House, Co. Roscommon, and Ditchley House, Oxfordshire. Rosalind's two maternal grandparents represent her only direct family connection with Ireland. [3] For George Howard (1843–1911), 9th earl of Carlisle, and for Rosalind, see the entries in the *ODNB*; there are also entries on Rosalind in Joseph O. Sullivan and Norbert J. Grossman (eds), *Biographical dictionary of modern British radicals*, vol. 3: *1870–1914, A–K* (New York, 1988), pp 458–63, and Olive Banks (ed.), *The biographical dictionary of British feminists*, vol. 2: *a supplement, 1900–1945* (New York, 1990), pp 102–5. See also two family memoirs by her daughter and son-in-law, Dorothy Henley, *Rosalind Howard, countess of Carlisle* (London, 1958), and Charles Roberts, *The radical countess* (Carlisle, 1962); and also

seriously annoy me if I were to think of my life henceforward to be taken up in a series of country visits'.[4] She believed that her privileged life conferred on her a moral responsibility to work and serve in the public sphere, and after asking her husband if she could manage the family estates (while he pursued his passion for painting), she wrote to him in 1888, outlining how she desired a life of purpose and recognition in her own right: 'I am glad I have boldly accepted the estate work as my own … Yet I too want a sphere, a definite one of my own which shall make my life have some definite, persistent effort about it, some incentive to learn and to achieve, not to flit merely'.[5]

She took over the management of the Howard estates in Yorkshire, Cumbria and Northumberland, while also caring for her eleven children born between 1865 and 1884 (fig. 12.2). Immersing herself in day-to-day issues, she worked with her agents and dealt with rents, forestry, farming, cottage improvements, taxation, finance and welfare issues such as village schools, religion and welfare.[6] Litigation held no fears for her either, and in 1907 she went to the High Court in London in a lawsuit with tenants over a water supply in Cumbria. Describing herself as land agent acting for her husband, who had become 9th earl of Carlisle in 1889, she was cross-examined in the witness box by Sir Edward Carson, and showed no signs of being intimidated by his reputation as a fierce and forensic prosecutor. For his part Carson found Rosalind combative and disinclined to follow the protocols of the courtroom, forced to remind her at one point, 'You must not ask me questions'. According to her son-in-law, Carson 'did not come off best in the encounter'.[7]

Local affairs led to national issues too. Rosalind was concerned by the lack of sobriety among the tenants on the estate in Cumbria, and its destructive effects upon families. In the nearby town of Brampton she formed abstinence societies, held temperance meetings, closed down pubs, opened a coffee house, and had some success in persuading tenants to give up drink. Her friend, the artist Walter Crane, designed a pledge card for the Blue Ribbon Army, which depicted St George vigorously slaying the dragon of drink, and in 1903 she was elected president of the National British Women's Temperance Association.[8] Her

Virginia Surtees, *The artist and the autocrat* (Salisbury, 1988).   **4** Rosalind Howard (hereafter RH) to George Howard (hereafter GH), undated, Sept. 1864 (Castle Howard Archives, J22/4). Unless otherwise stated all references are to the Castle Howard Archives.   **5** RH to GH, 15 Nov. 1888, J22/4.   **6** Rosalind's papers held at Castle Howard are extensive and cover all aspects of her family and public life. For estate management, comprising letter books, notes, and instructions to agents from 1899–1919, see F9/1–250, and also Roberts, *Radical countess*, pp 68–9, 136–50.   **7** Roberts, *Radical countess*, p. 131. Pasted into one of Rosalind's scrapbooks are two press reports of the hearing; the account in the *Daily Graphic*, 9 Feb. 1907, was entitled 'Lady Carlisle and Her Tenants, Amusing Cross-Examination', that in the *Daily Mail* described the encounter as a 'Battle of Wits', J23, 489/1, pp 158–9. For Carson's reputation in court see Geoffrey Lewis, *Carson, the man who divided Ireland* (London, 2005), pp 7–11, 24.   **8** For Rosalind's temperance papers see J23/144–301; these include her temperance pledge book, which she signed in 1882, J23/243; and Walter Crane's Blue Ribbon

12.1 Rosalind Howard, by Frederic Leighton, 1865, oil on canvas; Castle Howard Collection.

12.2 Rosalind and family on the steps of Castle Howard; Castle Howard Collection.

campaign against alcohol caused a national furore in 1916 when it was reported how she had destroyed hundreds of bottles of wine at Castle Howard. On 7 November 1916 the front page of the *Daily Express* contained six headlines, the first four of which were reports from various theatres of war, the Somme, the North Sea, the English Channel and Romania; the fifth column was headlined '1,000 Bottles of Wine Wasted, Countess pours them into the ground'; the sixth column was about the price of bread. Rosalind rebutted the story furiously, writing to the press to explain that the wine had gone off and become mouldy, and she thundered, 'not even a dipsomaniac, under the influences of his worst

Army pledge card, J23/240. Her temperance work is described in Henley, *Rosalind Howard*, pp 109–11; Roberts, *Radical countess*, pp 60–7, 91–101; Surtees, *Artist and autocrat*, pp 128–30, 138–9; more recently by Margaret Barrow, 'Teetotal feminists: temperance leadership and the campaign for women's suffrage' in Claire Eustace, Joan Ryan and Laura Ugolini (eds), *A suffrage reader* (Leicester, 2000), pp 69–89; and Ros Black, *Scandal, salvation and suffrage, the amazing women of the temperance movement* (Kibworth Beauchamp, 2015), pp 144–67.

drink craving, would have touched this mixture of fungus and smelly liquid'. Implicit in the public criticism was the suggestion that the wine could have been offered to convalescing soldiers.[9]

Along with temperance Rosalind's other great crusade in life was women's suffrage. In 1869, she read John Stuart Mill's volume *On the subjection of women*, and this was a defining moment. She recorded in her diary: 'Mill's book on the Subjection of women is splendid ... I go with him in every word he says throughout. He is a wonderful champion for women's cause[s] ... It has roused me to care more about women's liberty. I have always had liberty myself and so can well appreciate what value it would be to the mass of womankind'.[10] Her work began at a local level, and in 1887 the Women's Liberal Federation was formed, in response to the Conservative-founded Primrose League. Initially, she refused to join because it did not include female enfranchisement among its aims, but when she did become a member three years later she led a progressive wing that campaigned for votes for women. This led to a split in the WLF, and in 1892 Mrs Gladstone stepped down as president. Within two years Rosalind had been elected president and women's suffrage became central to WLF activities.[11]

Although Rosalind was a good public speaker she preferred to chair committees and draft pamphlets, recognizing that the key to political success was efficient organization and lobbying and not simply headline news. 'My quiet organizing work prospers and suits me vastly better than all this flashy London posturing', she wrote in 1891.[12] The direct action tactics of Suffragettes, founded by Emmeline Pankhurst in 1903, were counter to all that she believed in with regard to constitutional progress. After 1909, suffragette action escalated from heckling ministers to mass public disturbances, attacking property and vandalizing works of art. Rosalind described these militants as 'impatient, lawless, scolding women, with hate in their hearts'. It is ironic then that in 1913, and a year later, police surveillance confirmed the presence of activists in the neighbourhood of Castle Howard. Following an attack on one of Rosalind's

9 Her letter to the editor of *The Daily Mirror* is dated 9 Nov. 1916, and is followed by a further three letters explaining her action, J23/101/5, pp 360–3.   10 Entry for 8 Sept. 1869, J23/105/15.   11 For Rosalind's papers relating to suffrage and Liberal politics see J23/302–461; a summary of her activities is found in Roberts, *Radical countess*, pp 113–29, and more recently, Margaret Barrow, 'Teetotal feminists', who also shows how temperance and suffrage were closely intertwined issues. On Rosalind and the history of the Women's Liberal Federation and its schisms see David Morgan, *Suffragists and Liberals* (Oxford, 1975), pp 17–18; Lilian Lewis Shiman, *Women and leadership in nineteenth-century England* (New York, 1992), pp 132–4, 195–6; and Martin Pugh, *The march of the women* (Oxford, 2000), chapters 3 and 7.   12 RH to GH, 6 May 1891, J23/4. Henley described her mother as a hypnotic speaker and engaging conversationalist, *Rosalind Howard*, pp 38–9, and Roberts also attested to her abilities as a public speaker, *Radical countess*, p.130. However, she wrote to her mother confessing 'I greatly dislike speaking', 12 Nov. 1891, J23/7. For public speaking more generally see Joseph S. Meisel, *Public speaking and the culture of public life in the age of Gladstone* (New York, 2001), esp. chapter 5.

properties in Middlesex, there were real fears that Castle Howard would be subject to an arson attack, and extra night-watchmen were recruited.[13]

Active at a local level in relation to estate affairs, Rosalind was also elected a district councillor for Malton in Yorkshire and Brampton in Cumbria.[14] While she once described herself as a politician this was the nearest she could ever hope to come to being a publicly elected representative of the people. A political creature to her core, she could only follow the national picture second-hand through the pages of *Hansard*, or when discussing government affairs with members of her family, or assisting her sons and sons-in-law during their election campaigns.[15] Her favourite son, Geoffrey (1877–1935), sat as a Liberal, MP from 1906 to 1924, and was particularly close to the heart of government, first as parliamentary private secretary to Prime Minister Herbert Asquith from 1908 to 1910, and then as Liberal party whip from 1911 to 1918. Rosalind's son-in-law Charles Roberts (1865–1959), who had married her second daughter, Cecilia (1869–1947), sat as a Liberal MP from 1906 to 1923. The young Welshman Leifchild Jones (1862–1939), who became Rosalind's secretary in the 1880s, was a Liberal MP from 1905 to 1931 before becoming Lord Rhyader in 1932. This triumvirate of political confidantes was joined by another son-in-law, the classical scholar and public intellectual Gilbert Murray (1866–1957), who married Rosalind's eldest daughter Mary (1865–1956). All four men shared Rosalind's beliefs in Liberal causes, temperance and home rule. Politics could also divide her family as well as unite it, for she became estranged from her eldest son Charles (1867–1912), later 10th earl of Carlisle, on account of his opposition to home rule, and he sat as a Liberal Unionist MP from 1904 to 1911. Her daughter recalled how home rule 'helped to split many homes besides ours'; Rosalind's marriage nearly sundered as her husband and four of her sons supported the Union, but family discord was caused by strong and inflexible personalities as much as by political division.[16]

She supported all the Liberal leaders, out of loyalty to the party, even if she disagreed with them over specific issues. Like many she revered Gladstone, who

---

13 Roberts, *Radical countess*, pp 120–4. For the suffragette scare see F8/3/61, pp 416, 426; F8/4/1, 9 Apr. 1914 and 14 Sept. 1914; F9/71.   14 Sullivan, *Dictionary of modern British radicals*, p. 462. Among her estate papers is a notice for the 1910 Malton election, for the parish of Coneysthorpe on the Castle Howard estate, which reveals that Rosalind was the sole candidate and that consequently no poll was taken, F9/126. This suggests that feudal traditions of family influence in local political affairs still operated.   15 In 1908, Rosalind reported in a letter to Gilbert Murray how she had spent 'long joyous days' listening to debates in the House of Commons, 2 Mar. 1909, J23/26. Her correspondence regularly digested or circulated political news, especially at election time, and when in London she would often discuss the day's parliamentary business with family members. Typical is a comment in a letter to her daughter Mary Howard (hereafter MH) during the Boer War, 'We absorb ourselves in the war and politics here', no date, Jan. 1900, J23/26.   16 Henley, *Rosalind Howard*, p. 43; Roberts, *Radical countess*, p. 71. In 1886, husband and wife agreed to recognize their differences and not speak about them, RH to GH, 28 May and 11 June 1886, J23/4. See also Surtees, *Artist and autocrat*, pp 144, 148, who argues that emotional

12.3 Portrait of Gladstone, by George Howard, 1879, pencil on paper; Castle Howard Collection.

she had met through her husband. In 1873, Gladstone stayed at Naworth Castle, and six years later the couple met him in Surrey, when George captured Gladstone while reading in a pencil portrait that Gladstone described as 'a most clever sketch' (fig. 12.3).[17] Rosalind naturally welcomed Gladstone's home rule bill, going so far as to call him 'splendid'; but she also clashed with him over enfranchisement, disagreeing with his wish for women's suffrage to take second place to the campaign for home rule. In 1891 she was critical of his speech to the National Liberal Federation in Newcastle, declaring how he had 'missed his opportunity of rising to a great occasion'. But in the same year she spoke at an unveiling of his portrait, and referred to him as a 'great statesman', 'one of England's immortal possessions', and a 'great chieftain and beloved leader'. She reminded her audience how the WLF was fighting for women's causes, and advocating home rule, and with regard to Ireland she was convinced that 'triumph is near'. However, progress on enfranchisement still faced obstacles, not least of all attitudes on the part of Liberal MPs who were divided on the issue, either on principle or because they felt there were more pressing political

entanglements contributed to the breakdown of the marriage.   **17** Surtees, *Artist and autocrat*, pp 97, 120; H.C.G. Matthew (ed.), *The Gladstone diaries*, 25 vols (Oxford, 1968–94), ix, 5 June 1879, p. 419.

priorities. Her hyperbole over Gladstone was heartfelt, but precisely because she admired him so much she found it hard to accept his opposition to votes for women, and so used her speech of 1891 to argue the case for enfranchisement. She accused him of failing to understand how women did not wish 'to be condemned to a life of frivolity'. Nevertheless, she struck a conciliatory note, promising the campaign would not threaten party unity; this was unlikely to happen for she conceded, 'We have no force', but she urged her listeners not to forget the value and impact of women supporters and activists.[18]

A decade later she was still making the same arguments, and was convinced that Asquith favoured women's suffrage. In 1908, she refused to believe the MP John Morley when he told her that Asquith would, in fact, not support the suffrage bill; a year later she still held to the belief that he favoured the cause when in fact the opposite was the case. Notwithstanding this her support for him was such that when his premiership came under attack in 1915 she wrote, 'I shall work henceforth only with those who are loyal Party Liberals, and who do not attack Mr Asquith'. As with Gladstone her feelings for the Liberal leader were affectionate and loyal, especially after the party's catastrophic defeat in the 1918 election when she lamented, 'Only for Asquith do I mourn without finding any consolation. Asquith the magnanimous, slain foully'.[19]

She dismissed Winston Churchill as 'that new charlatan who has come into our ranks' after he had crossed the floor of the House of Commons from the Tory party to the Liberals in 1904. Like many people she was fascinated by Lloyd George but distrusted him, and first voiced her suspicions during the suffrage debates; during the war she expressed doubt over his 'insidious' attempt to regulate alcohol in the munitions industry, and by 1917 was accusing him of 'infamies' in the state control of liquor supplies.[20] Rosalind admired Queen

18 Roberts, *Radical countess*, pp 116–17; RH to GH 14 May 1884, 4 Oct. 1891, J23/4; *Speech by Lady Carlisle at the unveiling of a Portrait of Mr Gladstone in the Newcastle Liberal Club, August 18, 1891* (Brampton, n.d.), J23/350. For Gladstone on women's suffrage see Colin Matthew, *Gladstone, 1875–1898* (Oxford, 1995), pp 324–6, 363–4; and also Brian Harrison, *Separate spheres, the opposition to women's suffrage in Britain* (London, 1978), pp 40, 44. See also her letter to John Morley, 15 Oct. 1906, where she rehearsed the same argument and concluded, 'We knock at the door, Open it to us', Bodleian Library, MS Eng'd 3577.   **19** RH to MH, 2 Mar. 1908, 29 Nov. 1909, J23/26; RH to Miss Graham, 24 June 1915, J23/101/5, p. 284; RH to MH, 1 Jan. 1919, J23/26. For Asquith's views on women's suffrage see Harrison, op. cit., pp 48–51, 204–5, and Roy Jenkins, *Asquith* (London, 1964), pp 247–8. **20** RH to MH, 10 Dec. 1904, J23/26. In 1911 she held 'queer, pleasant interviews' with both Churchill and Lloyd George at Westminster, RH to MH, 30 Mar. 1911, J23/26. On Lloyd George and alcohol see her letter to Miss Johnson, 9 May 1915, J23/101/5, p. 192, and to MH, 25 Mar. 1917, J23/26. For discussion of alcohol during the First World War see, Robert Duncan, *Pubs and patriots: the drink crisis in Britain during World War One* (Liverpool, 2013), chapters 3 and 8. Gilbert Murray used a telling phrase when he described Lloyd George as 'a man of sudden curves', Bodleian Library, Murray MSS.462, correspondence with Mary Murray (née Howard), 8 Jan. 1918, no. 17. For Murray's dealings as a 'trusted agent to the government' in wartime, and his relationship with Lloyd George, see Duncan Wilson, *Gilbert*

Victoria and in 1897, the jubilee year, she wrote warmly of her reign as 'a good and faithful servant' to the nation; but only four years later during the Boer War she accused the monarch of ministering to 'the military spirit which is now degrading and cursing our nation'.[21] She held the aristocracy in low esteem, and shunned London society; as a consequence, her son-in-law observed, 'London Society in turn hit back and did not spare her'. And during the general election of 1895 she attacked the House of Lords, arguing for 'the necessity of clearing out of the way this ancient obstruction to all democratic reform'.[22]

She was similarly divided over other issues: she abhorred British jingoism, but admired Kipling's verses; was fiercely opposed to the Boer War, but pleased when both Mafeking and Ladysmith were relieved in 1900; and she was appalled at the treatment of Boer women and children, receiving a copy of the official consular report on concentration camps. At the same time she subscribed to William Stead's anti-war periodical *War Against War!* launched in 1899, and later she sat on the committee of the National Peace Council formed in 1908.[23]

Rosalind's political opinions were trenchant, and she once wrote, 'I was brought up in a fierce Whig atmosphere – we had no dealings with Tories'; such was her antipathy towards the Conservatives that she would often deliberately write the word 'tory' using a lower case 'T'.[24] She remained a Liberal all her life, but some of her actions show sympathies with the Labour movement. She sent donations to strike funds: in 1893 for confectioners at Barratt's north London factory, and the York Comb-Workers; to Scottish railwaymen in 1891; and the Miners' Federation in 1893. She also contributed to trade union and Labour party publications. Like many she felt that England was divided between a decadent upper class while much of the population suffered from poor wages and harsh working conditions. However, she was opposed to the Labour party because it occupied what she believed was the natural ground of progressive Liberals, and she held mixed feeling on the question of state intervention. But in 1895 Rosalind had declared that radical Liberals were challenging traditional

Murray (Oxford, 1987), p. 230.   **21** RH to MH, 22 June 1897, 4 Feb. 1901, J23/26. **22** Roberts, *Radical countess*, p. 72. Henley also described her as casting off aristocratic society, *Rosalind Howard*, p. 112. Her correspondence frequently raged at how she had been attacked in the press. Her attack on the hereditary legislative chamber came in her printed *Appeal to every member of the Women's Liberal Federation at the General Election, July, 1895*, J23/355. **23** Roberts, *Radical countess*, pp 72–3; her comment on Kipling is in a letter to GH, 9 Jan. 1902, J23/4; her remarks on the Boer War are in her correspondence with Mary Howard, 4 Mar. and 29 Aug. 1900, and 5 Jan. 1902, J23/26. For her papers relating to the Boer War, peace movements, and Stead's newspaper, see J23/467–71. Stead's *War against war!* was seen as extreme in its opposition to the war: W. Sydney Robinson, *Muckraker: the scandalous life of W.T. Stead* (London, 2012), p. 236. For Liberal attitudes to imperialism see D.A. Hamer, *Liberal politics in the age of Gladstone and Rosebery* (Oxford, 1972), and Colin Mathew, *The Liberal imperialists* (Oxford, 1973).   **24** Letter of 22 Apr. 1886, quoted in Roberts, *Radical countess*, p. 109; for her lower case use of the word 'tory' see her letters to GH, 22 Mar. 1901, J23/4; to MH, 25 Oct. 1907, J23/26; and to Geoffrey Howard, 29 May 1915, 17 Feb. 1917, J30.

laissez faire practices by shaping a 'policy that the State shall hold itself responsible for all the preventable misery which is still crushing down the toiling working classes'.[25]

This wide range of commitments and activities preoccupied Rosalind for her entire life. Her children had mostly grown up by 1900, but her work in managing the family estates proved unremitting and exhausting – at times she would be at her desk by 4.30 a.m. To this was added her involvement in public affairs, the WLF, the temperance movement, and other causes, many of which involved frequent travelling between Cumbria, Northumberland, Yorkshire and London. When heart trouble was diagnosed she attributed this to her 'eager nervous temperament added to that fatal stimulant coffee', and from the 1890s onwards she began to visit Bad Nauheim spa in Germany.[26]

By 1914, female enfranchisement had not materialized, but the passing of the third home rule bill two years earlier by the House of Commons had promised a settlement to the Irish question even though the thorny matter of Ulster was unresolved and parliament was wrestling over Asquith's amending bill. Not only had Rosalind long been a supporter of home rule, she also expressed a fondness for the Irish. She had written to her mother from Glengarriff, Co. Cork, during a two-week visit to Ireland in 1880 to say, 'I can only speak of Ireland in superlatives'; and in 1893 she declared, 'I like all the people from that country', going on to remark 'there is uncommonly little difference in social characteristics between Protestants and Catholics, I can get on with them all'.[27] For someone whose personal faith moved from conventional Anglican piety to a more ecumenical and eventually agnostic position, she had little time for religious sectarianism. While Rosalind will have met many Irish figures in England it is not clear how many times, if any, she revisited Ireland after 1880; her first-hand experience of the country was therefore limited. There is no evidence that she met Parnell, but she admired him, and in 1889 added a jubilant entry in her diary, 'Parnell is cleared. Hurrah!', following the collapse of the charges against him. She hosted the agrarian campaigner and labour activist Michael Davitt at a Liberal meeting in Brampton in 1895, and sent him a gift of money; writing to thank her, Mary Davitt praised Rosalind for her support for Ireland, recognizing how 'you have suffered in the estrangement of friends through your warm and

25 For papers relating to striking workers and trades unions see J23/462–6; and Roberts, *Radical countess*, p. 163. In 1894, she wrote to Ernest Williams to say that she would not contribute to the Social Democratic Federation parliamentary election fund because she felt that a second candidate on the ballot sheet would harm the Liberal vote, 27 June 1894, J23/462; her discussion of the 'Labour Question' came in the same election campaign in her *Appeal to every member of the Women's Liberal Federation*, pp 2–3, J23/355.   **26** For comments bemoaning her workload and sense of fatigue, see RH to GH, 7 Feb. 1886, n.d. Nov. 1885, 24, 26 June 1887, and 21 June 1909, J23/4; and RH to MH, 4 Mar. 1900, 5 Jan. 1902, 13 Apr. 1903, J23/26. Rosalind went to Bad Nauheim in 1897, 1898, 1902, 1907, and 1912–14, H2/1/55.   **27** Letter to her mother Henrietta Stanley while staying at Roche's Hotel, 8 May 1880, J23/7; RH to GH, 16 Apr. 1893, J23/4.

unceasing advocacy of the Irish cause'. Davitt's remark echoed that of her
contemporary at the other end of the social scale, Lady St Helier, who recalled,
'Nothing divided society like the Home Rule question'.[28] Rosalind's position as
a wife in favour of home rule married to a Liberal Unionist occasioned a passing
witticism in the *Pall Mall Gazette* in 1889 with the suggestion that George
Howard had declined to stand for parliament in 1886 for fear of 'a hostile canvas
by his wife'. Calling this 'a calumny', she felt further insulted since both the
magazine and its editor, W.T. Stead, were home rule supporters. Her reaction
was out of all proportion to the teasing one-liner from the section of the
magazine entitled 'Today's Tittle-Tattle'. She wrote to Stead, stopped taking the
Gazette, and complained to her husband: 'I don't care to go to London at all
where evidently all parties and everyone hates me and wishes to speak unkindly
of me'. Part of her fury, however, lay in the assumption that wives should not
hold opinions contrary to their husband but her letter elicited a fulsome apology
from Stead, with whom she corresponded warmly in the 1890s.[29]

Given the volume of her papers devoted to Liberal matters, suffrage and
temperance, it is surprising that there is not more material directly relating to
Ireland. However, there exists among all her copious papers a small packet
marked 'Special': dating from the summer of 1914, it contains a dozen letters
and a handful of press cuttings and leaflets, and the ordering of these particular
papers, like so much of her archive, is proof that they were reviewed, collated,
and deemed worth preserving.[30] In June, Rosalind sent a donation of £300 to the
Irish National Volunteers, as they were busy training a militia in response to the
formation of the Ulster Volunteer Force spearheaded by her old adversary Sir
Edward Carson. In her letter to the leader of the Irish Parliamentary Party, John
Redmond, Rosalind explained her action against the backdrop of sectarian
tension and dissension within the British army: 'should armed rebellion break
out in Ulster, it is high time that a Nationalist volunteer force should arise to
protect, should the unfortunate necessity for doing so occur, the rights now
secured to the Irish nation under the Home Rule bill'.[31] Although she described
herself as 'an advocate of peace' and 'an anti-armament politician', she can have
had little doubt that the funds would have been directed towards buying arms.
The *Irish Times* accused her of this in its headline, 'Money for Guns. Countess
of Carlisle a Subscriber'; and this was confirmed later in July when the
Volunteers famously unloaded a cache of arms at Howth before marching them
into Dublin. An intriguing footnote to this episode is that on the 9 June, Rosalind

---

28 Entry for 24 February 1889, J23/105/26; she also noted approvingly that the report on the
Parnell Commission was 'good', 14 Feb. 1890, J23/105/27. For the correspondence with
Davitt see J23/78/302–6. Lady St Helier's recollection is in her *Memories of fifty years*
(London, 1909), p. 210. 29 *Pall Mall Gazette*, 1 Apr. 1889; for her reaction, see the two
letters to her husband both written on 2 April, RH to GH, J22/4. For her correspondence
with Stead see J23/369. 30 'Special. Irish National Volunteers, June 1914, Lady Carlisle's
Contribution to funds', J23/472. 31 RH to John Redmond, 24 June 1914, J23/472; also

MONEY FOR GUNS.

COUNTESS OF CARLISLE A
SUBSCRIBER.

Mr. John Redmond has received the following letter from Rosalind Countess of Carlisle,
enclosing a cheque for £300 for the Irish
National Volunteer Fund :—

Boothby, Brampton, Cumberland,
June 24.

DEAR MR. REDMOND,—Seeing that Lord
Lansdowne and the Conservative party are
trying to overawe the Government by threats
of civil war, and seeing that the generals and
officers of the British Army stationed in Ireland have dared to question what their duty
would be should armed rebellion break out in
Ulster, it is high time that a Nationalist
Volunteer Force should arise to protect,
should the unfortunate necessity for doing so
occur, the rights now secured to the Irish
nation under the Home Rule Bill. I trust
that peace may prevail, but it will not make
for peace to let the fomenters of Ulster sedition underrate the power of resistance and
the determination of Nationalists in Ireland.
I have pleasure in sending £300 to the fund
which is being collected for organising "Irish
National Volunteers," and I hope you will receive a ready response to your appeal from
all parts of the world.

ROSALIND CARLISLE.

[Rosalind Countess of Carlisle is the widow
of the ninth Earl of Carlisle, who died in
1911. She is a daughter of the second Baron
Stanley of Alderley.]

12.4 Report on Rosalind's
donation, *Irish Times*, 2 July
1914; Castle Howard Collection.

presided at the annual Council of the WLF in London; also present at the
gathering was fellow committee member Molly Childers who moved a rider
urging the government 'to make no further concessions to the demands of
Ulster'. Just a few weeks later she was onboard the yacht *Asgard* with her
husband Erskine Childers (no stranger to surreptitious sailing) as it reached
Howth harbour laden with rifles. The closeness in time of each woman's action
raises the question whether either of them were aware of what the other was
planning when they had been in each other's company in London (fig.12.4).[32]
The 'Special' packet also contains letters criticizing her for the consequences of

J23/101/4, p. 908.   **32** *Irish Times*, 2 July 1914. Like the *Times*, the *Freeman's Journal* was in
no doubt as to the use to which the money would be put reporting Rosalind's donation under
the headline, '£300 for War Chest', 2 July 1914; two days later, on 4 July, it described the
contribution as 'magnificent in its generosity', J23/472. Childers' motion was reported in the
Freeman's Journal, 10 June 1914. The committee formed in June to raise money for arms for
the Volunteers included Alice Stopford-Green, with whom Rosalind had corresponded some
years earlier, J23/78/414–16. The standard account of the Howth landing remains F.X.
Martin, *The Howth gun-running and the Kilcoole gun-running: recollections and documents*
(Dublin, 1964, rpt. 2014).

12.5 Cartoon in *Punch* magazine, 17 December 1913, showing a heavily armed Carson alerting the customs officer to an unwitting John Redmond; Castle Howard Collection.

PUNCH, OR THE LONDON CHARIVARI.—December 17, 1913.

PROCLAMATION
OF
IMPORTATION
OF
ARMS

FORE-ARMED.

Sir Edward Carson (*in course of promenade on the quay, to Customs Officer Birrell*). "CAPITAL IDEA THIS OF STOPPING IMPORTATION OF ARMS. NOW THERE'S A DANGEROUS CHARACTER; YOU SHOULD SEARCH HIM. THAT'S JUST THE SORT OF BAG HE'D HAVE A COUPLE OF HOWITZERS CONCEALED IN."

her action. One was from an anonymous woman in Wicklow, signing herself 'An Irish Protestant and Unionist', who feared she would have to flee for her life, and warning her, 'It may come home to you one day, what a <u>very, very serious</u> thing you have done'. An antagonistic response from Captain William Molony of Kiltanon House, Co. Clare, echoed similar sentiments: describing the Volunteers as a cowardly rabble targeting defenceless men and women, he too levelled an accusation of ignorance at her as someone who had the luxury of living in a law-abiding country.[33] Several of these letters enclosed a press cutting about a recent incident at Mountshannon Regatta in Co. Clare, when a band of 200 Volunteers marched along Lough Derg singing 'God Save Ireland' before demanding that a Union Jack be lowered from a launch moored at the pier-side. The boat was filled with women who were intimidated by their conduct, and for many this action was not simply an example of boorish behaviour, it signalled a militant

33 J23/472, 2 July 1914; the correspondent concluded with the postscript, 'I do not wish to give my name, but will merely say I am a lady living on my own property here'; the letter from Molony is undated.

tendency that, if armed, would threaten lives. The voices in these letters are those of beleaguered southern unionists who despised and feared the Volunteers.[34]

Rosalind for her part held Carson's army in equally low esteem, describing the UVF as 'fomenters of Ulster sedition' intent on sparking civil war; and the British officer class was no better with their treacherous disobedience in the so-called mutiny at the Curragh military base in Co. Kildare.[35] As did many people she perceived the National Volunteers as a force for preserving law and order, and defending their own communities in a world of double standards that allowed the UVF to land guns and flout the rule of law – as memorably depicted in a *Punch* magazine cartoon of 1913 that showed a heavily armed Carson hoodwinking a customs officer into apprehending John Redmond (fig. 12.5).[36]

But this 'Special' packet also contains letters of approval, including a formal note of thanks from the Tyneside Brigade of the Volunteers; a piece of sycophantic doggerel by one J.H. Canwell; and expressions of gratitude from individuals as diverse as Belfast barrister Thomas Higgins (who enclosed a copy of his address on the rise of the Volunteers), and Bridget Meehan from Staffordshire, a Catholic spinster nursing her aged mother who had left Ireland at the time of the Famine. There is also a short note from John Redmond thanking Rosalind and asking permission to publish her letter in the press, to which she acceded, noting, 'I am not unaware that my action will be criticized'. Printed in several newspapers, this ensured she gained even greater notoriety. She was also particularly gratified to be congratulated by her son Geoffrey, who reported that Lloyd George was 'much pleased' on learning of her action; as well as by Gilbert Murray who wrote, 'I was delighted to see your letter to Redmond in the *Daily News* yesterday. You have always stood by the Irish when they most needed it, and I think it is most timely that someone in your position should show this confidence in them now. You are a known friend of peace, a known constitutional Liberal, and your letter makes it clear that you are looking to the National Volunteers as a force for the preservation of order and the carrying out of the will of the people'.[37] This split between letters from supporters and

34 The Mountshannon incident appeared under the heading 'Union Jack lowered at Mount-Shannon' in the *Irish Times* not only on the same day as it reported Rosalind's donation, but on the same page and in the same column, four articles further down. The incident was reported in the *Northern Whig* as 'Nationalist "Loyalty", Pull down the Union Jack', 3 July 1914, J23/472. On the plight of southern unionists see Ian d'Alton, 'Southern Irish unionism: a study of Cork Protestants, 1884–1914', *Transactions of the Royal Historical Society*, 23 (1973), pp 71–88; and R.B. McDowell, *Crisis and decline: the fate of southern Protestants* (Dublin, 2015), chapters 2 and 3.   35 RH to John Redmond, 24 June 1914, J23/472. For the action by British officers at the Curragh see Sir James Ferguson, *The Curragh incident* (London, 1964), and Pat Jalland, *The Liberals and Ireland* (Brighton, 1980), chapter 7.   36 For Carson and the UVF see A.T.Q. Stewart, *The Ulster crisis* (London, 1967); more recently Timothy Bowman, *Carson's army* (Manchester, 2007), and Alan Parkinson, *Friends in high places, Ulster's resistance to home rule, 1912–14* (Belfast, 2012).   37 J23/472; Redmond's letter of thanks is dated 26

Dear Lady Carlisle

I thank you very sincerely for your letter & your most generous contribution to the Irish Volunteers.

When I publish, later on, a list of subscriptions, may I publish your letter?

With heartiest thanks

Very truly yrs

J.E. Redmond

26 June 1914

My Lady that the latter are in earnest; and even we nationalists must acknowledge (in private) that they have right on their side, and would shoot our men down without compunction if we attempted to wrest the northern province from them. We must first ensure that the British army does its duty, and shoots those Orange bigots down, then, the "Irish National Volunteers" might come up, with the Reserve line, and see to the burning, and destruction of Protestant property, and the shooting down of the women and children of the Orangemen. Our ancestors did this in 1798, at Wexford Bridge

12.6a and b The two letters to Rosalind signed by John Redmond in 1914, the first with an authentic signature in June, the second, with a counterfeit signature in July, full of inflamatory rhetoric; Castle Howard Collection.

opponents is not in itself very surprising; Rosalind's public actions engendered similar levels of controversy throughout her life, but the fact that she took care to keep all of these communications – positive and negative – marks her as someone interested in preserving a balanced record of events.

However, one letter among this group is exceptional. It is purportedly a second letter from Redmond after his first note of thanks. Unlike the first letter, which was on official House of Commons stationery, this has just an inked address, 'House of Commons, Westminster', at the top. It begins by thanking Rosalind but then veers in a surprising direction. Her donation was very welcome since party funds had been severely depleted because, the correspondent claims,

June. Her original letter to Redmond was published in the *Irish Times*, the *Dublin Express*, the *Cork Examiner*, and the *Yorkshire Evening News*. For Lloyd George's reaction see Geoffrey Howard to RH, 1 July 1914, J23/23; and for Murray's response, dated 2 July, J23/27/131.

'It cost us an enormous sum (paid into Mr Asquith's private account) to persuade him to bring in the Home Rule Bill'. The charge of corruption is quickly followed by a naked display of sectarianism: 'We must first ensure that the British Army does its <u>duty</u>, and shoots those Orange bigots down; then the Irish National Volunteers <u>might</u> come up, with the Reserve line, and see to the burning, and destruction of Protestant property, and the shooting down of the women and children of the Orangemen. Our ancestors did this in 1798'. The surprise and shock of these statements will not have fooled Rosalind for very long; the letter is so clearly false, written in all likelihood by a Protestant unionist with the aim of casting Redmond as a bloodthirsty bigot. Purportedly signed by Redmond in his capacity as colonel-in-chief of the Volunteers, it deployed the usual vocabulary of fear and loathing in the face of inter-communal violence; a rhetoric that was mirrored by unionists and nationalists alike.

The counterfeit letter has a special place in this cache of documents alongside the genuine one from Redmond (figs 12.6a&b).[38] Rosalind would have been alert to the danger of counterfeit letters in relation to Irish affairs, for the Redmond forgery, although not published in the press, was a throwback to the forged letters that implicated Parnell in the Phoenix Park murders of 1882. These had been the work of the journalist Richard Pigott who was exposed in court during the proceedings of the Special Commission established by Lord Salisbury to investigate Parnell's alleged criminal behaviour; Pigott fled to Madrid where he committed suicide and *The Times* was forced to pay damages, which had occasioned Rosalind's cry of 'Hurrah' in her diary. She would also have had personal reasons to recall the Parnell libel case since George Howard's relatives had been involved in two aspects of the affair. His cousin Lord Frederick Cavendish had been one of the two officials murdered in Dublin, and another cousin, the journalist and politician Henry Du Pre Labouchere, had, together with Parnell, challenged Pigott over the letters in 1888.[39]

Rosalind may have admired Redmond as a parliamentary leader but she would have been disappointed at how the political role of women was less developed in Ireland where there was no equivalent to the Primrose League or the WLF. The attitude of the Irish Parliamentary Party towards female enfranchisement was at best ambivalent and she would not have received kindly John Redmond's admission to a group of ladies in Belfast in 1914 that this was the first time he had ever addressed an audience of ladies.[40] Some nationalist

---

38 The second 'Redmond' letter is dated 3 July, such was the ire of the correspondent that he/she penned the letter immediately on reading the report in the *Irish Times* just 24 hours earlier, J23/472.   39 See note 28 above. The best account of the Parnell Special Commission remains F.S.L. Lyons, *Charles Stewart Parnell* (London, 1977), pp 368–89, 404–32. But see also the chapters in Algar Labouchere Thorald, *The life of Henry Labouchere* (London, 1913), pp 334–70. Another figure active in the Parnell affair was W.T. Stead who had an uncanny ability to crop up regularly in people's lives.   40 Senia Pãseta, *Irish nationalist women, 1900–1918* (Cambridge, 2013), pp 32, 66–72; also Constance Rover, *Women's suffrage and party*

MPs supported female suffrage but once the party was in coalition with the Liberals after 1910 the priority was to pass the third home rule bill in 1912, and thereafter find a way to implement it successfully.[41] In the world of hung parliaments and coalition government a different kind of realpolitik had to be pursued in order to secure constitutional gains. Political agitation and advocacy of single causes had to be balanced against differing tactical and strategic objectives, which would ultimately be measured by how the House of Commons voted on any given issue. This was something those who were not accustomed to the day-to-day business of parliament didn't always find easy to grasp.

Rosalind's letters to Redmond recognized that her action went beyond normal conduct: 'for an advocate of peace and an anti-armament politician like myself to bless a volunteer movement may seem strange' she conceded. But in reaffirming her belief in constitutional politics she was also declaring that there came a time when it was necessary to act in other ways. The tipping point with regard to Ireland had been the Ulster crisis, and it was essential to defend 'the rights now secured to the Irish nation under the Home Rule bill'. But there is evidence of another kind that she may have anticipated the real prospect of armed conflict in the region, for amongst her library is a copy of George Birmingham's novel *The red hand of Ulster*, a fictional account of preparations for armed resistance in Ulster. This, along with a number of bound pamphlets on both home rule and the Union show her to have been ecumenical in her reading around the question.[42]

Thus arose the irony that in 1914 most people felt civil war was more likely to break out over Ireland than any conflict in Europe; all were caught by surprise over the consequences of the assassination in Sarajevo on 28 June, and the war suspended the deadlock over home rule. As late as 23 July even someone as informed as Gilbert Murray could write: 'The crisis is rather more puzzling but not I think quite so bad as it seemed at first'.[43] Rosalind's attitude towards violence and conflict was ambivalent. With the outbreak of war she continued to defy people's expectations by refusing to allow the army to use Castle Howard as headquarters for northern command, declaring, 'I do not like the military and never have done so'. Her response was to join in the mass movement for Belgian relief, taking in sixty refugee families, ensuring they were housed, employed and their children educated, across the estates in Cumbria and Yorkshire.[44]

politics in Britain, 1866–1914 (London, 1967), pp 143–6, and Rosemary Cullen Owens, *Smashing times: a history of the Irish women's suffrage movement, 1889–1922* (Dublin, 1984), pp 47–50. For Redmond's attitude towards suffrage see Dermot Meleady, *John Redmond, the national leader* (Sallins, 2014), pp 175–7; his position was very different from that of his brother Willie Redmond. **41** For this period see James McConnel, *The Irish Parliamentary Party and the third home rule crisis* (Dublin, 2013), and Paul Bew, *Ideology and the Irish question, Ulster unionism and Irish nationalism, 1912–1916* (Oxford, 1994). **42** RH to John Redmond, 24 June 1914, J23/472; also J23/101/4, p. 908. For Birmingham, the nom-de-plume of the cleric and novelist James Owen Hannay, see his entry in the *ODNB*. **43** Gilbert Murray to 'Prit', 23 July 1914, Gilbert Murray MSS, 462, Bodleian Library. **44** Her forthright opinion

As early as September 1914, Rosalind had advocated the need for men in civilian life 'to keep our Government to sane counsels'; and by 1919 she was troubled by the punitive terms of the Armistice.[45] She despised militarism but, as with so many, her attitudes shifted during the war. In the summer of 1915 she wrote of how she meant 'to keep alive and strong the opposition to national conscription and the Prussianizing of our nation'; a few months later she was of the opinion that eligible men ought to enlist, and she did not oppose conscription when it was introduced in 1916. The following year came the realization that German militarism had to be defeated at any price: 'It is a war of attrition with a vengeance – and it has got to be put through, that much is certain'.[46]

With society increasingly subordinated to the war effort she began to voice her fear that civil liberties were being eroded, and began to despair at Lloyd George's coalition government: 'We are told and indeed we believe that we are fighting and killing to get freedom on earth yet in our own country we are fast losing all our liberties and Parliament is scorned and ignored'. In the same letter she looked further afield and expressed satisfaction at the overthrow of the Tsar in early 1917: 'Strange to say the only actual achievement for Freedom in this war has been that of the Russian army as politicians and not as soldiers. They said with one voice, there shall be freedom in Russia and they made a bloodless revolution'. In the first instance she supported the downfall of what she saw as a corrupt autocracy, and the liberation of the people, a feeling she had voiced at the time of the 1905 revolution in Russia, which she had described 'as the one hallelujah joy on my horizon'. But Alexander Korensky's provisional government was rudely shouldered aside when the Bolsheviks seized power in October, heralding a more sanguinary phase of revolution. On this Rosalind remained silent.[47]

Like many in the war she paid a heavy price: in 1917, her young secretary James Mitchell was killed leaving her distraught: 'We are living in the lowest pit of abomination … I am desperately dejected, I see no light anywhere'; a few months later her youngest son Michael went missing at Passchendaele.[48] By 1918, she had the dubious privilege of seeing memorials to four of her sons, who had lost their lives in either military or colonial service, and yet for all her sorrow and anger at the war she strove to believe in a world beyond the conflict.[49]

on the military was in a letter to Geoffrey Howard, 10 Sept. 1914, J30; for her work with Belgian refugees see F9/212, F8/4/12 and J23/101/5. For Castle Howard during the First World War see Christopher Ridgway, *Duty calls: Castle Howard and the Great War* (Castle Howard, 2014). For the role of women in organizing refugee relief see Katherine Storr, *Excluded from the record: women, refugees and relief, 1914–1929* (Oxford, 2010). **45** RH to Geoffrey Howard, 17 Sept. 1914, J30: RH to MH, 1 Jan. 1919, J23/26. **46** RH to Mary Ramsay, 1 June 1915, J23/101/5, p. 228; Leif Jones to Charles Luckhurst, agent at Castle Howard, 28 Oct. 1915, F8/4/12; RH to MH, 8 Nov. 1916, J23/26. **47** RH to MH, 25 Mar. 1917, J23/26; for the earlier comment RH to MH, 26 Jan. 1905, J23/26. **48** For the deaths of James Mitchell and Michael Howard see J23/122 and J23/99; and RH to MH, 9 Feb., 16, 25 Mar. 1917, J23/26. **49** The plaques commemorating four of her sons are in Lanercost

How is one to assess this figure involved in such a wide range of public activity stretching well beyond conventional models of aristocratic good deeds and charity?[50] What did she help to achieve? Was she effective and successful as a campaigner? Temperance, suffrage and home rule were lifelong commitments, as well as a strong sense of social justice; but many of her interventions were brief and transient: her support for striking workers coincided with the upsurge in industrial unrest in the early 1890s; Belgian relief was obviously prompted by the outbreak of war; and for all her remarks to John Redmond she made no further mention of Irish nationalism after 1914 (her surviving correspondence is silent on the 1916 Rising as well as the War of Independence). Her commitment to peace changed from supporting the Norman Angell movement, to calling for Germany to be defeated; but by 1919 she recognized the need to treat the defeated enemy reasonably, and like her son-in-law Gilbert Murray placed great faith in the League of Nations.[51]

Renowned in her lifetime as a radical figure, she adhered to a binary, almost Manichean, view 'that one could not live in two worlds, the Dedicated and the Pleasureful. Things of the spirit could not be mixed with things of the world'. Inevitably her high-minded ideals collided with the intractability of real life, consequently her energy and commitment would battle with despair and anger, producing 'a confused state' as her daughter recalled.[52] She was thus a contradictory character, remembered with real warmth and affection by some but known too as someone who was capricious, intemperate and inflexible. Her robust personality, and trenchant opinions, as well as a propensity to provoke, coloured her actions. On the whole she was a political realist, and knew that with every action there lay a range of motives, objectives and consequences. Many of her actions helped others, financially, with housing and employment, towards sobriety or personal and social amelioration; and in so doing they affirmed for her a sense of worth, the fulfilment of a public responsibility as expected of aristocratic women who were socially and politically engaged. In some ways the

Priory, Cumbria. Hubert Howard had been killed at the battle of Omdurman in 1898, as a correspondent for *The Times*; Christopher who had been commissioned in the Royal Irish Hussars died suddenly from pneumonia in 1896; Oliver had died in Nigeria in 1908; and Michael was killed at Passchendaele in 1917. Her eldest son, Charles, had served in the Boer War before dying of cancer in 1912. Geoffrey Howard, who had served in the Royal Naval Brigade between 1914 and 1915 before returning to government, was the only son who did not predecease Rosalind.   **50** For a survey of this subject see F.K. Prochaska, *Women and philanthropy in nineteenth-century England* (Oxford, 1980).   **51** Norman Angell (1872–1967), Labour MP and author of the pamphlet *The great illusion* (1909), argued that the need for war between advanced industrial economies was both futile and redundant. Gilbert Murray's thinking during the war followed an almost identical trajectory to that of Rosalind, from dismay at the outbreak of the conflict, to arguing the case for opposing German aggression in his pamphlet *How can war ever be right?* (1914), to worries at censorship and the suppression of civil liberties, and a fear that the war was being prolonged unnecessarily, Gilbert Murray to Mary Murray, 7 Sept. 1914, 18 Apr. 1917 (Bodleian Library, Murray MSS.462); see also Wilson, *Gilbert Murray*, chapter 17.   **52** Henley, *Rosalind Howard*, p. 112.

need to act, and to be seen to act, was paramount, whether this was agreeing to a rent reduction in 1892, organizing thirty tenant farmers to visit the House of Commons in 1889, or lending £500 to printers on strike in Berlin.[53] And while she might rage at how she was reported in the press, she recognized that her reputation ensured that these matters were receiving public attention.

But what she could accomplish at a local level with clear results, whether on the estates in Yorkshire and Cumbria, or by helping to organize committees and mount campaigns, was not always so easy to replicate at a national level. She may have been part of a collective, working for grand causes such as suffrage or temperance, but her strong personality often led to tensions with colleagues, or sudden outbursts of unexpected behaviour. In some ways these can be explained as acts of protest or frustration on the part of someone who refused to acquiesce to particular expectations and orthodoxies. Many such interventions were public statements that said as much about her as the causes themselves, but in the eyes of some they came increasingly to be regarded as the actions of a quirky controversialist. Her reputation may have gained her notoriety but ironically this could weaken the political force of her actions, which came to be seen as quixotic.

One of the best ways of measuring her life is to see what regard she was held in at the time of her death. Her obituary in *The Times* described her as 'A fearless champion of causes', and *The Westminster Gazette* called her both 'A great lady' and 'a conscientious worker'. These were testimonials she would have appreciated, given that public engagement was what mattered most to her. In his lengthy memoir in the *Daily Telegraph* the Irish MP and journalist T.P. O'Connor captured a sense of her restless and articulate intelligence: 'she had intense vitality', he wrote, but she was also 'feverish and in a way clamorous'; and 'If you chanced to pass her by, you were sure to observe that she walked with a brisk step and that she was talking vividly and emphatically'.[54] While she relished debate, argument, and confrontation, as she grew older she would brusquely put down views that did not accord with her own.

Her memory lingered in the minds of her family too, her sons-in-law Charles Roberts and Gilbert Murray both offered astute summaries. For Roberts, she was a 'Radical below the gangway', someone in favour of government of the people for the people but not wholly by the people; in the end he considered her to be 'déclassé', and fully aware that her radical views would 'break down the aristocracy to which she originally belonged'.[55] Gilbert Murray recognized this dimension too, calling her a 'Whig aristocrat in an extreme form, with all the authoritarianism and fearlessness of the aristocrat and the rebellious nature of

53 For rent reductions in 1892 and 1893 see F8/19/5, pp 32, 46; for the visit by farmers to London see Roberts, *Radical countess*, pp 46–7, and J23/489/2, p. 10; also RH to GH, 22 and 23 June 1889, J23/4 and RH to Henrietta Stanley, 14 June 1889, J23/7; for her support for Berlin printers in 1891 and 1892, see J23/462.   54 All three obituaries appeared on 13 Aug. 1921.   55 Roberts, *Radical countess*, p. 162.

the radical', but he also discerned a puritanical streak in her. Both assessments affirm the sense of a divided character or, as her daughter Dorothy Henley remarked in her candid memoir, someone with a 'two-sided personality'.[56]

Rosalind also found literary fame of sorts as the model for George Bernard Shaw's character Lady Britomart in his drama *Major Barbara*. Shaw also caricatured Gilbert Murray and his wife, Mary, in the play, who appeared respectively as the Greek scholar Professor Adolphus Cusins, and the character of Major Barbara Undershaft, Lady Britomart's daughter, an officer in the Salvation Army and who is wooed by Cusins. Shaw collaborated with Murray over parts of the dialogue and structure, and the play appears to have caused no offence to the family when they attended a performance in December 1905.[57] Rosalind, who was a regular theatre-goer, saw a number of Shaw's plays, greatly enjoying *John Bull's other island*, and finding his *Misalliance* 'intensely amusing'; she was less complimentary about *Great Catherine*, and only cared 'moderately' for *Pygmalion*.[58]

The imperious Lady Britomart has unmistakeable affinities with Rosalind, Shaw gives her some amusing lines, as for example when she rounds on her son Stephen to say that she has never treated her children as children but always as friends and companions, 'with perfect freedom to do and say whatever you liked so long as you liked what I could approve of'. In choosing the name Britomart Shaw was alluding to the heroine who appeared in Book 3 of Edmund Spenser's epic poem *The Faerie Queene* first published in 1590; Shaw's literary model would have pleased Rosalind in many ways, perhaps not so much because Britomart, the only female knight in the poem, was an allegorical figure of chastity, but because she was a representation of Elizabeth I, the ultimate national matriarch (at least before Queen Victoria). Shaw may or may not have known that Rosalind was also exceptionally fond of Spenser's poetry.[59]

But Shaw also managed to capture the contradictory nature of Rosalind's personality as recalled by her family. At the beginning of the play Lady Britomart is described as 'a woman of fifty or thereabouts, well dressed and yet careless of her dress, well bred and quite reckless of her breeding, well mannered and yet appallingly outspoken and indifferent to the opinion of her

---

56 Both assessments are in Henley, *Rosalind Howard*, pp 143, 145–8.   **57** For the way in which Shaw quarried his material from the Howard family see, Wilson, *Gilbert Murray*, pp 94–5, 108–12; see also Stanley Weintraub (ed.), *Shaw: an autobiography, 1898–1950, the playwright years* (Toronto, 1971), pp 152–3, 284; Bernard Shaw, *Collected letters, 1898–1910*, ed., Dan H. Laurence (Toronto, 1972), pp 565–6, 585–6; Michael Holroyd, *Bernard Shaw, 1898–1918: the pursuit of power* (London, 1989), pp 108–12.   **58** RH to MH, 6 Mar. 1905, 20 Mar. 1910, 8 Dec. 1913, 19 June 1914, J23/26; Rosalind and her daughter attended a matinee performance on 8 Dec. 1905; Bernard Shaw, *Major Barbara* (London, 2000), p. xi.   **59** For her lifelong pleasure in reading Spenser, 'one of my most loved poets', see RH to GH, 23 and 26 Nov. 1872, and 18 Feb. 1898, when she was overjoyed to receive a copy of Walter Crane's illustrated six-volume edition of *The Faerie Queene*, J23/4. See also her diaries, 19 Nov. 1872, J23/102/16, and 9 and 14 May 1883, J23/102/19.

interclocutors, amiable and yet peremptory, arbitrary and high-tempered to the last bearable degree'. The play revolves around who will inherit her husband's business as an armaments manufacturer, but Andrew Undershaft wishes to preserve a tradition that the fortune can only be passed to a foundling who would then marry into the family. Their son Stephen Undershaft is passed over and the factory is left to Adolphus Cusins who is revealed to be a foundling, and who then marries Barbara Undershaft. As with so many Shavian dramas the plot device is there to service a fable, but what Shaw cannot have realized is that within a few years a similar discussion over inheritance would occur between Rosalind and her husband as they decided to disregard the custom of primogeniture and divide the family estates among their surviving children.[60]

The negative image of Rosalind Howard has persisted to the point where she has become a caricature, a stereotypical Victorian harridan. There is much to admire in her life, which should not be eclipsed by episodes and actions of a less sympathetic nature. It is too easy to forget that in Victorian Britain aristocratic women received little or no formal education, even if they were skilled conversationalists, avid readers, fluent linguists, and independent thinkers. They operated within what has been termed a 'separate sphere', in a world polarized by gender. In the case of Rosalind this could reinforce a wilful sense of isolation that manifested itself almost in a need to be at odds with the world, as seen by her reaction to the remark in the *Pall Mall Gazette* in 1889.[61] Such headstrong individualism made her an embattled figure who cared little for what the world said about her but who was still capable of being angered by personal criticism. As a political campaigner she was efficient and effective, and for her the success of meetings was not measured by performance and oratory: instead, she asserted, 'All we have to judge is whether the <u>truth</u> is spoken whether the ideas put forward are enlightened and progressive and therefore helpful to our world'.[62]

But her partisan stance in a world of diverse values – social, political, moral, cultural – meant that like Lady Britomart she had difficulty in accepting viewpoints contrary to her own. In some respects she was disadvantaged too by the fact that her husband stepped aside from politics after 1885, devoting the rest of his life to pursue his passion for painting, something she warmly encouraged him to do. Her motives here were mixed: Howard's retreat from public life defused political differences especially over home rule; but she was genuinely glad that he had forsaken the 'present angry and bitter turmoil of politics'.[63] As a consequence she presented a more solitary political profile, to all intents and purposes married to a non-political husband. She had little opportunity to act

60 Roberts, *Radical countess*, pp 156–9.   **61** For the role and status of women in this period, see K.D. Reynolds, *Aristocratic women and political society in Victorian Britain* (Oxford, 1998), pp 153–87, and Pat Jalland, *Women, marriage and politics, 1860–1914* (Oxford, 1988), pp 189–220. Both books offer a number of examples of politically active women who show how untypical Rosalind was in many regards; Reynolds reviews the debate around 'separate spheres', pp 3, 20–1, 189–90.   **62** RH to MH, 12 May 1901, J23/26.   **63** RH to GH, 18 Jan.

as partner to a spouse who was either an engaged parliamentarian or an active member of government. Therefore, neither a political hostess nor a political wife, she could not exercise patronage and influence in the way other aristocratic women did. But this isolated stance can also be read in another way, as proof that a woman such as Rosalind did not necessarily need the platform of a politically engaged husband. She could, quite simply, make her own way through public life although this meant her reach was limited. She hosted no salon, and No. 1 Palace Green, Kensington, the family house in London designed by the architect Philip Webb in 1868, and decorated by William Morris and Edward Burne-Jones, was an artistic salon and a family home rather than anything else.[64] There were few if any regular gatherings of political figures, actual or aspirant, nor was it a locus of influence in the capital. If she had a coterie it was a small one consisting of family – her son Geoffrey, son-in-law Charles Roberts, secretary Leif Jones and her other son-in-law Gilbert Murray who refused to stand for parliament but was a politically respected figure. When Geoffrey started to rise through the Liberal party, and Charles Roberts also achieved office, then she had more contact with Westminster, and was able to meet directly with leading politicians.

Two of her closest aristocratic activists were Lady Henry Somerset (1851– 1921) and Ishbel Marjoribanks, 2nd marchioness of Aberdeen (1859–1939). Both women espoused temperance, and were Liberals. Somerset was in many ways a closer model to Rosalind. Divorced from her husband she had to make her own way through life, but she was wealthy in her own right, and this allowed her to set up temperance associations, travel widely, and eventually found an Industrial Farm Colony in Surrey that was a refuge for women. Unlike Rosalind she was adept at building alliances with other organizations and influential leaders, including William Booth of the Salvation Army, and the American temperance campaigner Frances Willard who she met in the United States. Rosalind enjoyed Somerset's company, finding her 'full of fun' with a 'vivid and crisp personality'.[65] If Somerset led an independent life, Aberdeen, by contrast, assumed a more conventional role, acting as consort to her husband when he was viceroy of Ireland, and governor general of Canada, but she also found time to raise her family and campaign on Liberal and women's issues. Gladstone referred to the Aberdeens as 'an edifying couple', so close were their beliefs and

1881, 4/5 Mar. 1885, 28 May 1886, 15 Nov. 1888; on Howard giving up the parliamentary seat for East Cumberland see Surtees, *Artist and autocrat*, p. 144.   **64** For Palace Green see Surtees, op. cit., pp 51–7, 84–5; and Christopher Ridgway, 'A privileged insider, George Howard and Edward Burne-Jones', *British Art Journal*, 3:3 (Autumn 2002), 9–13.   **65** RH to MH, 2 Aug. 1910, J23/27; for her correspondence with Lady Somerset between 1894 and 1906 see J23/200; Claire Niessen, *Aristocracy, temperance and social reform: the life of Lady Henry Somerset* (London, 2007), and Ros Black, *A talent for humanity: the life and work of Lady Henry Somerset* (Chippenham, 2010). By a curious coincidence W.T. Stead likened Lady Somerset to Spenser's heroine Britomart, Niessen, op. cit., p. 231. The application of chivalric identities and modes of behaviour to Victorian women is something not considered by Mark Girouard in *The return to Camelot: chivalry and the English gentleman* (London, 1981).

activities; and in 1925 they even wrote a joint autobiography, *We Two*. Rosalind confided to her daughter that she had taken 'a rare liking and affection' to Lady Aberdeen, but felt that she was not sufficiently strong as a leader to stamp out dissent in the WLF.[66]

Nor was Rosalind ever to achieve the sort of standing held by Theresa, 6th marchioness of Londonderry (1856–1919). Diametrically opposed to Rosalind in politics, especially over suffrage and home rule, she acquired a reputation as the foremost political hostess of the day, closely linked to the heart of the Conservative and Unionist parties, and deploying her home in the capital, Londonderry House, as well as the family seats of Wynyard Park in Co. Durham, and Mount Stewart in Co. Down, in the service of her friends and allies. At the height of her prowess Londonderry has been described as 'privy to advice from the highest echelons of unionism; entrusted with politically sensitive information; pumped for political news and holding the largest assemblage of political women in Ireland's history'[67] Rosalind never came anywhere close to exercising such power and influence. Besides which she had an aversion to the grand, she disliked smart society, and was careless of social etiquette. When she entertained it was for estate tenants and staff, or small handfuls of visitors: not for her receptions with lavish dinners for hundreds of people. She felt that she could exercise influence in a quiet, behind-the-scenes manner, but she never entirely gave up the idea of being a significant hostess. Her daughter noted that towards the end of her life, in 1919, when Rosalind moved from Palace Green, she was making plans for a new home in London: 'with pathetic and deluded optimism she meant to rebuild a brilliant social circle, political this time, and to be the centre of the Liberal parliamentary party'. These were the dreams of an ageing woman struggling to adjust to a new political landscape, following the collapse of the Liberal party in the general election of 1918.[68]

But her public life was always balanced with a sense of domestic duty. In choosing to educate some of her children at home she never abandoned her responsibilities as a mother despite the presence of nurses and governesses; her youngest daughter Aurea did not come of age until 1905 – by which time her eldest daughter Mary was aged forty and through whom Rosalind was a grand-mother. The arc of family and domestic life therefore spanned a long time.[69] Equally, her insistence on managing the family estates only added to her workload, causing her to lament, 'this effort to live in two homes is killing work and spoils both places'.[70] To begin with, like so many new owners, she was

66 RH to MH, 13 May 1902, 27 June 1906, J23/26; for her correspondence with Lady Aberdeen between 1890 and 1911 see J23/429; and Veronica Strong Boag, *Liberal hearts and coronets: the lives and times of Ishbel Marjoribanks Gordon and John Campbell Gordon, the Aberdeens* (Toronto, 2015), pp 76–115, 135–40, 168. 67 Diane Urquhart, *The ladies of Londonderry: women and political patronage* (London, 2007), chapter 2, and p. 116. 68 Henley, *Rosalind Howard*, pp 141–2. One bright moment was partial enfranchisement for women in 1918. 69 On tutoring her children at home see Roberts, *Radical countess*, p. 73.

doubtful as to the abilities of her deputies and reticent to delegate; but eventually she came to appreciate the professional skills of her agents, clerks and staff, and entrusted them with greater responsibility; thus in the course of a single year she went from viewing her agent in Cumbria, R.E. Turnbull, as 'not wildly clever' and someone unable to read a compass, to 'the best agent I have seen'.[71]

Rosalind's energy, fuelled by an invincible belief in Liberal values, burned brightest in the service of just or moral causes. Her actions may not always have been consistent, and she changed or modified her stance on more than one occasion; if some of her behaviour seems erratic then that is because all public causes demand sooner or later some degree of adjustment. Her egalitarianism was perhaps selective; nor was she troubled by apparent contradictions, on the one hand declaring herself an anti-armament campaigner yet able to give money to a physical-force movement like the Irish National Volunteers. Her view undoubtedly would have been that changing circumstances sometimes necessitate different responses. Notwithstanding her periodic bouts of fatigue and ill-health she was a woman of immense drive and conviction; contemporaries may have described her as extreme, feverish or clamorous, but what remains uppermost in any assessment is the vigour and engagement of a well-intentioned, independently minded woman. Dorothy Henley likened Rosalind's conversational powers to a flow of lava: a figure of speech that encompassed the sensation of heat and intensity, as well as a force that was unstoppable and fiery.[72] More widely her presence did indeed flow in every direction, and while she may have recognized the concept of separate spheres, all that she did or said bridged the differences between gender, as well as the dichotomy between public and private life. No endeavour could be denied her if she set her mind to it, and it is no coincidence that the epitaph on the tomb she shares with her husband in Lanercost Priory reads, 'They served their generation'. But she made for a difficult servant, for she wished, also, to be mistress of all that she did and said. Or in the words of Gilbert Murray, 'She was good when charging at the head of her troops, but I suppose if she was not quite the head she left the troops altogether'.[73]

---

70 RH to GH, 26 June 1887, J23/4.   **71** RH to GH, 9, 10, 12, 16 May, 5 July 1888, J23/4.
72 T.P. O'Connor, note 49 above; Henley, *Rosalind Howard*, pp 38–9, where she also comments on her mother's stamina in meetings, p. 80.   **73** Quoted in Henley, *Rosalind Howard*, p. 148.

Elite women and their recipe books: the case of Dorothy Parsons and *her Booke of Choyce Receipts, all written with her owne hand in 1666*

REGINA SEXTON

In recent years, growing academic interest in food and culinary history has directed attention to manuscript receipt (hereafter recipe) books, printed cookery books, and the women who wrote them. The concept of the recipe filtered downwards in the later medieval period from court and royal collections, and by the sixteenth century, cookery manuals were entering into the workings of the food culture of the nobility. While cooking at court was dominated by men, aristocratic and gentry women developed a strong and lasting association with compiling, bequeathing and inheriting manuscript recipe books. In time women infiltrated the print industry, giving rise in the eighteenth century to the 'age that we think of English country cooking at its best, represented in cookery books written mainly for women'.[1] This feminization of the cookbook in England opens rich entry points into understanding aspects of the lives of the women who wrote them.[2] Recent studies have not only broadened the understanding of these texts, and how they were circulated and transmitted, but also have encouraged deeper analysis, with the books being viewed as sources of a lived tradition.[3]

Irish manuscript recipe books share common characteristics in their content and cookery styles that point to the existence of a distinctive culinary culture amongst the gentry in pre-Famine Ireland, a culture that was heavily influenced by, if not indistinguishable from, British practice. A number of recent publications have addressed the Irish manuscript recipe books, focusing mainly on the collections in the National Library of Ireland.[4] A number of books are also

I would like to express my gratitude to Lord and Lady Rosse, Birr Castle, Co. Offaly, for their permission to work on the Birr Castle Archive manuscript and for their hospitality and welcome on my visits to the castle. I would also like to thank Lisa Shorthall, archivist, Birr Castle Archive, for her help. Particular thanks go to Lorna Moloney (APG & SoGUK), Merriman Research & Training Ltd, genealogist and medieval historian, for her work in tracing Dorothy Parsons the younger's family trees and for her generosity in sharing with me her unpublished research. **1** Stephen Mennell, *All manners of food: eating and taste in England and France from the middle ages to the present* (Illinois, 1996), p. 95. **2** For discussion see Gilly Lehmann, *The English housewife: cookery books, cooking and society in eighteenth-century Britain* (Devon, 2003), pp 61–3 and ibid., pp 95–9. **3** See, for example, Michelle and Sara Pennell (eds), *Reading and writing recipe books, 1550–1800* (Manchester, 2013). **4** See Madeline Shanahan, *Manuscript recipe books as archaeological objects* (London, 2015); idem,

held in private collections and the best-known of these is Dorothy Parsons' 1666 *her Booke of Choyce Receipts*, which is held in Birr Castle (formerly Parsonstown House), Co. Offaly. Despite the reputation of the book as possibly the oldest recipe collection to be associated with Ireland, surprisingly little has been written about either Dorothy Parsons or her recipes.[5]

This chapter will redress the lack of attention to the 1666 text. It will consider the book as a typical representative of the genre and it will argue that far from being merely an item of ephemera, the book can be seen to have multiple meanings: it is at once a very personal document, but it is also sophisticated, modern and outward-looking in terms of its construction and in shaping the culinary culture of Dorothy Parsons and her household. However, the manuscript also presents a tangle of problems common to handwritten recipe collections: its relationship with Birr Castle is uncertain; the women responsible for influencing the content of the collection and for compiling and writing the recipes, namely Lady Elizabeth Parsons and Dorothy Parsons, have not been conclusively identified to date as the compilers and it is difficult to pinpoint with any degree of certainty the place of composition. The first task, therefore, is to attempt to untangle these uncertainties and to suggest a contextual background for the manuscript and the women involved in its production. Indeed, a consideration of the problems associated with provenance, ownership and authorship is useful to a discussion of how the family and marital relationships of the elite, especially as these relate to communities of women, may have helped to spread and establish new foods and culinary styles from England to Ireland in the seventeenth century.[6]

In the 1980s, the recipe book was acquired by the Birr Castle Archive from a bookseller in England on the premise that it had strong links to the Parsons of Birr.[7] A pen and pencil drawing of 'Parsonstown House, 1668', in the fly-leaf of the remedies section, shows improvements made to the castle, with the humorous and playful heading, 'An excellent receipt to spend 4,000 pound', in a hand which seems similar to that of Dorothy Parsons.

The Parsons of Birr are related in the paternal line to the powerful Parsons brothers, Sir Laurence Parsons (1575–1628) of Youghal and Birr, and William Parsons (1570–1650). The Parsons came to Ireland from England around 1590

'"Whipt with a twig rod'": Irish manuscript recipe books as sources for the study of culinary material culture, *c.*1660 to 1830', and Regina Sexton, 'Food and culinary cultures in pre-Famine Ireland', *Proceedings of the Royal Irish Academy, section C, volume 115* (Dublin, 2015). **5** The fullest treatment of the manuscript (hereafter Birr Castle Archive (BCA), MS A/17) is given by Lady Alison Rosse, 'Birr Castle' in C.A. Wilson (ed.), *Traditional country house cooking* (London, 1993), pp 124–55. **6** Shanahan, in reference to her own work on the National Library of Ireland's collection of Irish manuscript recipe books and to the work of Jane Ohlmeyer, *Making Ireland English: the Irish aristocracy in the seventeenth century* (New Haven, CT, and London, 2012), discusses the evidence for the transmission of recipe-based cookery from the New English settlers to elite Gaelic families in the context of marriage. See Shanahan, '"Whipt with a twig rod'", pp 199–200.

and 'as tough and capable men, they pioneered the resettlement of the country
after the wars of the sixteenth century'.[8] William held offices including that of
surveyor-general of Ireland and commissioner of the plantations of Leinster,
Ulster and Connaught and was created baronet of Bellamont, Co. Dublin, in
1620. Laurence worked with him as joint supervisor and extender of crown lands
in Ireland, and after 1622 he established himself at Birr.[9] By the early 1650s, the
Parsons of Birr held additional properties in Dublin and in Youghal, Co. Cork,
together with the manor of Rathanghan in Co. Kildare.[10]

    In 1636, Laurence's son, William (1604–52) married Dorothy Philips
(1609–71), daughter of Sir Thomas and Lady Alicia Philips of Limavady,
Londonderry (hereafter identified as Dorothy the elder).[11] Through her
maternal line, Dorothy the elder, was related to the Ussher and Loftus families.
Her maternal grandfather was Sir William Ussher of Donnybrook, a family that
had provided several mayors of Dublin during the fifteenth and sixteenth
centuries, while her grandmother, Isabella Loftus, was daughter of Adam Loftus,
archbishop of Dublin, lord chancellor of Ireland and first provost of Trinity
College Dublin.[12]

    Dorothy's eldest daughter, Dorothy Parsons (Dorothy the younger), was born
at Birr in 1640. Dorothy the younger's siblings were Laurence, for whom the
baronetcy of Birr was created in 1677, William, John, and younger sisters
Margaret and Elizabeth. In the 1650s the Parsons were forced to leave
Parsonstown House for London and by 1653 they had experienced a number of
deaths in their immediate family over a short period of time: William's death in
November 1652 was followed by the death of his daughter Elizabeth in
December 1652, while his son John died in January 1652, and his brother ffenton
Parsons, of Lincoln's Inn, London, died in September 1652.[13] Before his death,
William provided in his will for the maintenance and inheritance of his (then
pregnant) wife Dorothy and their children.

    Along with a yearly income, Dorothy the elder was to 'have my dwelling house
at Youghall with the Yards Courts Stable Malthouse Gardens Coach house
outhouses Gardens orchards and all other Appurtenances'.[14] William also
provided well for the inheritance, portions and education of his sons. He
stipulated particular conditions for the education of his daughters and their

---

7 Personal communication, Lady Alison Rosse, Aug. 2016.   **8** A.P.W. Malcomson, *Calendar
of the Rosse papers* (Dublin, 2008), pp 8–9.   **9** Ibid.   **10** Copy, made *c*.1820, of the will of Sir
William Parsons, Kt and 1st Bt, the former lord justice, proved in the Prerogative Court of
Canterbury, together with an incomplete, typescript copy (made by Rolf Loeber, [*c*.1990]) of
the will of William Parsons of Parsonstown, proved 1653, and typescript notes by Loeber on
both wills (Birr Castle Archive (BCA), MS A/11).   **11** Ibid.   **12** Lorna Moloney, A
genealogy report for Dorothy Parsons (Clare, 2016), pp 1–47 [compiled for Regina Sexton,
UCC, 9 Nov. 2016; another copy in possession of Lady Alison Rosse, Birr Castle, Co. Offaly].
13 A thick folio volume of accounts of money, debts, payments, prices of articles, clothes,
allowance, and other matters connected with the family of Parsons, 1652–96 (BCA, MS
A/12), p. 18.   **14** BCA, MS A/11, p. 9.

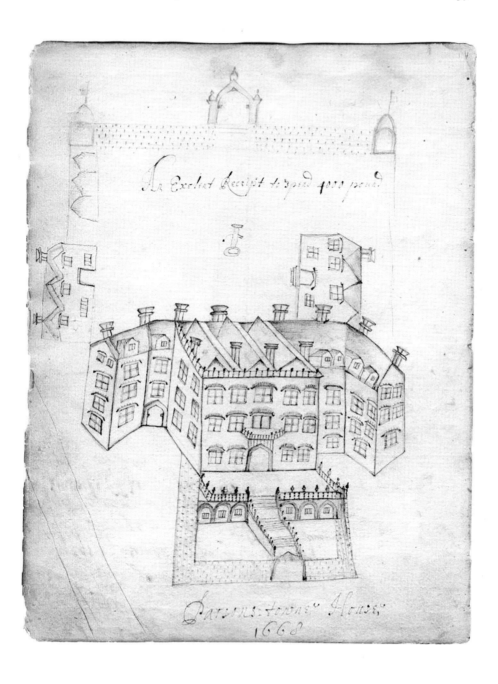

13.1 Pen and pencil drawing of Parsonstown House (now Birr Castle) showing improvements made to the house in the late 1660s. BCA MS A/17. Image courtesy of Birr Castle Archive, Birr, Co. Offaly.

marriage portions, in particular that of his eldest daughter, Dorothy. Provision was made for their 'maintenance, breeding and education' while living with their brother Laurence; however, if he and the executors of his will deemed fit, the daughters could either be sent abroad or live elsewhere for their 'better breeding'.[15] Provision for the social, cultural and educational betterment of the daughters rendered them more valuable on the marriage market and William was particularly keen to secure a good marriage for Dorothy.

Securing a good marriage for Dorothy the younger was of no small significance socially or economically, in maintaining existing connections or establishing new networks of influence. In anticipation of an advantageous marriage, William granted his daughter the substantial marriage portion of £1500[16] provided she married 'that person [unnamed] whom I have nominated to her Mother and Grandmother'.[17] Her refusal to marry the pre-selected candidate would see her portion reduced. In 1655, the marriage of Dorothy the younger and William Parsons (1627–61/2) of Langley Marish, Buckinghamshire, took place in St Margaret's Church in Westminster.[18] Her final marriage settlement was £1700 together with £100 'for her clothes and for her wedding expenses – £16 (and £5 for the repair of a cabinet)'.[19] By accepting her father's nomination, connections were now established between the Buckinghamshire Parsons, for whom a baronetcy was created in 1661, and with the notable Kedermister family of Langley Park, in Langley Marish.

Dorothy's husband William was the son of Sir John Parsons (c.1590s–1653) and Elizabeth Kedermister (1599–1663).[20] Generations of the Kedermister family had worked as keepers of the royal lands at Langley (known as Langley Park) and in 1626, Charles I granted Elizabeth's father Sir John Kedermister (c.1570s–1631) a lease on the estate.[21] In his lifetime, Sir John founded the Langley almshouses and the library attached to the church of St Mary the Virgin. Sir John stocked the library with printed books of a theological nature, but he also gifted the family's 500-page illuminated manuscript herbal, *Pharmacopolium; or, A booke of medicine*, which he compiled around 1630 with his wife Mary.[22] The almshouses and library were endowed in his will with a further stipulation that his wife Mary Kedermister (1577–1637) extend the library's holdings with the purchase of books to the value of £20. His estate passed to his sole heir Elizabeth and her husband John Parsons.

It was against this backdrop of political upheaval, displacement and relocation in the milieu of Cromwellian and Restoration London that work on the recipe

15 Ibid., p. 6.   16 BCA, MS A/11, p. 5.   17 Ibid.   18 Dorothy Parson – marriage – 1655, Society of Genealogists (UK), Boyd's marriage index, 1538–1840.   19 BCA, MS A/12, unnumbered page.   20 'Parishes: Langley Marsh' in *A history of the county of Buckingham*, vol. 3, ed. William Page (London, 1925), pp 294–301, British history online http://www.british-history.ac.uk/vch/bucks/vol3/ pp 294–301 [accessed 7 June 2017] .   21 Ibid. 22 Slough history online http://www.sloughhistoryonline.org.uk/asset_arena/text/pdf/sl /sl/sl-sl-max_chapter15–d-02–000.pdf [accessed 25 Feb. 2017].

book commenced in 1666. A close reading of the book together with evidence from the will of Dorothy the younger leaves little doubt that she was the lead compiler of the recipe collection. There is a brief mention of her son, John (1656–1704), second baronet of Langley, in a margin note in the remedies section of the book. As well as the recipe 'A drink Good for those yt are subject to sore Eyes', Dorothy recalls of the recipe that 'the Dr Tuberfield apoynted [this remedy] for my son John at Salisbury in 1665.'[23]

Furthermore, a number of recipes ultimately sourced from a Mrs Jewkes,[24] and attributed to Elizabeth Parsons, are important clues not only in identifying the compiler but also the figure of Lady Elizabeth Parsons, Dorothy's mother-in-law. The recipes from Mrs Jewkes circulated between Elizabeth and Dorothy, thus making her known to both women, and Dorothy the younger refers twice to Mrs Jewkes as her 'good friend' in her will of 1668 when she bequeathed her an item of her jewellery.[25] Clearly, the three women enjoyed each others' company and friendship between the time of Dorothy's marriage in 1655 and the death of her mother-in-law in 1663. It is also reasonable to suggest that the emphasis on remedies in Dorothy's book, and the volume of medicinal recipes she inherited from Elizabeth, is a reflection of the Kedermister interest in the science of medicine as illustrated in John and Mary Kedermister's *Pharmacopolium*. Dorothy integrated knowledge of cookery and medicine inherited from two generations of her husband's family. Dorothy's blending of inherited material with her own recipes makes her part of a multi-generational process of securing and extending knowledge in the science of medicine and the art of cookery. Indeed, her engagement with the process may have been not only a gender expectation but also a family obligation given the Kedermister interest in book culture.

The book itself is a leather bound small quarto volume (height 24cm x width 19cm). It is in handsome condition,[26] the majority of the pages are free of foxing or food staining, tearing or environmental damage, and the clarity of the handwriting enables easy reading of the recipes. In this respect, the book stands apart from other near-contemporary Irish manuscript recipe collections, many of which are in a poor state of preservation.[27] The *Booke of Choyce Receipts* is

23 A small quarto volume of medicinal and culinary recipes of Dorothy Parsons of Birr (1640–1688) (BCA, MS A/17), remedies section, p. 72.   24 For example, see recipes from the cookery section of BCA, MS A/17, 'To make Bunes', p. 1; 'To make small mead', p. 2; 'To make mince Pies', p. 12, and in the remedies section 'to make orange water good to Expel wind and comfort the Stomach', p. 12.   25 Will of Dorothea Parsons of Langley, 8 Feb. 1669 (TNA, Will registers, PROB 11, piece 332).   26 The volume was sent to England for rebinding within the last twenty years. The covers are intact and without damage and the pages are securely bound to the spine. Personal communication, Lady Alison Rosse, Aug. 2016.   27 NLI holds a small collection of manuscript recipe books with commencement dates of *c.* late seventeenth century. See, for example, two recipe collections, authors unknown, associated with the Smythe family of Barbavilla, Co. Westmeath (NLI, papers of the Smythe family of Barbavilla, Co. Westmeath, MSS. 11,688 and 11,689). The cover and binding of both books are in a poor state of preservation.

comprised of un–ruled, hand-numbered paper pages and it is divided into two distinct halves: one contains culinary recipes totalling more than eighty-seven pages 'of Preserves & cookery', and the other half runs to 147 pages of 'Salves, Oyles, waters & other Physican Receipts'. There is evidence to suggest that Dorothy Parsons intended a carefully organized collection of recipes: the culinary and medicinal recipes are alphabetically arranged into contents pages.[28] There is also some evidence of an attempt to categorize the recipes; for example, those for enriched breads, puddings and preserves are often grouped together. However, this attempt at imposing order is more a feature of the early sections of the book, particularly those recipes associated with Elizabeth and Dorothy Parsons. Indeed, apart from Elizabeth and Dorothy, there seems to be six other unnamed contributors to this volume, each adding either a single or a block of recipes over time. These additional recipes date from after Dorothy had ceased her recipe-writing, and so extended the life of the volume into the eighteenth century.

Malcomson has dated the volume to between 1666 and *c.*1720.[29] However, the nature of the recipes from what is referred to as 'Hand 3' (H3) and their attending culinary styles may push the period of composition later into the eighteenth century. This contributor (H3) has peppered recipes throughout the volume, many of which are short, concise entries, at times no more than a few sentences in length. It appears that this contributor identified empty spaces on pages with earlier recipes and took advantage of these blank sections, and possibly abbreviated the recipe instructions to fit the available space. H3 provides twenty-four recipes and of these six are for puddings. These pudding recipes were baked in a dish with a puff crust at the rim rather than being boiled in a cloth or casings, thus suggesting the early decades of the eighteenth century when baked puddings grew in favour and fashion over the gut and cloth-cooking versions.[30] The continued use of bone marrow in these recipes may also indicate an early seventeeth-century date. The final recipe in the collection, 'To stew Pigeons white', is written in a bold and fluid hand and the recipe is typical of the eighteenth century in its use of a concentrated gravy in which to stew or braise the pigeons.[31] In comparison to recipes of an earlier period, it takes a more restrained approach to flavouring, letting the sharp properties of herbs (chives and parsley) lift the dish rather than spices. The dish is served strewn with parsley and more chives, bringing a fresh finish. A later date for continued work on the collection is evident in margin notes which include the dates 1746 and 1769 in H3's hand in the remedies section of the book.

---

28 The culinary recipes are listed in ten incomplete and unpaginated pages of contents. Five of these pages precede the culinary recipes, while the other five are contained in the medicinal remedies section of the book. The table of contents for the medicinal remedies runs to over eleven pages.   29 Malcomson, *Calendar*, p. 8.   30 Anne Wilson, *Food and drink in Britain* (London, 1973), p. 318.   31 BCA, MS A/17, p. 87.

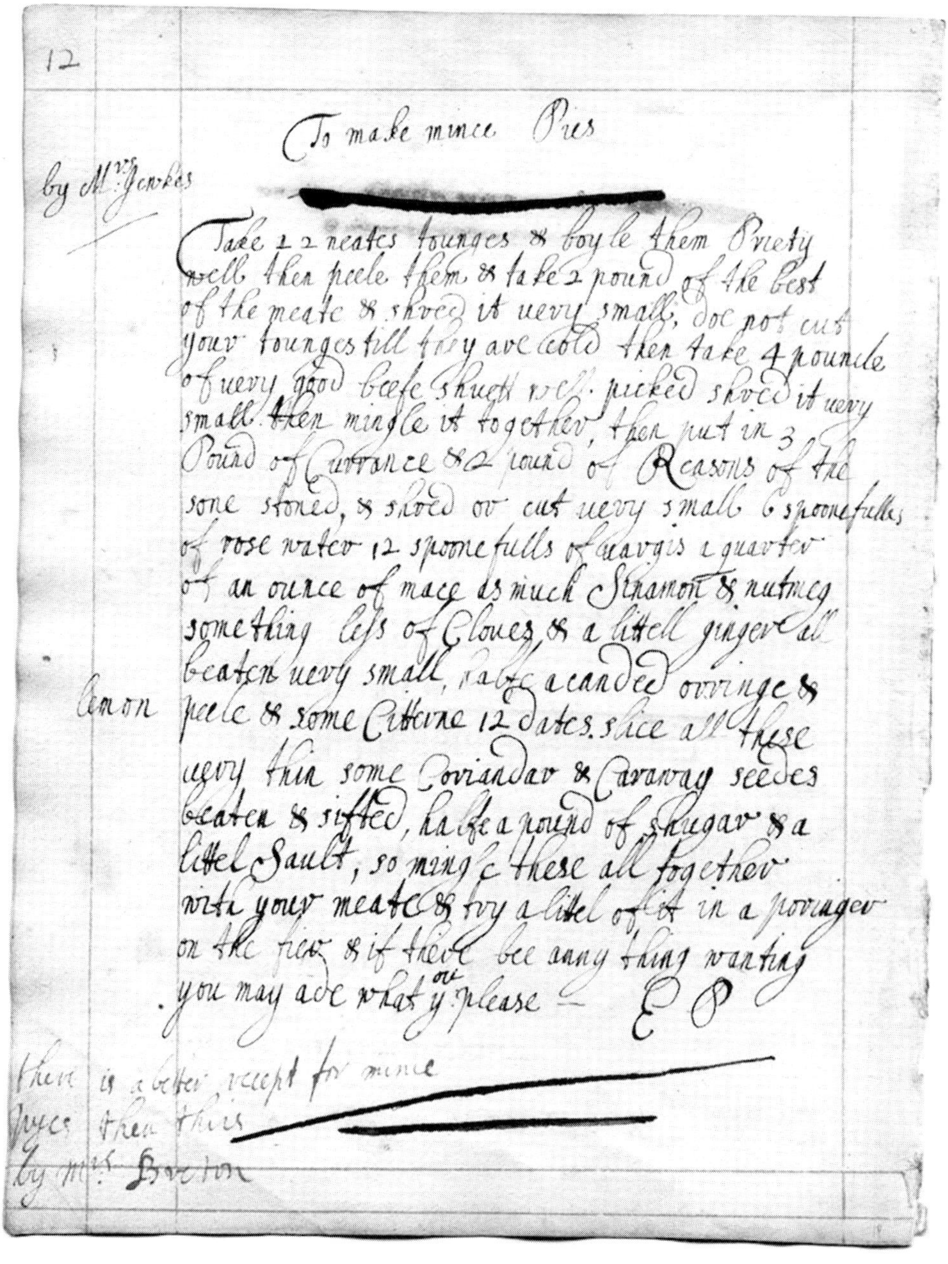

12

To make mince Pies

by Mrs Jewkes

lemon

Take 2 neates tounges & boyle them Prety
well then peele them, & take 2 pound of the best
of the meate & shred it uery small, doe not cut
your tounges till they are cold then take 4 pounde
of uery good beefe shueh well picked shred it uery
small then mingle it together, then put in 3
Pound of Currance & 2 pound of Reasons of the
sone stoned, & shred or cut uery small 6 spoonefulls
of rose water 12 spoonefulls of uargis a quarter
of an ource of mace as much Sinamon & nutmeg
something lefs of Cloues, & a litell ginger all
beaten uery small, take a canded ouringe &
peele & some Citterne 12 dates slice all these
uery thin some Coriandar & Caraway seedes
beaten & sifted, halfe a pound of shugar & a
litell Sault, so minge these all together
with your meate & try a litell of it in a porriager
on the fier & if there bee anny thing wanting
you may ade what you please ——   E P

there is a better receipt for mince
pyes then this
by mrs Breeton

13.2 A recipe 'To make mince Pies' attributed to Mrs Jewkes, approved by Lady Elizabeth Parsons and included in Dorothy the younger's 1666 collection of recipes. BCA MS A/17. Image courtesy of Birr Castle Archive, Birr, Co. Offaly.

A further complication in attempting to trace a chronological order for the community of contributors is that H3 and 'Hand 5' (H5) may have been entering recipes concurrently. It is very difficult to determine where Dorothy Parsons finally ceased working on the collection. It is likely that her work on the volume ceased at some point between the recipe 'to makes sausages' on page 60 and the entry 'to collar pig' on page 67. A final recipe attributed to Elizabeth is given on page 63, 'to pickell cowcumbers', and it would seem that after this Dorothy makes just a few more entries. By page 63, the handwriting exhibits a deterioration away from the tendency towards exuberant looping of letters to lettering that is more ragged, and the words have a looser spacing on the page. However, a comparison of recipes for making sugar cakes, one on page 14, and a later version on page 49, indicates that Dorothy is still contributing to the collection, and the changed nature of her handwriting may be as a result of declining health or upheavals in her personal affairs. Thereafter, considerations of authorship are complicated further by a variety of additional hands.

The recipes that this chapter is most concerned with are those of Lady Elizabeth Parsons and Dorothy Parsons. Dorothy marked the start of the collection in 1666 with the inscription:

> *Dorothy Parsons her Booke of Choyce Receipts, all written with her owne hand in 1666*
> *But those are most Especialy Exelent that are marked with EP being all aproved & tryed by ye Lady Eliz: Parsons in her Life time*

From the outset, Dorothy intended to establish ownership of the collection. She made implicit reference to her own abilities of discernment and good taste, but she also evoked the past through the memory of her mother-in-law to bring further gravitas and authority to her collection. In establishing a relationship with Elizabeth, Dorothy can be seen as the inheritor of a cache of 'Especialy Exelent' recipes, the details of which would be revealed through the act of recording them. There is no indication of how Dorothy acquired Elizabeth's recipes and we can only surmise that she may have transcribed them from an existing collection, possibility loose-leaf or bound, that may have been held by the family. By recording or re-recording these recipes, Dorothy was the link between the past and the future; in effect she was the guardian of this culinary inheritance and by committing the collection to paper she was safeguarding them for the future.

She left little doubt as to the nature of these recipes: they were selected on the basis of their superior qualities: they are 'Choyce' and 'Exelent' and those attributed to Elizabeth (initialized EP) carried the additional benefit of guaranteed reliability; they are 'aproved' and 'tryed'. The concept of quality for Dorothy was built on tangible, results-based considerations (ensuring that the recipes worked) but also on more subtle notions of taste and refinement. On the practical side, numerous recipe notes, and tips and recommendations for the optional addition of improving or embellishing ingredients, indicate a commitment to improvement, be it in technique or ingredient choice. Elizabeth's recipe 'To Hash a Caulfes head' has a note in the margin on how to improve the flavour and presentation of the dish: 'you may fry bacon & put among it [?] it very good, & fry some of the brain in the yolke of an egg for garnish.'[32] Margin notes also alerted the reader to the fact that there was a better version of this recipe later in the collection; similarly, Dorothy's recipe for 'Livery Pudings' has a margin note that 'there is a better receipt to make livery pudding than this.'[33] Such comparisons are repeated with recipes 'to make Custards'[34] and 'to make a very good Custards'; as well as 'to preserve respas [raspberries]' and 'to preserve respas the best way'.[35] This was a working collection of recipes and the marginalia, with their recommendations to add, change and insist on the 'best', brought together a particular community of people who engaged with the activity – the cook, the consumer, the compiler, the reader and Lady Parsons herself. Therefore, the recipe often came to be seen as 'an embedded discourse with a variety of relationships within the social context'.[36] However, these relationships were not simply confined to local communities of family, friends and kitchen staff; for it is clear from the contents of Dorothy's cookbook, and from the design plan and construction of the collection, that she also engaged with the wider world of printed cookbooks and with the burgeoning interest in new foods and cookery styles. She balanced this wider awareness with an eye on the past and through her invocation of Elizabeth Parsons, she blended the excellence of a mostly Elizabethan-style of sugar cookery with the more contemporary trends of her day. In this selective commandeering of the past it could be said that Dorothy Parsons was creating a personalized culinary history for her family.

Dorothy Parsons was not alone in her approach; these features and characteristics are typical of the manuscript cookbook genre. The tendency to reach backwards in time for material and to blend that with contemporary recipes was standard practice for recipe book compilers and authors. Depending on how the book was compiled, this could lead either to a chronological ordering, with the old recipes presented first and followed by the new, or else to the creation of a blended volume where 'the additions of the previous owner were incorporated into the manuscript according to category so that the book would have to be re-copied and re-indexed', thus shattering chronological continuity.[37] In more scattered collections, there is often a mishmash of old recipes and new ones with no clear attempt to distinguish between them, and very often there are

32 BCA, MS A/17, p. 13. **33** Ibid., p. 24. **34** Ibid., pp 32, 33. **35** Ibid., pp 7, 45. **36** Janet Floyd and Laurel Forster (eds), *The recipe reader: narratives, contexts, traditions* (Nebraska, 2010), p. 2. **37** Karen Hess, *Martha Washington's booke of cookery* (New York, 1995), p. 452.

no contents or index pages. Karen Hess states that 'until sometime in the seventeenth century … manuscripts were usually accretive, as distinguished from collected ones. It was a question of station: the nobility, even the gentry, had their recipes [accretive collections], but the wives of rising merchants had to collect them.'[38] Lehmann points out that Hess' broad categorization of manuscript collections into just two forms is an 'over-simplification', and a number of hybrid forms can also be found depending on when the manuscript was produced, and the circumstances and context of how the book was produced.[39]

Dorothy's collection is in a hybrid style: the volume contains 147 culinary recipes and of these 46 are attributed to Elizabeth Parsons and 59 belong to Dorothy. Most of Elizabeth's recipes are entered in the earlier pages of the book but there is no clear attempt to separate the entries according to ownership and Dorothy enters her own recipes between those of Elizabeth. This organization is based on an attempt to order the recipes by category rather than by ownership. Therefore, the volume groups together Elizabethan and pre-Restoration-style recipes with no attempt to separate the entries by date. And while this mixing of times and styles was a common practice of manuscript collections, it is also likely that Dorothy modelled her volume on contemporary trends in cookbook design, and these trends may have had a particular resonance with the Parsons family.

Lehmann points out that by the mid-seventeenth century, the aristocratic origins of recipes was a selling-point and that [printed] books began to emphasize their upper-class sources. She argues that the content of recipe books was shaped by three trends: an interest in the cookery of the aristocracy and of royalty, a fascination with the recipes of the past, and the growing influence of French cookery.[40] She notes that 'nostalgia for the old order' is obvious, and would become even more so at the Restoration, when the cook and cookery book author, Robert May, commenting on his own (much-quoted) instructions for producing a set-piece for a banquet, concluded:

> These were formerly the delights of the Nobility, before good House-keeping had left England, and the Sword really acted that which was only counterfeited in such honest and laudable Exercises as these.[41]

There is clear evidence that each of these trends impacted to varying degrees on the contents of Dorothy's book. Her recipes, like those of her mother-in-law Elizabeth, are lavish, exceedingly rich, highly flavoured, and generous in their use of expensive and exotic ingredients. There are traces of French influence and the recipes have much in common with aristocratic and court cookery. Up to a third of the recipes are very similar to those found in May's *The accomplisht cook* (1660), and other printed volumes. The elite nature of the recipes that Dorothy

---

38 Ibid., p. 451.   **39** Lehmann, *The British housewife*, p. 33.   **40** Ibid., pp 38–9.   **41** Ibid., p. 39.

selected for her volume is an unequivocal statement of the Parsons' high standing and good taste.

The period in which Dorothy compiled the book was a period of recovery for her family. In the decade between 1640 and 1650, the Parsons of Birr were embroiled in the wars of the Irish Rebellion and the Cromwellian wars, and the family spent much of the 1650s in London. Recovering the past, therefore, may have brought a sense of comfort to Dorothy and in creating a tradition of inheritance, she justified her current position in directing and controlling the food economy and culinary culture of her own household.

Her decision to compile her book of recipes may have had more to do with more personal upheavals rather than the political impact of war in Ireland. In 1666, Langley Park, the manor and estate, was leased to Sir Henry Seymour (1612–83), MP for the borough of East Loe (and groom of the bedchamber and comptroller of the customs), who eventually bought the estate in 1669.[42] In the same year, Dorothy was the defendant in a dispute with Sir Charles Cleaver and Rowland Jenckes, of Inner Temple, London, about the implementation of the terms of her husband's will in providing properties for his younger children, William, Elizabeth and Alice at Dorney, Burnham and Cippenham, in Buckinghamshire.[43] Indeed, Dorothy's own will of 1668 indicated that her personal property was scattered in a number of different locations.[44] Her practice of compiling and collating recipes may well reflect a wider desire to establish a semblance of order in a world beset with national and family conflicts. Her work can be seen as a demonstration and affirmation of her important role in managing the culinary aspects of the house, and the knowledge too that the collection would memorialize her achievements after death.[45]

What is clear is that Dorothy Parsons went beyond simply compiling a list of recipes. This was a deliberate exercise in re-enforcing her expertise and her control over areas of preserving, confectionary and high cookery. Her time in London no doubt brought her into contact with established and emerging tastes of food, cookery and dining. The period was also an active one for cookbook production: Lehmann notes that between 1650 and 1659, eight new titles appeared, several going into many editions. Clearly, there was a demand for such publications, and the enthusiasm with which these books were bought, read and copied demonstrates that Puritanism did not have the deadening effect on English cookery sometimes attributed to it.[46] The print trade deliberately targeted wealthy women with promises to throw open the 'closets' and reveal the

42 J.B. Burke, *A genealogical and heraldic history of the extinct and dormant baronetcies of England* (2nd ed., London, 1847), p. 478 and G.E Cokayne (ed.), *Complete baronetage vol. iii, 1649–1664* (Exeter, 1903), pp 183–4.   **43** Court case 1666. C6/398/2, 'Cleaver v Parsons', TNA, *Discovery Series*, http://discovery.nationalarchives. gov.uk/details/r/C5280572 [accessed 14 May, 2017].   **44** Will of Dorothea Parsons of Langley, 8 Feb. 1669.   **45** G.E. Cokayne, *Complete baronetage*, p. 184, gives the date of her death as 20 Feb. 1668 and 24 Feb. as the date of her burial in Dublin.   **46** Lehmann, *The British housewife*, p. 38.

'secrets' of the aristocracy. Exemplars of the period include A.W., *A book of cookrye* (1591); Thomas Dawson's *The good huswifes jewell* (1585); Sir Hugh Plat's *Delights for ladies* (1609); Gervase Markham, *The English huswife* (1615) and of course Robert May's collection of 1300 recipes, *The accomplisht cook*; although the latter was not published until 1660 it contains recipes from the pre-Restoration era. While these books were compiled by men they took the manuscript recipe books of women as their source material. It is likely that Dorothy was a witness to these developments while in London and later worked these influences into the style and design of her own book. She must also have realized the prestige and practical value of Elizabeth Parsons' manuscript, most especially her recipes for sugar-based cookery.

Lehmann notes that by the early seventeenth century, women's areas and spaces of work were changing, due largely to the increased use of sugar in cookery. The preparation of remedies (many sugar-based) and confectionary engaged women in the specialist work of the still-room, but soon women were involving themselves in cookery as well. According to Lehmann, 'sugar seems to have been the ingredient which drew all three strands of household receipts together.'[47] The elaboration of sugar cookery brought it beyond the production of sweetmeats for the 'banquet' course. Throughout the first half of the seventeenth century, the blending and extension of work from the still-room and the kitchen gave rise to an extensive range of sweet goods from the preserves and sweet wines of the still-room to the sweet creams, custards, syllabubs, puddings and jellies and sweet baked and fried goods – cakes, biscuits, pastries, pancakes and fritters – of the kitchen. Working with sugar was a modern and appropriate pursuit for women and not surprisingly their manuscript recipe collections reflected their desires to be involved in the fashion. Referring to Lady Fettiplace's 1604 manuscript collections, with which Dorothy's book has much in common,[48] Lehmann observes that 'The proportion of the three types of receipt in this collection indicate a hierarchy of prestige; remedies were foremost, followed by confectionary, with cookery at the bottom of the pile.'[49]

Dorothy Parsons clearly aligned herself with these current and emerging trends. Her collection focused on preserving fruit and working with sugar to produce cream dishes, puddings and baked goods. These areas of activity would continue to occupy elite women and influence the contents of their recipe books into the nineteenth century,[50] and Dorothy's collection is the earliest extant evidence of how the tradition may have been transmitted to Ireland.

However, as the contents of her recipe book are highly selective, they fall short in offering a rounded and inclusive description of upper-class food and culinary practices in the first half of the seventeenth century. The contents

47 Ibid., p. 33.   **48** See Hilary Spurling (ed.), *Elinor Fettiplace's receipt book: Elizabethan country house cooking* (London, 1986).   **49** Lehmann, *The British housewife*, p. 33.   **50** For a fuller discussion see Sexton, 'Culinary cultures', pp 258–96.

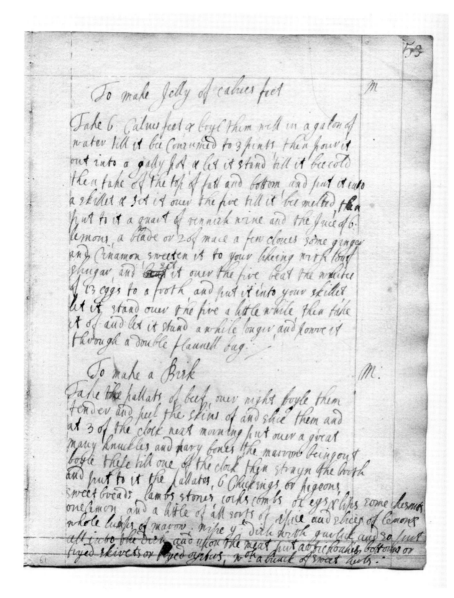

13.3 Dorothy the younger's recipe for a French-style bisk, which was a lavish stew of mixed meats, offal and broth/sauce. BCA MS A/17. Image courtesy of Birr Castle Archive, Birr, Co. Offaly.

satisfied her own areas of interest and they deliberately neglected to mention the more routine and mundane kitchen activities such as bread-making, and roasting and boiling meat, fowl, wild fowl and fish. It is likely that she concerned herself predominantly with the areas where she had a direct or supervisory role in executing. Yet many of her recipes expected an inherent relationship with other specialized areas of work – the dairy and the brew- and bakehouses. Mention of ingredients like ale yeast for cakes suggests that if these were not home-produced, it is most likely they were acquired from local suppliers. References to the standardized, though hopelessly regulated, penny loaf in a number of Dorothy's recipes suggests a local supplier.[51] The diversity and range of luxury ingredients that her recipes demanded, or at least aspired to, indicate a healthy trade with commercial suppliers and it is possible that exotic items were acquired in bulk at particular times. Therefore, the successful creation of recipes and the preparation of dishes of elite consumption were dependent upon reliable suppliers, healthy trade networks and sound infrastructural supports.

Furthermore, given that the successful creation of the dishes was contingent on wealth, access to ingredients and kitchen staff with requisite skills, it is quite possible that many of the recipes were associated with times of special celebration, such as luxury dinners and gatherings of family, friends and notables within their networks of influence. For such occasions of display, lavish dishes and various other elements of vicarious display denoted wealth, privilege, prestige and a sense of *à la mode*. In this 'social atmosphere of commensality'[52] the recipe was crucial to demonstrating and distinguishing the elite culture of a household. The house's recipe collection was a very powerful symbol of communication and it is not surprising that women like Dorothy Parsons took such care in structuring and selecting their contents. Her inclusion of key dishes of the court style (a bisk, four recipes for fricassees, together with a Spanish-style olio)[53] owed as much to the influence of French cookery writers like the founder of French classical cooking Francois Pierre La Varenne (*c.*1615–78),[54] often mediated through English printed cookbooks, as it does to the family's own ambitions to appear forward-looking and 'universal'.[55]

However, it is also possible to catch faint glimpses of what may have been more commonplace items of eating. Dorothy includes two recipes for pease porridge and one for pease potage, dishes that were more usually associated with a simpler food culture. Her first recipe 'to make ordinary Pease Porridge' contains white peas, new milk and mint and the instructions are concise:

---

51 For discussion of the penny loaf see Elizabeth David, *English bread and yeast cookery* (London, 1979), pp 226–32.   52 J.P. Daloz, *The sociology of elite distinction: from theoretical to comparative perspectives* (Hampshire and New York, 2010), p. 74.   53 Bisks and olios were elaborate stews made with a variety of meats and served with/in a sauce and often elaborately arranged for presentation at table. For more information see Wilson, *Food and drink*, p. 101. 54 For further information on La Varenne, his recipes and influence, see Philip and Mary Hyman, *The French cook, Francois Pierre La Varenne* (East Sussex, 2001).   55 Robert May, *The accomplisht cook*, facsimile edition (Devon, 2000), un-numbered page. In an overdone testimonial to May's work, his friend John Town describes him as 'so universal, he'l not miss, the Pudding, nor Bolonian Sausages. Italian, Spaniard, French, he all out-goes, Refines their Kickshaws, and their Olio's [sic].'

boyle a quart of white pease wth some mint till they are broke & strain them through a Collender & put some new milke to them.[56]

This recipe is immediately followed by a second, superior one attributed to a 'JP'.[57] Here peas are boiled with a leg or neck of beef. Additional ingredients such as bacon, bread, leeks and butter are added and the porridge is flavoured with mint and anchovies. Spinach is suggested as an optional extra. It appears that JP may also have supplied the recipe 'To make french Potage' in which a shin of beef is used as the base of a broth with spinach, charnell, sorrel, ox palates and cox combs. The recipe explains that this dish may be turned into a pease potage by adding in the cooking liquor of boiled peas. This ordering of pea dishes is perhaps guided by taste preferences and the ingredients to hand but the recipes may also have reflected the hierarchy of eating within the household, with simpler dishes being prepared for staff and servants. The sheer size of other food items, and the volume of ingredients they contained, may also indicate that these items were shared amongst household staff. Dorothy's collection has four recipes for plum cake, which is raised with ale yeast/barm and therefore is more akin to a heavily enriched bread.[58] The cakes are large, starting out with a gallon or peck of flour, and up to two pounds of butter, six pounds of currants, four nutmegs, and a pint of cream and a pint of ale yeast. Caraway comfits (sugar-coated caraway seeds) are used in one recipe and the margin note recommended the addition of the 'perfumes' musk and ambergris. These were exceedingly rich and large fruit cakes that demanded not only luxury ingredients but also the preliminary preparations of making ale yeast and caraway comfits. Both operations demanded a high level of skills – barm was notoriously temperamental to work with and making comfits required excellent confectionary skills. These cakes may have been prepared for social gatherings or else they stored well and may possibly, on occasion, have been shared with staff or upper servants.

Overall, the recipes in Dorothy Parsons' collection and the style of cookery promoted conformed closely with styles and fashions that are found in English manuscript collections and printed cookbooks of the first half of the seventeenth century. One of the bestsellers of the period was Gervase Markham's *Country contentments or the English huswife* (1615), which had run to nine editions by 1683. In his section on 'skill in cookery' he recommends the following as dishes proper and fitting to a good kitchen: pottages, broths, salads, meat collops, eggs, tansies, fritters, pancakes, puddings, sausages, boiled and spit-roasted meat, fish, fowl and wild fowl, sauces, pastry, pies, tarts, fools, trifles, florentines, banqueting stuff-preserves, cakes, jumbals and sugar leaches, wafers, fricassees, quelque choses, carbonados, pauperdies and oleputringes.[59] Over half of these types of

56 BCA, MS A/17, p. 60.   **57** Ibid., p. 61.   **58** Ibid., pp 16, 20, 35, 49.   **59** Gervase Markham, *Country contentments or the English huswife* (London, 1623), pp 57–115. http://digital.library.lse.ac.uk/objects/lse:heh898zor [accessed 9 Mar. 2016].

dishes are variously represented in Dorothy's recipes and the collection also has much in common with that of Robert May's. However, it was also a food and culinary culture that was in transition. Hess points out that 'the seventeenth century was the golden age of the English kitchen. Medieval excesses were being sloughed off; the heavy standing pottages (stews thickened with cereals) were largely being replaced with more bracing soups, especially among the wealthy; spices were being used lightly and more discreetly except for the ubiquitous nutmeg; the use of fresh herbs was becoming more skilled; and the sauces were never cheapened by flour.'[60] Dorothy's collection of recipes was still heavy in spices and the continued use of items such as ginger, rose and orange waters and the perfuming ingredients lingered from an earlier period. New approaches to flavouring dishes are evident, most especially the use of citrus juice and anchovies, and of course the use of sugar was extensive.

A number of ingredients and dishes are notable by their absence: there is no mention of New World ingredients such as turkey, kidney beans and, most especially, chocolate that together with tea and coffee were assimilating quickly in the food habits of Europe and England. In the fifteenth century, the European voyages of discovery to the east and to the Americas brought a range of new ingredients and new culinary practices to Europe and in time generated demand for these exotics. The commercial activities involved in their cultivation, production and trade, most especially in the case of sugar, 'would alter global food systems in dramatic and unexpected ways.'[61] The most significant and high profile New World ingredient in Dorothy Parsons' collection is sugar and her use of this ingredient falls in line with contemporary developments that saw 'the dramatic growth of sugar production and consumption after the mid-seventeenth century, [and which] enabled the articulation of a rather new distinction within the European understanding of food taste, namely the difference between "savoury" and "sweet".'[62] The process of separating the sweet from the savoury, which continued throughout the eighteenth century, would change the ways in which sugar was used in cookery, resulting in a new classification of dishes into sweetened dessert dishes and unsweetened savoury ones. Dorothy's collection is at the cusp of these emerging developments. Her collection of cake recipes, for instance, is instructive in comprehending the transformative effect of sugar when used in baking, and the evolution and separation of breads and cakes. Her cake recipes, using ale yeast rather than eggs as the leavening agent, are at the mid-point between a traditional enriched bread and a more modern cake. Yet many of her pudding recipes followed older tendencies of mixing sweet and savoury in the one dish. Similarly, fashionable

---

60 Hess, *Martha Washington*, p. 4.   **61** Rebecca Earle, 'The Columbian exchange' in J.M. Pilcher (ed.), *The Oxford handbook of food history* (Oxford, 2012), pp 341–57, at p. 342. **62** Brian Cowen, 'New worlds, new tastes: food fashions after the Renaissance' in Paul Freedman (ed.), *Food: the history of taste* (London, 2007), pp 197–231, at pp 219–20.

hot beverages like chocolate, coffee and tea are not mentioned and her recipes are more concerned with caudles[63] and possets[64] – the hot drinks of an older culinary order. What is striking however is the inclusion of a recipe using potatoes. The potato was unknown in Europe until the sixteenth century and it was slow to feature in the dietary practices of the wealthy, not least because of the suspicions about its similarity to the poisonous nightshade plant family.[65] Her decision to include the recipe may relate to the novelty value of this relatively new ingredient rather than its culinary merits. And her recipe treats it as a starch foundation for a pudding that would at once be sweet, spicy and savoury. Nonetheless, Dorothy's recipe 'To make a Potata pie' is quite possibly the earliest recipe for a potato dish connected with Ireland.

Dorothy Parsons' collection reflects a range of food trends and culinary developments. The inclusion of French-style recipes is significant as it indicates an awareness of the latest trends, particularly those pertaining to aristocratic and court cookery. It is doubtful, however, that the refinements in the use of spices, fruit and sugar, as encouraged by the French chefs of nouvelle cuisine, had reached or gained support in Dorothy's household, and in this respect the collection reflected the somewhat confused attitude that the English held in deciding whether to embrace or distance themselves from the principles of this new approach to cooking. Indeed, the broad collection of meats, offal and fowl contained in her folio recipes seems staid in comparison to that of Robert May's, and yet the astonishing array of ingredients in her bisk recipe (beef palates, knuckles, chickens, pigeons, sweetbreads, lamb stones, cocks combs, ox eyes and lips, marrow, skirrets, oyster, artichokes, chestnuts and lemons) would indicate that the French tendency for restraint was missed in the transmission of these recipes.

The case of Dorothy Parsons is significant in illustrating how recipe-based cooking was established in Ireland. As an example of a marriage out of Ireland, she was positioned to re-direct and share her learning with her family in Birr and Dublin. Thus, as Shanahan has pointed out, the network of marriages amongst gentry families in Ireland and England supported the transmission of food tastes and sensibilities and no doubt encouraged a lively trade in ingredients, utensils and wares.[66] The late seventeenth century (*c.*1668–70) account book of David Johnston of Dublin, for instance, offers an insight into the range of luxury and specialist goods and cooking equipment available in the city.[67] The account book records payments to him for commodities such as spices (cloves, nutmeg, mace, ginger, cinnamon, ginger, pepper, saffron and aniseeds), sugar (powdered sugar,

---

63 A caudle was a hot alcoholic drink that could be sweetened and spiced and often enriched with the addition of breadcrumbs and eggs. Caudles were also added to pies towards the end of the cooking time to moisten the contents. **64** A posset was a thickened alcoholic drink. Dorothy Parsons' rich variety was composed of wine, ale, eggs, cream, sugar and spice. **65** Cowen, 'New worlds', p. 213. **66** Shanahan, '"Whipt with a twig rod"', pp 199–200. **67** Account book, of uncertain provenance, belonging to one David Johnston of Dublin, *c.*1668–75 with the inscription, 'A copie booke of accompts belonging to David Johnston, Dublin 1669' (BCA, MS A/16).

brown sugar, muscovado sugar and brown candy), molasses, dried fruit (currants, raisins and prunes), rice, alum (an astringent salt used in pickling and bread-making),[68] sweet oil, vinegar and tobacco. An entry *c.*1670 lists goods delivered to an Alin/Elin Smith for what seems to be the stocking of a kitchen with utensils and wares.[69] The variety of goods is similar to those listed in Dorothy's recipes.

Shanahan also makes the case that English gentry women brought with them a portfolio of knowledge that promoted recipe-based cooking among the Gaelic elite. In this sense the recipe was a cultural marker. The willingness to embrace and practice recipe-based cookery differentiated the new settlers from their Gaelic counterparts, whose food culture was systematically denigrated by commentators and propagandists for the crown in blanket tones of shock, revulsion and disgust, and which ranged from the extreme anti-Irish bias of the artist and engraver John Derricke[70] to John Dunton's comic, almost histrionic, accounts of grinding and making butter and oatcakes in the west of Ireland.[71] Presented as primitive, disordered and unhygienic, the food culture of the Gaelic Irish became a convenient symbol with which to represent the general disarray and barbarity of 'the other'. The text to accompany *The image of Ireland* details an outdoor feast of boiled and roasted meat with its unwashed puddings (possibly the casings), dirty strips of meat and offal that were cooked directly over coals for the 'want of a gridiron'. In such a system there was no need for a cook since, 'Each knave will play the cook, to stand his lord in stead. But tag and rag will equal be when chiefest rebel feed.'[72] Equally, a recipe written in English had no place here as the approach to cooking was presented as fundamental and intuitive rather than guided by instruction. For instance, Edmund Campion (1540–81), English Jesuit writer and scholar who lived in Dublin from 1569 to 1571, describes what was a rudimentary form of black puddings eaten by the Gaelic Irish ('*their kine they let blood*, which, grown to a jelly, *they* bake and overspread with butter and so eat in lumps'),[73] that is at a considerable distance from the black puddings described in the recipe books. Dorothy Parsons' recipe (attributed to Elizabeth) 'To make Black Pudings', which is very close to that of Robert May's,[74] is rich and exquisite and highly flavoured:

---

68 Christopher Driver (ed.), *John Evelyn, cook: the manuscript receipt book of John Evelyn* (Devon, 1997), p. 179.   **69** BCA, MS A/16, unnumbered page.   **70** John Derricke, *The image of Irelande with a discoverie of woodkarne* (London, 1581), facsimile edition with introduction, transliteration and glossary by D.B. Quinn (Dublin, 1985), p. 192. The aim of Derricke's work was to illustrate in glorious terms the achievements of Lord Deputy Henry Sidney (1529–86), governor of Ireland, 1575–8.   **71** John Dunton, *Teague land; or, a merry ramble to the wild Irish: letters from Ireland, 1698*, published as an appendix in Edward MacLysaght, *Irish life in the 17th century* (Dublin, 1939). Dunton (1659–1733) was an English author and bookseller who wrote about his travels to Ireland in the late seventeenth century. **72** Derricke, *The image of Irelande*, p. 192.   **73** Edmund Campion, *A history of Ireland written in the yeare 1571*, quoted in A.T. Lucas, *Cattle in ancient Ireland* (Kilkenny, 1989), p. 201. **74** May, *The accomplisht cook*, pp 126, 189–91.

Take a pottle of great oatmeal, pick it very Clear take 3 quarts of milk make the milk boyle then put in the oatmeal & let it boyle a little then putt in to a basin & Couer it Close & let it stand all night Couered; then in the morning take of the topp of the otmeale & put to it a quart of hogs blood then work it well together whith yr hands then put in quarter of an ounce of mace a few cloves & a little peper beaten small 2: nutmegs grated. Season it well with sault then put in a good deale of Peneroyall greene fennell, time sweet mariojeme all shred very small 10 eggs Leaving out of the whites stird in [inked out] pound of beef shuett shred very small thicking itt with grated bred & soe fill itt into oxes Gutts, iff it bee to stiff to fill putt in a little Creame or milk that hath being boyled & cold againe.[75]

The base ingredients were oatmeal, milk/cream and blood, high ranking and popular items in the Gaelic tradition, so what separated the cultural groups was not exclusively the ingredients, rather the treatment of these ingredients. A recipe would set down, order, measure, and recommend method – all of which would refine the objectionable, thus the art of cookery could be seen as a civilizing force delivered through the agency of the recipe. Familiarity with recipe-based cookery was a gateway to a different food culture and it is quite possible that adopting recipes was one dimension of the cultural re-adjustments and re-alignments made by the Gaelic nobility to secure and advance their positions. And contrary to the extreme and prejudiced accounts mentioned above, it is likely that the power of the recipe was realized by the Gaelic Irish, the old English and the urban elites much earlier than is commonly held. One of the earliest manuscript collections in the National Library of Ireland identified by Shanahan is from the Inchiquin O'Briens. She states that 'while the Inchiquin O'Briens had ancient roots in Ireland, the books within their collection dating to this period were largely written by women marrying into them, often directly from England'. For example, the earliest manuscript recipe in their collection 'was potentially started by the English Lady Frances Keightley, but more likely by her daughter, who was born in Ireland, but whose family and connections were chiefly English aristocrats, including Queen Anne and Queen Mary II.'[76] The Inchiquin O'Briens' manuscript was started in the mid-to-late seventeenth century,[77] close in time to when Dorothy Parsons began her collection, and a comparison between them could well reveal the degree to which an English food culture was received amongst elements of the Gaelic community.

In her will, Dorothy Parsons bequeathed items that were very personal – her beds, bed linen, pewter, jewellery and items of tableware[78] – 'two silver spoons,

---

75 BCA, MS A/17, p. 23.   **76** Shanahan, *Manuscript recipe books*, pp 85–6.   **77** For discussion on the commencement date of the Inchiquin O'Briens' book of recipes see Shanahan, "'Whipt with a twig rod'", p. 119.   **78** Will of Dorothea Parsons of Langley, 8 Feb. 1669 (TNA, Will Registers, PROB 11, piece 322).

her caudle pott and her porringer'.[79] Spoons and bowls represent the very
fundamentals of feeding with a strong association with soft, comforting foods
and beverages, thus re-enforcing her role in nurturing and symbolically locating
her in the domain of food and care-giving within the household. Her marriage
into the Parsons of Langley brought her into contact with Mary and Elizabeth
Kedermister, women who were engaged in the quintessential female activities of
cookery, preserving, home remedies and almsgiving. Dorothy's book perpetuated
and extended these traditions, aligned her with the cultures of wealthy and noble
women, and affirmed her position within the group. In this regard she is
conformist in meeting the social norms and expectations of respectability. As the
subject of her father's strategic marriage-planning, she is used as a device in
sealing three branches of the Parsons families, all of whom had established
connections to the court, thus bolstering the ambitions of the Parsons of Birr in
insecure times.

Dorothy Parsons' life experiences and her movement among communities of
aristocratic women informed her approach to food and cookery. Her choice of
recipes defined not only the food culture of the house but it also defined her
relationship with food fashions. And while cookery resided in the private world
of the home, the implications of how Dorothy built her food and culinary
cultures had wider and public implications. The art of cookery brought a gloss
of prestige to the dining affairs of the house, which no doubt had aided the social
ambitions of her husband. Furthermore, the willingness of Dorothy Parsons and
her contemporaries to embrace new styles of cooking and new ingredients,
together with the heavy use of spices, encouraged a trade in consumer goods, in
particular kitchen utensils and tableware, and in luxury ingredients, notably
sugar. The world of the kitchen, therefore, linked not only to the estate with its
kitchen gardens, orchards, malt and bake houses and fish ponds but to networks
of local, international and transatlantic trade. However, what is most notable
about Dorothy's book is its significance in helping to illustrate how culinary, food
and material cultures may have moved from England to Ireland in the mid-
seventeenth century. In this regard, Dorothy Parsons' *Her Booke of Choyce
Receipts* stands as a culinary landmark for Ireland.

---

79 A porringer was a shallow bowl/cup-like utensil usually with two handles. Porringers were
made in a variety of materials including wood, ceramic, pewter and silver.

'I will do myself the pleasure of now writing to you':[1] Louisa Conolly's letters to her sister, Sarah Bunbury

BRENDAN TWOMEY

INTRODUCTION

The quotation in the title of this chapter is taken from the first of several hundred letters that were written between 1759 and 1821 by Louisa Augusta Conolly, née Lennox (1743–1821), to her sister Sarah Lennox (1745–1826).[2] It is part of a collection known as the Conolly/Bunbury letters now owned by the Irish Georgian Foundation and deposited with the Irish Architectural Archive (IAA) in Dublin. This corpus of letters is just one part of a surviving archive of over 2000 letters that were exchanged between the Lennox siblings and other family members, in England and Ireland, in the second half of the eighteenth century and the early decades of the nineteenth century.[3] In the 1990s these letters formed the most important source for the narrative of Stella Tillyard's best-selling book *Aristocrats* and the subsequent hit TV series.[4] One attraction of these letters, both to the general public and also to historians, is not only the smorgasbord of topics addressed by the authors, but also the apparent modernity of many of the sentiments expressed. For example, in 1777, when referring to the possibility of a further pregnancy of her sister Emily FitzGerald (1731–1814), who had already experienced twenty births by this point, Louisa noted:

> For I am not clear about those miscarriages, the People about her ought to know, and are positive about the reality of them, But Doctor Carter will not

---

1 Louisa Conolly, Stretton Hall to Sarah Lennox, 22 Mar. 1759 (IAA, MS 94/136).   2 Over the course of this correspondence the marital status of the recipient Sarah Lennox changed. She married Charles Bunbury in June 1762 and was divorced from him in May 1776. She married George Napier in 1781. In this chapter Sarah is named according to her marital status at the time of the date of the letter.   3 Between 1949 and 1957 the Irish Manuscripts Commission published three volumes of Conolly letters that totaled nearly 1,800 items; Brian FitzGerald (ed.), *Correspondence of Emily, Duchess of Leinster (1731–1814), vol. i; Letters of Emily, duchess of Leinster: James, 1st duke of Leinster: Caroline Fox, Lady Holland* (Dublin, 1949); idem, *Correspondence of Emily, duchess of Leinster (1731–1814), vol. ii; Letters of Lord Edward FitzGerald and Lady Sarah Napier (née Lennox)* (Dublin, 1953); and idem, *Correspondence of Emily, duchess of Leinster (1731–1814), vol. iii; Letters of Lady Louisa Conolly and William, marquis of Kildare (2nd duke of Leinster)* (Dublin, 1957).   4 Stella Tillyard, *Aristocrats: Caroline, Emily, Louisa and Sarah Lennox, 1740–1832* (London, 1994); also idem, *Citizen lord: Edward FitzGerald, 1763–1798* (London, 1998).   5 Louisa Conolly to Sarah Lennox, 31 Aug. 1777 (IAA, MS 94/136).

<u>credit</u> them, and says that her constitution <u>is wore out for the Office of child bearing</u> and that the way she is in denotes a change, He is such an old Woman that I am very apt not to mind what he says in general; tho' to be sure if he has any sense of knowledge about anything it must be in those matters, and therefore I wish her to be as cautious as possible.[5]

'Quaint' language aside, this letter could be a contemporary and somewhat wry take on the perils of large families, and on litigation-wary, and over-cautious doctors today. Such apparent modernity can however give rise to an inappropriate and anachronistic sense of familiarity, or empathy, with the letter writers. The past is indeed a foreign country and, despite the obvious temptations, the life experiences and perspectives of historical figures do not readily conform to our twenty-first-century sensibilities and expectations; *caveat lector* is therefore advisable. Nonetheless, for historians of eighteenth-century Ireland, who perforce must work with a relative paucity of official, business and legal sources, such caches of letters stretching over an extended period of time can offer significant insights into many aspects of the *mentalité*, preoccupations, and actions of the elite in Ireland in the second half of the eighteenth century.

The letter cited above was the first in a series from Louisa Conolly to her sister Sarah, or Sally, or Sal as she was variously addressed. However, despite the enduring fame of the lives, loves, scandals and letters of the Lennox sisters, Irish historians have not given the corpus of Conolly/Bunbury letters the attention that they perhaps deserve. The collection is important for a number of reasons. As would be expected these letters are replete with anecdotes of Louisa's busy social life and they also recount Louisa's response to the complicated, and on occasion very public, squabbles and scandals of various members of her extended family. The letters also give details of Louisa's various improvement projects in arguably Ireland's most important eighteenth-century country house and garden at Castletown, Co. Kildare.[6] There is, however, much more to these letters. A close reading of the letters reveals material on at least thirty separate themes or topics that are of interest to historians of political, social, economic and women's history, of both Ireland and Britain in this period.[7] This chapter, primarily by means of numerous citations of Louisa Conolly's letters, explores a number of these themes in order to highlight the wealth of material contained in this collection, and to offer a better understanding of her lived experience and her actions, as well as gain some modest insight into her worldview.

6 The contemporary scandals of the Lennox siblings, the details of which are beyond the scope of this chapter, were extensively reported in the contemporary press, including elopement, divorce, extramarital affairs, and Emily's marriage to her children's tutor; these events have been recounted in Tillyard's *Aristocrats*; for details of Louisa's improvements at Castletown, see Gillian Byrne, 'The redecoration and alteration of Castletown House by Lady Louisa Conolly, 1759–76' (MA, NUIM, 1997).   **7** The text of this first letter in the Conolly/Bunbury letters dated 31 Aug. 1759 is reproduced as an appendix to this chapter.

I

The Lennox sisters, Caroline (1723–74), Emily, Louisa and Sarah, and their brothers Charles (1735–1806) and George (1737–1805) were the children of the 2nd duke of Richmond. Following the death of their parents, Emily, who had married James FitzGerald, 20th earl of Kildare in 1747, assumed a guardianship role for her younger sisters at Carton House, Maynooth, Co. Kildare. In December 1758 the 15-year-old Louisa married the 20-year-old Thomas Conolly (1738–1802), of nearby Castletown, reputedly Ireland's richest man. The two sisters resided in Ireland for the remainder of their lives.

To date, with the exception of the historiography of the country house, it has proven somewhat problematic to fully accommodate the epistolary evidence of Irish elite women, such as Emily FitzGerald and Louisa Conolly, into the grand narrative of eighteenth-century Irish history.[8] Likewise, the content of the Conolly/Bunbury letters and similar collections have not been prominent within the narrative of Irish women's history.[9] British and North American historiography has more readily incorporated the letters of elite women into their narratives of this period.[10] In the 1950s the publication by the Irish Manuscripts Commission (IMC) of a substantial corpus of the correspondence of Emily FitzGerald, and others, was the subject of some criticism. Brian Inglis wondered about the selection criteria and the priorities that had facilitated the publication of 'the correspondence of a silly woman', and Richard Pares concluded that the 'political gleanings in this volume are small', and that the second volume contained 'very little that is of public interest'.[11] Even a more sympathetic reviewer only concluded that 'this is a book which will be of value to the social historian'.[12] Surely this is an inadequate response to a corpus of 2000 items and it is gratifying to note

---

8 Neither Emily FitzGerald nor Louisa Conolly are referenced in Ian McBride's recent important and comprehensive overview of eighteenth-century Ireland; Ian McBride, *Eighteenth-century Ireland: the isle of slaves* (Dublin, 2009). 9 For a broad consideration of issues in women's history in Ireland see Mary O'Dowd, *A history of women in Ireland* (Harlow, 2005); Margaret MacCurtain, *Ariadne's thread: writing women into Irish history* (Galway, 2008); Margaret MacCurtain, Mary O'Dowd and Maria Luddy, 'An agenda for women's history in Ireland, 1500–1900', *Irish Historical Studies*, 28:109 (May 1992), 1–37. 10 For example, see Maxine Berg, *Luxury and pleasure in eighteenth-century Britain* (Oxford, 2005); Amanda Vickery, *Behind closed doors: at home in Georgian England* (New Haven, 2009); John Styles and Amanda Vickery (eds), *Gender, taste, and material culture, in Britain and North America, 1700–1830* (New Haven, 2006). 11 Brian Inglis, 'Correspondence of Emily, duchess of Leinster (1731–1814) by Brian FitzGerald' in *Irish Historical Studies*, 10:38 (Sept. 1956), 236–8; Richard Pares, 'Correspondence of Emily, duchess of Leinster by Emily Mary Lennox FitzGerald, Caroline Fox, ed. Brian FitzGerald', *English Historical Review*, 65:254 (Jan. 1950), 139; and R. Pares, 'Correspondence of Emily, duchess of Leinster by Brian FitzGerald', *English Historical Review*, 70:275 (Apr. 1955), 336. 12 E.M. Johnston, 'The correspondence of Emily, duchess of Leinster by Brian FitzGerald', *English Historical Review*, 73:287 (Apr. 1958), 361–2.

the IMC commitment to the publication of a forthcoming volume of letters of Katherine Conolly.[13]

To be sure, elite Irish women such as the Lennox sisters can be accused of 'only talking to themselves' and of being out of touch with the quotidian reality of contemporary tradesmen and farmers, and even of their own employees, or the mass of their tenantry, to say nothing of their social and cultural distance from the 'hidden' world of Gaelic Ireland.[14] This criticism is however to ignore the reality that, in *ancien regime* or ascendency Ireland, a small landed elite had a near-complete monopoly on both local and national political, economic and social power. Three recent works by Rachel Wilson, Deborah Wilson and Karen Sonneliter have, at least in part, addressed this lacuna. These volumes include a review of elite women's role in the creation of an Irish salon culture, in the management of country houses and estates, and their active involvement in charity and philanthropy.[15] While financial issues were not foregrounded to any great extent in Louisa's letters to Sarah, especially in the early years, other surviving records from Castletown are ample testament to her involvement in important aspects of the financial management of the household and the estate. The point is that, while even elite women of the standing of the Lennox sisters were subject to arranged marriages, were unrepresented at a formal level in the world of eighteenth-century politics, and were only marginally represented in the public sphere of print, these women nevertheless exercised considerable social, economic and cultural power.[16] In this context the abusive behaviour of the 1st earl of Belvedere, who locked up his 'reputedly' unfaithful wife for over thirty years, can be seen as an exception. The lived reality for most elite wives in this period was more in line with the notion of a happy, or at least a companionable, partnership. This was certainly the case of the over fifty-year marriage of Louisa and Thomas Conolly. Without pushing any naïve notion of marriage equality, or of the 'separate spheres' hypothesis, too far, it should be acknowledged that responsibility for managing the health, education and even psychological well-being of children, and the control of important elements of the financial management of the household, and on occasion of the estate, was devolved to such women.

II

Louisa Conolly's letters, mostly from Ireland, to her sister Sally in England are not unknown to historians. Some of these letters have been cited, not only for

13 Marie-Louise Jennings and Gaye Ashford (eds), *The letters of Katherine Conolly, 1707–1749* (Dublin, forthcoming).   **14** For a recent consideration of Catholic Ireland in the eighteenth century, see Vincent Morley, *The popular mind in eighteenth-century Ireland* (Cork, 2017). **15** Rachel Wilson, *Elite women in ascendancy Ireland, 1690–1745* (Woodbridge, 2015); Deborah Wilson, *Women, marriage and property in wealthy landed families in Ireland, 1750–1850* (Manchester, 2009); and Karen Sonnelitter, *Charity movements in eighteenth-century Ireland: philanthropy and improvement* (Woodbridge, 2016).   **16** See Vickery, *Behind closed doors.*

the biographies of the Lennox sisters, but also as sources for research on the development of Castletown, the pre-eminent house 'within the canon of Irish country houses', and one of the 'great designed landscapes of Ireland'.[17] The letters have been cited to authenticate the dating of various refurbishment projects in Castletown; for instance Louisa wrote in 1760 'our stair case is finish'd all to putting up the banisters. The Gallery will be done in a fortnight.'[18] Brian FitzGerald used the letters as a primary source for two short popular history books on Emily and Louisa.[19] Patricia McCarthy, in her *Life in the country house in Georgian Ireland*, cited Louisa's letters in her discussion of country house renovations and decoration, domestic entertainment for and by elite parents and children, and the evolution of private spaces such as closets.[20] Karol Mullaney-Dignam has used the correspondence to explore music, dance, and entertainment in Castletown.[21] Finola O'Kane has noted that 'the history of landscape design in eighteenth-century Ireland reveals, somewhat surprisingly, that many of the principal players were women.'[22] She has drawn on the letters in respect of Louisa's free hand in landscaping, in the development of the Liffey riverbank, and in the construction of a parkland landscape replete with follies and cottages.[23] In 1767, Louisa wrote, 'We have begun a new piece of work, which will make Castletown beautiful and that is dressing the Banks of the River, you like that sort of work, for it is scooping some parts of the ground, and adding it to the other to make a little rising ground, for alas that is what this pretty Dear place wants, but if it had that, it would be too beautiful, for I think it lovely as it is.'[24]

However, there is much more to be 'gleaned' from the Conolly/Bunbury correspondence. The first letter is representative of a 'chatty' and personal epistolary style that Louisa retained throughout her life, and it can be viewed as a *fons et origio* for the entire collection. Individual letters, which typically ran to approximately 1000 words, could rehearse snippets of information on a dozen, or more, incidents, events, thoughts, feelings, responses, ideas or questions, in a

---

17 Patrick Walsh, 'Biography and meaning of an Irish country house: William Conolly and Castletown' in Terence Dooley and Christopher Ridgway (eds), *The Irish country house: its past, present and future* (Dublin, 2011), p. 21; Finola O'Kane, *Landscape design in eighteenth-century Ireland: mixing foreign trees with the natives* (Cork, 2004), p. 55.   **18** Louisa Conolly to Sara Lennox, 15 Dec. 1760 (IAA, MS 94/136).   **19** Brian FitzGerald, *Emily Duchess of Leinster, 1731–1814: a study of her life and times* (London, 1950); idem, *Lady Louisa Conolly, 1743–1821: an Anglo-Irish biography* (London, 1950).   **20** Patricia McCarthy, *Life in the country house in Georgian Ireland* (New Haven, 2016), pp 91, 157, 187, 222; J.S. Lewis, 'When a house is not a home: elite English women and the eighteenth-century country house', *Journal of British Studies*, 48:2 (Apr. 2009), 336–63.   **21** Karol Mullaney-Dignam, *Music and dancing at Castletown, County Kildare, 1759–1821* (Dublin, 2011).   **22** Finola O'Kane, 'Design and rule: women in the Irish countryside, 1715–1831', *Eighteenth-Century Ireland / Iris an dá chultúr*, 19 (2004), 56–74; Vandra Costello, *Irish demesne landscapes, 1660–1740* (Dublin, 2015).   **23** O'Kane, *Landscape design*, pp 55, 59; Finola O'Kane and Stephen Bending, 'Melancholy amusements: women, gardens, and the depression of spirits', *Studies in Literary Imagination*, 44:2 (Fall 2011), 41–62.   **24** Louisa Conolly to Sarah Bunbury, 5 May 1767 (IAA, MS 94/136).

torrent of words. The original autographs show very few signs of revision or corrections and they do not appear to have been fair copy transcriptions from earlier drafts. The letters are typically signed off 'Affectionately, L.A. Conolly'.

While the first letter in the sequence reflected the youth and inexperience of the writer, this letter also introduced a number of themes that recurred frequently over the course of the ensuing decades. As she grew older in years and in experience Louisa's letters became more opinionated both in respect of personal matters, and, in particular, Irish politics and the economic well-being of Ireland. Over time, while the letters retained a strong focus on her large extended family, she became less self-obsessed and more reflective on the wider world. A typical early example of her youthful self-absorbed expression of frustration comes in the letter of March 1759: 'It has rained so much of late I can't think of riding out before I go from this, as I had wish'd for the roads are so wet'.[25] The benefits of riding, walking and bathing, both for pleasure and for exercise, and comments on the weather, were to be recurring themes. A second regular theme also present in this first letter is Louisa's endearing references to her various nieces and nephews: 'Kissing sweet Dr. little Charles and Charlot at Carton'. This early example also shows that even at 15 Louisa was already assuming an 'adult' tone vis-à-vis her younger FitzGerald nieces and nephews; 'I do love them so much Pretty little dear Souls.'[26] When describing her feelings about close family members, she could be rather effusive: 'I should rather wish to make her happy by your remaining in Ireland, than myself by seeing you here'.[27] This generous, and by times light-hearted, tone is maintained throughout and the FitzGerald children in Carton were routinely referred to as the 'brats'. Given her decades-long role in rearing and educating her various nieces and nephews, whom on occasion she called '<u>my</u> Children', her conclusion was that 'In generally I am against teaching Children too young, but depend on their genius's'.[28] In respect of Louisa Napier she commented: 'she learns so well that it is quite an entertainment to me to teach her and as I find it is no sort of punishment to her to learn, rather a diversion, I think it a pity not to make use of her talents'.[29] In the same letter, in one of her rare attempts at a joke, she commented, 'I fancy Louisa has skipped a generation for sense, for her good mother had a very small share of it, her father's in the common run, so that I believe she has taken it from her Grandmother.'[30]

Over the course of the correspondence Louisa's abiding concerns and her evolving personality emerge as she steadily matured from the sheltered 15-year-old *ingénue* of 1759 to the more self-assured mature woman of the later letters. The first letter offers an example of her youthful *naiveté* in respect of the moral

---

25 Louisa Conolly to Sarah Lennox, 22 Mar. 1759 (IAA, MS 94/136).   **26** Louisa Conolly to Sarah Lennox, 22 Mar. 1759; ibid.   **27** Louisa Conolly to Sarah Lennox, 22 Mar. 1759; ibid.   **28** Louisa Conolly to Sarah Bunbury, 28 Nov. 1771; ibid.   **29** Louisa Conolly to Sarah Bunbury, 28 Nov. 1771; ibid.   **30** Louisa Conolly to Sarah Bunbury, 28 Nov. 1771; ibid.

economy and her understanding of the expected behaviour of the social elite. Louisa recounted how a Mr Barbor, who 'everybody says he's mad', had sent Mr Conolly 'a pig, pine aple & offer'd to send some Carp & tench, and at the same time, begging him to send him a joint of meat, some ale and wine'. The young Louisa concluded: 'what a strange thing to beg provisions and send some at the same time.' The older and more mature Louisa would have understood the reciprocal world of the gift.[31] As can be seen from the above quotations her language was, for the most part, plain, straightforward and direct with almost no use of colourful adjectives, complex metaphors, or classical allusions. Her spelling, with some notable exceptions (rid for rode), was good and reasonably consistent. By and large she made only sparing use of irony or caricature. In December 1777, in one of her very few explicit jokes, she commented, 'as I am alive, my birth day 34 years of Age, what an old Creature!'[32] However, over time the letters became more self-reflective and in 1776, in a rare flash of irony, she averred that 'I am grown a <u>great</u> Philosopher' and she then added 'and I hope a little wiser'.[33] It is also worth noting that while her numerous references to her husband are invariably affectionate and considerate, he was always referred to as Mr Conolly.

Expressions of personal political opinions were not a major theme of the letters. It should however be remembered that these were personal and not business letters. Her political comments tended to be reflections on her husband's immediate electoral concerns, or of his views on contemporary matters of controversy. For example, in 1768 she noted in respect of political tensions between Lord Lieutenant Townshend and some members of parliament arising from the debate in respect of the Octennial Bill that 'Mr Conolly thinks him so frank and honest, and is so persuaded that he means the good of this Kingdom, that he intended supporting him yesterday if there had been any occasion, against the violent attacks which had been threaten'd, but it was much pleasanter to have it all end quietly.'[34] Nevertheless it is clear that Louisa was well informed on both the minutiae and the broad themes of contemporary Irish, British, European and also American politics. Her few comments on political developments also have a distinctly Irish tone. However, Louisa was not a power broker, either in her own right, or even as a representative of her husband, in the

31 Louisa Conolly to Sarah Lennox, 22 Mar. 1759; ibid. See also Felicity Heal, 'Food gifts, the household and the politics of exchange in early modern England', *Past & Present*, 199 (May 2008), 41–70. 32 Louisa Conolly to Sarah Lennox, 5 Dec. 1777 (IAA, MS 94/136). 33 Louisa Conolly to Sarah Lennox, 17 Aug. 1776; ibid. 34 Louisa Conolly to Sarah Bunbury, 14 Feb. 1768; ibid. The Octennial Bill for limiting the duration of parliaments (7 George III, ch.3) was debated in the House of Commons on 12 Feb. 1768. Dr. Charles Lucas was involved in this particular dispute and later letters made a number of disparaging references to Louisa's opinion of the Dublin MP. Louisa made several other positive comments on Townshend, who experienced a very difficult tenure as lord lieutenant of Ireland, and who was later famously involved in duel with Lord Bellamont; see James Kelly, *'That damn'd thing called honour': dueling in Ireland, 1570–1860* (Dublin, 1995), pp 106–11.

mode of her illustrious predecessor as *châtelaine* of Castletown.[35] In the 1720s
and 1730s the childless Katherine Conolly had used, the still uncompleted,
Castletown House as a locus of political patronage and display in continuation
of the work of her husband. Louisa, although also childless, sought to create a
more homely atmosphere and engaged in what Gillian Russell has termed
'domiciliary sociability'.[36] Nevertheless, entertainment at Castletown remained
lavish in the second half of the century, and when her husband was on good
terms with the lord lieutenant, it retained a political edge. For Louisa, however,
family living centred on the numerous FitzGerald children, and also fulfilling
her social obligations both to her husband's horse-racing coterie and for the local
gentry.

Thomas Conolly is not a major figure in Irish historiography. He is cited most
often in respect of his ownership of Castletown House and his reputation as
Ireland's richest man. His second claim to fame is as a minor politician who was
a long-serving MP in both the Irish and the British parliaments. Conolly was
effectively an independent member and he gained a reputation for 'illogical' U-
turns.[37] Louisa has little to say about the day-to-day political activities or
commitments of her husband but in January 1767, in an unusually lengthy and
detailed report, she noted that:

> All last Week I was detained in Dublin on a tiresome business for Mr
> Conolly, for he was on a Jury, to judge whether a Lord Ely was an Idiot or
> not, this Lord Ely is Son to a Mr Loftus Hume (whom you may have
> heard of) who was the cruellest Creature I ever heard of, he treated his Son
> in a most shocking manner, he is Dead lately and some of his relations
> wanted to prove the Son an Idiot, but they could not, so that he has got
> peaceable possession of his Estate, but think of all the Judges shut up from
> ten o'clock in the morning till five in the Evening for a week together, and
> yet Mr Conolly was very patient and did not grumble.[38]

Examples of similar insights on contemporary politics from the letters
include comments on election campaigns and the details of the election results.
In 1776, Louisa noted that in the recent election 'Mr Cary carried by about 200
majority, and Mr Conolly by very near 600'.[39] Thomas Conolly is also
remembered today as an emblematic representative of the eighteenth-century

---

35 Lewis, 'When a house is not a home', pp 336–63; Conor Lucey, 'Keeping up appearances:
redecorating the domestic interior in late eighteenth-century Dublin' in *Proceedings of the
Royal Irish Academy. Section C: Archaeology, Celtic Studies, History, Linguistics, Literature*,
111C (2011), 169–92.   36 See Gillian Russell, *Women, sociability and theatre in Georgian
London* (Cambridge, 2007), p. 11.   37 E.M. Johnston-Liik, *History of the Irish parliament,
1692–1800*, 6 vols (Belfast, 2002), vol. iii, pp 467–74.   38 Louisa Conolly to Sara Bunbury,
29 Jan. 1767 (IAA, MS 94/136).   39 Louisa Conolly to Sarah Lennox, 16 June 1776; ibid.

horse-obsessed and lavishly hospitable Irish squire. He was an ardent supporter of all aspects of horse racing – as a horse owner, competent rider, hunting enthusiast and as a frequent visitor to race meetings in Ireland and England.[40] Louisa's letters are replete with stories of Mr Conolly being away at the Curragh, or other racing venues. He attended race meetings even when ill, as in 1776 when Louisa reported that 'Mr Conolly grew so much better that nothing would keep him from going to the Curragh'.[41] Louisa only rarely expressed any sense of grievance at these absences – these were reserved for his absences on political business; for the most part she simply reported the fact of his absence and moved on to report the next factoid that took her interest.

While some of her political observations may amount to nothing more than family household political gossip they do provide some insight into aspects of the background political thinking of at least part of the Protestant ascendancy at that point in time. Louisa noted how Lord Townshend, the lord lieutenant, 'is at present very popular for having obtain'd the Bill some much wished for, here, for the limitation of Parliament, we are to have an Octennial Parliament'. She continued with a more personal observation (with perhaps another rare flash or irony), 'which I fear will create great confusion in this kingdom, for the plague of elections every eight Years, will I think encourage quarrelling and drinking, two things we have enough of, already however People who must know better than I do, say that it will be a great means of promoting the Protestant Interest, that indeed, will be a good thing, and I wish heartily that it may turn out to be so.'[42] In this letter she also recorded a nuanced view of the duplicity of *realpolitik* when she noted, 'for many People are much disappointed at it having pass'd the House, tho' they pretended to be very eager for it, before it came from England, while they thought that it would not be sent over to us.'

Not surprisingly Thomas Conolly was a supporter of the status quo, reminding his fellow MPs that 'You represent property not numbers'. However, his wealth and social standing meant that he remained at the heart of Irish politics for over forty years.[43] He did not sponsor many pieces of legislation although his involvement in the 1771 act 'For badging such poor as shall be found unable to support themselves by labour, and otherwise providing for them, and for restraining such as shall be found able to support themselves by labour or industry from begging' elicited one of the most comprehensive social and political comments from Louisa.[44] As she observed,

> Mr Conolly has brought his poor Bill thro' the House of Commons. We meet with vast discouragement about it, everybody says it won't do, I am

40 James Kelly, *Sport in Ireland, 1600–1840* (Dublin, 2014), pp 82–4. 41 Louisa Conolly to Sarah Lennox, 16 June 1776 (IAA, MS 94/136). 42 Louisa Conolly to Sarah Bunbury, 14 Feb. 1768; ibid. 43 For a brief overview of his political career see Johnston-Liik, *History of the Irish parliament*, iii, pp 467–74. 44 See http://www.qub.ac.uk/ild/?func=simple

sure it won't do as much as one can wish, but still if it does a little, 'tis better now, and when one thinks that is the case, one cannot with satisfaction omit the trying. Perhaps I am woring in regard to my Ideas of society, but my notion is, that the division is very unfair between rich and poor. A distinction I know is necessary, for the sake of subordination.[45]

Economic concerns are only fleetingly mentioned but always with a sense of a realistic appraisal of the news; in July 1778 Louisa noted: 'The country is certainly in a most deplorable way at present. The Potatoes were bad last year, which add greatly to the distress of the North'.[46] Over time her views became increasingly radical and in one of her last letters she observed that 'The labouring class are the most populous in all countries, it is thro' their bodily labours that the productions of the Earth are to be had, and justice calls for their receiving that share of them, that is necessary for their maintenance and comfort'. And later in the same letter: 'The Labouring class have no power to redress themselves but by violence (the most destructive mode possible for them and their superiors).'[47] These sentiments are a world and a lifetime away from those that were penned by the newly married *ingénue* in 1759.

While Thomas Conolly was undoubtedly one of the richest men in Ireland the burden of debts inherited from his father, the payment of his mother's jointure, which continued until 1797, and the payment of portions for (at least six) sisters, combined with his own and Louisa's expenditure, meant that over time his patrimony became burdened with debt.[48] On the rare occasions when financial matters are mentioned in the letters it is clear that Louisa had an intimate knowledge of both the business at hand and of the mechanisms for making the required payments. In 1760, she reported: 'I have put off from post to post writing to her on account of the Bill she sent me, but the thing is Mr Conolly did not know the name of his Banker was till a day or two ago'.[49] The consequences of the deterioration in the financial well-being of the Conolly estate in this period were visited on later generations. Louisa, however, was not unaffected by this change and in the first two decades of the nineteenth century the now-aging Louisa was subject to some financial difficulties.

_search&search_type=name&search=true&search_string=0459&&session_from=1692&sessi on_to=1800 [accessed, 1 Feb. 2017].   **45** Louisa Conolly to Sarah Bunbury, 5 Feb. 1772 (IAA, MS 94/136).   **46** Louisa Conolly to Sarah Lennox, 5 July 1778; ibid.   **47** Louisa Conolly to George Lennox, 3 Oct. 1720 (IAA, MS 94/136).   **48** For a detailed review of the techniques used by gentry families to manage marriage settlements, wills, jointures, long-term debt and portions, see Jerzy Habakkuk, *Marriage, debt, and the estates system: English landownership, 1650–1950* (Oxford, 1994).   **49** Louisa Conolly to Sarah Lennox, 15 Dec. 1760 (IAA, MS 94/136).

III

Detailed reports on her own ailments and those of various servants, acquaintances, her sisters and their families, and not infrequently those of Mr Conolly, were an ever-present theme of Louisa's letters. These reports are worthy of more detailed study for the light they shine on medical practice in elite circles, causes of illness, interpretation of symptoms, contemporary cures and prescriptions, the reputation of various medical practitioners, and the specifics of contemporary practice, including the frequent resort to what she referred to as the 'purge' or 'blooding'.[50] Louisa, Sarah and Emily all read and discussed the popular, and influential, *Domestic medicine* by William Buchan (1729–1805).[51] In 1776 she noted: 'I read Buchan like anything, and find so much encouragement in it, to become a Doctor that I mean to be one'.[52] Louisa was too socially conservative to entertain such a notion. Four years earlier, Louisa had positively and knowledgably referred to William Cadogan's frequently printed book on gout.[53] Louisa felt that women were entitled not only to become literate in medical matters, but that they should be able to use that expertise in their interactions with the medical world, and especially in the case of childbearing.[54] In June 1776, in an unusually lengthy report, Louisa recorded that

> Mr Conolly was so ill as to frighten me very much. Thank God he is now well again, but he requires much attention and care having neglected that bad cold he caught at Newmarket when I was at Stoke, which had fouled his blood, that upon the least attack he was liable to be very ill. I did not think him well in London but I imagined it was owing to the being so much in Town, and that upon getting home to the Country air he would recover, instead of that the journey heated him, and the day after he got here, he was very indifferent, and determined to be blooded, Mr Power found his blood in a most inflamed state, and very bad, the next day sitting by the fire he was so overcome with the heat, as to faint away and was so weak and ill as to be obliged to go to Bed again … However, Mr Conolly grew so much better that nothing would keep him from going to the Curragh where you may be sure I went with him to nurse him, he rid a

50 Louisa Conolly to Sarah Lennox, 19 Jan. 1760; ibid. Louisa Conolly to Sarah Lennox, 16 June 1776; ibid. See also J.S. Lewis, 'Material health in the English aristocracy: myth and realities, 1790–1840', *Journal of Social History*, 17:1 (Autumn 1983), 97–114. 51 Buchan's treatise went through at least 67 editions (London, Dublin, Edinburgh, Philadelphia, Boston, Hartford, New London, CT, Waterford, Fairhaven, New York) between 1769 and the end of the century. There were ten separate Dublin printings, the first of which was in 1773; William Buchan, *Domestic medicine: or, a treatise on the prevention and cure of diseases by regimen and simple medicines. By William Buchan, M.D.* (Dublin, 1773). 52 Louisa Conolly to Sarah Lennox, 16 June 1776. 53 William Cadogan's book on gout was reprinted on at least twenty occasions in 1771 and 1772 in London, Dublin, New York, Boston and Philadelphia; William Cadogan, *A dissertation on the gout* (Dublin, 1771). 54 For Louisa's acerbic view of the

little, and was very good in all other respects, so that I don't think it has done him harm, he has had great evacuations which have left him low, but as the symptoms of his fever are all gone, I hope he will soon recover entirely.[55]

Sicknesses, and as a consequence death, were never far from the minds of the elite of this period. In June 1776, in one of several references to bereavement Louisa noted that Lady Roden 'is in affliction just now poor woman with the loss of her youngest Girl.'[56] In 1767, Louisa wrote in respect of the death of Lord Tavistock, following an accident, 'surely he was releas'd from great suffering then and from still greater supposing him to have recover'd'; and later in the same letter she remarked, 'People have such different ways of expressing their grief, that there is no judging from appearance what they feel'.[57] Even at sixteen years of age Louisa noted that 'the Small pox, is such treacherous disorder ... we have been so unlucky to lose three of our Servants by this dreadful distemper one was in Danger 22 Days with it, and after having been just pronounced out of Danger there came on a purging which he not being strong enough to bear it carry'd him off; This man was a Groom that we were so fond of'.[58] However, it should also be noted that some of her interests in things medical were less traumatic. In the first letter of March 1759 Louisa wrote: 'Pray ask my Sister if she could advise me anything that would do my neck good for the Scarr is redder than it was tho' I keep it more cover'd'.[59] The details of the circumstances in which Louisa got the 'Scarr' on her neck were not recorded.

Other contemporary books were cited regularly throughout the correspondence. An interesting citation occurred in 1763 when she noted the publication of a report on the notorious Knox 'heiress' murder in 1761. The young 18-year-old Louisa noted: 'think how shocking the story was to me, who knew them both ... when we were in the North, we were at their House sometime. And she was one of the sweetest prettiest Girls that ever was.'[60]

Other recurrent themes in the letters, and worthy of brief consideration, include the weather, pictures, the outdoor life and pets. In early 1760, Louisa reported that it is 'so cold' and 'What shocking dismal weather', and two weeks

knowledge of some male doctors, Louisa Conolly to Sarah Lennox, 31 Aug. 1777; see also James Kelly, 'Health for sale: mountebanks, doctors, printers and the supply of medication in eighteenth-century Ireland', *Proceedings of the Royal Irish Academy. Section C: Archaeology, Celtic Studies, History, Linguistics, Literature*, 108C (2008), 75–113.   **55** Louisa Conolly to Sarah Lennox, 16 June 1776 (IAA, MS 94/136).   **56** Louisa Conolly to Sarah Lennox, 16 June 1776; ibid.   **57** Louisa Conolly to Sarah Bunbury, Mar. 1767; ibid.   **58** Louisa Conolly to Sarah Lennox, 19 Jan. 1760; ibid.   **59** Louisa Conolly to Sarah Lennox, 22 Mar. 1759; ibid.   **60** Louisa Conolly to Sarah Bunbury, 26 Jan. 1763; ibid. For the broader context of this incident see James Kelly, 'The abduction of women of fortune in eighteenth-century Ireland', *Eighteenth-Century Ireland / Iris an dá chultúr*, 9 (1994), pp 7–43. The text of the book was also printed in the *Annual Register 1761* (London, 1762), which could also have been a source for Louisa.

later, 'It's a wretched bad Day, and Sunday & we don't go to Church.'[61] For art historians, Louisa's letters contain comments on the pictures of family members that she acquired. Her focus was always on the likeness, or otherwise, of these images, 'I was vastly flatter'd by them all who told me they thought her Picture was very like me'.[62] Louisa recorded on 1 January 1767 that 'I was a lucky Creature to get that Picture of you, for I do think it is much the most like of any that has been done of you.'[63] It is also clear from the letters that Louisa enjoyed the outdoors for walking, riding and bathing. She was fond of horses and the letters record several falls while riding. The first letter cites in some detail an incident as to how she had now become 'quite a Convert about dogs'. She went on to report how her dog 'is the cleanest thing in the World & never dirtys the House, is fond of me and follows me when I am below, but never thinks of coming upstairs unless she is made.'[64] A later letter referred to 'my little Sally has puped [sic] 5 beautiful little wretches, but since I came from Kildare she is so glad to see me that she won't stay with them and I am obliged to have them up in my room for that reason.'[65]

In one letter there is a passing reference to shopping, 'I send my Sisters list of what I was to get for her'. Later letters contained more detailed requests in respect of haberdashery, jewellery and clothing. A good example is from February 1761 when Louisa commenced a letter to Sarah, 'I should be vastly obliged to you if you would be so good as to execute the Commission I am going to tell you for me.'[66] She continued: 'The first is that you will send this pearl cap of Caroline Hamilton to a Mrs Passavant upon Ludgate Hill in the Cyty with commands to have it strung like mine'.[67] Instructions for the purchase of 'black velvet ribbon' and 'a dozen of fine large Chip Hatte' were set out in the same letter. She gave specific details of the potential suppliers for the various goods that included a 'Mrs Labords' and a 'Mrs Charlier'. Sarah was however warned, somewhat tongue-in-cheek perhaps, in respect of Mrs Charlier: 'rather than not getting them I beg you'll go to Mrs Charlier for I know that toad has all these pretty things, but don't let her know its for me till you have bought it as she would give you the worse having a great quarrel with me'.[68]

61 Louisa Conolly to Sarah Lennox, 15 Dec. 1760 (IAA, MS 94/136); Louisa Conolly to Sarah Lennox, 30 Dec. 1760; ibid.   62 Louisa Conolly to Sarah Lennox, 22 Mar. 1759 (IAA, MS 94/136).   63 Louisa Conolly to Sarah Bunbury, 1 Jan. 1767; ibid.   64 Louisa Conolly to Sarah Lennox, 22 Mar. 1759; ibid.   65 Louisa Conolly, Castletown, to Sarah Lennox, 17 Sept. 1760; ibid. I.H. Tague, *Animal companions: pets and social change in eighteenth-century Britain* (Pittsburgh, 2015); and idem, 'Companions, servants, or slaves? Considering animals in eighteenth-century Britain', *Studies in Eighteenth-Century Culture*, 39 (2010), 111–30. 66 Louisa Conolly to Sarah Lennox, 7 Feb. 1761.   67 Suzanna Passavant was a leading London retailer of jewellery and luxury goods with a shop at the Plume of Feathers on Ludgate Hill. See Ambrose Heal, *The London goldsmiths, 1200–1800: a record of the names and addresses of the craftsmen, their shop signs and trade cards* (Cambridge, 1935), p. 217.   68 Louisa Conolly to Sarah Lennox, 7 Feb. 1761 (IAA, MS 94/136).

Louisa's religious belief was sincere if somewhat understated and conventional. In particular, she drew comfort from her faith in the prospect of what she termed 'future happiness'. She also displayed a typical condescension, albeit without overt bigotry, towards any acquaintance who maintained a continued adherence to Roman Catholicism. A good example (worth quoting at some length) of the interaction of these various religious impulses is seen in respect of the travails of a Mrs Hussey when, in 1768, Louisa noted:

> The last time I saw my Sister, she told me, that she had been to see poor Mrs Hussey whom she says is a melancholy object, she endeavours very much to get the better of her grief, poor soul! but she is vastly affected with her misfortune; I own I fear'd from the first that it would make sad impression on her, from a thought which came into my heart, with regard to her situation, which I will tell you, tho' I don't care to mention it, in general; She, you know, is a most strict Roman Catholick, and he had, within these few years, read his recantation, and was quite a Protestant; now I much fear, that with her strong feelings, and the terrible notions she must have of him (from being so strict a Catholick herself) she must be very miserable; I hope in God I am mistaken about her, but if it should be so, her situation is deplorable indeed; I feel more fore her now, than ever I did, for thro' Gods goodness to me, at the time of my sweet Thomas' illness, one of my greatest comforts was, in thinking that if I was to lose him, I had nothing to disturb me with regard to his future happiness, and felt an inward satisfaction that all the misery of losing him would fall upon me.[69]

Finally, the letters give insights on contemporary letter writing culture when in 1766 the youthful Louisa wrote, 'I hope that this will convince you, that 'tis a very ill-natured thing of you ever to think of burning your letters, and 'tis a crime I can never forgive and the Idea of you having intended to burn that long letter, make me outrageous.'[70] In the same year she felt that a breach of confidence was 'unpardonable of Mrs Fortescue to go and publish' opinions on a proposed match of some their acquaintances.[71] Three years later she asked Sarah to avoid disclosing confidences and to 'be so good as to write upon a separate paper. I don't mean to give you this trouble often, only now and then.'[72]

69 Louisa Conolly to Sarah Bunbury, 14 Feb. 1768 (IAA, MS 94/136).   70 Louisa Conolly to Sarah Bunbury, 16 Mar. 1766; ibid.   71 Louisa Conolly to Sarah Bunbury, 7 Apr. 1766; ibid.   72 Louisa Conolly to Sarah Bunbury, 10 June 1769; ibid.

CONCLUSION

There is no doubt that in eighteenth-century Ireland, female agency, even for the elite, was limited, and on occasion could be severely restricted by contemporary legal and cultural constraints. Coverture, failure to implement the terms of marriage settlements, and primogeniture were real issues with real legal, social and financial consequences for women. But it also clear from the letters of Louisa Conolly that elite women were not uninformed about current events, that they were not short of opinions about their world, and that despite many barriers their individual agency was not extinguished.[73]

The richness of the content of the Conolly/Bunbury letters means that they should be seen as more than just another collection of domestic letters by an elite Irish woman. At a minimum, by recounting the movements of, and the opinions of Thomas Conolly, by their references to interactions with other leading figures of the period, and through other *obiter dicta* and personal asides, the letters provide both corroborative detail, and on occasion some interesting background and colour and other 'gleanings' in respect of political events in Ireland in this period. This chapter has argued that the letters of Louisa Conolly are much more. From the perspective of elite women in the country house in Ireland the Conolly/Bunbury letters provide detail of familial, social, cultural, and decorative and landscape activities, over a sixty-year period, in one of the most important families, houses and landscapes in Ireland. Over time Louisa's views on theatre, politics, medical matters, childrearing and politics mature and become more sophisticated, nuanced and opinionated.

It must be acknowledged that Louisa Conolly was not an intellectual figure and that despite her sociability and her charitable work, she could not be considered as a proto-Bluestocking for Ireland. She was, however, an educated, articulate, well-connected, prolific, and, for the most part, a disarmingly, clear recorder of her views on all manner of subjects. Her words provide a contemporary and unmediated testimony on a vast range of topics that are of enduring interest to historians of the political, social, architectural/landscape and economic world of elite women in eighteenth-century Ireland.

73 Amanda Vickery, 'Golden age to separate spheres? A review of the categories and chronology of English women's history', *Historical Journal*, 36:2 (June 1993), 383–414.

APPENDIX: LETTER FROM LOUISA CONOLLY TO HER SISTER SARAH
LENNOX, 22 MARCH 1759[74]

My Dear Sarah

As we had agreed we should write to my Sister and you in turns I will do myself the
pleasure of now writing to you, and acquaint you I am extremely well; we go to London
next Sunday and propose dining with Lady Anne next Tuesday. It has rained so much of
late I can't think of riding out before I go from this, as I had wish'd for the roads are so
wet, I thought of you for these two or three last Evening and imagined you at all the
Benefits that were to be this week, after which I suppose you will go, kissing sweet Dr:
little Charles and Charlot at Carton. I wish I could kiss them also, I do love them so much
Pretty little dear Souls. Pray whenever you see Counselor Macmanus, give my Compts:
to him and tell him he must no longer find fault with the poor little Doctors riding hard
upon the road, for that our Parson here goes a hunting & rides like a D—l, therefore 'tis
the fashion. Mr Conolly made him drunk yesterday. he dines here with Mr Congreve
(Nephew to Mr Congreve the author of the mourning Bride), who seems a very pretty
sort of Man. There is a Miss Edgington in this neighbourhood who is a might pretty sort
of Woman. She is tall as my Sister but fatter and a very good Complexion, We dined with
them last Monday at a place call'd Cammock, from whence there is a very pretty view.
Pray give my love to my Sister and tell her I was vastly flatter'd by them all who told me
they thought her Picture was very like me. I must tell you (if it gives you any plesure) that
I am quite a Convert about Dogs for there is one here call's Gruff very large, black, & the
hair all ruff. That comes & dines with us. but she is the cleanest thing in the World &
never dirtys the House, is fond of me and follows me when I am below, but never thinks
of coming upstairs unless she is made, and I love her vastly. there is a Mr Barbor who
lives near this, that was a Parson, then went into the Army & now is turn'd to a Collier he
has wrote twice to Mr Conolly since he has been here & has sent a pig, pine aple & offer'd
to send some Carp & tench, and at the same time, begging him to send him a joint of
meat, some ale and wine. on account he says of so many misfortunes which have befallen
him, everybody says he's mad tho'. but what a strange thing to beg provisions and send
some at the same time, there are a vast many stories about him he is such a …d mad
Creature. I will not make you any excuses for this paper as I am obliged to write on it
having no better. Pray my Dr Sarah have you heard anything about my Jewels and
whether Tallant is in Dublin or not. I had a letter from my Sister Caroline since I came
here, she mentions poor Ste's continuing very ill I don't hear anything of Dr: George or
William, I hope they were well when my Sister heard from them, as soon as I have the
pleasure of seeing them I shall certainly let my Sister know how I find them and exactly
what alterations I find in them since we saw them last. Pray ask my Sister whether she
ever had an opportunity of speaking to Mr Nelson about Mr Cullens little Cottage, as
she intended, I hope we shall get it as I like the appearance of so much. Pray let me hear
from you soon, I am just going to dinner therefore will finish this afterwards. Mr Conolly
desires his love to you. Pray have you or my Sister seen poor Mrs Crofton lately, how
does she do? I hope that now that the great shock is over she will recover soon. Pray my

---

74 Original spelling and grammar have been retained in the text.

Dr: Sarah let me know (if you possibly can) whether I may flatter myself with the pleasure of hopes of seeing Lord Kildare and my Sister this Summer. I am more anxious now (if possible) than I was before, for their coming, it already seems so long since I have had the pleasure of seeing them. as to your coming it would certainly make me happy to see You (that I believe you have no doubt of) but if they don't come I do believe I should be vastly divided which to wish for, as I love my Sister so much, I should rather wish to make her happy by your remaining in Ireland, than myself by seeing you here, I do assure you my Dr: Sarah I speak sincerely and from the very bottom of my heart. and my Sister and you find I shall always act according to what I say now. I wish I knew any news that could entertain you, but I really do not. In London I hope to pick up a little more than what I do here to write you about. Pray never forget me to my Dr: sweet Sensible little Emily, Cecelia & Harriott, also & believe me my Dr: Sal: no one can love your better nor more Sincerely that you ever Affecate Friend and Sister L:A: Conolly:

P.S. If anybody ever asks you after me pray let me know, for it flatters my vanity most prodigiously if anybody does me that favour especially if it is people I like. My love to Lucy. Pray ask my Sister if she could advise me anything that would do my neck good for the Scarr is redder than it was tho' I keep it more cover'd. I send my Sisters list of what I was to get for her

Stretton Hall March the 22d: 1759

Louisa Moore of Moore Hall: a life in letters

FIONA WHITE

This chapter is an examination of some of the correspondence of Mrs Louisa Moore (*née* Browne, 1788–1861) of Moore Hall, Co. Mayo. It will shed light on the life of a female Catholic landlord and a member of the Anglo-Irish gentry who ran the day-to-day affairs of her estate, while tending to her ailing husband and raising very troublesome offspring. The letters show the role and the agency of women at a time when women were often ostensibly invisible.

Louisa Browne was the daughter of the Right Honourable John Browne, sixth son of the 1st earl of Altamont of Westport House, and his second wife Rosalind Gilker (d.30 April 1812) (fig. 15.1).[1] The couple resided at Elm Hall near Belcarra. Louisa's father, who was the tax collector of Foxford and Newport, became high sheriff in 1790. Elm Hall was deliberately burnt during the rebellion of 1798 and John Browne died later that same year. The Altamonts were among the first families of the Irish Protestant ascendancy, but Louisa had been brought up as a Catholic and remained a staunch believer all her life.

Situated on the banks of Lough Carra, and close in proximity to Elm Hall, Moore Hall was built by George Moore of Alicante, Spain. He made his fortune in the 1780s in Alicante in the wine and grain trade. George Moore's original Irish home was Ashbrook near Straide, Co. Mayo, where he was raised as a Catholic. He married Catherine de Kilkelly who was brought to Spain by her father Dominick Kelly of Castle Lyndican, Galway, at an early age. Catherine had adopted the customs and language of the Spanish and was naturally reluctant to leave to reside at Moore Hall. With the passing of the Relief Acts in Ireland, which allowed Roman Catholics to inherit and purchase land, the Moores returned and built Moore Hall between 1792 and 1795. The couple had four sons, all educated in the finest Catholic schools abroad.

Their eldest son, the unfortunate John Moore, became embroiled in the 1798 conflict in Mayo and received the title 'president of the Republic of Connacht' from the general of the French forces, Jean Joseph Amable Humbert. John was later arrested and tried by the English forces and died in captivity in Waterford. Shortly after his son's death, George Moore of Alicante also died. His successor was his second son, also named George, known as 'the Historian', who took over

---

1 Sir Bernard Burke, *A genealogical and heraldic dictionary of the peerage and baronetage of the British empire* (London, 1868), p. 1014.

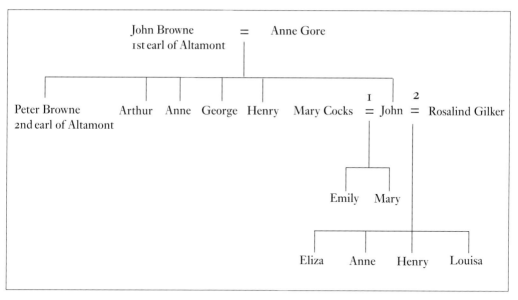

15.1 Louisa Browne family tree.

the running of Moore Hall. He was a scholar and Whig historian and unlike his brother supported the Union with Britain. During his days in London, he wooed and won the hand of Louisa Browne (fig. 15.2). The match would have been considered an excellent one, but for the fact that Louisa's cousin, Denis 'The Rope' Browne, had prosecuted George's brother John at a vindictive trial in Castlebar.[2] Catherine, George's mother, never forgave this marriage and retired to London on her jointure of £11,000, where she lived until her death, never again setting foot inside Moore Hall.[3]

Louisa, as the new mistress of Moore Hall, ignored the criticism of her in-laws. George Henry Moore's biographer, Joseph Hone, portrays her as a haughty, passionate and domineering woman, fond of money and good at figures. She did not discourage her ailing husband from his reclusive habits, and gladly took on responsibility for the finances of the family and the management of the property, as is apparent from her correspondence. There is evidence to show that

2 The home of Denis Browne (1763–1828) in Claremorris was destroyed by the rebels during 1798. He took revenge by arbitrarily hanging many of the local people who had joined the French and earned the nickname 'Denis the Rope' for his zeal in stringing up suspected rebels. His persecution of Moore may have been less of a personal grudge and more of a display of power. See Desmond McCabe, '"A small expense of blood": Denis Browne and the politics of Westport House, 1782–1809' in Sheila Mulloy (ed.), *Victory or glorious defeat: biographies of participants in the Mayo rebellion of 1798* (Westport, 2010), pp 23–95. 3 Joseph M. Hone, *The Moores of Moore Hall* (London, 1939), p. 47.

15.2 Portrait of Louisa Moore, from Hone, *The Moores of Moore Hall* (London, 1939), artist unknown.

she was acting on behalf of her husband in most matters associated with the estate. Two examples are particularly striking: one is ordering cattle to be distrained for unpaid rents and Louisa is mentioned as the acting person; the second is the dismissal of Moore Hall's domestic chaplain after she did not agree with his political stance on the payment of tithes.[4] Such actions could excite reactions, as was clear from a newspaper reference to Louisa:

> A male aristocracy have already nearly ruined the country – are we now to be cursed with a female aristocracy, who without distinction thinks fit to blend religion and politics for evil purposes.[5]

There were three sons from the marriage, George Henry (1810–70), John (1812–29) and Augustus (1817–45) (fig. 15.3).[6] Both John and Augustus would die as a result of falls from horses. George Henry was sent to Oscott, a Catholic school

4 Louisa is mentioned for dismissing her chaplain on Christmas Day 1832: *Connaught Telegraph*, 9 Jan. 1833.   5 *Connaught Telegraph*, 22 Apr. 1835.   6 Burke, *Genealogical and heraldic history of the landed gentry of Great Britain and Ireland*, p. 942.

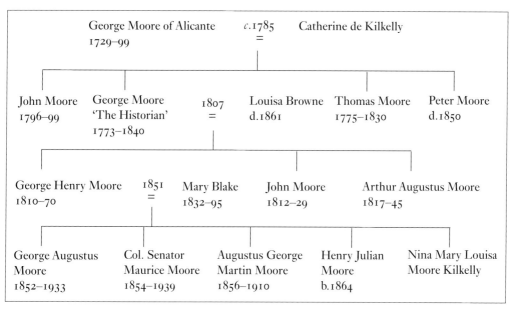

15.3 Moore family tree.

near Birmingham, to be educated, a common practice of the Irish gentry at this time.[7] He seemed to show considerable ability at school and was sent to Cambridge, and his parents hoped that on leaving Cambridge he would become a resident and improving landlord. George Henry, however, wasted his time gambling among wealthier contemporaries.[8] And his father soon realized that his son's prospects were poor, handing over the decision-making regarding his future to Louisa. Mother and son loved each other but fought as fiercely as they loved. George Henry had learned little at Cambridge except skill at billiards. He emerged as an affable young extrovert who preferred horse racing, hunting and gambling to more scholarly pursuits.

It was during this period that the Moores became friendly with Maria Edgeworth (1768–1849). The Moores met Edgeworth through a common friend, Charles Strickland of Lough Glynn in Roscommon. Edgeworthstown was situated about a day's ride from Moore Hall and it is perhaps surprising that the two families had not come into contact with each other at an earlier date. Maria was approaching her seventieth year when they became friends but her friendship with Louisa would last another twelve years. Maria admired the works

---

7 Oscott School was deliberately designed to offer a public school education along the lines of an Eton or Winchester. The fees were expensive and the school had strong Irish sympathies. Daniel O'Connell presented its rector with a fine carved armchair, 'embroidered in Irish green'. See Ciaran O'Neill, *Catholics of consequence: transnational education, social mobility and the Irish Catholic elite, 1850–1900* (Oxford, 2014), p. 77.   8 Maurice George Moore, *An Irish gentleman George Henry Moore: his travel, his racing, his politics* (London, 1913), p. 8.

of George Moore 'The Historian' on the French revolution and his *History of the British revolution*. In his youth in London, George Moore had been an esteemed member of the circle of Sir John Macintosh, the Whig philosopher, and it was after reading Sir John's memoirs and coming upon his appreciation for Moore, that Maria introduced herself to the owner of Moore Hall and to his wife. She wrote to a friend: 'They are not, of the poet's race of Moores, but of more ancient and aristocratic lineage.'[9]

Early in 1836 George and Louisa Moore were guests at Edgeworthstown where Maria, her stepmother, half-sister Honora and an aged aunt received them hospitably. In September 1836, Maria and her stepmother toured Mayo and stopped for some days with the Moores. In a letter Maria did not mention the beautiful scenery of Lough Carra but was impressed with the courtesy and scholarly refinement of her host:

> We took care to tell our aunt on our return to Edgeworthstown of Mr Moore's taking the trouble to return into the drawing-room that last night when he was so unwell, on purpose to give his message of remembrance to Mrs Mary Sneyd.[10]

The letters between the two women demonstrate a strong friendship and deep mutual admiration. For the liberal-minded Moores, Maria was a recognized authority on education, and Louisa Moore hastened to confide in Maria her griefs and anxieties concerning her sons, George Henry and Augustus, both of whom had been brilliant schoolboys but were now running wild. Maria's letters to Moore Hall, therefore, consisted largely of advice and sympathy. She assured the anxious mother that the young men would not always prefer a racehorse to Pegasus, and the *Racing Calendar* to transcendental mathematics.[11]

Maria and Louisa discussed a range of matters that would have concerned women of their class, sometimes resorting to gossip. Maria provided information on contemporary events like the effects of the great storm of January 1839, and the murder of Lord Norbury in the same year. She mentioned the custom of gale days and dealing with the collection of rents, and there were lengthy discussions on the Famine and the government's response to it. Maria offered Louisa plenty of updates from her acquaintances in London, including, for example, Lord Lansdowne's reactions to a week of activities in London during the coronation of Queen Victoria. He wrote to Maria, 'Nothing is so fatiguing as the business of pleasure. I only hope I may find when it is all over my faculties are what they were before it began.'[12]

9 Maria Edgeworth was referring to Thomas Moore, poet, singer and songwriter and who was still living. He died in 1852; see *New Statesmen and Nation*, 3 Apr. 1937. **10** Maria Edgeworth to Mrs Louisa Moore, 29 Sept. 1836 (NLI, typescript copies of letters of Maria Edgeworth, mainly to Mrs Moore, 1835–49, MS 495). **11** *New Statesmen and Nation*, 3 Apr. 1937. **12** Maria Edgeworth to Mrs Louisa Moore, 30 July 1838 (NLI, MS 495).

The role of elite women in household management and the selection of staff can be gleaned from the letters describing the difficulties of finding and keeping servants. Generally a high turnover of servants existed due to innumerable grievances and disputes between domestics and employers.[13] Several letters between the two women provide assistance in locating and recommending staff, such as in this letter of July 1837 from Maria:

> Could you find a place for a person who for some years was housekeeper (kept house for my brother's school)? Mrs Lowe is a perfectly trustworthy person who had never flattered in the presence nor ever abused or complained in the absence of her employer. Though she suffered almost total loss of her employment never did she utter a word of complaint. She had £32 a year. She has since engaged herself whenever she could at lower salary. She is not fit for a housekeeper in any gentleman's family because she does not understand confectionary and arrangement of grand dinners and so forth, though she would be inestimable for trust worthiness and care. But she is exactly fit for a house keeper in any public institution, hospital, infirmary or convent …[14]

Two years later she wrote to Maria with another set of enquiries:

> Are you still in quest or in want of a steward and gardener? And if you are will you tell me again what you require from such a person? And what would be his remuneration? Whether you give a house and cow's grass? Or whether you lodge and board your gardener and land steward in your house?[15]

There are also some comical moments in the correspondence as when Maria complained of tedious dealings with servants:

> And now to descend at once to the creature comforts or creature plagues of life. The laundry maid who lived with you some time ago my dear Mrs Moore would be very glad to leave her poor home and to go or come to you if you pleased and she won't make objections to nothing but be very agreeable to everything and everybody in life.[16]

During the 1830s George Henry was sent to London to study law. Racing and hunting filled his life but on an allowance of £400 a year he was soon heavily in debt. In one incident Louisa had to pay off a bond to an unsavoury character to

---

13 Susan Durack, 'Maynooth – towards a community profile, 1750–1911' (MA, NUI Maynooth, 2001), p. 9.   14 Maria Edgeworth to Mrs Louisa Moore, 9 July 1837 (NLI, MS 495).   15 Maria Edgeworth to Mrs Louisa Moore, 29 Sept. 1836 (ibid.).   16 Maria Edgeworth to Mrs Louisa Moore, 14 June 1842 (ibid.).

whom George Henry had promised a horse. She sent concerned messages both to her lawyer and her banker in London, demanding that he return home at once but received the following discouraging reply from her lawyer:

> My dear Mrs Moore, I have directed to send off your son directly, and to arrange as best I can his affairs here … We must cut the knot and he must return to you and I hope learn wisdom by reflection. He appears to me not to have an idea of the value of money and from all I see if left here will soon run into debt again without really finding out that he is doing anything outrageous.[17]

George Henry was also involved romantically with a well-known married socialite from Cheltenham, much to his mother's dismay. Louisa's sister, Anne Browne, lived in Bath and was able to keep her informed of the gossip of the affair. Louisa sent her son letters blotted with tears, she accused him of treachery and called upon him either to cease his attentions upon her or to forfeit the affection of his parents.[18] In fairness to George Henry, he does seem to have genuinely loved this woman and he stated in his diary that he found it very difficult to get over her. As a result of this affair, his mounting debts and the constant pressure from his mother to return to Mayo, George Henry felt the time was right for him to travel abroad, and from 1834 to 1839 he visited Russia, Syria and Palestine, where he explored the Dead Sea. Maria Edgeworth, on her visit to Moore Hall, enjoyed listening to his communications from the Middle East, and admired the pen and pencil sketches that adorned the letters. George Henry reached many conclusions on his travels and was contrite for his earlier behaviour:

> The love of a woman, that but yesterday seemed passionate and eternal, may today have passed, like a shadow on the waters, from her false and reckless heart; but a mother's love lives on alike through storms and sunshine, follows to the grave and the throne alike with unchanged and unchangeable devotion; and yet for how vile a thing would I once have bartered my mother's heart.[19]

Members of the Irish landowning classes played a key role throughout the nineteenth century in the promotion and organization of horse racing. They were able to use this pastime as a way of enhancing and maintaining their social status, both locally and nationally. Their influence was obvious in every aspect of the sport – as promoters, administrators, owners, breeders and as amateur riders. Aided by improvements in transportation and communication, horse racing became a mass betting industry. Gambling was a key component in their

---

17 Hone, *The Moores of Moore Hall*, p. 62.   18 Ibid., p. 64.   19 Ibid., p. 73.

involvement in horse racing, and some Irish landowners lost their entire estates through gambling.[20]

In 1830 George and Louisa's second son John had been killed as a result of a riding accident, and for a while Louisa declared she never wished to see a horse again at Moore Hall. However, in time, she become reconciled to the place of horses in the lives of the family. Her two sons George Henry and Augustus were soon noted for their skills as horse riders and horse breeders and Moore Hall became a centre of equine activity. Castlebar was the main centre of horse racing in Mayo. The races were held at Breaffy outside the town and were second in Connacht only to the Galway races. They were attended by the distinguished families of the county, such as the Knoxes and Gores, but the Moores of Moore Hall were the most prominent, known especially for their training of racehorses and hunters.

During this period Louisa wrote her *Life of Christ: for the use of the young*. She must have obtained approval from her own bishop to publish this and also from Dean John Hamilton, secretary to Archbishop Murray of Dublin, with whom she was in correspondence about her book. Louisa wrote to Hamilton:

> My sons won a steeplechase last week; I think racing the least sinful of young men's pursuits; in my young days it was the gambling tables and profligacy of all kinds. I wish the clergy would stop attacking one another in the public press; it scandalizes the people and is cause for joy to enemies of the church.[21]

Louisa also looked to Maria Edgeworth for advice on both her sons and her book. Of her book, fellow author Maria wrote:

> Your book, will show from one of our well-informed, well-educated ladies of the higher class, that the reading of Scriptures without note or comment is approved by the Catholics, and this will be a most essential service in Ireland as the contrary belief has tended to keep Christians at variance with each other.[22]

Following the death of his father in 1840, George Henry returned to Mayo and took charge of the family estate, but in the years immediately prior to the Famine it seems he continued to live the life of a leisured member of the ascendancy class, with the estates providing the funds necessary for maintaining his lifestyle. Louisa still had a hand in managing the estate, and her philanthropic activities

20 Gina M. Dorré, *Victorian fiction and the cult of the horse* (London, 2006), p. 101; Máire Kelly, 'Manners and customs of the gentry in pre-Famine Mayo', *Cathair na Mart*, 8:1 (1988), 47–57. **21** Mary Purcell, 'Dublin diocesan archives: Hamilton papers (9)', *Archivium Hibernicum*, 52 (1998), 42–72, at 43. **22** Maria Edgeworth to Mrs Louisa Moore, 14 Mar. 1841 (NLI, MS 495).

included donating money for the establishment of a church in the locality, and providing blankets for the poor.[23]

By 1841, George Henry and his brother Augustus had given up all else and devoted themselves heart and soul to racing and riding. George Henry was commonly called 'Dog Moore' during the 1840s after his celebrated racehorse Wolf Dog, and he was noted throughout the country for his blood stock and his reckless courage when hunting.[24]

Maria Edgeworth also commented on Louisa's sons and horse racing:

> The account you give of your sons being so carried out of the course of science and literature by the horse fever, I would deplore, but that I am convinced it will soon come to a crisis with such men, and that it is a disease which they will have but once in their lives, wish them well through it and well married all in good time.[25]

A tragic setback and certainly the incident which changed George Henry's life was the death of his brother Augustus from injuries received while riding Mickey Free at Liverpool in 1845. George Henry's passion for racing continued but he sold a lot of his horses and curbed his gambling. Maria Edgeworth wrote to Louisa after Augustus' death:

> but truth I do pity George; we know how fond they were of each other; but I have no doubt that such a great shock, instead of being permanently weakening as sorrow sometimes is to the mind, will be serviceable and strengthening and consolidating to his character. He will turn more to quiet literary pursuits, and he will feel in them, along with resource against sorrow, something congenial to his hereditary nature and pleasing and comforting to his mother. His higher nature, his superior tastes and abilities will come out. You will pardon me for this prophecy. I am an old woman.[26]

Louisa lamented her son's death in a letter to Dr Hamilton:

> I have had a cross. My son died. Two days before his death, I walked my estate selecting a site to build a house for him. Now I will build two schools, one for boys, one for girls, on that site.[27]

But Maria Edgeworth was proved right: his brother's death and the Famine that now overwhelmed the country called George Henry to a sense of duty.

23 See Hone, *The Moores of Moore Hall*.   24 Kelly, 'Manners and customs of the gentry', p. 51.   25 Maria Edgeworth to Mrs Louisa Moore, 17 May 1841 (NLI, MS 495).   26 Maria Edgeworth to Mrs Louisa Moore, 15 Apr. 1845 (ibid.).   27 Purcell, 'Hamilton papers', p. 18.

Documentary sources in the Valuations Office, the Land Commission and the National Library of Ireland provide a clear picture of the structure and management of much of the Moore estate under George Henry's proprietorship, and during the period of his mother's influence.[28] Sources indicate that the Moores owned over 12,000 acres near Ballintubber, Partry and Ballycally. Agricultural land on the Ballintubber estate, near to Moore Hall, fell into the categories of arable, pasture and mountain-commonage. The quality of the land, according to the field valuations of 1843, varied from poor mica-slate soil to rather good arable.[29]

The functions of the middleman on Irish estates in the nineteenth century were important to the landlord, particularly an absentee one. By using a middleman, the landlord facilitated his rent collecting and ensured his cash-flow, but by letting land on long leases to middlemen on advantageous terms, the landlord received much less in rent than he otherwise would have done. Land on the estates was let by Moore either directly to a tenant or to a sub-tenant via a middleman. Louisa, rather than George Henry, is also listed as the immediate lessor for a number of holdings on the estate, in both the baronies of Carra and Gallen. An agent, William Mullowney, was employed to oversee the running of the estate, combining this duty with those of butler and steward.[30] Tenants included cottiers who paid their rents with their labour, tenant farmers who paid rent either in cash or in kind, and graziers who rented pasture for their cattle. There was also a full staff employed at Moore Hall.

There was always the temptation for middlemen to rackrent and this most certainly happened on the Moore Hall estate.[31] Looking at the holdings of three middlemen in particular, Malachy Tuohy, Peter Tuohy and Mr Cheevers, it would seem that they were sub-letting their holdings at between two and three times the rent paid to George Henry Moore. The power of the Tuohys stemmed in part from the long leases they had been given; they had secured a lease for lands of Kiltarsaghaun for a period of four lives from George Henry Moore's grandfather, George of Alicante, as early as 1793.[32] Griffith's valuation shows that Tuohy's property is recorded at a very low value (ten shillings) and that he held thirty acres of land. A valuations officer, prior to the Famine, judged that rent for portions of the Ballintubber townland were 'greatly too high' and prompted him to conclude that Mr Moore was a rackrenting landlord.[33] George Henry and

28 David Barr, 'George Henry Moore and his tenants, 1840–70', *Cathair na Mart*, 1 (1988), 66–79.   29 Ordnance Survey field name books for the county of Mayo 1838, book 14, parish of Ballintober, p. 430.   30 George Moore, *Hail and farewell*, ed. Richard Allen Cave (Buckinghamshire, 1976), p. 730.   31 'In the eighteenth and nineteenth centuries landowners increasingly tried to maximize their incomes by moving away from long leases to annual agreements with their tenants. Such "rack rents" came to be regarded as extortionate, but in practice landowners were able to get only what the market would stand': David Hey, *The Oxford companion to local and family history* (Oxford, 1996), p. 387.   32 Barr, 'George Henry Moore and his tenants', 69.   33 Barr, 'George Henry Moore and his tenants', 69.

Louisa could have reviewed this situation on numerous occasions but chose for the sake of convenience to let things stand. Maria Edgeworth in a letter to Louisa Moore wrote:

> … forty guineas taken from these wretched tenants it is beyond anything my wickedest imagination could have conceived for a bad Irish agent (see Jane Quirke in my *Castle Rackrent*).[34]

Yet, rackrenting of the sort observed by Maria in *Castle Rackrent* was prevalent on Louisa's family estate. Despite the rent levels in the early 1840s there is no evidence that George Henry evicted any of his tenants for non-payment. During his later life and that of his sons rent levels on the estate fell generally. In 1843, Peter Tuohy offered £200 to rent pasture in Carn townland; the same land was being let for £120 in 1895.[35]

Grazing was a highly emotive national issue at this time when it became an increasingly attractive financial proposition for large farmers. Extensive grazing reduced employment and forced the eviction of smallholders to make way for cattle. Moore Hall included a livestock farm. At the time George Henry took over the management of the estate from Louisa, cattle and sheep produced an estimated turnover of £1500 per annum.[36] It seems, however, that Moore could have yielded much more profit if other parts of the Ballintubber estate had been let out as grassland, yet the Ballintubber estate in particular saw no mass clearance of tenantry for cattle, despite the financial benefits such an action would have brought for George Henry.

During the period 1840 to 1845 no forceful measures to improve the condition of his estate were taken by George Henry. He did, however, begin to respond to the distress experienced among his tenants, particularly around the Ballybanaun and Partry estate, by sending donations as early as July 1842. When the Famine reached the region around Louisa's home at Moore Hall, the effects were hard. The population decline overall for the country was about 20 per cent but in Mayo the population fell by 29 per cent, from 388,887 to 274,830, due to death and emigration.[37]

In a letter to Louisa dated 30 July 1847 Maria Edgeworth discussed the larger significance of the Famine and its consequences for Irish–British relations:

> The conduct of Irish proprietors during these distresses must convince England as it has convinced the Irish of their good will by their good deeds … I see also that the feeling excited in England by Irish distress still more than the munificent contributions they have made towards the relief of our

34 Maria Edgeworth to Mrs Louisa Moore, 12 Oct. 1841 (NLI, MS 495).   **35** Barr, 'George Henry Moore and his tenants', 69.   **36** Ibid., 71.   **37** Statistics referenced from www.mayolibrary.ie/en/LocalStudies/TheFamineinMayo.

poor has created gratitude and has counteracted that mischievous spirit of national hatred which O'Connell … raised between the Irish and the Saresenach [*sic*].

The effects of the Famine were particularly bad in Mayo because of the power of the 'middle men', the dependency on the potato and the unsustainability of small holdings. A lack of both industry in the region and an alternative food supply ensured that Mayo, as well as most of the counties on the western seaboard of Ireland, suffered the most.

Fr Browne, the parish priest of Ballintubber, wrote that of 1600 houses standing in his parish in 1844 at least 800 had been levelled, 3000 lives had been lost and 500 persons had fled to either America or England. Four thousand souls remained and some families had been forced to pawn their clothes in order to buy seed in a desperate bid to plant the land and feed themselves.[38]

The areas referred to included parts of George Henry Moore's estates. Local landlords received much criticism from Fr Browne and other local priests for their lack of response. George Henry seems to have been an exception. He chaired two relief committees at Ballintubber and Partry and was actively involved in the management of relief measures.[39] A notably generous act on behalf of Moore was the provision of funds as a result of a win of one of his horses, *Coranna*, which he had entered, in association with Lord Waterford, in the Chester Cup in May 1846. He wrote to his mother Louisa in May 1846:

> Coranna won the Chester Cup this day. I win on the whole £17,000. Deducting Lord Waterford's share and other expenses … I shall realize about nine thousand pounds all good money. This is in fact a little fortune and I am received on all sides by congratulatory friends. I shall lodge £500 in the Westport Bank to your account and leave the whole direction of the sum to your judgement with the sole limitation that every tenant of mine or living on my land whether tenant or squatter shall receive immediate full relief.[40]

Much of the money went on settling his debts but he sent £1000 pounds to his mother at Moore Hall with instructions for its distribution. Five hundred pounds was to be used to finance relief works, and the balance was to be distributed in charity to the very poorest because he believed that the 'horses would gallop all the faster with the blessings of the poor'.[41] Fr Michael Heaney,

---

38 Barr, 'George Henry Moore and his tenants', 71.   39 'Ballinrobe relief committee record' (NLI, correspondence of George Henry Moore regarding administration of his estates and other family, financial and political matters 1826–70, MS 891, p. 132).   40 George Henry Moore to his mother Louisa Moore, 6 May 1846 (NLI, Correspondence of George Henry Moore, 1826–70, MS 892).

parish priest of Mayo Abbey, mentions that every widow on George Henry's property received a milch cow, rents were waived on holdings under £5 in rent and relief was given to others paying up to £20 in rent.[42]

As chairman of two relief committees, George Henry often wrote to the lord lieutenant describing the situation in his region. He wrote on 21 January 1847:

> Able-bodied men can no longer obtain two quarts of meal for a day's work, which has to be divided amongst six individuals … We have sent from this house several times to Westport within the last fortnight without being able to procure meal. The merchants in this county … are apprehensive that the enormous profits they have been making will soon be interfered with … There is a necessity of having provisions in government depots, sold to the people at a reasonable price … If not done, serious and alarming outbreaks are likely to take place. A meeting which will be attended by enormous crowds of people has been convened for Monday next.[43]

Moore was one of a trio of Mayo landlords, along with Lord Sligo and Sir Richard Blosse, who jointly financed the voyage of the *Martha Washington* that shipped a large cargo of foodstuffs from New Orleans to Westport Quay in June 1847.[44] Flour and meal imported were sold to famine-stricken tenants at highly subsidised rates, the deficit being met by the three men. The venture required £10,000 in capital and incurred an overall loss of £4800. Maurice Moore said his father George Henry's deficit share was approximately £900.[45]

Unfortunately, despite his best intentions, the distribution of relief was not trouble-free. Louisa, who had been placed in charge of the fund from the Coranna win while George Henry was in Westminster as an elected member of parliament, found herself in dispute with local priests who encouraged tenants to refuse to work except for double wages in the Ballybanaun area. George Henry wrote to his mother to suspend all relief to this region until he returned from England. In this instance both parties were doing what they felt was best for the tenants but there were other, less scrupulous, individuals prepared to profit from the crisis. For example, one Tom Lawless of Ballintubber was convicted of using false weights when selling flour and meal.[46]

Years of Famine relief, low or often cancelled rents, high poor law union rates, and gambling debts left Moore in acute difficulty. His estate fell into debt forcing

---

41 Hone, *The Moores of Moore Hall*, p. 138.   **42** Barr, 'George Henry Moore and his tenants', 71.   **43** Liam Swords, *In their own words: the Famine in north Connacht, 1845–9* (Blackrock, Co. Dublin, 1999), p. 117.   **44** Consignment record for the *Martha Washington*, 23 Apr. 1847 (NLI, Correspondence of George Henry Moore regarding administration of his estates and other family, financial and political matters 1826–70, MS 890, p. 153).   **45** Moore, *An Irish gentleman*, p. 125.   **46** Barr, 'George Henry Moore and his tenants', pp 72–3.

15.4 Kiltoom Cemetery, Moore Hall, Co. Mayo.

him during 1854 to sell half his property for £5900. Some of the lands were purchased by the proselytizing Bishop Plunkett, much to the chagrin of the Catholic Moore and the local clergy.[47] Moore owed money to his cousin Lord Sligo, who reminded him on more than one occasion of this debt. His later political career would involve further expenses, and when when he died in 1870 the family estate was in financial crisis.

In the 1840s George Henry had embarked on a political career and was elected MP for Mayo during the 1847 general election. He was a prominent figure in the Tenant League and the Catholic Defence Association. This meant that he was, once again, absent from Moore Hall and Louisa was left to manage the estate. It was a sad period for Louisa as her friend and correspondent Maria Edgeworth died in 1849. The last letter of the series saw Maria announce the death of her stepdaughter; shortly afterwards, on 25 May, Maria died in her eighty-fourth year.

Louisa Moore gained, however, another companion in the form of George Henry's new bride. He had married Mary Blake from the nearby Ballinafad estate who was a Catholic. Mary's brothers Joseph and Llewellyn were racehorse enthusiasts. The marriage was a happy one. The presence of the young wife at

47 Ibid., p. 74.

Moore Hall acted as much-needed relief. As Moore's parliamentary duties often took him to London, it was suggested that Louisa should remain at Moore Hall as company for his wife. To this the younger woman readily assented, saying that she had found in her mother-in-law the most witty and agreeable woman in the world. When George Henry was in London they spent long evenings together talking of him, reading his travel-diaries and his letters from the East.[48]

Louisa was pleased that George Henry was now taking responsibility for his estate and engaging in a successful parliamentary career. During the 1860s, Louisa met with an accident and was confined to two rooms at the top of the house. Mullowney, the steward, pushed her about the garden in a bath chair, or she was carried around in a sedan chair; she died in 1861 (fig. 15.4). George Augustus Moore, the novelist and eldest son of George Henry, wrote of Louisa, his grandmother:

> I remember her as a cripple going along the passage with her to the dining-room and hearing her say the gingerbread nuts were too hard and my first disappointment was at seeing them sent back to the kitchen. She promised that some more should be made. But a few days or a few weeks after she was picked up at the foot of the stairs. She never recovered from that fall, she never walked again but was carried out by villagers in a chair on poles. I remember seeing her dead and the funeral train going up the narrow path through the dark wood to Kiltoom where the family cemetery-tomb was. Half-way up that pathway is a stone seat. It was she who had it put there, she had walked to Kiltoom every day to visit my grandfather; she is there now.[49]

George Henry continued in politics, in addition to maintaining his passion for racing and breeding horses. He supported Gavin Duffy's tenant-rights movement, which alienated him from many of his own class. He was returned again in 1852 but was unseated after winning the 1857 election on the grounds that two priests had intimidated voters in his favour. He returned to parliament in 1868. His Mayo tenants, whom he had strove to protect during the Famine, suddenly refused to pay their rents in 1870. He travelled to Moore Hall to investigate the matter and died suddenly and inexplicably. The doctor said he had had a stroke, the local priest that he had died of a broken heart brought on by his tenants' deception and ingratitude.

His son George Augustus, a controversial but successful novelist, took over the estate in 1870 but had little interest in it. His brother, Col. Maurice Moore, who would become a senator in the Free State, managed it to the best of his ability. The house was eventually burned in 1923 by anti-treaty forces and with

48 Moore, *An Irish gentleman*, pp 303–4.   49 Moore, *Hail and farewell*, p. 410.

15.5 Moore Hall today in ruins.

it, much of the material culture associated with Louisa and her family's life (fig. 15.5).

An examination of Louisa's correspondence with Maria Edgeworth and with her son, George Henry, provides an insight into their daily lives as well as the management of Moore Hall against the backdrop of George Henry's political life, his landlord-tenant relations, and the impact of the Great Famine and his relief efforts on the estate. Louisa Moore was a strong-minded, formidable woman of great business ability who combined the roles of wife and mother with that of managing the estate. She was a product of turbulent times, resilient and determined to see her family succeed; she certainly embodied the Moore family motto *Fortis Cadere cedere non potest*: 'He who proceeds with courage will never fail.'

Contributors

AMY BOYINGTON is a postdoctoral research associate at Queens' College, University of Cambridge. She recently completed her PhD entitled 'Maids, wives and widows: female architectural patronage in eighteenth-century Britain'.

KERRY BRISTOL is a senior lecturer at the University of Leeds where she has taught architectural history and country house studies since 1999. She is currently writing a book on the Winns of Nostell Priory.

PHILIP BULL holds an associate research fellowship at the Centre for the Study of Historic Irish Houses and Estates at Maynooth University and is an adjunct professor in history at La Trobe University in Melbourne.

JONATHAN CHERRY is a lecturer in Geography in the School of History and Geography, Dublin City University. His main research interests are in historical and cultural geography, with a particular focus on the role of the landowning elite in Irish society and their influence on the Irish landscape. He co-edited *Cavan: history and society* (Dublin, 2014).

ARLENE CRAMPSIE is an historical geographer in the School of Geography, University College Dublin. Her research interests lie at the intersection of historical, social and cultural geographies with her main research to date focussing on the social, cultural and political landscapes of the late nineteenth and twentieth centuries in Ireland. She is chairperson of the Oral History Network of Ireland and co-editor with Francis Ludlow of *Meath: history and society* (Dublin, 2015).

CAROLINE DAKERS is professor of cultural history at Central Saint Martins, University of the Arts, London. She is the author of *A genius for money: business, art and the Morrisons* (London, 2011), and is working on *Fonthill recovered, a cultural history* (to be published by UCL Press in 2018) and *Bohemians and gentlemen: the image of the artist in British society, 1850–1950* (Princeton).

TERENCE DOOLEY is associate professor of history at Maynooth University and director of the Centre for the Study of Historic Irish Houses and Estates. His most recent book is *The Irish revolution, 1912–23: Monaghan* (Dublin, 2017).

JUDITH HILL is a Moore Institute visiting research fellow at National University of Ireland, Galway. She recently completed her PhD at Trinity College Dublin on meaning in post-Union Irish Gothic revival, funded by an Irish Research Council Government of Ireland Postgraduate Scholarship. She has published widely on Irish architecture.

EDMUND JOYCE is an architectural historian who lives near Borris in Co. Carlow. He is a lecturer at the Institute of Technology Carlow and the author of *Borris House, Co. Carlow, and elite regency patronage* (Dublin, 2013).

RUTH LARSEN is a senior lecturer in history at the University of Derby. Following a PhD at the University of York on the role of elite women in the Yorkshire country house, she has continued to research and publish on the aristocratic family, religious history and material culture studies.

MAEVE O'RIORDAN completed her IRC-funded PhD in University College Cork in 2014 and was IRC postdoctoral fellow at the Centre for the Study of Historic Irish Houses and Estates, History Department, Maynooth University to September 2016. She has contributed to a number of volumes and journals. Her book *Women of the Irish country house, 1860–1914* will be published in 2018.

ANNA PILZ is a scholar of nineteenth-century Irish literature and women's writing with research interests in the environmental humanities. She is co-editor with Whitney Standlee of *Irish women's writing, 1878–1922: advancing the cause of liberty* (Manchester, 2016), and is currently working on her first monograph, *Woody island: trees, inheritance, and estates in Irish writing.*

LOWRI ANN REES is a lecturer in modern history at Bangor University. Her research interests centre on eighteenth- and nineteenth-century Wales, in particular the landed elite and their country estates. She has published on paternalism and rural protest, the Rebecca riots, Welsh sojourners in India, and is currently researching upward social mobility in Wales.

CIARÁN REILLY is a historian of nineteenth- and twentieth-century Ireland. He is author of *The Irish land agent: the case of King's County, 1830–60* (Dublin, 2014); *Strokestown and the Great Irish Famine* (Dublin, 2014) and *John Plunket Joly and the Great Famine in King's County* (Dublin, 2012).

CHRISTOPHER RIDGWAY is curator at Castle Howard in England, and chair of the Yorkshire Country House Partnership. He is also an adjunct professor in the Centre for the Study of Historic Irish Houses and Estates, History Department, Maynooth University, and his recent publications include *The Morpeth Roll, Ireland identified in 1841* (Dublin, 2013).

REGINA SEXTON, University College Cork, is a food and culinary historian, food writer, broadcaster and cook. She has been researching and publishing in the area of Irish food and culinary history since 1993.

BRENDAN TWOMEY is a retired banker. His publications and research interests are focused on all aspects of early eighteenth-century Ireland with a particular emphasis on banking and personal financial management in this period and on Jonathan Swift and the development of Dublin city. He is presently completing a PhD thesis on 'Personal financial management in early eighteenth-century Ireland'.

FIONA WHITE is a lecturer in heritage studies at Galway-Mayo Institute of Technology, Mayo Campus. Her main academic interests are the big house and landed estate.

Index